Collins

children's food bible

Collins

children's food bible

JUDITH WILLS

First published in 2004 by Collins
an imprint of HarperCollins*Publishers*
77–85 Fulham Palace Road, London, W6 8JB

everything clicks at:
www.collins.co.uk

Text © 2004 Judith Wills
Photography and design © HarperCollins*Publishers*

Designer: Colin Brown
Photographer: Nikki English
Food Stylist: Lucy Knox
Illustrator: John See
Copy Editor: Lewis Esson
Indexer: Janet Smy

For HarperCollins:
Publishing Director: Denise Bates
Senior Managing Editor: Angela Newton
Art Direction: Luke Griffin
Editor: Alastair Laing
Editorial Assistant: Lisa John
Production: Chris Gurney

A CIP catalogue record for this book is available
from the British Library

ISBN 0007164432

Colour reproduction by Colourscan
Printed and bound in Great Britain by Scotprint

CONTENTS

INTRODUCTION

What is it that every parent wants the most for his or her child? I believe it is good health. We want our children to be healthy now, to stay healthy throughout childhood, and to grow into healthy and long-lived adults. And one of the most significant – and simple – ways to achieve this is through diet. What you choose to feed your children and, later, what advice you give them about making their own choices will have wide-ranging effects on their physical and even mental health throughout life.

In theory, feeding our children well should not be a problem since the volume of research into, and information about, children's diet and health has never been greater. But ironically, both world and UK statistics show that a high proportion of children's diets in the West are having negative, rather than positive, effects on their health – and the situation is getting worse.

According to the Royal College of Paediatrics, we are raising a generation of children who are overweight but poorly nourished. The National Diet and Nutrition Survey (UK) published in 2000 showed that children are eating too much saturated fat, far too much sugar and salt, and only 50% of the optimum amount of fruits and vegetables. In the week of the survey, only a fifth of children ate any citrus fruit at all, only a half ate salad and only a third any leafy greens. Oily fish, whole grains and natural yogurt hardly figure at all in the diets of our schoolchildren, while their consumption of sweets and soft drinks has gone up 25-fold in 50 years.

The Sodexho UK Meals Survey 2002 found that children spend £1.3 billion on food outside the home every year, most of this on fast foods, crisps, sweets, chocolates and fizzy drinks. No wonder then that one recent survey found that four out of five parents worry about their children's diet, but feel guilty because they don't invest enough time or effort in making that diet better.

In the USA, up to 80% of children aged up to 9 were found to have a diet that needed improvement, according to the last official Healthy Eating Index,

while teenagers of both sexes rated the worst scores of all on the same index.

One UK Government health minister revealed in 2000 that the current young generation may well not live as long as their parents – a prediction endorsed by various child health and obesity specialists. But why have our eating habits changed for the worst? Experts cite the modern fast food culture, peer pressure and advertising, in addition to the poor monitoring and standard of school meals, and the decline of parental influence, home cooking and family meals.

As a direct consequence of poor diet and a decline in physical activity amongst children, we are now experiencing record levels of childhood obesity. The World Heart Federation says that 22 million children under five are obese, while in the UK, the number of overweight children has doubled in a decade to nearly 20%.

In turn, poor diet and overweight have led to a rapidly increasing incidence of 'modern' illnesses such as diabetes and heart disease in young adults, while early signs of artery disease are showing in children as young as 7 and early markers for diabetes are evident in young teenagers. It is also becoming apparent that very many other childhood complaints, such as asthma, behavioural problems and eczema may be influenced by diet.

But even the most health-conscious parents often feel that they are battling against the tactics of the huge multinational food conglomerates, who are more concerned with healthy accounts than healthy eating. Indeed these companies often seem to have a diametrically opposed view to that of the nutrition experts about what children should eat. There isn't so much profit in fruit and vegetables!

But it is becoming increasingly clear that we *do* have a choice. The multinational fast food chains' profits are beginning to slow or even decline; many parents' organisations have been formed to support the need for good, healthy food for our children. Slowly, very slowly, government is beginning to get the message and hopefully we will see improvement in how schools sell food and teach healthy eating, and in legislation for better control of food labelling, safety, marketing and so on.

Meanwhile, this book is my own contribution. My aim has been to produce an unbiased reference resource for parents of children of all ages, hopefully answering all the 'whats', 'whys' and 'how-tos' that you regularly find yourself asking. I also aim to reassure. For though the current statistics make depressing reading, it *is* true that most of us have easy access to what could be the most varied, balanced, interesting and healthy diet that children have ever known.

By increasing your knowledge I believe you will then have the confidence, and the power, to give your children exactly that – a healthy and enjoyable diet, right through their growing years.

Judith Wills

FEEDING YOUR CHILD

This first section of the book provides advice for parents at each of the particular stages of a child's development and is divided into three chapters – from weaning through pre-school, then the primary school years and finally the teenage years.

These chapters highlight the changing dietary needs of children as they grow and as their circumstances alter, and give nutrient tables for each stage. I have also addressed the different eating problems that are typical for each age group and how they may affect health. From allergies in toddlers to food refusal in teens, you will find help in this section. There is also plenty of advice on meal planning, with 'blueprint' eating plans for each age group, including specific advice and meal plans for feeding the vegetarian child.

The information in this section is best used in conjunction with the A–Z of Child Health & Diet on pages 68–197, which provides more detailed advice on dozens of topics – cross-references on most pages will lead you to the relevant areas of the A–Z. You can also consult the Appendices on pages 240–53, where you will find comprehensive lists of food sources for key nutrients, age-related growth charts and a list of websites and contact details for food, diet and health organisations.

WEANING AND THE PRE-SCHOOL YEARS

When our children are small, we have a never-to-be-repeated chance to instill good eating habits into them – as well as the opportunity to encourage them to enjoy food and feel good about their relationship with it. Good nutrition is key to the future health and development of any child. It is probable that every child's short- and long-term health can be improved if parents wean at the right time, and then provide a nutritious and suitable diet from weaning onwards.

And yet studies show that a significant percentage of children aged 1–4 are regular consumers of sweets, biscuits and other highly processed foods of dubious nutritional value, and that this age group are on average getting double the recommended amounts for both sugar and salt, while less than half regularly eat fruit or leafy greens.

While it isn't necessary to be overprotective about what your children eat as babies and infants, almost all the research shows that this is the ideal time to encourage them to develop healthy tastes in food – and to do so is probably easier than you might imagine. These few years are, in effect, the only time that you will have the opportunity for 100% control of what your children eat and drink. Making the most of them is what this chapter is all about.

SUCCESSFUL WEANING

A baby's first natural food is breast milk. In the UK, according to the Department of Health, 71% of new mothers now breast-feed their babies for at least two weeks. Bottle-feeding with a formula based on cows' or soya milk is an alternative. If possible, however, you should try to breast-feed, as there are many natural advantages to be had.

Studies have shown that, in addition to building up the immune system, there is evidence that breast milk can also help visual development and improve mental skills and brain power (though formula milk with added essential fats has been shown to produce similar results). The long-chain fatty acids in breast milk could also protect your baby against high blood pressure, helping to prevent heart disease and strokes in later life. One recent study published in the US magazine *Pediatrics* found that breast-fed children had a 55% lower risk of obesity in later life.

The current consensus of expert opinion is that breast or bottle milk should be the only food you provide for your infant for the first four months, and that weaning before this age is detrimental. Indeed, the UK Department of Health has issued new guidelines (2003) advising women that breast-feeding as the sole source of nutrition is preferable for the first six months. The British Nutrition Foundation (BNF) suggests that it may be time for weaning when the baby's weight reaches 7kg (or doubles from birth weight).

ADVANTAGES OF BREAST MILK

- Hygienic, temperature-controlled – and free!

- Protects your baby against infection

- Helps build a healthy immune system

- May aid visual development and mental skills

- Protects against high blood pressure

- May protect against becoming overweight

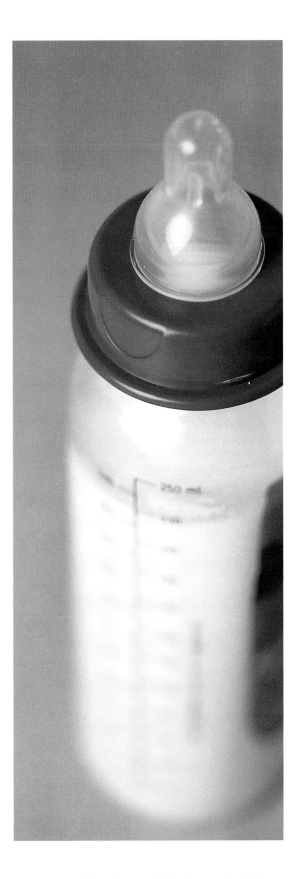

EARLY WEANING PROBLEMS

There are numerous good reasons for not weaning your child too early:

Baby's digestion. The digestive system and kidneys of young babies may not be able to cope readily with solid foods.

Development of allergies. It may help to prevent infant and childhood allergies from developing, especially if there is a family history of allergy.

Tendency towards obesity. There is some evidence to show that children weaned on to solids at an early age tend to be fatter.

Problems with arteries. A study backed by the Medical Research Council found that early weaning is linked with hardening of the arteries later in life.

LATE WEANING PROBLEMS

Although early weaning isn't advisable, neither is late weaning if delayed much beyond six months, which has been linked with:

Malnutrition. Breast milk alone is unlikely to provide all the nutrients and calories that a growing baby needs after 6 months. There is little iron or vitamin D in breast milk, for example, and by 6 months the baby's own stores will be used up. (With formula milk, this isn't a problem.)

Slow development of eating skills. Babies may find it harder to develop the correct chewing response or learn to accept 'lumpy' food if weaning doesn't start at 6 months.

Development of fussy eating. Experts say that children exposed to a wide variety of tastes and textures between the ages of 6 and 9 months are less likely to become faddy eaters.

See also: 'Allergies and Infants' pp16–17, 'Feeding Problems Aged 1–4' pp26–7, Food Allergies pp117–19, Fussy Eating and Food Refusal p131.

FOODS TO WEAN YOUR INFANT ON

A child is described as an infant from birth to aged 12 months. At this time your baby is growing rapidly and so he or she will need enough calories from fats, carbohydrates and protein, and a range of vitamins and minerals. The table opposite shows how much of each of several selected nutrients the average infant requires.

Don't worry about trying to calculate whether or not your baby is getting precisely these amounts of nutrients – as long as you give him or her a range of suitable foods (see opposite) and they appear to be thriving and growing well, you are almost certainly giving your baby a nutritionally balanced diet.

There are no precise weights given for the amount of fat and carbohydrate that your baby should receive – but, in general, his or her fat intake (as a proportion of his or her total calorie intake) should be higher than that for an adult. Breast and formula milks are about 50% fat.

The first weaning food is often baby rice mixed to a creamy consistency with breast or formula milk, or boiled water, and served slightly warm. Vegetable purées can be introduced after a week or two – the sweeter vegetables, such as carrot, sweet potato and squash, are usually well received. Fruit purées, such as apple, pear and banana, can then follow. All purées should be lump-free at this stage, to avoid choking or refusal, and purées should be introduced one at a time in small amounts on the end of a flat plastic baby spoon. Once babies have been taking solids for several weeks you can introduce a more varied diet. At 6–7 months, most will enjoy a range of cereals, mild fish, eggs, dairy produce, chicken, turkey and a variety of fruit and veg – purées can be slightly thicker.

By 9–12 months, most babies will enjoy food which is more textured and will enjoy eating finger foods, such as cooked carrot or broccoli sticks or pieces of ripe banana. After one, your baby will enjoy meals similar to the rest of the family.

FEEDING INFANTS AFTER WEANING

After weaning, your child regularly needs a variety of foods from each of the following four food groups:

Milk and dairy foods. Provide calcium for bone growth and health, protein for muscle growth, fat and carbohydrate, vitamins and a variety of minerals.

Meat, fish, eggs, pulses. Provide protein, fats, and a wide range of vitamins and minerals. Pulses also contain carbohydrate and fibre.

Cereals, bread and potatoes. The starch foods provide an important source of energy (calories) in the diet as well as fibre, vitamins and minerals.

Fruit and vegetables. Provide your child's main source of vitamin C and other vitamins and minerals, and also contain important plant chemicals (phytochemicals) and fibre.

See also: Phytochemicals p160.

See also: Phytochemicals p160.

VITAMIN SUPPLEMENTS FOR YOUNG CHILDREN

The UK Department of Health recommends that children from 6 months to at least 2 years old, or perhaps up to 5 years of age, should receive a supplement of vitamin D in liquid form – these ensure adequate growth and bone development.

Having said that, if a child eats well and is provided with a good-quality varied and balanced diet, including plenty of fruit and vegetables, and receives adequate sunlight (from which the body can manufacture vitamin D), a supplement may not be necessary.

INFANT DAILY NUTRITIONAL REQUIREMENTS (BASED ON DOH•, 1991)

Age (months)	Calories	Protein	Vit A	Vit C	Vit D	Vit K	Calc	Iron	Zinc
0–3	530	12.5g	350mcg	25mg	8.5mcg	10mcg	525mg	2mg	4mg
4–6	670	12.7g	350mcg	25mg	8.5mcg	10mcg	525mg	4mg	4mg
7–9	790	13.7g	350mcg	25mg	7mcg	10mcg	525mg	8mg	5mg
10–12	890	14.9g	350mcg	25mg	7mcg	10mcg	525mg	9mg	6.5mg

Sodium – new daily target average intakes are less than 1g salt (less than 0.4g sodium) a day for babies up to 6 months, and 1g salt (0.4g sodium) a day for infants 7–12 months.

• Department of Health's Scientific Advisory Committee on Nutrition.

FOODS TO AVOID

It is important to follow official guidelines on which foods to offer and which to avoid giving your baby in infancy. Some foods can cause allergic reactions, others are difficult to digest, while others are unsuitable for small children for other reasons. The chart opposite shows what foods to offer and what foods to avoid at each age.

GENERAL TIPS ON FEEDING INFANTS

Meal routines. Aim to get him or her settled into a three-meals-a-day routine, with breast or formula milk snacks in-between meals. Most infants exercise their own portion control, refusing food when full.

Home-cooking or jars? Try to provide your infant with as many home-cooked meals as possible, but commercial baby foods can be convenient from time to time, especially when travelling. Don't feel guilty for having a few jars as standbys!

Batch cooking. This can save time and effort – freeze small portions in ice trays, then bag them and defrost as necessary. Reheat thoroughly and allow to cool to the required temperature.

Food safety. When preparing, cooking and feeding, keep hands and equipment scrupulously clean.

Weight issues. Although many people seem to prefer 'chubby' babies, and infants do naturally have a higher body-fat percentage than adults, it is important that your baby doesn't put on too much weight in their first year. If you think that your infant may be too fat, take him or her to the doctor, who will arrange for the baby to be weighed and assessed by a professional who will give you further advice. Similar advice applies if you think he or she is not gaining enough weight.

See also: Food Safety pp123–6, Growth Charts pp250–1.

SUITABLE FOOD AND FOODS

AROUND 6 MONTHS

SUITABLE FOODS

At first, 1–2 small spoonfuls of baby rice offered halfway through a milk feed. Introduce mashed potato, polenta (fine cornmeal), puréed vegetables such as carrot and squash, puréed fruits such as apple and pear, and then purées of other fruits and vegetables, such as peas, parsnips, plums and bananas, as the early weeks of weaning progress. Small amounts of cooked meat, such as chicken, may be introduced to the purées towards the end of the first weaning period.

AVOID

Don't ever add salt to baby foods, and only add sugar to sweeten sharp fruits. Avoid all types of nuts especially groundnuts (peanuts), seeds, gluten-containing grains e.g. wheat, oats, barley and rye, honey which can cause a type of food poisoning called infant botulism, eggs – particularly egg white and uncooked or lightly cooked egg yolks, cheese, yoghurt, cows' milk, offal, fish.

TIPS

- Don't add baby rice or other foods to a drinks bottle as the baby may choke.
- Introduce new foods one at a time, a little at a time. Your baby will dictate how much they eat, usually just a couple of spoonfuls at this age.
- Make a purée by peeling, chopping and de-seeding, if necessary, the vegetable or fruit, then steam or boil in a little unsalted water until tender. Blend in an electric blender with a little breast or formula milk or boiled water, until you have a smooth creamy consistency. As the baby gets older, make the purée less liquid.

AGE 6-9 MONTHS

SUITABLE FOODS

The age to try many foods. An increasing variety of fruits (e.g. avocado, papaya, melon, peach) and vegetables (e.g. cauliflower, swede, sweet potato, broccoli), along with some high-protein foods, such as red lentils and other dried pulses, chicken, turkey, white fish (like cod or coley), natural bio yoghurt, lean red meat. Gluten-containing grains – wheat, oats, barley and rye – are fine for most babies now, as are small quantities of hard cheese, such as Cheddar and pasteurized soft cheeses, hard-cooked egg yolk and small amounts of cows' milk as part of a dish (not as a drink). A tiny portion of offal can be given once a week – it is rich in iron, but contains high levels of vitamin A, too much of which can be dangerous for infants.

AVOID

Groundnuts (peanuts) and other nuts, seeds, offal, egg white and uncooked or lightly cooked egg yolks, soft cheeses and blue cheeses, shark, swordfish or marlin, added sugar except to sweeten sour fruits, added salt, honey.

TIPS

• At 6 months, make the purées a little thicker and with more texture, to encourage chewing.
• Between 7 and 9 months, gradually change from blended to mashed or well-minced food. Many babies are keen to eat their 'solid' meals at this age and slightly less interested in their milk.
• From 8 months, offer plenty of finger foods, such as slices of peeled fruits, lightly cooked broccoli or carrot, or fingers of bread or unsalted rice cakes or breadsticks. Some baby rusks contain added sugar and these are best avoided, so always read the label.

AGED 9–12 MONTHS

SUITABLE FOODS

Try reintroducing foods that your baby may not have enjoyed a few months ago – stronger tastes will be more acceptable. All fruits and vegetables are suitable now – try sieved berry fruits, seedless satsumas, tomatoes. You can now offer egg white and yolk (well cooked), and it is a good time to try tiny amounts of oily fish such as tuna.

AVOID

Groundnuts (peanuts) and other nuts, shark, swordfish or marlin, salty foods, foods containing much added sugar, sweets, soft and blue cheeses, shellfish, honey, raw or lightly cooked eggs.

TIPS

• Always make sure that any fish is completely bone-free.
• Your baby can eat with the family – mash or chop his or her food and don't add salt or use it in cooking.
• Encourage the baby as much as possible to try to feed him- or herself.

DRINKS FOR INFANTS

It is very important that infants have plenty of fluids. From weaning to 12 months the most suitable drink for your baby is still breast or formula milk. In the early days of weaning, a baby will still want milk at every meal and weaning foods will form a fairly small, but gradually increasing, part of his or her diet. It is best to start offering milk in a baby cup rather than a bottle as soon as you can when weaning begins. The baby can still have a bottle before bedtime up to one year old – if he or she needs it.

Aim to give your infant 600ml of breast or formula milk a day up to 1 year of age. 'Follow-on' formulas are available for babies over 6 months – for some babies these may be more suitable than early infant formula as they contain more nutrients – but if a wide variety of foods are being eaten, follow-on milk may not be necessary. Babies under one year old shouldn't be given ordinary cows', goats' or ewes' milk as a drink, as it doesn't contain enough nutrients.

If your baby is thirsty, offer plain cooled boiled tap water. Avoid sparkling mineral water and any mineral waters with a high mineral content. For safety, bottled water still needs to be boiled until your baby is six months old.

> • Avoid all drinks with added sugar or artificial sweeteners, and all caffeine-containing drinks which can hinder mineral absorption and may cause other problems.
> • Don't leave your baby with a bottle of milk or juice – continual sucking of such drinks can cause tooth decay over time.

If you want to give your infant any other drink, give him or her an occasional unsweetened fruit juice, well diluted with cooled boiled water, but in a cup not a bottle, as the sugars and acids in fruit juices can contribute to tooth decay. High intake of fruit juice has also been linked with diarrhoea and overweight in infants. The American Academy suggests that intake of fruit juice should be limited to 170ml per day for children aged 1 year (therefore less than that may be permitted for younger infants) and some paediatricians advise withholding all juice until at least 6 months of age.

See also: Caffeine p85, Drinks pp103–4, Milk p146–7, Teeth and Gums p189–90, Water p196.

ALLERGIES AND INFANTS

Several everyday foods which most infants can eat with no problem may cause an adverse reaction in some babies. Food intolerance (including allergy) is much more prevalent in babies and children up to the age of 5 than it is in other age groups – official estimates are that between 1 in 5 and 1 in 10 are affected by intolerance and 1–2% by 'true' allergy.

The foods most likely to cause an adverse reaction are cows' milk (up to 2% of infants are allergic to cows'-milk protein), egg (prevalence of actual allergy estimated in one recent study at 1.3%), soya, peanuts (groundnuts – but not groundnut oil) and other nuts, fish and shellfish. Wheat and other gluten-containing grains can cause coeliac disease in susceptible infants, while reports of allergy to sesame seeds are on the increase. Reactions have also been reported to citrus fruits, chicken, all dairy produce, goats' and ewes' milk, other seeds and exotic fruits, such as mango.

The infants most susceptible to an allergic reaction or intolerance are those who have a family history of allergy. Breast-feeding for up to 6 months will give some protection – and the mother may be advised to avoid the potentially allergenic foods while breast-feeding. For mothers who don't breast-feed and have infants who are allergic to cows' milk, various other infant formulas are available, such as soya formula (which can also cause allergy in approximately 5-10% of children who have a cows' milk allergy), or a hydrolysed milk formula. Unmodified goats' and sheep's milks are unsuitable for infants. For susceptible infants, weaning on to solid foods before 6 months is discouraged. None of the known common food allergens should be offered before 6 months at the earliest, according to the Department of Health, while other experts feel that avoidance of these foods for the first year is better.

Because not all adverse reactions to food occur in children with a family history of allergy, parents/carers of all infants are also advised to avoid foods that most commonly cause an adverse reaction until various age milestones are reached – lists of these foods and appropriate times to introduce them appear in the charts on pages 14–15.

Symptoms of a food allergy or intolerance can include vomiting, abdominal pain, diarrhoea, eczema, rashes, swelling (e.g. around the mouth), asthma and breathing difficulty. A severe and immediate allergic reaction called anaphylaxis is a rare but possible occurrence – peanuts are the leading cause of anaphylactic shock and there is evidence that 'sensitisation' often occurs in the first year. About 1 in 200 children is thought to have a peanut allergy (though some experts put the figure as high as 1 in 30). In any case, peanuts and other nuts should never be fed to infants, as they can cause choking.

If you suspect that your infant does have a food allergy or intolerance, or you have any food allergy in your family and are thinking of becoming pregnant, are already pregnant or have an infant, you should go and get professional advice from your GP, who should, in turn, refer you to a State Registered Dietitian.

The good news is that a high percentage of infants simply outgrow their food allergies, especially an allergy to milk. Peanut allergy, however, is much less frequently outgrown and gluten intolerance is usually a lifelong disease.

> " "Up to 90% of children will have outgrown an allergy to cows' milk by the age of 3.
> **Royal Society of Medicine (1997)**

Above all – *don't panic!* If you follow these guidelines, your baby has a 90%-plus chance of no adverse reactions to food at all. Don't go avoiding hundreds of different foods, other than those listed above, on the off-chance there might be a problem. Children need a wide variety of foods at this time and you could cause other problems, including fussy eating or even malnutrition. If you are ever at all worried about food allergies – see *your doctor!*

See also: Food Allergies pp117–19.

TOP ALLERGENIC FOODS

- Cows' milk
- Eggs
- Soya, peanuts (groundnuts) and other nuts
- Fish and shellfish

EATING PLAN

AGED AROUND 6 MONTHS

DAY 1

Early morning
150 ml milk feed

Mid-morning
100ml milk feed

Lunch
Few spoons of baby rice purée
100ml milk feed

Tea-time
Few spoons of banana or apple purée (or combine both once baby is used to each flavour)

100ml milk feed

Bed-time
150ml milk feed

DAY 2

Early morning
150ml milk feed

Mid-morning
100ml milk feed

Lunch
Few spoonfuls of potato and/or parsnip purée

100ml milk feed

Tea-time
Few spoonfuls of pear purée
100ml milk feed

Bed-time
150ml milk feed

AGED 6–9 MONTHS

DAY 1

Early morning
150ml milk feed

Breakfast
60-100ml baby porridge cereal made with breast or formula milk

DAY 2

Early morning
100ml milk feed

Mid-morning
100ml milk feed
Unsweetened baby rusk (for older babies in this group)

Lunch
60ml carrot and red lentil purée
100ml well-diluted apple juice

Tea-time
Stewed plum and bio yoghurt purée

100ml milk feed

Bed-time
150ml milk feed

DAY 3

Early morning
150ml milk feed

Breakfast
60-100ml baby rice and puréed apple

Mid-morning
100ml milk feed

Lunch
75ml Cod, Potato and Cheddar Pie (page 221)

100ml milk feed

Tea-time
Broccoli and sweet potato purée
100ml milk feed

Bed-time
150ml milk feed

AGED 9–12 MONTHS

DAY 1

Early morning
150ml milk feed

Breakfast
60-80ml baby rice cereal blended with ripe banana

100ml milk feed

Mid-morning
100ml milk feed

Lunch
Beef and Vegetable Hash (page 214)

100ml milk feed

Tea-time
80-100ml Creamed Pasta with Vegetables (page 225)

100ml well-diluted grape juice

Bed-time
150ml milk feed

DAY 2

Early morning
150ml milk feed

Breakfast
100ml sieved strawberry compote with full-fat fromage frais

100ml milk feed

Mid-morning
100ml milk feed

Lunch
Well-cooked scrambled egg
Fingers of white bread and butter
100ml well-diluted orange juice

Tea-time
Tuna and Potato Fishcakes (page 224) with pea purée

Slices of peeled ripe peach or nectarine

Bed-time
150ml milk feed

DAY 3

Early morning
150ml milk feed

Breakfast
100ml baby porridge topped with 1 dessertspoon prune or sultana purée

100ml well-diluted orange juice

Mid-morning
100ml milk feed

Lunch
Chicken and Mushroom Pasta (page 219)

Peeled apple slices
100ml milk feed

Tea-time
Red Lentil and Tomato Soup (page 200)

White bread fingers with butter
Baby rice with apricot purée
100ml milk feed

Bed-time
150ml milk feed

DAY 4

Early morning
150ml milk feed

Breakfast
1 Weetabix with mashed banana and milk

100ml well-diluted orange juice

Mid-morning
100ml milk feed

Lunch
Vegetable and Butter Bean Hotpot (page 215)

Fromage frais with apple purée
100ml milk feed

Tea-time
Well-scrambled egg

White bread and butter

Peeled peach slices or satsuma segments

Bed-time
150ml milk feed

• All milk feeds are breast or formula. All amounts are guidelines only; feed amounts according to your baby's needs. Give extra milk or boiled water as necessary, and for older infants, finger foods such as unsweetened rusks or rice cakes if hungry between meals.

• Meals with capitalized names indicate recipes in the Recipes section and are followed by their page number.

THE VEGETARIAN CHILD

The parents of infants and young children who are vegetarian may have to work a little harder to ensure they don't fall short on iron, as meat is the main dietary source of easily-absorbed iron for non-vegetarians. Lentils and other pulses, dried fruits, eggs and leafy greens are all good sources. Iron absorption is helped if the iron-rich food is eaten with a vitamin C-rich food or drink. Tea, coffee and high-fibre foods can hinder absorption. Dairy produce should provide sufficient protein and calcium in the diet and a wide variety of cereals, pulses, fruits and veg should provide all the vitamins and minerals.

If your infant is vegan (eating no dairy produce or eggs either), you need to ensure that he or she receives enough calcium. Continue breast-feeding for as long as possible. Other good vegan sources of calcium are mineral-enriched soya formula, tofu, fortified baby breakfast cereals, leafy green vegetables and dried fruits. He or she may also need a vitamin

B12 supplement unless you are feeding B12-fortified soya products or breakfast cereals.

Both vegetarian and vegan babies may benefit from a supplement of omega-3 (long-chain) fatty acids. These essential fats are vital for the maintenance of health and development, and our main source in the diet is usually oily fish, although breast milk contains variable amounts of essential fats and some formula feeds also contain added omega-3s. The main non-fish source is flaxseed (linseed) oil.

The good news for parents of vegetarian children is that the long-term health profile of vegetarians who receive a varied, balanced diet is very good. Several reports have linked vegetarians with lower incidence of cancer and heart disease, and a longer lifespan than that of carnivores.

See also: Fats and Oils pp110–12, Supplements pp185–6, Appendix 1 pp240–5 for a list of sources of iron, calcium, vitamin B and vitamin C.

TODDLERS AND PRE-SCHOOL CHILDREN

Once your child starts becoming more active, learning to walk and run, he or she will need plenty of good food to support all the extra energy he or she is using, as well as for growth and development.

Small children still need a wide range of foods from the four groups:

- Milk and dairy foods
- Meat, fish, eggs, pulses
- Cereals, bread and potatoes
- Fruit and vegetables

The table on page 22 gives the amounts of key nutrients that should be sufficient for most children, from ages 1 to 4 (UK Department of Health).

AGED 1–2

Because toddlers have small stomachs and therefore do not have a great capacity for a lot of bulky foods, it is important not to provide them with the type of low-fat, high-fibre diet that is healthy for most adults. A high-fibre diet will be difficult for them to digest and cope with, and could mean they may not eat enough calories to provide all the energy they need.

A diet fairly high in fat will provide those much needed calories. Fat contains over twice the calories, gram for gram, of either carbohydrates or protein, and a diet containing up to 50% fat is appropriate at this age. For an average two-year-old girl this is about 65g a day, for a boy that age about 68g a day.

After the age of 1, children can have cows' milk as part of their balanced diet, and full-fat milk – as well as other dairy produce, eggs and meat – will provide this fat. Whole milk and other dairy produce also provide the vital vitamin A and calcium that toddlers need, and eggs and meat (as well as pulses and fish) are good nutrient-dense sources of protein. Children aged under 2 shouldn't be given skimmed or semi-skimmed milk as they need the calories and vitamin A that whole milk provides.

Into their second year, toddlers should be managing food similar to that eaten by the rest of

Avoid offering sweet and savoury snack foods and drinks as a 'treat', otherwise children may perceive these foods as more desirable than others. Don't ever offer them as a 'reward' for, say, eating their vegetables.

the family, chopped up small if necessary – but it is still important to avoid adding extra salt or sugar to their meals. Continue to offer new foods – one or two a week is about right. Children over one-year-old can be offered all types of cheese, including soft and blue cheeses. It's at this time that parents should be wary of allowing their toddler to eat too many highly-processed sweet or savoury 'snack' foods and drinks – items such as sweets, packet cakes and biscuits, packet desserts, crisps or sugary drinks – as these are the types of foods that provide a high

proportion of the salt and sugar in many young children's diets, and research has shown that small children eat approximately twice as much of both these as recommended.

See also: Junk Food pp140–3, Salt pp171–4, Snacks p178, Sugar and Sweeteners pp182–5.

IRON

The National Diet and Nutrition Survey of Pre-School Children found that the average iron intake of children in the 1½–2½ age group was low. Iron-deficiency anaemia may result, which is associated with increased risk of infections, and poor weight gain and development. Make sure to include enough iron-rich foods in the diet, such as lean red meat, pulses, dried fruits, dark leafy green vegetables or fortified breakfast cereals. Adding a vitamin C-rich food (e.g. red pepper, orange) to an iron-rich meal helps to increase iron absorption.

See also: Appendix 1 pp240–5 for sources of iron and vitamin C.

AGED 2–4

Small children will need a similar diet to toddlers but, as they grow, their calorie needs will increase, along with the need for a little more of many of the nutrients (see the chart below). A good rough guide to how many calories your own pre-school child needs is his or her weight in kilos × 100. For example, a two-year-old toddler weighing 12 kg would need around 1,200 calories a day.

During this time the overall percentage of fat in the diet can be gradually reduced from around 50% at

weaning, so that by the time your child is 5 he or she is getting no more than 35% of calories as fat. By age 2 you can move your child over to semi-skimmed milk if you prefer – this may be a good idea if he or she is slightly heavier than average – but don't start giving children skimmed milk until they are 5. As he or she needs less fat now, it is even more important to keep intake of high-fat snack foods, such as crisps and chocolate, and fatty sugary foods low.

ENERGY REQUIREMENTS FOR BOYS AND GIRLS AGED 1–4 (KCALORIES)

Age	Girls	Boys
1–3	1,165	1,230
4	1,545	1,715

NUTRITIONAL REQUIREMENTS FOR GIRLS AND BOYS AGED 1–4 (DEPARTMENT OF HEALTH)

Age	Protein (g)	Vit C (mg)	Vit A (mcg)	Vit D (mcg)	Calcium (mg)	Iron (mg)	Zinc (mg)
1–3	14.5	30	400	7	350	6.9	5.0
4	20	30	500	–	450	6.1	6.5

Sodium – the new average daily target is no more than 2g of salt a day, which equals not more than 0.8g sodium a day for children aged 1–3 and 3g a day (1.2g sodium) for children aged 4–6.

SALT

Continue to watch your child's salt intake. The Food Standards Agency suggests 2g salt (or 0.8g sodium) a day as a maximum for children aged 1–3 and 3g (1.2g) for children aged 4–6 – much less than most young children eat. Remember when reading food labels, that salt (sodium chloride) is 40% sodium and 60% chloride e.g. a sodium content of 0.4g per 100g food translates to 1g of salt per 100g. (Multiply any sodium content by 2.5 to get the salt content.)

See also: Salt pp171–4.

PEANUTS AND FOOD ALLERGIES

Unless your child is at high risk of allergy (i.e. you or they suffer from allergies, asthma or eczema), you can feed him or her smooth nut butters (e.g. peanut butter) from age 1 onwards – they contain good amounts of protein, as well as essential fats, and are especially useful for vegetarian or vegan children.

For high-risk children, the British Dietetic Association Paediatric Group advise waiting until age 3 before trying them with peanuts and peanut products. Some other experts advise waiting until age 5. It is also wise to avoid any foods to which other members of the family may be intolerant – e.g. peanuts (groundnuts) and other nuts, eggs, wheat – or ask your dietitian for further advice.

> **Don't ever think of giving any whole nuts to children who are under 5 years of age, as there is quite a considerable risk that they could choke on them. Provide them instead with nutritious nut butters such as smooth peanut butter.**

FRUIT AND VEGETABLES

Most of us are probably aware that fruits and vegetables are rich in vitamins, minerals, plant chemicals and fibre, and that the official advice is to eat 5 portions a day – but does this advice apply to small children?

The Food Standards Agency advises that between weaning and five years old, you should gradually increase your child's intake of fruits and veg so that by age five, he or she is getting 'five a day'. I believe that the best way to do this is to offer a wide variety of fruits and vegetables right from the start but to offer them in very small portions, and in plenty of soups, purées and composite dishes. Then, gradually over these important years, increase portion sizes (1 tablespoon, say, at age 2, up to 2 tablespoons by age 4) and offer them in more 'adult' form, e.g. sliced, chopped, shredded or whole, as appropriate, so that your child learns to enjoy the natural crunchiness, flavour and form of all the delicious range of fruits and veg.

If you hold off too long it may become harder to get your children to enjoy their 'five', as they do form much of their taste for food in the first couple of years. The eating plans in this chapter give many suggestions for serving fruits and vegetables (with recipes for many dishes in the Recipe section), and there are numerous tips for encouraging your child to eat fruit and veg in the A–Z section. For serving sizes for small children, see the box 'What is a serving?' below.

See also: 'Eating Plans' pp28–31, Fruit pp129–30, Fussy Eating and Food Refusal p131, Greens pp133–4, Vegetables pp191–4.

DRINKS

The great majority of your child's liquid intake should still be in the form of milk, water and, if liked, a small amount of diluted fruit or vegetable juices. You should avoid offering your child fizzy drinks and caffeine-rich drinks.

See also: Caffeine p85, Drinks pp103–4, Milk pp146–7, Teeth and Gums pp189–90, Water p196.

VEGETARIAN CHILDREN

Continue with the advice that appeared on page 19, providing vegetarian children with a good range of non-animal sources of protein, including pulses and dairy products, and ensuring that they don't miss out on essential minerals such as iron, and vitamins such as B12.

See also: 'The Vegetarian Child' p39.

FEEDING STRATEGIES AGED 1–4

Try to match the size of servings to your child's appetite – paradoxically, for poor eaters it is best to offer portions that are slightly smaller than you might think, as you can always offer more. A typical day's eating for a child aged 1–4 should try to include:

Fruit and vegetables. 4–5 servings of fresh or frozen fruits and vegetables, cooked or raw.
Starchy carbohydrates. A starchy carbohydrate food with each meal – bread, cereals, potatoes, rice, etc. Most of these should be in as 'unadulterated' a form as possible, for example a slice of bread rather than a sticky bun.

Protein. 2 servings of meats or alternatives – e.g. lean beef, chicken, fish (avoiding marlin, shark or swordfish), pulses, egg. For safety, still cook the egg well; don't serve children raw or lightly cooked eggs.
Calcium. 600ml of milk (whole under 2, semi-skimmed or whole for ages 2–4; alternatively, substitute 25g cheese per 100g for some of this milk) plus one or two daily snacks/desserts based on yoghurt or fromage frais. For vegan children, calcium-fortified soya milk and soya milk yoghurts and tofu are alternatives.

HOW MANY MEALS A DAY?

Small children often can't face or manage big meals, yet their nutrient needs are high, so 'little and often' is a good maxim. Breakfast is important and shouldn't be skipped; lunch is a vital refuelling meal for active pre-schoolers and also gives a breathing space in the day, and early supper/tea is a good time for the whole family to share a meal. Mid-morning and mid-afternoon are good snack times – as long as these snacks aren't too calorie-rich – while a milk drink and a semi-sweet biscuit at bedtime will help children to sleep.

See also: 'Eating Plans' pp28–31.

WHAT IS A SERVING?

For an average pre-school child, a portion may be:

• 1 x 30g slice of bread or 2 tablespoons breakfast cereal or pasta or rice or 1 x 150g baked potato

• 40–50g meat, poultry, fish or pulses, or 1 whole egg

• 30g hard or cream cheese or 60g cottage cheese or fromage frais, or 1 small individual tub of yoghurt or fromage frais

• 1 small whole fruit (e.g. plum) or ½ large fruit (e.g. large apple, orange, pear), 2 tablespoons berry fruits, 8 grapes or cherries (stoned)

• 1–2 heaped tablespoons cooked vegetables, 2 broccoli florets, 1 whole carrot (sliced)

FEEDING PROBLEMS AGED 1–4

Toddlers and young children can be notoriously difficult about eating what you want them to eat, when you want them to eat it. The tantrums of the 'terrible twos' can be just as bad at the dining table as they are in your supermarket or at nursery school.

❝ ❞ Experiencing food problems is a normal and common stage of development in pre-school children. One-third of under-5s practise food refusal or selective eating.
The Royal College of Psychiatrists

This is partly because children are experimenting with, or being asked to try, new textures and tastes, and partly because they are testing their parents' reactions and seeing what effect their behaviour has. The majority of children will grow out of any problems, but you can help minimize mealtime tantrums and raised stress levels (and that's only in you, the parent!) with the following tips.

See also: Fussy Eating and Food Refusal p131.

DON'T WORRY, STAY CALM

Almost all children aged around 2–3 have their food favourites and take against certain foods that they have previously liked, or refuse certain foods just from looking at them, or try a little and then refuse that food next time. Many will use food refusal as a way to get your attention – or a reaction. If they are not underweight and seem healthy, and are eating some foods from each of the groups (see page 13), then you shouldn't worry too much. Getting agitated, or forcing them to eat, will make the situation worse.

POSSIBLE PHYSICAL CAUSES OF REFUSAL

Teething. If your child is teething, he or she may feel off-colour, his or her gums will be sore and he or she may be off his or her food. Offer sugar-free rusks or rice cakes to chew on and plenty to drink until the child feels better.
Illness. If your child is ill, this may cause them to be off their food. See a doctor and give plenty to drink.

Tiredness and stress. If your child is more tired than usual, or worried about anything, such as the arrival of a new child minder, or picking up on the fact that you yourself are troubled, he or she may go off his or her food.

See also: Convalescence pp96–7.

SMALL RANGE OF FOODS

Small children who will only eat a few different types of food – say, milk, bread, cheese, apples – can be a worry, but seem to do better on such limited diets than you might think. Try to build on a favourite food and work others in. For example, if he or she loves milk, then add a small amount of blended fruit to make a milkshake and gradually increase the amount and variety of fruits used. If your child loves bread, try it toasted, plain, white, brown, with butter, with spread, and then try a tiny bit of peanut butter or mashed banana in a small sandwich. Your community dietitian may advise vitamin and mineral drops – A, C and D are commonly given to small children.

INTRODUCING NEW FOODS

Early conditioning. Research shows that if your child has been introduced to a wide range of foods straight from weaning, they are more likely to accept them. Only 4% of new foods are accepted after the age of 2. Also, delayed weaning (after 6 months) can cause later faddy eating, as can delay in offering textured foods or chunks of food.

Keep trying. One UK study has shown that the best way to offer children a new food is in very tiny amounts, and you may need to offer it numerous times. Most parents give up on a new food after offering it twice, but it takes 8–10 times for the child to accept the new taste.

Don't mention the 'H' word! Research also shows that children who are told that they must eat up a food because it is 'healthy' or 'good for them' are actually less likely to like or accept the food being offered.

SMALL APPETITE

Be guided by whether your child is a reasonable weight or not – if he or she is, then don't worry. Many small children don't have much of an appetite for their main meals because they have filled up on snacks and drinks between meals. A child needs to be hungry to enjoy a meal, so try offering only water or diluted juice for drinks, and snacks of fresh fruit or vegetable batons between meals.

See also: Appetite Loss p74.

A HEALTHY START

Dislike of vegetables. If your child only dislikes some vegetables then that isn't too much of a problem as he or she can get all the nutrients they need from the ones they do like.

Junk foods and snacks. By and large, if the young child doesn't have access to these foods he or she won't want them. Sadly, a lot of parents do offer their small children crisps, sweets and so on. As at this age you have control over what your child eats, don't introduce the idea that these items are treats or rewards. This is especially important for overweight children and those with a poor appetite.

Sweet tooth. Tastes for salty and sweet foods are developed early in life, and though they can be reversed, it is hard when entrenched. However, there is nothing wrong with many puddings – like custards, fruit desserts and rice puddings – which can offer a range of important nutrients such as vitamin C, calcium and protein. If your child eats a general balanced diet, the small amounts of sugar in such desserts are acceptable.

See also: Desserts pp99–100, Fruit pp129–30, Greens pp133–4, Junk Food pp140–3, Sugars and Sweeteners pp182–5, Vegetables pp191–4.

MAKING FOOD ENJOYABLE

Some parents worry so much about a good diet for their child that meals become tense and anxious affairs. This can make small feeding problems worse, as children can easily be put off food by tension – or learn to like the attention that food refusal brings. Give your child the idea that good food is wonderful,

FOODS TO LOVE AND HATE

Top ten foods that children aged 4–5 HATE MOST:
• avocado • leeks • marrow • melon
• cottage cheese • sweet pepper • onion
• liver • cabbage • parsnips

Top ten foods that children aged 4–5 LIKE MOST:
• chocolate • chocolate biscuits • crisps
• yoghurt • ice cream • ice lollies • fruit squash
• bread • chicken • plain biscuits.

Source: survey by University College London (2002).

to be enjoyed. Help them develop a love of real food and home cooking. Let them enjoy sitting with you, and other family members if you have them. Even small children can help prepare food – washing fruits or vegetables, mixing, kneading, then taste testing.

If a child really doesn't want his or her meal, never force them to sit there with uneaten food for ages after others have finished. Set a time limit on each meal of 20–30 minutes.

WEIGHT CONTROL

The number of overweight and obese pre-school children is rocketing in both the UK and USA, so much so that, according to a recent survey by Liverpool University, almost a third of under-fours in the UK are now overweight and 1 in 10 are obese.

These figures are worrying because there are many links between childhood obesity and later health problems. For instance, a 2002 study at the University of Southampton found that children who gained the most weight between ages 1 and 5 had the highest blood pressure in adulthood. Childhood obesity is linked with adult obesity, heart and circulatory diseases, diabetes and insulin resistance, and joint problems.

Although parents should not feed their children a low-fat, high-fibre, low-calorie type of diet (see page 21 for the reasons), most experts consider the overweight triggers to be lack of exercise and too many sweet, fatty, calorie-dense fast foods, snack foods and drinks. If you follow the healthy feeding principles, recipes, menus and tips in this book, you should be providing your child with a balanced healthy diet that won't make him or her put on too much weight.

However, if you think that your child may be overweight, check out the Growth Charts in Appendix 2 and see your doctor, who should refer you to a dietitian for specialist advice. It is also important that your child isn't undernourished – some children are naturally thin without being short of any nutrients, but if your child is thin (see Growth Charts again) and appears to be failing to thrive in any way (pale, listless, lacking in strength or energy), then you should also see your doctor for a referral.

See also: Obesity pp152–5, Appendix 2 pp250–1 for Growth Charts.

EATING PLANS

FOR CHILDREN AGED 1–4

- Portion sizes for all meals, unless otherwise specified, should generally be guided by your child's appetite.
- Chop or finely chop any food as necessary for younger children.
- Provide 2 between-meal snacks if your child is hungry (one mid-morning, one mid-afternoon), choosing from: a handful of dried fruit (e.g. apricots, sultanas), a piece of fresh fruit, a small slice of bread with a little honey or thinly-spread Marmite or peanut butter, a rice cake, a small pot of fromage frais, a breadstick with a little Cheese Dip (page 203), a small chunk of Cheddar or similar cheese with a low-salt oatcake, a small slice of Fruit Cake (page 234), half a toasted teacake with thinly spread butter.
- Provide about a litre (2 pints) of fluid a day – half of which should be milk (whole up to aged 2, semi-skimmed aged 2–4), the remainder should be water or up to 2 small cups of fruit juice diluted with an equal quantity of water.
- Meals with capitalized names indicate recipes that are to be found in the Recipes section and are followed by their page number.

EATING PLAN FOR AGE 1–2

DAY 1

Breakfast
Weetabix with milk
Banana

Lunch
Fish Fingers with Potato Wedges (page 220)
Small portion of peas (lightly mashed)
1 pot of fruit fromage frais

Evening
Baked beans on white toast topped with 1 tablespoonful of grated hard cheese
1 seedless satsuma

DAY 2

Breakfast
1 medium egg, boiled
Toast soldiers with butter
½ kiwi fruit or pear

Lunch
Chicken Dippers (page 214), batons of lightly cooked carrot and apple slices, served with a savoury dip of light mayonnaise mixed with low-fat bio yoghurt, a dash of tomato purée and some lemon juice to taste

Evening
Cooked pasta shapes served with Tomato Sauce (page 237)

DAY 3

Breakfast
Porridge served with milk and a little runny honey
Seedless grapes, halved

Lunch
Beef and Carrot Casserole (page 226)
Mashed potato
Cauliflower

Evening
Peanut butter or ham sandwich
2 cherry tomatoes, quartered
Small pot of fruit yoghurt

DAY 4

Breakfast
Small bowlful of Special K with milk and fresh fruit (chopped as necessary)
Slice bread or toast with butter and reduced-sugar jam

Lunch
Baked, microwaved or poached white fish (e.g. cod, haddock, coley) served with Cheese Sauce (page 235)
Mashed potato
Broccoli

Evening
Scrambled egg on toast
1 seedless satsuma

DAY 5

Breakfast
1 small pot of Greek yoghurt with runny honey
Apple slices
1 slice of toast with butter and reduced-sugar jam

Lunch
Plain basmati rice served with Lentil Ragu (page 237)
Seedless satsuma or pear slices

Evening
1 small baked potato with grated cheese and butter
Quartered cherry tomatoes

DAY 6

Breakfast
Porridge with milk and brown sugar
1 banana

Lunch
Cottage Pie (page 211) made using Basic Minced Beef recipe (page 220) and a mashed potato topping (brown under grill)
Broccoli and ½ grilled tomato

Evening
Ready-made pizza fingers
Apple slices

DAY 7

Breakfast
Ready Brek with milk and honey
1 seedless satsuma
1 slice of toast with butter and reduced-sugar jam

Lunch
Roast chicken with roast potato
Broccoli and carrot
Gravy
Apple and custard fool made by blending apple purée with ready-made custard

Evening
Sandwich filled with well-drained tuna canned in water or oil mixed with a little ready-made mayonnaise or mayo/bio yoghurt mix and finely chopped cucumber
Cherry tomatoes, quartered
Slice of Date Loaf (page 232)

EATING PLAN FOR AGE 2-3

DAY 1

Breakfast
Natural bio yoghurt with runny honey and chopped banana

Toast, butter and reduced-sugar jam or a little Marmite

Lunch
Home-made Burger (page 225)
Potato Wedges (page 220)
Peas
Plum or pineapple slices

Evening
Mini pitta bread filled with Hummus (page 205) and a little chopped salad

Few seedless grapes, halved

DAY 2

Breakfast
Banana sandwich on white bread
Glass of apple juice

Lunch
Grilled turkey or vegetable escalope
Grilled tomato quarters
Green beans
Mashed potato

Evening
Boiled egg and bread soldiers
Seedless satsuma

DAY 3

Breakfast
Shreddies with milk and chopped apple
Toast with butter and honey

Lunch
Fish and Tomato Bake (page 215)
Broccoli
Greek yoghurt with stewed dried apricot purée

Evening
Cheese sandwich
Halved cherry tomatoes

DAY 4

Breakfast
Berry and Banana Milkshake (page 239)

Toast with butter and a little Marmite

Lunch
Pasta shapes or chopped spaghetti served with Basic Minced Beef (page 220)

Small side salad (e.g. thin wedges of Iceberg lettuce, cucumber batons)

Evening
Carrot and Orange Soup (page 201)
Small soft roll and butter
Small pot of fruit fromage frais

DAY 5

Breakfast
Boiled egg
Slice of toast and butter
Glass of orange juice

Lunch
Chicken breast slices fried in a little sunflower oil

1–2 croquette potatoes or Potato Cakes (page 206) cooked in the same pan

Sweetcorn kernels and carrots
Small pot of fruit fromage frais

Evening
Sandwich of drained canned tuna in oil mashed with a few cooked butter beans and a little ready-made mayonnaise

Apple slices

DAY 6

Breakfast
Weetabix with milk
Toast with butter and honey
Seedless satsuma

Lunch
Chunky Vegetable and Kidney Bean Soup (page 201)

Vanilla ice cream with ready-made fruit coulis and a few sliced strawberries or other fruit

Evening
Chicken wrap (mix cooked chicken breast with a little ready-made mayonnaise and lemon juice and some shredded lettuce and fill a tortilla-type wrap), cut into bite-sized pieces to serve

Slice of Fruit Cake (page 234)

DAY 7

Breakfast
Porridge with milk and brown sugar
Few seedless grapes, halved

Lunch
Roast lamb
Roast potatoes
Mashed swede
Peas
Gravy
Banana Split (page 230)

Evening
Cheese Dip (page 203)
Selection of vegetables, bread sticks, etc. to dip
Apple slices

EATING PLAN FOR AGE 3–4

DAY 1

Breakfast
Special K with milk
Chopped berry fruits
1 slice of bread with butter and
reduced-sugar jam

Lunch
Tuna and Egg Kedgeree
(page 221)

Greek yoghurt with stewed
blackcurrants or plums

Evening
Baked beans on toast
Ready-made or home-made rice
pudding with apricot purée

DAY 2

Breakfast
Porridge with milk and honey
Orange segments

Lunch
Lentil and Vegetable Soup (page
202)

Small soft roll
Pot of fruit fromage frais

Evening
Baked potato filled with grated
hard cheese and chopped ham
blended with natural fromage frais

Cherry tomatoes and lettuce
wedges

DAY 3

Breakfast
Berry and Banana Milkshake (page
239)

Toast and butter with a little
Marmite

Lunch
Salmon and Egg Flan (page 222)
Box of cress, tomato and
cucumber salad
Pear slices

Evening
Chicken Soup (page 202)
Soft brown roll
Pot of fruit fromage frais

DAY 4

Breakfast
Boiled egg and toast soldiers
Kiwi fruit or orange slices

Lunch
Reduced-fat good-quality chipolata
sausages

Mashed potato
Baked beans
Seedless grapes

Evening
Cheese Dip (page 203)
Selection of crudités (e.g. lightly
cooked baby corn cobs, carrot
batons, breadsticks, apple slices)

Slice of Date Loaf (page 232)

DAY 5

Breakfast
Apple Smoothie (page 238)
Toast with peanut butter or soft
cheese spread

Lunch
Chicken Casserole (page 223)
Plain basmati rice
Broccoli

Evening
Egg mayonnaise wrap
Seedless satsuma

DAY 6

Breakfast
Weetabix with milk and chopped
pear

Slice of toast with butter and
reduced-sugar jam

Lunch
Fish Fingers (page 220 or use
ready-made if preferred)

Mashed potato
Peas
Grilled tomato

Evening
Grated Cheddar cheese and apple
chutney sandwich

Fruit yoghurt
Orange slices

DAY 7

Breakfast
Greek yoghurt with honey and
berry fruits or peach slices

Slice of toast with butter and a
little Marmite

Lunch
Roast beef
Roast potatoes
Shredded cabbage
Carrots
Gravy
Fresh Fruit Trifle (page 231)

Evening
Apricot and Brown Rice Salad
(page 209)

STARTING SCHOOL UP TO ELEVEN

By the time children start school, many of the 'toddler' feeding troubles will have vanished. For most parents, having to cope with table tantrums are well in the past. But, of course, there will be new food dilemmas once children reach the primary school years. At this age, children become more independent and opinionated, are away from home for some meals, and are able to make their own choices about what they eat. Many parents find children begin to demand foods they haven't wanted before, and often these are 'junk foods'.

For example, school lunches are the main meal of the day for many kids, and helping them make wise choices – or going the lunch-pack route – can be a minefield. And, however well you have previously managed a 'no sweets' policy with your young children, competing with peer pressure in the playground can be hard. At home they can be influenced just as much by the power of marketing. Primary-age children now watch an average of 2½ hours of television a day and 63% have their own TV set, so no wonder the many ads for crisps, sweets and fast foods result in a phenomenal level of 'pester power'.

In this section we look at whether or not you should be worried by these influences, and how to combat them. We also look at the growing problem of obesity in young schoolchildren and what to do to try to ensure your children maintain a reasonable weight.

NUTRITIONAL NEEDS OF PRIMARY SCHOOL CHILDREN

Once children reach about 5 years old, their healthy diet is more or less similar to an adult's healthy diet, but there are several important considerations at this age. At age 5, unless your child has problems such as food allergy or specific health difficulties, he or she can now be given a diet based upon that of an adult. Here are the main points of difference between a 5-year-old's diet and that of a pre-school child.

Fat. The need for a higher proportion of fat in the diet is now over and the level to aim for is about 30–35% of total calories, the same as for adults. This means that he or she can use skimmed milk instead of whole milk or semi-skimmed milk. Indeed, as obesity levels in young children are rising, it is wise to keep a careful eye on total fat intake.

Long-chain omega-3 fatty acids are special health-giving fats, found in oily fish and some other foods (see pages 248–9). In the recent National Diet and Nutrition Survey of young people aged 4–18, average intake of omega-3 fatty acids was found to be very low, at 0.8% of total food energy, and the British Nutrition Foundation in its report Nutrition, Health and Schoolchildren (2002) recommends doubling this amount.

Nuts. Children can now be given whole nuts (unless they have a nut allergy).

Fish. Children under 16 shouldn't eat marlin, shark or swordfish because of the mercury levels in these fish.

Fibre. You can increase the fibre content of your child's diet so that he or she is eating more whole grains, pulses and so on. This is important if the child tends to suffer from constipation, and less necessary if he or she is underweight and/or has trouble eating normal child-sized portions.

Although there is no UK official dietary reference value for fibre, the American Academy of Pediatrics (AAP) offers a simple way of calculating a reasonable fibre intake for your child and, using these guidelines, many children have a low intake. The AAP says that a child's fibre intake in grams should equal his or her age plus 5. For example, a six year old should have 11g of fibre

a day, while a 10 year old should have 15g a day. The average UK child (aged 4–18) has only 11.2g/day (boys) and 9.7g/day (girls).

> Our children, on average, eat a diet that is too high in sodium. New recommendations in the UK suggest that children aged 4–6 should have no more than 3g salt a day in their diet (1.2g sodium) and children aged 7–10 should have no more than 5g salt (2g sodium).

Nutrient intake. If you give your child a good varied diet, with plenty of fruits, vegetables, grains, proteins and some fat, you shouldn't really need to worry about exactly how much of each nutrient you are providing.

❝ ❝ The more colour on a child's food plate, the more varied and comprehensive the selection of nutrients that plateful is likely to contain – reds, yellows and greens in particular. ❞ ❞
The American Academy of Pediatrics

As a reference, however, the table on page 35 shows the amounts of some of the most important nutrients for 5–11-year-olds which the UK

Department of Health consider will be enough for the needs of most children. The charts at the back of the book show which foods are the best sources of these nutrients.

See also: Dietary Fibre pp101–2, Fish pp113–14, Food Allergies pp117–19, Salt pp171–4, Appendix 1 pp240–9 for sources of nutrients.

GIRLS AND BOYS

During the course of this age range, girls and boys will be found to have slightly differing needs for a few of the major nutrients.

Throughout the primary school years, most boys will need a steadily increasing number of calories – a few more than girls normally need at that age – as they are beginning to become, on average, slightly bigger, with resulting greater energy needs.

When boys get into the 'double figures' in age, their need for protein and calcium, to help them build the extra muscle and bone needed for growth at this age, will also be found to be slightly higher than that for girls.

As they enter puberty, aged around 11, girls will then begin to need more iron than boys, but their need for calories is slightly less, on average, at this age than it was between 7 and 10.

AMOUNTS OF ENERGY AND SELECTED NUTRIENTS SUFFICIENT FOR AVERAGE CHILDREN (DEPARTMENT OF HEALTH)

	Cals	Protein (g)	Vit A (mcg)	Vit C (mg)	Calc (mg)	Iron (mg)	Zinc (mg)
Boys Age							
5–6	1,715	19.7	500	30	450	6.1	6.5
7–10	1,970	28.3	500	30	550	8.7	7.0
11	2,200	42.1	600	35	1,000	11.3	9.0
Girls Age							
5–6	1,545	19.7	500	30	450	6.1	6.5
7–10	1,940	28.3	500	30	550	8.7	7.0
11	1,845	41.2	600	35	800	14.8	9.0

MAXIMUM RECOMMENDED DAILY FAT INTAKES (DOH)

The table here shows the maximum number of fat grams that a child should have daily in order to provide a maximum of 35% of his or her calories.

Age	5–6	7–10	11
Boys	67g	77g	86g
Girls	60g	75g	72g

THE FOOD PYRAMID

The Food Pyramid illustrated on page 37 is a simple guide to the different types of food we need and in what proportions we need to eat them for good health. (For children under 6 there is a slightly modified pyramid on page 36.)

This Pyramid is based on the ones designed by the United States Department of Agriculture and is, in essence, the same as that used by the Australian Department of Health. In the UK, the Nutrition Forum at the Food Standards Agency (FSA) uses a plate divided up into segments, but I feel that the Food Pyramid is the easiest and best guide to follow as it contains actual portion guidelines and also includes nuts, which the FSA plate does not.

The Pyramid is for adults and children over 6 alike. The only major alteration I have made is to include potatoes in with the starchy carbohydrate group – the US pyramid includes only grains (bread, rice, pasta, breakfast cereals, etc.) in this band. I have done this because, in the UK, potatoes are classed as a starchy carbohydrate and don't count towards the day's fruit and vegetable intake.

The Pyramid is suitable for all children, even those who have special needs (for example, vegetarians, vegans or those with food allergies), as there is no need to eat any one particular food, as long as you choose foods from each group to make up the total recommended servings.

INTERPRETING THE FOOD PYRAMID

A glance at the food pyramid shows you that the 'base' of your child's diet should be starchy carbohydrates – grains (and foods made from grains) and potatoes. Vegetables and fruits together form the next layer and should make up the next largest part of a child's food intake. Then the 'protein' foods come next – dairy foods, meats, poultry, fish, pulses (including tofu), eggs and nuts. The tip of the pyramid is made up by naturally occurring and added fats and sugars – the foods your child should eat in the smallest quantities.

Recommended servings a day are given for all the food groups except fats and sugars, which simply say 'eat less' and should be used sparingly. Younger children may need only the lower number of servings of the foods as their calorie needs may

be lower, but once children reach 10 or 11 they may require the higher number of servings stated. Actual serving sizes for children aren't given against the Pyramid, but the American Academy of Pediatrics (AAP) has published guidelines which I have adapted (see the panel on page 38). At first glance the number of serving sizes may seem quite high but then, if you check the size of what a 'serving' is, in fact there isn't too much to eat at all.

For example, a serving of bread for a 6-year-old is only half a slice, so one normal 2-slice sandwich would give 4 servings from the starchy carbs group. And half a piece of fruit is one serving, so a whole apple would be 2 servings of fruit. The AAP says that you don't need to worry about meeting these serving requirements every single day – it is what your child eats over a period of 1–2 weeks that counts.

See also: 'Eating Plans' pp49–51 for more guidance on converting the pyramid recommendations into actual meals.

FOOD PYRAMID – 2–6 year olds

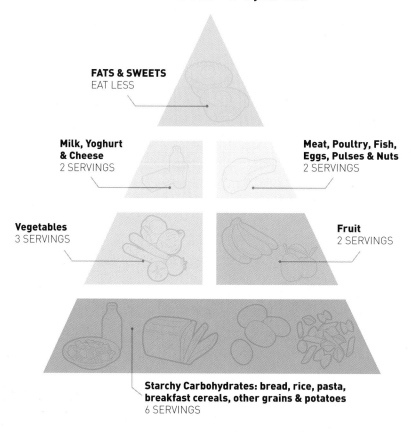

FATS & SWEETS
EAT LESS

Milk, Yoghurt & Cheese
2 SERVINGS

Meat, Poultry, Fish, Eggs, Pulses & Nuts
2 SERVINGS

Vegetables
3 SERVINGS

Fruit
2 SERVINGS

Starchy Carbohydrates: bread, rice, pasta, breakfast cereals, other grains & potatoes
6 SERVINGS

FOOD PYRAMID – 6 years and over

FATS & SWEETS
EAT LESS

Milk, Yoghurt & Cheese
2–3 SERVINGS

Meat, Poultry, Fish, Eggs, Pulses & Nuts
2–3 SERVINGS

Vegetables
3–5 SERVINGS

Fruit
3–5 SERVINGS

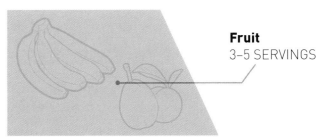

Starchy Carbohydrates: bread, rice, pasta, breakfast cereals, other grains & potatoes
6–11 SERVINGS

SERVING SIZES – WHAT IS A PORTION?

The American Academy of Pediatrics (AAP) says that portion sizes should be guided by the 'Three As' – age, appetite and activity levels. If a child is growing well and is of around average weight, then the portion sizes they receive are probably about right. The panel below shows my adaptation of the AAP's own portion charts. In practice, most children will gradually increase portion sizes between ages 5 and 10, until by 10 or 11 they are eating adult-sized meals. As you will see from the table of energy and nutritional requirements, a 7–10-year-old's calorie needs are similar to those of an adult woman – a woman aged 19–50 needs 1,940 calories a day.

See also: Fruit pp129–30, Vegetables pp191–4 for more detailed guidance as to what makes a portion.

SERVING SIZES FOR CHILDREN AGED 5–10
(BASED ON THE NUMBER OF SERVINGS RECOMMENDED IN THE USA FOOD PYRAMID)

NOTE: For ease of use I have retained the American cup sizes for some items. A US cup measurement is a cup that holds 225ml liquid. That is roughly equivalent to a small mug, but if you have a measuring jug you could test your mugs with 225ml water until you find one that is 'cup' size. It is much easier to measure both dry and liquid foods like this than weighing them.

Food group	Portion size for ages 5–6 for 1 serving	Portion size for ages 7–10* for 1 serving
Starchy carbohydrates	bread – ½ slice cooked rice/pasta – ⅓ cup breakfast cereal – ½ cup potato – ⅓ cup (2 small chunks)	bread – 1 slice cooked rice/pasta – ½ cup breakfast cereal – ⅔ cup potato – ½ cup (3 small chunks)
Vegetables	cooked vegetables – ¼ cup salad – ½ cup	cooked vegetables – ½ cup salad – 1 cup
Fruit	cooked or canned – ¼ cup fresh – ½ average piece juice – ⅓ cup	cooked or canned – ⅓ cup fresh – 1 piece juice – ½ cup
Dairy	milk – ½ cup cheese, hard – matchbox size yoghurt – small (125g) pot	milk – 1 cup cheese, hard – matchbox size yoghurt – 1½ small pots
Meat, poultry, fish	All – 30g or 2x2.5cm cubes	All – 60-90g or 4-6x2.25cm cubes
Eggs	1 egg	1–2 eggs
Pulses	All pulses, cooked – ⅓ cup	All pulses, cooked – ½ cup
Nuts, seeds	1 small palmful (20g)	1 medium palmful (30g)

* From age 11, adult portions

INTERNATIONAL RECOMMENDATIONS

I think it is worth giving you here some general recommendations that various Governments have made regarding diet, which seem to add up to a pretty strong consensus of opinion.

The USDA (United States Department of Agriculture), in its newly revised recommendations which apply both to adults and school-age children, says:
• Choose a diet that is low in saturated fat and cholesterol, and moderate in total fat.
• Choose beverages and foods that limit your intake of sugars.
• Choose and prepare foods with less salt.
• Eat a variety of grains, especially whole grains, fruit and vegetables daily.
• Let the Food Pyramid guide your food choices.

The National Health and Medical Research Council of Australia says in its 'Dietary Guidelines for Children and Adolescents':
• Enjoy a wide variety of nutritious foods.
• Eat plenty of vegetables (including legumes/pulses), fruits and cereals (preferably whole grain).
• Include lean meat, fish, poultry and/or alternatives such as legumes (pulses) and nuts.
• Include reduced-fat dairy foods and/or alternatives.
• Choose water as a drink.

Care should be taken to:
• Limit saturated fat and moderate total fat intake.
• Choose foods low in salt.
• Consume only moderate amounts of sugars and foods containing added sugars.

The UK Food Standards Agency says that children should eat:
• A variety of different foods.
• A diet rich in starchy foods.
• A diet that includes large amounts of fruit and vegetables.
• A diet that includes moderate amounts of meat, fish or alternatives, such as eggs, beans and lentils.
• Moderate amounts of dairy products.
• Small amounts of fatty or sugary foods.

THE VEGETARIAN CHILD

The UK National Diet and Nutrition Survey found that less than 2% of children aged from 5 to 10 are vegetarian or vegan. At the age of 11, the number of vegetarian girls increases but the number of vegetarian boys doesn't. The same survey found that levels of iron in the blood were significantly lower in vegetarians than in meat-eaters – but on the positive side, LDL cholesterol levels were lower and intake of several vitamins and selenium were higher in the vegetarians.

If your child is vegetarian and gets a varied diet (see the Food Pyramids pages 36–7) with plenty of vegetables, fruits and pulses, and with not too much dairy produce as a substitute for meat – although dairy is a good source of calcium and protein, a high-dairy diet can also be high in fats and saturates – then you probably have no cause to worry. However, iron deficiency may be a problem, and you should ensure good sources are included in your child's diet.

See also: Anaemia p73, Appendix 1 pp244–5 for sources of iron.

THE VEGAN CHILD

A vegan diet can be very healthy if it contains a wide variety of vegetables, pulses, fruits, nuts and seeds. But a vegan child – eating no dairy produce or eggs as well as avoiding meat, poultry and fish – does have a greater risk of nutrient deficiencies simply because the range of foods is restricted. Pay particular attention to the following needs:

Calories. Vegans tend to consume fewer calories than both carnivores and vegetarians. This may be no bad thing, but if your child is underweight you may need to provide extra snacks during the day.

Protein. Adequate protein is vital for muscle and other tissue development in a growing child but, while animal protein is 'complete', containing all the amino acids necessary for humans, plant proteins (with the exception of soya beans) are not complete. The best way round this is to offer 'mixed protein' meals that contain all the amino acids that are needed. This means combining pulses with grains (e.g. beans on toast), or pulses with a starch (e.g. potato and lentil casserole) or nuts with grains (e.g. peanut butter sandwich).

Calcium. Vital for bone development, some good vegan sources of calcium are fortified soya milk, white bread, baked beans, dried figs, leafy green vegetables, tofu, nuts, muesli, pulses.

Iron. Pulses, leafy green vegetables (e.g. broccoli) and whole grains are all good sources of iron. Absorption from pulses and grains is increased if the meal contains a rich source of vitamin C.

Vitamin B12. Normally found only in animal produce, B12 can be obtained by vegans from sea greens, fortified breakfast cereals, fortified soya milk, Vecon and fortified bread.

Vitamin B2. Vecon, fortified soya milk and fortified breakfast cereals will supply this vitamin for vegans.

Vitamin D. Children who are regularly outdoors are unlikely to shortfall on vitamin D, which the body makes when the skin is exposed to the sun. Otherwise, choose vitamin-D-fortified vegan margarines/soya milk/cereals.

See also: 'Meal Ideas for Vegetarians' p51, Anaemia p73, Underweight pp190–1, Appendix 1 pp240–7 for sources of nutrients.

THE SCHOOL DAY

What your children eat really does have a significant effect upon their intelligence and their ability to concentrate at school, so it makes sense to supply them well with good fuel every day.

THE IMPORTANCE OF BREAKFAST

If a child eats nothing after supper, their blood sugar levels will be very low by the following morning. If he or she doesn't then eat breakfast, blood sugar will dip dangerously low and this can produce various physical symptoms, such as headache, physical and mental tiredness and dizziness.

Several studies have established a strong link between good nutrition early in the day and a child's brain-power. Eating breakfast has been shown to affect the ability to solve problems, and can significantly aid concentration and memory. Other research has found that children who eat breakfast are more creative, have more energy and endurance.

Provision of breakfast means that children are much less likely to snack on sugary, fatty foods during the morning, which has implications for both health and obesity. Breakfast-time is also an important meal for providing calories for energy and growth, and a wide variety of nutrients. People who skip breakfast are unlikely to make up their daily requirement for some vitamins and minerals, and this is especially important for growing children.

 those [children] who ate breakfast had a significant better overall diet... consuming breakfast was associated with a higher grain, fruit, milk and variety scores. Breakfast is a very important contributor to... schoolchildren's overall diet quality.
US Department of Agriculture (1999)

WHAT IS THE BEST BREAKFAST?

A good breakfast for children will include protein, fat and carbohydrate, and will also include some vitamin C. Protein and fat take longer to digest than carbohydrates and so will help to keep the child feeling full and keep his or her blood sugar levels even until lunchtime. Carbohydrates are the main fuel for the brain, while vitamin C, vital for the formation of neurotransmitters in the brain, has been shown to be directly linked with increased IQ.

One study carried out at Reading University in 2001 found that a breakfast of a bacon sandwich was one of the best at improving brain power, while one of cornflakes and milk was one of the poorest – although other experts have disputed these findings. Another study in Denmark and Sweden of 200 children, however, also found that nutrient-packed breakfasts, such as those containing muesli, ham and fruit juice, produced better test results in grammar, maths and physical endurance than breakfasts of only a jam sandwich and fruit squash.

On schooldays, few parents have time to cook a full breakfast – but there are numerous cold breakfasts that will provide a good range of nutrients and enough calories during the week (see the box on the right), while the weekend may be a good opportunity to have something cooked.

See also: 'Eating Plans' pp49–51 for further breakfast ideas, Breakfast Cereals pp83–4.

Some items made and promoted as good breakfast foods are probably best avoided. These include:
• **Breakfast and cereal bars**
– many of these are very high in sugar and fat and even salt.
• **Kiddies breakfast cereals**
– many of the cereals specifically promoted to children via ads and sponsorship contain high levels of sugar and salt.

START THE DAY RIGHT...

A good breakfast should offer a high nutrition profile without too much fat, saturated fat, sugar or salt. Here are several good breakfasts for children:

• Bowl of no-added-sugar-or-salt luxury muesli with skimmed or semi-skimmed milk and a portion of fresh fruit chopped over the top OR with a glass of fruit juice (preferably citrus not apple, which has much less vitamin C).
• Bowl of porridge made with equal parts semi-skimmed milk and water, sprinkled with a little sugar or honey; slice of white or wholemeal toast with a little butter or spread and some reduced-sugar jam, marmalade or Marmite; glass of fruit juice or a piece of fresh fruit.
• 1–2 Weetabix with skimmed or semi-skimmed milk; fruit juice; slice of wholemeal bread with a little butter or spread and a thin coating of peanut butter.
• Bowl of whole milk or low-fat natural bio yoghurt topped with fresh chopped fruit or berries and a handful of luxury muesli.
• Home-made fruit milkshake (see page 239) and a slice of wholemeal bread with a little spread, Marmite or reduced-sugar jam.
• Home-made fruit smoothie (see pages 238–9) with a small pot of fruit fromage frais and a slice of wholemeal bread with spread.
• Sandwich made of 2 slices of wholemeal bread with a little low-fat spread and filled with 2 slices of grilled extra-lean back bacon; glass of orange juice or portion of citrus fruit.
• 1 boiled egg; wholemeal bread with a little butter or spread; pink grapefruit segments.
• Low-sugar, low-salt baked beans in tomato sauce on 2 slices of toast with a little butter; orange juice.

SCHOOL LUNCHTIME – PACKED LUNCH OR CAFETERIA MEAL?

Although nearly half of parents rely upon the school cafeteria to provide their children's lunchtime meal, packed lunch can be a good alternative. Both options have their plus and minus points (see the box on the right) from a convenience and health point of view, though sometimes a packed lunch may be more expensive.

In April 2001, basic nutritional standards for school meals were reintroduced by the UK Government. These are based upon eating a balance of foods similar to the Food Pyramids on pages 36–7, and include dictates such as two chip-free days a week for primary schools, and a menu that contains foods from all the major groups every day. Some feel that these guidelines don't go far enough, and that a child can still choose an unbalanced meal from the items on offer – for example, choosing a meal of, say, burger and chips but declining the vegetables and salad that are available. It helps if you talk about school lunches with your child and encourage him or her to make good choices, and it also helps if you've already established good eating habits at home.

Another problem is cost – it has been reported that although the average cost of a school meal is now £1.56, school caterers spend only 35p on each school meal. Another concern is that many children don't actually spend their school 'dinner money' on lunch in the school cafeteria at all – they often spend it on snacks, sweets and drinks on the way to and from school, or in the school vending machines. Some schools offer a 'credit card'-type scheme (you pay money into your child's lunch account and his or her card is swiped when a meal is chosen) to get round this, while others offer vouchers.

Some schools try very hard to find ways around the problems inherent in the school meals system, but others don't. Perhaps the best advice is to see your school head and find out exactly how their lunch system works before making a decision on whether or not to opt for packed lunches. Ask if the school has a School Nutrition Action Group (SNAG). Ask to see menus, and to visit one lunchtime to see for yourself. Do the salads look fresh and interesting? Are the main courses swimming in fat? What sort of fresh fruit is on offer?

SCHOOL MEALS VS PACKED LUNCHES

School meals pros:
- Quicker and easier for you
- Hot meal option especially good in winter
- Child may prefer to choose his or her own meal
- Basic standards of nutrition now mandatory

School meals cons:
- You have no real control over your child's choices
- Not all school meals caterers follow good practice – vegetables cooked early and kept warm for hours lose much vitamin content, for example
- It may be possible for your child to spend his or her school lunch money on snacks or 'junk foods'

Packed lunches pros:
- You have control over what goes in the lunch-box
- You can provide a completely balanced lunch
- Knowing what's for lunch means you can organize the rest of the day's diet for a balance of nutrients

Packed lunches cons:
- Takes time to shop for and prepare
- Many items sold as good for children's lunch-boxes are, in fact, high in fats/ salt/ sugar/ additives
- Slight risk of food poisoning if lunch-box stored in hot room and/or not in insulated container.

WHAT MAKES A HEALTHY PACKED LUNCH?

Try to ensure that it contains something from each of the following groups:

Starches. For example, bread or pasta – this should form a large part of the lunch-box.
Protein. Lean or medium-fat protein food – either as a sandwich filling or as part of a salad, e.g. cheese, ham, chicken, tuna, egg, peanut butter.
Salad. Either as part of the sandwich or mixed with protein and starch into a salad (e.g. tuna, pasta and tomato salad), or perhaps carrot or celery crudités, or a small bag of cherry tomatoes.
Fruit. The equivalent of 1 piece of fresh fruit, e.g. an apple, satsuma, kiwi fruit, pear. Try to pack things that won't bruise easily. Or make a fruit salad and pack it in a little container with a tight-fitting lid and supply a spoon. If the lunch-box has plenty of salad, you could pack a mini-bag of dried fruits

instead. Mini-containers of ready-prepared fruit salad are available from the supermarket chains, but choose fruit in juice and use these only occasionally.

Dairy. Yoghurt or a milk drink or fromage frais – these are full of calcium and always popular.

Cake. Slice of good-quality cake – e.g. home-made Fruit Cake (page 234), or Banana Bread (page 235), or Carrot Cake (page 234).

Drink. Water or diluted fruit juices are best. Try to avoid fizzy and caffeinated drinks.

Other items, such as crisps, salted nuts, commercial cakes and biscuits, are best kept for very occasional use. If you don't pack these items, your child will simply eat what you have packed. Also try to avoid the convenience lunch-box items that are crowding the supermarket shelves, such as instant noodles, brightly coloured dips, cheese and biscuit packs, which are usually full of salt and/or saturated or trans fats.

Ensure that the content of daily lunch-boxes doesn't get boring – spend time and imagination to provide enough variety of texture, colour and taste. Vary the types of bread used, go for as many different sorts of salad filling and fruits as you can.

SCHOOL VENDING MACHINES

It is now common for schools to sell a variety of snacks, sweets and drinks from vending machines. According to the UK Food Commission, schools rely on the income that these machines make them to fund the shortfall in their budgets.

Schools are also happy for food manufacturers to provide school equipment in return for their being able to plug their wares. For example, exercise books may be sponsored by chocolate manufacturers or soft drinks makers. Or children may be given free samples of fatty, sugary, salty foods – all with the school's blessing. Practices such as these won't stop unless enough parents make their feelings known. The Food Commission has an active and vocal Parents' Jury which you can join. In the USA, similar practices are already in decline or even banned.

See also: 'Eating Plans' pp49–51 for further suggestions for packed lunches, Artificial Sweeteners p75, Brain Power pp81–2, Confectionery pp95–6, Drinks pp103–4, Fats and Oils pp110–12, Junk Food pp140–3, Obesity pp152–5.

AT HOME AND OUT AND ABOUT

What we, and our children, eat is a direct reflection of our lifestyle. In recent years there has been a huge shift away from 'home-cooked' family meals over to fast foods, snacking and eating ready meals. The modern way of life can seem to leave little room for giving food the consideration it deserves.

Most parents of school-age children now work, and working life itself has become increasingly busy, with longer hours, shiftwork, more stress and long commuter journeys. Many parents haven't the time or energy to direct much thought to how they feed their children. Meanwhile, TV, computers and peer culture exert their influences on children's habits and preferences, and more children are left to use their spare time as they wish, visiting friends or shopping, with snacks, foods and drinks available everywhere they go.

The phrase 'family meals' is becoming redundant and in one survey adults who prepared meals such as bottled pasta sauce with spaghetti, or jars of curry with rice, described these as 'home-cooked meals'. It may be little wonder, then, that we are raising nations of children who aren't interested in good, healthy home-cooked food – or indeed, in learning to cook.

REVERSING THE TRENDS

There is little doubt that in order to reverse the negative food patterns described above, time and thought is needed at every level, from government down to individual parents. And there are signs that the importance of good food and good diet is being recognized at corporate level. For instance, several supermarkets have been involved in healthy eating for children initiatives, and the labelling of fresh fruit and vegetables in supermarkets has begun to include cooking and serving suggestions. Even some fast-food outlets are cutting fat in their foods and offering salads and fresh fruit for sale.

Children's cookery clubs and cooking schools are proving that, if given the right encouragement, kids do enjoy cooking and eating 'real' food. The message is that children need to be taught and encouraged to enjoy food in all its variety, and to enjoy cooking – not feel frightened of it. Experts also agree that these ideas need to be instilled at an early age – the primary school years, or even earlier, are ideal.

EVENING MEALS AFTER SCHOOL

After a packed lunch, it's usually a good idea to provide a hot meal in the evening – except perhaps on hot summer days, when a salad may fit the bill. After a school lunch, I would still tend to provide a 'proper' meal in the evening, not just a snack or a sandwich, as, for reasons already examined, the school lunch may or may not have been nutritionally adequate.

On school days it's also best to serve the evening meal no later than around 6pm for younger children and certainly no later than 7pm for 11-year-olds – any later and your child's sleep may be disrupted by his or her digestive activity. A late meal may also encourage excessive snacking before dinner, though all children benefit from a small snack when they get in from school – this should be something like a banana, a slice of bread and reduced-sugar jam, a handful of dried apricots, or a pot of yoghurt.

See also: 'Eating Plans' pp49–51, Recipes pp198–239 for ideas for healthy evening meals.

This is not all intended to make you, the parent, feel guilty about not having spent enough time or energy on feeding your children or encouraging them to develop their own cooking skills. However, it is not too hard or time-consuming to make a few minor changes that can, overall, have a great effect.

> " Parents have a responsibility to educate children about healthy eating, as many bad habits are learnt at an early age. To change these habits you often have to change the whole culture of eating within the family. "
> Spokesperson for Institute of Child Health, London

ENCOURAGE YOUR CHILD TO COOK, AND TO EAT WITH YOU

Whenever you do cook a simple meal, have your child help you. Between 5 and 10, most children are keen to cook, but get little encouragement or lead from their parents. Think of cooking as another 'fun' pastime you can do with them – like playing hide-and-seek or reading a story. Whatever the recipe, there is nearly always something your child can do to help.

What they need to know is that almost all food is good to eat if you know how to go about preparing it. Try to have at least a few real family meals together in any given week, and encourage their interest in 'real' food by taking them with you to markets, looking at cookery books together and so on.

BATCH COOKING

Batch cooking is an ideal way to cook for a family – when you do have some spare time, make up large quantities of pasta sauces, soups, casseroles, basic mince and freeze them in individual portions and/or in family-sized portions. Many people find that a wet Sunday afternoon or winter's evening spent cooking can actually be quite relaxing and satisfying.

ADDING VALUE TO MEALS

The nutritional profile of many fast-food type meals can be improved with the addition of a side salad or a fruit dessert, or with a good-quality drink such as a fruit smoothie. These won't take away fat, sugar or salt from a meal, but they will help your child towards 5 portions of fruit and vegetables a day.

HEALTHY MEALS IN NO TIME

At home, make use of quick and easy meals you can cook yourself – there is no need to spend more than half an hour cooking, except for special occasions.

• Make quick and easy Tomato Sauce or Vegetable Sauce (see pages 236–7) to serve with pasta, couscous or baked potatoes.
• Use eggs and leftover cooked potatoes to make a Spanish omelette and serve with ready-washed salad and bread.
• Serve egg thread noodles with stir-fried ready-sliced chicken or turkey and a pack of ready-shredded stir-fry vegetables.
• Cook some rice, adding petit pois halfway through, and steam salmon or undyed smoked haddock fillet over the top of the pan. Flake the salmon and stir it through the rice with chopped tomato and cucumber.
• Of course, not all food that is good for kids has to be cooked. You can serve simple salads with canned tuna or pilchards, chicken or lean ham.

JUNK FOOD

There is nothing wrong with feeding your children convenience foods some of the time – almost all foods have at least some good points. Lean burgers, chips cooked in oil, fried eggs, chocolate, pizza, cake and many more foods can easily be a part of your child's diet, with real nutritional benefits. It is just the overall balance of the diet that you need to watch, because a diet too reliant on fried, fast, convenience, junk-type foods is also likely to be too high in fat, saturated fat, sugar, salt and calories.

Many parents say to me that their children 'just won't eat' anything except fast foods, chips, burgers and so on, and that they hate fresh vegetables, salads and fruits. Research shows that children who are given a variety of fresh foods from an early age continue to accept, and like, these foods – so first rule is to start as you mean to go on.

I have also found children who do like decent food but their parents just can't cook – overboiled veg and overcooked roasts are never going to be appetising whatever your age. For children who don't like 'grown-up food' like proper fish for example, there are recipes at the back of the book that should help.

It also helps if you can provide good-quality food in terms of raw materials. Whatever the nutritional benefits or otherwise of organic food, I do find that organic meat, eggs, vegetables and fruit taste better than their mass-market factory cousins.

See also: Fruit pp129–30, Fussy Eating and Food Refusal pp131–2, Vegetables pp191–4.

ALTERNATIVES TO 'JUNK FOODS'

As drinks and snacks and foods such as colas, crisps and sweets now account for a large percentage of school-age children's total diet, it makes sense to find ways to reduce their consumption:

- Make sure your child has breakfast, so that they won't need to use the school vending machines.
- Give your child only enough cash for an emergency phone call – then they can't buy junk food.
- Pack a lunch so they don't have to take lunch money which is often spent on snacks rather than lunch.
- When they get home from school (and in other between-meal situations), ensure there is bread and honey or bananas for a quick starchy snack.
- If he or she is out with friends, pop a pack of fresh shelled nuts or dried fruit in a pocket as well as some designer fizzy water in their bag. Make sure they have a nutritious meal/ snack before they go.
- Remember what you don't buy, your children can't eat.

If your child has got out of the habit of eating decently, the best way to get him or her to eat more healthily is by stealth. At first, add vegetables to casseroles or finely chopped in mince mixtures and burgers. Purée them in soups. Purée fruits and serve them stirred into yoghurt or custard.

PESTER POWER

Don't feel angry with your child if he or she pesters you for a food or drink you'd rather they didn't have. They are being influenced by the huge food companies, who profit every time he or she gets you to spend money on their value-added items.

All the food multinationals have now perfected their seduction techniques. They influence your child to pester via TV ads, via packaging, via special offers and free gifts, by linking up with favourite characters

'BETTER' CONVENIENCE FOOD

If you need to choose convenience foods, try to bear these points in mind:

- Buy the best quality you can afford. With food, as with much else, you get what you pay for. Premium-quality beefburgers made from organic meat, for example, will make you feel better about feeding burgers to your child. Similarly with organic eggs versus battery eggs. And if you can't make your own cake – go for cakes from your local Women's Institute or farmers' market rather than those that come packaged with long lists of additives.

- Add fresh fruit and salads to ready meals, such as chicken nuggets (see picture below), fish fingers, burgers, pizza, etc.

- Buy frozen or chilled counter items rather than those in cans or packets (e.g. soups), which will usually contain more additives. Chilled counter items are also likely to have a better nutritional profile.

from books or TV; via sponsorship of sports events – even by sponsorship at school and of school products and school events.

They cash in on the fact that young children like bright colours so they make packaging bright and even the food itself bright with artificial additives. They know that young children have an inherent sweet tooth and so they push sugary foods and artificially sweetened foods. They also know that children are actually brand loyal, and pride themselves on holding seminars to tell others how to cash in on that child loyalty.

This would all be not too bad if the products that are pushed weren't those most likely to be nutritionally poor – the Food Commission found that 77% of foods marketed to children contain high levels of fats, sugars and/or salt. But you don't find adverts for fresh fruit or carrot batons aimed at your kids, because there is little profit in that.

No – you don't have to feel angry with your child. You should only feel angry with the marketing men. But you do have to exercise your right to say 'no' to a child's demands. You have one huge advantage over your child – you hold the purse strings. Though it may be convenient to give in to your child's demands, the short-term relief can never outweigh the long-term negative health effects of a poor diet.

If you feel angry enough, you could join a pressure group or form one yourself to campaign for change – in some countries, TV advertising of foods during children's TV hours is banned. The Food Commission Parents' Jury is a good starting point, or you could write to the Advertising Standards Authority.

NOT ALL BAD NEWS!

Many supermarkets are making efforts to reduce the amount of fat, sugar and salt in their brands, while others, such as the Co-op, campaign to outlaw certain food adverts to children. And research has found that if a free gift is offered, or the packaging is made more attractive, children are as happy to try 'healthy' foods and drinks as they are the less healthy ones.

See also: Confectionery pp95–6, Fried Foods p128, Junk Food pp140–3, Ready Meals p168, Snacks pp178–9, Takeaways pp186–8, Appendix 3 pp252–3 for contact details for pressure groups.

CONFECTIONERY – TO BAN OR LIMIT?

First, limit – bans rarely work and only make the child feel guilty or resentful.

Secondly, when you do allow your child chocolate or sweets, make sure they are good-quality.

Thirdly – at home, make sure confectionery is part of a meal rather than a between-meal snack.

Fourthly – never offer sweets as a reward or bribe.

Finally – all children seem to like a sweet taste, so remember that fresh and dried fruits are high in natural sugar and make a good alternative with added nutrient value.

WEIGHT PROBLEMS

Overweight and obesity levels are soaring in primary-school-age children across much of the world, from the USA to the UK, China to South America, and in many areas obesity in young children is doubling every decade. In the UK, for example, 20% of 6-year-olds are overweight and 10% are obese, according to a report from the Association for the Study of Obesity.

Childhood overweight is linked with a sedentary lifestyle and a decline in sports participation, and an increase in consumption of fatty, sugary foods and drinks. For instance, children in the UK eat 25 times as many sweets and drink 30 times as many soft drinks as they did fifty years ago.

One study has found that consumption of sugary drinks is directly linked with obesity. Another has linked obesity with the increase in portion sizes, particularly of fast foods. Meanwhile, children take little exercise. A study at Bristol University has found that only 5% of children now walk to school – 20 years ago the figure was 80%. Many do less than half an hour of 'moderate' exercise a day (which includes walking around in the home and school) and virtually no heart-healthy, calorie-burning aerobic exercise, as sports participation in school has decreased and children watch more and more television or play computer games.

 Obesity is having serious repercussions on child health – and later adult health – with childhood incidence of high cholesterol, high blood pressure and insulin resistance, which is an early sign of type-2 diabetes. In the US, Yale University found 25% of children aged 4–10 had signs of insulin resistance.

SOLUTIONS

Prevention is definitely better than cure – and a general healthy diet which follows the principles of the Food Pyramid (see pages 36–7), plus regular exercise, should ensure that your child doesn't become overweight. If a child is already overweight (check the Growth Charts in the Appendix), however, experts advise that the best method of dealing with this is to try to maintain the current weight while the child

ENCOURAGING DAILY EXERCISE

Try to encourage your child to take at least an hour's proper exercise a day:

• Make the exercise something they will enjoy – for example, take them swimming or cycling.
• Rather than 'boring' walking, how about orienteering or walks with a theme, such as bird-watching or car-spotting.
• Encourage him or her to join a sports club, e.g. football or cricket, for children who like team games, or a gymnastics or athletics club for others.
• If possible, try to walk your child to where you have to go rather than taking the car.
• In summer, encourage ball games in the park or garden and put a time limit on indoor activities such as TV or computer games.

grows. That is, you don't put the child on a diet to lose weight, but as they get taller they will gradually 'grow into' their weight and slim down. For more information of practical ways to achieve this, see Obesity in the A-Z. The strategies outlined there should be enough to reduce an overweight child's calorie intake sufficiently. You might also visit your doctor and ask to see your local dietitian.

BE DIPLOMATIC

There is evidence that even young children can become over-worried about their weight. Some children lose confidence if their parents make them feel fat, and some even show signs of anorexia. So try to keep weight control in your child as a low-key issue. There's no need for them to feel hungry or deprived, so concentrate on all the foods he or she can eat, rather than on the ones they should cut down on. It's best to avoid the 'diet' word and don't weigh the child regularly. Lead by example – eat healthily yourself and show a positive attitude.

See also: Eating Disorders pp105–7, Fats and Oils pp110–12, Junk Food pp140–3, Obesity pp152–5, Snacks pp178–9, Sugar and Sweeteners pp182–5, Appendix 2 pp250–1 for Growth Charts.

EATING PLAN: AGE 5–6

- For portion sizes for all meals, unless specified, be guided by your child's appetite and/or need to control weight.
- Allow at least 300ml skimmed or semi-skimmed milk a day for use as a drink. Ideally the remainder of the drinks should be water or fruit juice diluted with water. Total fluid intake should be around 1–1.5 litres.
- If a child has school cafeteria lunch, check what he or she has (preferably advise him or her what to have). The school meals listed here are sample 'healthier' choices.
- Meals with capitalized names indicate recipes in the Recipes section and should be followed by their page number.

MONDAY

Breakfast
Weetabix with milk
Banana

Packed school lunch
Peanut butter sandwich on wholemeal bread
Satsuma
Slice of Fruit Cake (page 234)
Small pot of fromage frais

Late-afternoon snack
Slice of bread and honey
A handful of sultanas

Evening
Cottage Pie (page 211)
Shredded spring greens or runner beans
Fruit Fool (page 230)

TUESDAY

Breakfast
Toast with a little butter and reduced-sugar jam
Kiwi fruit
Small pot of fromage frais

School cafeteria lunch
Vegeburger or beefburger in a bun
Side salad
Banana

Afternoon snack
Date Loaf (page 232)
Handful of dried apricots

Evening
Pasta with Vegetable Sauce (page 236)
Summer Fruit Compote (page 230)
Ice cream

WEDNESDAY

Breakfast
Real porridge made with semi-skimmed milk and with handful of raisins added
Orange juice

Packed lunch
Tuna or salmon (canned in water) and sliced tomato sandwich on wholemeal bread
Slice of Banana Bread (page 235)
Apple
Fruit yoghurt

Afternoon snack
Pear
Low-salt cracker with a small piece of Cheddar cheese

Evening
Spanish Omelette (page 226)
Crusty bread
Salad

THURSDAY

Breakfast
Special K with fruit pieces
Semi-skimmed milk
Peach or plum

School cafeteria lunch
Cheese and tomato pizza
Side salad
Fruit yoghurt

Afternoon snack
Apple and satsuma segments with natural fromage frais used as dip

Evening
Chicken and Vegetable Pie (page 229)
Spring greens
New potatoes

FRIDAY

Breakfast
Luxury muesli with skimmed milk
Berry fruits

Packed lunch
White bap with low-fat spread filled with lean ham and chopped salad
Small bag of Home-made Vegetable Crisps (page 204)
Fruit fromage frais
Satsuma

Afternoon snack
Banana and handful sultanas

Evening
Tuna, Pasta and Tomato Bake (page 218)
Broccoli or green salad

SATURDAY

Breakfast
Boiled egg with wholemeal toast and low-fat spread

EATING PLAN: AGE 7–11

Apple

Lunch
Baked potato with Home-made
Baked Beans (page 204)

Orange juice

Afternoon snack
2 Fruit and Nut Cookies (page
233)

Kiwi fruit

Evening
Macaroni and Broccoli Cheese
(page 216)

Side salad

SUNDAY

Breakfast
Grilled lean back bacon

Grilled tomatoes

Wholemeal toast with low-fat
spread

Lunch
Lean roast beef

Roast potatoes cooked in
groundnut oil

Carrots, green beans

Plum Crumble (page 231)

Afternoon snack
Apple and orange segments

Evening
Home-made Baked Beans (page
204) on toast with low-fat spread

or Peanut Butter, Banana and
Honey Toasties (page 205)

MONDAY

Breakfast
Special K with semi-skimmed milk

Banana

Packed Lunch
Wholemeal pitta pocket filled
with Hummus (page 205) and
chopped salad

Small packet of mixed nuts and
raisins

Fruit fromage frais

Orange segments

Afternoon snack
Slice of Date Loaf (page 232)

Evening
Southern-fried Chicken (page 223)

Baked potato

Sweetcorn and carrots

TUESDAY

Breakfast
Low-fat natural bio yoghurt
topped with selection of chopped
fruit and a handful of Branflakes

School cafeteria lunch
Fish and chips with peas

Apple

Afternoon snack
Berry and Banana Milkshake (page
239)

Fruit and Nut Cookie (page 233)

Evening
Pasta Shells with Peppers (page
211)

Side salad

WEDNESDAY

Breakfast
Luxury muesli with skimmed milk
and chopped apple

Packed lunch
A sandwich of Cheddar cheese,
cucumber and cress on
wholemeal bread with low-fat
spread

Small packet of mixed fruit and
nuts

Apple Muffin (page 233)

Satsuma

Afternoon snack
Fruit fromage frais

Evening
Lamb and Cherry Tomato Kebabs
(page 218)

Mixed leaf side salad

Boiled rice

THURSDAY

Breakfast
Weetabix with semi-skimmed milk

Peach or nectarine

School cafeteria lunch
Ham salad with a roll

Fruit yoghurt

Afternoon snack
Wholemeal bread with low-fat
spread and reduced-sugar jam

Glass of orange juice

Evening
Vegetable Burgers (page 224)

Potato Wedges (page 220)

Side salad

FRIDAY

Breakfast
White bread toast with low-fat
spread and reduced-sugar
marmalade

Yoghurt Smoothie (page 239)

Packed lunch
Chicken and Pasta Salad (page 208)

Home-made Vegetable Crisps

(page 204)

Fruit fromage frais

Apple

Afternoon snack
Handful of dried apricots

Evening
Prawn, Salmon and Egg Pie (page 219)

Peas or broccoli

SATURDAY

Breakfast
Scrambled egg on toast with low-fat spread

Orange juice

Lunch
Potato Soup (page 203)

Wholemeal roll

Fruit yoghurt

Afternoon snack
Pear

Evening
Traditional Pizza (page 212)

Side salad

SUNDAY

Breakfast
Low-sugar, low-salt baked beans on toast

Lunch
Roast chicken (remove skin before serving)

Roast potatoes

Spinach or spring greens

Carrots

Baked Bananas (page 232) with Greek yoghurt

Afternoon snack
Apple

Handful of sultanas

Evening
Brie and Tomato Toastie (page 203)

MEAL IDEAS FOR VEGETARIANS

Vegetarians can follow the eating plans on the previous pages and can substitute one of the following where there is a meat or fish meal. Recipes suitable for vegans are marked with a vegan symbol in the Recipes section.

Cold Breakfasts:
As for the Eating Plans; vegans can use soya milk or yoghurt and margarine.

Hot breakfasts:
Vegetarian sausages with grilled tomato and baked beans, bread and vegetarian spread; beans or tomatoes or mushrooms on toast; porridge with milk or soya milk and dried fruits.

Packed lunches:
Add yoghurt or fromage frais, fruit and cake to make a complete meal.
• Any bread, roll or pitta (vary wholemeal and white), with butter, vegetarian margarine or low-fat spread, plenty of salad and either cheese, egg, vegetable pâté, Hummus (page 205) or cooked vegetarian sausage.
• A salad based on cooked pasta or rice (chill cooked rice immediately and use within 24 hours) with chopped egg, cheese or tofu, chopped salad items, nuts, seeds, dried fruits. See Fruit and Nut Pasta Salad (page 207), Apricot and Brown Rice Salad (page 209), Cheesy Coleslaw (page 209), etc.
• A flask of home-made soup – see Red Lentil and Tomato Soup (page 200), Carrot and Orange Soup (page 201), Chunky Vegetable and Kidney Bean Soup (page 201), Lentil and Vegetable Soup (page 202), Potato Soup (page 203) – or chilled-counter vegetable soup, roll, nuts, fruit.
• A bean or cheese dip – see Hummus (page 205), Cheese Dip (page 203) with crudités, dried fruit, Home-made Vegetable Crisps (page 204).

School cafeteria lunches:
There should be one vegetarian hot lunch on the menu. Look for cheese/egg flan, cheese and tomato pizza, omelette, cheese or egg salad, baked potato with baked beans, chilli vegetables and rice, chunky veg soup followed by cheese and roll. Fruit and/or yoghurt is best dessert option.

Afternoon snacks:
Many of those listed on the plans are suitable for vegetarians. Vegans can choose nuts, fresh fruit, dried fruit and soya yoghurt.

Main meals:
Many main-meal recipes in this book are vegetarian, including: pasta with Vegetable Sauce (page 236), Macaroni and Broccoli Cheese (page 216), Pasta Shells with Peppers (page 211), Baked Eggs and Peppers (page 227), Traditional Pizza (page 212), Vegetable Burgers (page 224), Greek Cheese and Spinach Pie (page 228).

Any main-meal recipes in this book containing minced meat can be made using minced Quorn or textured vegetable protein (TVP). Many of the soup and snack recipes would be suitable for a main meal, especially if salad is served. For example, Roast Mushroom and Tofu Sandwich (page 206), Brie and Tomato Toastie (page 203), Home-made Baked Beans (page 204).

Quick and easy main meals can be made from pasta (check label for egg-free variety if vegan) with stir-fried vegetables and tofu or with cheese; from cooked rice with Tomato Sauce (page 237) and nuts or cheese stirred in.

Bakes and desserts:
All the recipes for bakes and desserts are suitable for ovo-vegetarians. Some are suitable for vegans – e.g. Plum Crumble (page 231), Summer Fruit Compote (page 230) and Baked Bananas (page 232). Fruit Fool (page 230) can be made suitable for vegetarians by using soya yoghurt.

THE TEENAGE YEARS

Most teens want to grab more and more independence and many realize that what they eat is one area in which they can take control. This chapter discusses the problems this can cause and some possible solutions.

The eating habits of Western teenagers are coming under increasing scrutiny. A recent study found that teenage girls are leading unhealthier lives than the boys. They drink more alcohol, skip more meals, have more of a sweet tooth, worry more about their weight and take less exercise. Boys, on the other hand, drink more fizzy drinks and eat more fatty foods. For both sexes the trend for fast and 'junk' food is not abating. Half of all teens eat between 3 and 4 burgers a week. If given school dinner money, a third of it is spent on sweets, fizzy drinks and even cigarettes. Meanwhile, eating disorders, often stemming from poor body image, are common amongst teenage girls and becoming increasingly common in boys, too – the dilemma for parents is to encourage healthy eating habits without taking concern too far.

Full of contradictions and 'attitude', teenagers often provide the biggest challenge, nutritionally speaking, of all the age groups. A research study published in 2002 found that two-thirds of teenagers aged 14 and 15 think that they are eating unhealthily, but 50% admitted that they would feel happier if they worked on making improvements. It may be helpful to keep that thought firmly in mind.

NUTRITIONAL NEEDS

Teenagers – particularly older teens – have higher nutrient and energy needs than almost any other group. Here we look at the factors to consider.

The UK National Diet and Nutrition (NDN) Survey of Young People aged 4–18 (2000) found that it was the older children, aged from 11 to 18, who appeared to be most likely to have inadequate diets. Levels of intake of iron, calcium, zinc, magnesium, some B vitamins and long-chain fatty acids were low in a significant proportion of that age group, while intake of salt, fat and sugar was higher than recommended.

CALORIES

Younger teenagers need about the same amount of calories as adults, while older teens (15–18) need even more than an adult. Boys aged 15–18 have particularly high needs. Teenagers often have big appetites to match these needs, but it is important that they don't fill up on too many sugary drinks, confectionery and snacks, or fatty snacks and meals.

Healthier ways for teenagers to get their calorie intake are to eat nuts, seeds and dried fruits, all of which contain important nutrients as well as being calorie-dense. Breakfast is just as vitally important for teens as it is for younger children (see 'The Importance of Breakfast' pages 40–1) and a good-quality muesli is the ideal way to provide these nuts and fruits. Dairy produce and meat also provide vital vitamins and minerals.

PROTEIN

Boys have a greater need for protein than girls in their teens, because they are continuing to build more muscle than the average girl does and are also increasing in height and becoming taller than the average girl. See the box on the right for good sources of protein.

FAT

Fat is the most calorie-dense of all the nutrients, at 9 calories per gram, and although teens should, like adults, watch their intake of saturated and trans fats (see Fats and Oils), regular consumption of moderate amounts of 'healthy' oils such as olive oil,

---

GOOD SOURCES OF:

PROTEIN
- lean meats and poultry
- fish
- dairy produce
- pulses and nuts

CALCIUM
- dark leafy greens
- nuts and seeds
- pulses
- dried fruits
- fortified white bread and flour

IRON
- red meat, offal
- liver pâté
- dark leafy greens, seaweed
- seeds, nuts, pulses,
- eggs
- pot barley
- baked beans in tomato sauce
- dried fruits
- fortified breakfast cereals
- wholemeal bread
- soya mince and vegeburger mix

'HEALTHY' FATS
- olive oil
- groundnut oil
- oily fish
- flaxseeds
- rapeseed oil
- walnuts

---

groundnut oil and oily fish should be encouraged. Use oils 'cold' if possible, to retain maximum health-giving properties, in salad dressings, and as the oil of preference for frying and cooking.

LONG-CHAIN FATTY ACIDS

The omega-3 long-chain fatty acids EPA and DHA are found in oily fish and fish oils, and can be converted in the body from another fatty acid, alpha-linolenic acid, which is contained in good

intake and nearly 40% of girls aged 11–14 were found to have low zinc intake. Nuts, seeds and pulses are good sources of both magnesium and zinc, while red meat and hard cheese are also good sources of zinc. Potassium is found in most fruits and vegetables.

Although the NDN survey didn't include selenium, this mineral is vital for normal growth, thyroid action, healthy skin and hair, and it may help to prevent miscarriage. One study found that selenium intake in the UK is only about half of that recommended. Good sources are fish, nuts and seeds.

VITAMINS

The NDN survey showed that vitamin A, riboflavin (vitamin B2) and folate were in shortfall in a significant percentage of 11–18-year-olds. Vitamin A is essential for healthy growth, vision and skin, and is found in dairy produce. It can be made in the body from beta-carotene, found in many fruits and vegetables. Riboflavin is a B vitamin essential for the release of energy from food and for healthy skin, and is found in offal, dairy produce and fortified

amounts in flaxseeds (linseeds), rapeseed oil and walnuts. Adequate intake of these fatty acids in children has been shown to be linked with improved brain power and concentration, and in all age groups with protection against heart disease and other problems. Yet intake of these fats in teenagers is very low.

CALCIUM

The need for calcium is higher in the teens than at any other age, as calcium is vital for building strong bones and teeth, and for many other functions. At this age, bone density increases rapidly, but the NDN survey found that about 20% of all teenage girls and 10% of boys get inadequate calcium. See the box on the previous page for sources.

IRON

Iron is important for healthy blood, and it is especially important to watch teenagers' iron intake as the NDN survey found that about 50% of teenage girls have levels below those recommended. Once they begin menstruation, girls' need for iron is greater than boys', as iron is lost in the blood each month. Iron-deficiency anaemia affects one in four girls aged 11 to 15. Scientific trials have shown that iron deficiency in the teens may affect academic performance. See the box on the previous page for sources of iron.

OTHER MINERALS

The NDN survey found that zinc, magnesium and potassium were all in shortfall in some teenagers. Over half of girls aged 11–18 had low magnesium

cereals. Folate is needed for healthy blood and normal foetal growth, and low intake is linked with CHD. It is found in offal, pulses, whole grains, vegetables and fortified cereals.

See also: Anaemia p73, Bone Health pp80–1, Fats and Oils pp110–12, Minerals pp148–9, Vitamins pp194–6, Appendix 1 pp240–9 for sources of nutrients.

GOOD NUTRITION FOR TEENAGERS

The Food Pyramid shown on page 37 is a standard blueprint for healthy eating that should provide most teenagers with all the nutrients they need – it should be used in conjunction with the notes above, so that intake of nutrients likely to be in shortfall in teenagers is especially considered. The teenage appetite should guide the actual number of servings a day (between those limits

DAILY CALORIE, PROTEIN AND FAT NEEDS FOR AVERAGE TEENAGERS

	Calories•	Protein•	Total fat••	Saturated fat•••
Boys Age				
12–14	2,220	42g	74–86g	25g
15–18	2,755	55g	92–107g	31g
Girls Age				
12–14	1,845	41g	61–72g	20g
15–18	2,110	45g	70–82g	24g

- • Department of Health Dietary Reference Values
- •• 30–35% of total calories as a maximum
- ••• 10% of total calories as a maximum

SELECTED DAILY VITAMIN AND MINERAL NEEDS FOR AVERAGE TEENAGERS•

	Vit A (mcg)	Vit C (mg)	Calc (mg)	Iron (mg)	Zinc (mg)	Mag (mg)	Sel (mcg)
Boys Age							
12–14	600	35	1,000	11.3	9.0	280	45
15–18	700	40	1,000	11.3	9.5	300	70
Girls Age							
12–14	600	35	800	14.8	9.0	280	45
15–18	600	40	800	14.8	7.0	300	60

- • Department of Health Dietary Reference Values

recommended on the Pyramid), although most teens, especially boys, should eat the larger portion numbers given – e.g. 11 portions from the starch group rather than 6. Portion sizes again should be guided by appetite and by any need to control weight. The table above gives average portion sizes adapted from the US Department of Agriculture recommendations, to use as a rough guide.

TEENAGERS AND VEGETARIANISM

A vegetarian diet can be very healthy but, as with a carnivorous diet, it can also be less than healthy – it all depends on achieving a good balance of nutrients. Many teenage vegetarians live in a meat-eating household – i.e. they have become vegetarians of their own choosing while the rest of the family are carnivores. It is these 'lone veggies' who need careful dietary supervision, otherwise they may simply choose to leave the meat out of main meals and not replace it with a suitable vegetarian item, giving rise to the possibility of shortfalls in nutrients, such as iron or B vitamins.

In the NDN survey, blood levels of iron were consistently lower in vegetarians than non-vegetarians. Vegetarians might also rely too heavily on dairy produce, which could give them a diet too high in fat and saturated fat. Other vegetarians, particularly girls, eat a lot of chocolate, cakes and biscuits.

On the plus side, vegetarian teenagers have a better LDL ('good') cholesterol profile than carnivores, and their status of several vitamins and minerals including selenium is higher than average. The vegan diet (eggs and dairy-free) is likely to be higher than average in fibre and plant chemicals, and lower than average in fat and saturated fat.

See also: 'The Vegetarian Child' and 'The Vegan Child' pp39–40, 'Eating Plan for the Vegetarian Teenager' pp66–7, Appendix 3 pp252–3 for details of the Vegetarian Society.

WEIGHT CONTROL

Estimates of overweight and obesity in adolescents range between 15% and 30% across countries including the USA, UK, and much of Europe. In the USA, the obesity figures for people under 19 have doubled in thirty years and in the UK they have doubled in ten years.

There are also important studies which show that obesity in the young tends to persist into adulthood. So it is vital that your child maintains a reasonable

weight through his or her teenage years – but calorie needs are greater at puberty. Studies show that there is a definite increase in preference for fatty (and often, in the case of girls, sugary) foods around this time, and appetite usually increases. This increased calorie intake is used in girls to deposit extra fat on their breasts, hips and thighs. Boys become taller and broader with extra muscle. These developments are normal and not to be confused with a weight problem.

Check out the Growth Charts in Appendix 2 pages 250–1 to see whether your child is within a normal weight range. If he or she is in the normal range, then simply try to offer a healthy diet as outlined on these pages and give portions to suit appetite. If your child does have a surplus weight problem, then follow the guidelines for younger children on page 28, first cutting out – or down on – the less healthy food items.

It is also important to try to increase the amount of activity that youngsters take. Research shows that regular daily exercise – walking, cycling, swimming, football, netball – is the best way to keep surplus weight off in the long term, and is, of course, vital for healthy heart and lungs.

" " Excess body weight is now the commonest childhood disorder in Europe and North America, with links to various life-threatening complaints including heart disease and diabetes. **" "**
The Association for the Study of Obesity

66 Children today expend 600 calories a day less energy than they did fifty years ago.
British Nutrition Foundation 99

While increasing numbers of teenagers are overweight, there is also a problem with underweight and various eating disorders, such as anorexia, which may affect 10% of teenage girls. Research indicates that around 60% of teenage girls think that they need to lose weight even if they really don't – so great care needs to be taken to ensure that normal-weight teens don't try to diet or become obsessive about nonexistent weight problems. Even where there is no sign of an actual eating disorder, teenage girls who try to maintain too low a body-weight may well suffer from lack of periods and/or infertility.

See also: Eating Disorders pp105–7, Obesity pp152–5.

HELP CONTROL THEIR WEIGHT

First check out the Growth Charts in Appendix 2 to see if your child is under or overweight, then if necessary try the following strategies:

• Encourage adolescents to eat with the family and to take an interest in cooking.
• Try to limit opportunities for fast food and sweet and fatty snacks.
• Controlling the size of portions you offer is an excellent way to control weight.
• Nagging teenagers about anything rarely works and nagging to control food intake is no exception.
• Encourage regular exercise – could he or she walk or cycle to school instead of taking the car or bus?
• Don't be afraid to take your teen to see the family doctor about their under/overweight problem and ask to be referred to a dietitian. Many children do respond well to personal supervision by someone outside the family – although some don't.

EATING PROBLEMS

Teenagers are the group of youngsters with the second highest (after pre-schoolers) incidence of embracing eating fads. Here we look at some of the most likely fads and how they may affect your child's nutritional status and health.

EATING FADS

One of the most obvious reasons for faddy eating is that from puberty onwards many children are desperate to show that they are becoming independent – and making their own food choices is a way of showing that. Unfortunately, many of these choices are nutritionally unsound – if understandable. Making food decisions that may baffle, worry or annoy their parents may all be part of the fun.

Many fads are short-lived and will leave your child with no lasting damage – so, at first, the best advice may be to stay quiet and keep watchful. Intervention and/or hints of bullying can antagonize many a teenager and just serve to make the 'fad' more entrenched.

The next strategy is often to embrace the fad and attempt to ensure a healthy diet nevertheless. The most popular teenage eating behaviour (particularly for girls) is to become vegetarian. Vegetarianism and even veganism can be a very healthy way to eat if it is managed properly (see pages 56–7).

Two other growing trends in adolescents are to give up wheat and to give up dairy produce (while still perhaps eating meat or fish, so this isn't the same as vegetarianism). As wheat is a major staple in the Western diet, a wheat-free diet can bring nutritional and logistical problems, and has few benefits for most people.

Dairy produce is a good source of dietary calcium and there is little advantage to be gained for most teenagers in giving up all dairy foods, although overweight children may benefit from a reduction in intake of full-fat dairy produce.

> Many teens have poor body image and find it hard to live up to the perfect bodies displayed in the media, and 40% of teenage girls and 25% of boys display at least some signs of faddy eating, anorexia, bulimia or comfort eating.

EATING DISORDERS

An eating disorder is a much more serious matter than a food fad. Eating disorders, such as anorexia and bulimia nervosa, can actually be life-threatening. The box below offers a few pointers on how you might get an early warning of a potential eating disorder in your adolescent child. Research has shown that busy parents often fail to spot the signs until late.

DETECTING EATING DISORDERS

• Typical signs of early anorexic behaviour include:
– skipped meals
– obsessive interest in food (without eating a lot)
– an obsessive desire to exercise
– obsessive interest in changes in weight

• Bulimia is harder to spot, as people tend to eat fairly normally and then make themselves sick.

• Sometimes the beginning of an eating disorder may be masked by faddism. For example, your daughter may say she is going vegetarian, or giving up wheat or dairy, in order to restrict her calorie intake without giving you cause to worry. Occasionally eating fads can turn into eating disorders even when that wasn't the intention in the beginning.

COMFORT EATING AND BINGE EATING

Teenagers can come under a lot of pressure – from school work, exams, parents – and may have problems with friendships and relationships. No wonder that, like adults, many may turn to food as a comfort. Comfort and binge foods tend to be those that aren't so good for health or weight – chocolate and confectionery are favourites with girls, while boys may eat more fatty foods such as crisps and chips.

Habitual comfort eating is unlikely to disappear unless the cause is identified and help offered – e.g. school work worries may be resolved with extra tuition or by you visiting the school – or the problem resolves itself in time – e.g. getting over a first love affair. The teenage years are turbulent, and few adolescents get through these years without some emotional problems. A parent's best course is to offer as much support as possible, and as much help and advice as can be given without antagonising. Some adolescents may welcome the opportunity to see a counsellor.

Research shows that girls are particularly prone to comfort-eat before menstruation. PMS is often at its worst in teenage girls and pre-menopausal women and at this time they are likely to feel more emotional or depressed than usual.

 To help avoid cravings for sweet or snack food pre-menstruation, make sure your daughter always has a few healthy snack items in her schoolbag or pocket – nuts, seeds, dried fruit and fresh fruit are good. Try to make sure she eats regularly to avoid low blood sugar, which makes the cravings worse.

See also: Dairy Alternatives p98, Dairy Produce p98, Eating Disorders pp105–7, Food Allergies pp117–19, Periods and PMS p160, Appendix 3 pp252–3 for details on counselling.

FAST FOOD, GOOD FOOD AND PREPARING TO LEAVE HOME

There is a great deal of circumstantial evidence that links the huge growth over recent years in the fast food and snack food industries with the increase in obesity and obesity-related problems in the young. It is certainly true that the rise of our fast-food culture has coincided with an increase in a wide range of health and behavioural problems in our youth.

And, as consumption of takeout meals, ready meals, convenience foods and sweet and savoury snacks continues to grow, so the trend away from home cooking and family meals continues, with fewer and fewer of our teens learning to cook even basic meals and more and more rarely eating anything cooked by their parents.

If you do choose to serve ready meals and takeaways, try to restrict them to just one or two evenings a week, always add salad or vegetables and choose the best quality you can find, reading the labels of ready meals to select the most healthy and nutritious available.

READY MEALS AND TAKEAWAYS VERSUS FAMILY FOOD

READY MEALS
Pros:
• Many are reasonably low in fat or saturated fat.
• If you choose carefully, a ready meal can represent a nutritionally balanced meal.

Cons:
• Some ready meal portion sizes are not big enough for teenagers.
• Some are high in fat and some are high in salt.
• Some are low on vegetables and you'd need to serve a salad or vegetables as well to make them a balanced meal.
• Can be costly, weight for weight, compared with home-made meals.

TAKEAWAY MEALS
Pros:
• If you choose very carefully, some takeaway meals fine now and then.

Cons:
• Research shows that many takeaway meals are very high in fat and saturated fat, and may be too high in calories even for teenagers' needs.
• Often no choice of salad or vegetables.

ENCOURAGING COOKING SKILLS
This worrying trend away from home cooking is compounded by schools who no longer teach cooking to our children. With no role models, it is little wonder that cooking is fast becoming a lost skill. For all parents who care about the future health of their teens, it is vital that we do help our children learn nutrition and cooking skills, and to care about eating good food.

There is much that can be done to give teenagers a real enthusiasm for home cooking, even in the busiest of households. The motivation will probably need to come from you, the parent, but I accept that most of us have less time to cook these days. There are various ways to reduce time spent on cooking home meals, without resorting to ready meals or takeouts.

Recipe books. Invest in a couple of the many 'quick cook' books that are in the shops – or at the library. Check through the recipes in the Recipes section of this book, many of which are quick to prepare and cook.

Time-saving ingredients. Choose basic ingredients that have a time-saving element in them – e.g. ready-washed and/or peeled root vegetables, ready-mixed and chopped stir-fry vegetables. Though, if you are teaching basic preparation skills to children, you need to do things from scratch some of the time.

The joy of casseroles. With the possible exception of during summer, you can include at least two or three casserole-type meals a week, which can be prepared the night or day before and left to cook all day, so that there is little to do near the time to eat.

These types of meals – which can include curries and sauces for pasta as well as more basic stews – are home cooking at its simplest and best, and all they need is a little forward planning, after which they can generally be left alone to cook. Again, you will find several suggestions in the Recipes section of this book.

The importance of planning. Don't shy from those words 'forward planning' – we do it at work and in other areas of our lives and yet working out menus for a week and doing one major shop is a great way to save time and wasted food and wasted money in the kitchen.

Work out which is the best day for you to do a proper shop and spend 20 minutes the evening before planning meals and drawing up a shopping list – try to ensure the kids are there to offer suggestions as to what they would like to eat in the week ahead.

Reheatable meals. If, on occasion, all the family has to eat at different times, then plan for meals that will be suitable for this – again, casserole-type meals are ideally suited.

Bulk-freezing. Clear out the freezer and make some space so that you can cook double quantities of some meals and freeze them. Label them properly, otherwise they will get forgotten.

Audience participation. Try to cook when your children are around, so that they can get drawn into the process. If they can play music they enjoy at the same time this may help them to linger.

HOME-MADE MEALS AS QUICK AS TAKEAWAYS:

- Pasta or couscous

- Microwaved baked potato with defrosted home-made sauce and side salad

- Omelette and salad.

- Grilled meat or fish with easy vegetables such as peas, mangetout, broccoli and new potatoes

- Salad with cooked meat or canned fish and crusty bread

- Stir-fries using ready-cut vegetables and meat with a good-quality sauce

Try to explain what you are doing, and why you are doing it, as you go along. Discuss the ingredients, why you like them, why they take a long or short time to cook. It's important to get across the idea that good-quality ingredients make all the difference to the taste of dishes.

Ask them questions to get them thinking for themselves: 'Why do you think organic carrots might be better than others?'; 'Why are we sautéing the onions for a few minutes first before we put the other ingredients in?' and so on.

Have mini-tasting sessions as you go along – encourage the idea that real, home-made food is good because it tastes good.

Let the apprentice have a go. Think of a few occasions when your child might like to attempt to cook a meal: on Mother's Day, Father's Day, when they have a day off school, when they have a friend round. Don't let them attempt a dish or meal that you know will be hard for them to pull off, especially when they're just starting to explore cooking, as this can have the effect of denting their confidence so that they may be loath to try again.

TEENS, BEDSITS, FLAT-SHARES AND FOOD

Many teenagers choose to leave home when they've finished schooling, or are obliged to live away from home when they begin university – 'degree malnutrition' is a common phenomenon. Here's how to help your child avoid it.

Both cooking facilities and cash are often lacking when your child leaves home for the first time. But, whether it's a single-ring cooker in a bedsit and only a pound or two a day to spend on food, or if he or she stretches to a share of a proper flat with a decent kitchen, the more he or she knows about

It is very important that young people, stressed out with moving home, new surroundings and new people, get enough vitamin C in their diet. Vitamin B group is another vital anti-stress nutrient, so persuade them to go for whole grains rather than refined – see Appendix 1 pages 240–2 for sources of vitamins B and C.

good food and cooking before they set off the better. At the very least, make sure your child knows the rudiments of food safety.

Pack a students' cooking paperback and make sure they know that someone who can rustle up something tasty to eat in student/bedsitland will always be very popular! Typical stand-by meals are soups, chillies, curries, spaghetti bolognese, omelettes and something on toast – and there is nothing wrong with any of these.

A few cans of pulses and chopped tomatoes will ensure some kind of nutritious meal can always be prepared. Don't bother giving them dried pulses – they'll never go through the hassle of cooking them – canned ready-cooked ones are better.

STUDENT/BEDSIT HEALTHY SNACKS AND MEALS:

• Beans or eggs or cheese or fried tomatoes or mushrooms on toast.

• Canned tuna, sardines or mackerel with ready-prepared salad and bread.

• Chilled soup (ready-made) with grated cheese and wholemeal roll.

• Baked potato with baked beans or ready-made chilli con carne.

• Pasta with an easy home-made tomato, vegetable or meat sauce (see Recipes, pages 220 and 236–7), ready-prepared side salad or fresh fruit to follow.

• Couscous reconstituted with nuts, seeds and chopped dried fruit mixed in plus any fresh salad vegetables if available.

• Hummus with pitta bread and tomato.

• Lean bacon and scrambled egg.

• Spinach and ricotta pizza with some ready-prepared side salad.

Few young people bother to prepare and cook many fresh vegetables, so it will help if there is fruit in the fridge and some easily prepared salad items, such as tomatoes and green leaves that keep a while – Cos lettuce or Chinese leaves are both tasty and relativity long-life.

Check to see if there's any cool storage area apart from the fridge. The vitamin C content of fresh fruit will diminish rapidly in warm, light conditions, so warn your child against storing fruit in a bowl in a warm room – even a dark cupboard is better in this respect.

If fridge or freezer space is limited or non-existent, canned fish, vegetables and fruits will be needed. Packets of dried pasta, rice, couscous and noodles can be stored anywhere and are all quick and easy to prepare.

If possible, visit your child's new home and see what facilities there are, then help them decide what food will be a possibility. Check out the cooking equipment: if there isn't a good-quality frying pan, saucepan and smallish casserole pan, and a few good knives, buy them. And make sure there is at least some crockery!

See also: Food Safety pp123–6, Appendix 1 pp240–9 for sources of nutrients.

EATING PLAN 1: TEENAGE GIRLS

- Portion sizes for all meals unless specified to be guided by appetite and/or need to control weight. See also 'Serving Sizes for Teenagers' on page 56.
- Allow at least 300ml skimmed or semi-skimmed milk a day for use as a drink. Ideally the rest of the drinks should be water or fruit juice diluted with water. Total fluid intake should be around 1.5–2 litres.
- The Tuesday and Thursday cafeteria meals are examples of the kind of food a teenage girl taking school lunches might be able to choose. If possible, find out what she is having at school lunch time and adjust the evening meal accordingly.
- The daily snack can be eaten any time, but is best eaten in the late afternoon or about 1 hour before bedtime.
- Meals with capitalized names indicate recipes in the Recipes section and are followed by their page numbers.

MONDAY

Breakfast
Weetabix with semi-skimmed milk
Wholemeal bread with low-fat spread and honey
Orange juice

Packed lunch
Cheddar cheese and salad sandwich
Small pot of fromage frais
Slice of Date Loaf (page 232)
Home-made Vegetable Crisps (page 204)
Apple

Evening
Baked Eggs and Peppers (page 227)
Poached plums with custard

Snack
a few walnut halves and dried ready-to-eat apricot halves

TUESDAY

Breakfast
Bowl of low-fat bio yoghurt with a handful of luxury muesli on top and some berries
1 banana

Cafeteria lunch
Ham and pineapple pizza
Side salad
Blueberry muffin

Evening
Turkey and Vegetable Stir-fry (page 216)
Brown basmati rice

Snack
1 apple and a handful of sunflower seeds

WEDNESDAY

Breakfast
Cornflakes with semi-skimmed milk and a few chopped dried apricots
Slice of white toast with low-fat spread and reduced-sugar jam
Orange juice

Packed lunch
Hummus (page 205) with slices of white pitta and vegetable crudités
Peach or nectarine
Slice of Carrot Cake (page 234)
Individual pot of fruit fromage frais

Evening
Cottage Pie (page 211)
Green beans and spring greens
Baked Banana (page 232)

Snack
a few almonds and a handful of pumpkin seeds

THURSDAY

Breakfast
Berry and Banana Milkshake (page 239)
Slice of wholemeal toast with low-fat spread and reduced-sugar jam
1 apple

Cafeteria Lunch
Beefburger or veggieburger in a bun
Baked beans
Fruit yoghurt

Evening
Potato and Vegetable Gratin (page 212)
Side salad with olive oil vinaigrette

Snack
a few almonds and walnut halves
handful of sunflower seeds

FRIDAY

Breakfast
Bowlful of muesli with skimmed milk and chopped fresh fruit
Slice of wholemeal bread with low-fat spread and reduced-sugar jam

Packed Lunch
Ham and Rice Salad (page 210)
Pot of fruit bio yoghurt
Apple Muffin (page 233)
Home-made Vegetable Crisps (page 204)
Satsuma or kiwi fruit

Evening
Salmon Fishcakes (page 227)
Ready-made tomato salsa
Broccoli
Fruit Fool (page 230)

Snack
Apple
Handful of dried ready-to-eat apricots

SATURDAY

Breakfast
Natural 8%-fat fromage frais with honey

Peach or pear

Slice of white toast with low-fat spread and Marmite

Lunch
Lentil and Vegetable Soup (page 202)

Wholemeal roll

Orange

Evening
Chicken Enchiladas (page 229)

Large side salad with olive oil French dressing

Snack
Piece of Cheddar cheese and 2 dark rye crispbreads

Handful of pumpkin seeds

SUNDAY

Breakfast
Poached egg, baked beans and grilled extra-lean back bacon

Wholemeal bread, low-fat spread

Lunch
Lean roast beef

Baked potato with a little butter

Spring greens, carrots, peas

Fat-skimmed gravy, horseradish sauce

Apple pie and Greek yoghurt

Evening
Large mixed salad with canned tuna

White bread with low-fat spread

Snack
Apple and orange

• Portion sizes for all meals unless specified to be guided by appetite and/or need to control weight. See also 'Serving Sizes for Teenagers' on page 56.
• Allow at least 500ml skimmed or semi-skimmed milk a day for use as a drink. Ideally the rest of the drinks should be water or fruit juice diluted with water. Total fluid intake should be 1.5–2 litres.
• The Tuesday and Thursday cafeteria meals are examples of the kind of food a teenage boy taking school lunches might be able to choose. If possible, find out what he is having at school lunch time and adjust the evening meal accordingly.
• The daily snack can be eaten any time, but is best eaten in the late afternoon or about 1 hour before bedtime.
• Meals with capitalized names indicate recipes in the Recipes section and are followed by their page numbers.

MONDAY

Breakfast
Yoghurt Smoothie (page 239)

White bread with low-fat spread and peanut butter

Packed lunch
Chicken Soup (page 202)

Wholemeal roll with butter

Slice of Fruit Cake (page 234)

Packet of mixed nuts and raisins

Apple

Evening
Vegetable Burgers (page 224)

Potato Wedges (page 220)

Peas, grilled tomato

Snack
Cheese scone with a little butter

Banana

TUESDAY

Breakfast
Weetabix with skimmed or semi-skimmed milk

Orange juice

Wholemeal bread with low-fat spread and reduced-sugar jam

Cafeteria Lunch
Fish and chips

Apple

Fruit yoghurt

Evening Meal
Chilli con carne made using Basic Minced Beef (page 220, see note)

Basmati rice

Side salad, olive oil French dressing

Banana

Snack
Slice of Carrot Cake (page 234)

WEDNESDAY

Breakfast
Greek yoghurt with fresh berries

Bread, low-fat spread and Marmite

Packed lunch
Chicken and Pasta Salad (page 208)

Slice of Banana Bread (page 235)

Slice of melon

Packet of mixed nuts and raisins

Pot of fruit fromage frais

Evening
Extra-lean premium pork sausages, grilled

Mashed potato, baked beans

Summer Fruit Compote (page 230)

Snack
Home-made Veg Crisps (page 204)

Apple

TEENAGE BOYS CONT.

THURSDAY

Breakfast
Bowl of luxury muesli with chopped fresh fruit and skimmed milk

Wholemeal bread with low-fat spread and Marmite

Cafeteria lunch
Beefburger in bun
Side salad
Banana

Evening
Prawn, Salmon and Egg Pie (page 219)
Green beans
Vanilla yoghurt

Snack
Peach or nectarine
Handful of dried ready-to-eat apricots
Slice of Date Loaf (page 232)

FRIDAY

Breakfast
Pot of fruit bio yoghurt
White bread with low-fat spread and reduced-sugar jam
Orange

Packed lunch
Wholemeal pitta bread with Hummus (page 205)
Side salad
Home-made Vegetable Crisps (page 204)
2 Fruit and Nut Cookies (page 233)

Evening
Chicken and Vegetable Curry (page 217)
Basmati rice, chutney
Fruit Fool (page 230)

Snack
Dark rye crispbreads with peanut butter

Kiwi fruit
Yoghurt Smoothie (page 239)

SATURDAY

Breakfast
Boiled eggs
White bread with low-fat spread
Peach and Mango Smoothie (page 239)

Lunch
Peanut Butter, Banana and Honey Toastie (page 205)
Apple

Evening
Traditional Pizza (page 212)
Potato Wedges (page 220)
Salad with olive oil French dressing

Snack
Orange
Pack of mixed nuts and raisins

SUNDAY

Breakfast
Extra-lean back bacon, grilled
Fried egg, baked beans
Grilled tomatoes and mushrooms
Wholemeal toast and low-fat spread

Lunch
Roast leg of lamb with mint sauce
Baked potato
Spring greens, carrots, peas
Fat-skimmed gravy
Fresh Fruit Trifle (page 231)

Evening
Brie and Tomato Toastie (page 203) or Roast Mushroom and Tofu Sandwich (page 206)

Snack
Banana
Slice of Date Loaf (page 232)

PLAN FOR

All notes for the boys' and girls' plans also apply here
Plus:
• Calcium-fortified soya milk and yoghurt can be used instead of the cows' milk and yoghurt mentioned if preferred.

MONDAY

Breakfast
Bowlful of low-fat bio yoghurt
Fresh berries
Handful of luxury muesli
Wholemeal bread and low-fat spread with reduced-sugar jam or marmalade

Packed lunch
Fruit and Nut Pasta Salad (page 207)
Slice of Carrot Cake (page 234)
Home-made Vegetable Crisps (page 204)
Pot of fruit fromage frais

Evening
Vegetable Burgers (page 224)
Potato Wedges (page 220)
Side salad with olive oil French dressing
Pancakes (page 232) with lemon juice and caster sugar

Snack
Orange
Handful of pumpkin seeds

TUESDAY

Breakfast
Berry and Banana Milkshake (page 239)
Wholemeal toast with low-fat spread and honey

Cafeteria lunch
Cheese and tomato pizza

Side salad

Apple

Evening

Chickpea and Spinach Pasta (page 213)

Fruit Fool (page 230)

Snack

Crudités with tzatziki (yoghurt and cucumber dip)

a few Brazil nuts and dried ready-to-eat apricot halves

WEDNESDAY

Breakfast

Porridge made with semi-skimmed milk and handful of sultanas

Orange juice

Wholemeal bread with low-fat spread and Marmite

Packed lunch

Sandwich of 2 slices white bread with low-fat spread filled with a slice of vegetarian pâté (ready-made from deli), watercress and cucumber

Slice of Fruit Cake (page 234)

Fruit yoghurt

Packet of mixed nuts and raisins

Evening

Baked Eggs and Peppers (page 227)

Baked Banana (page 232) with Greek yoghurt

Snacks

Mini bread sticks with Cheese Dip (page 203)

Apple

THURSDAY

Breakfast

Weetabix with semi-skimmed milk

White bread with low-fat spread and reduced-sugar jam

Peach or nectarine

Cafeteria Lunch

Baked potato with baked beans

Mixed salad or orange

Blueberry muffin

Evening

Vegetable and Butterbean Hotpot (page 215)

Fresh Fruit Trifle (page 231)

Snack

a few Brazil nuts and walnut halves

Slice of Date Loaf (page 232)

FRIDAY

Breakfast

Wholemeal toast with low-fat spread and honey

Pot of fruit fromage frais

Orange juice

Packed lunch

Slice of good-quality ready-made cheese and onion quiche

Slice of Carrot Cake (page 234)

Apple

Home-made Vegetable Crisps (page 204)

Evening

Stir-fry of Quorn pieces with thinly sliced carrot, broccoli, mange tout and spring onions with light soya sauce and hoisin sauce

Wholewheat noodles

Summer Fruit Compote (page 230)

Snack

2 rice cakes with peanut butter

a few dried apricot halves

SATURDAY

Breakfast

Bowlful of luxury muesli with skimmed milk

Peach or nectarine

Lunch

Cheesy Coleslaw (page 209)

Crusty wholemeal bread with low-fat spread

Satsuma

Evening

Pasta Shells with Peppers (page 211)

Fruit yoghurt

Snack

Fruit and Nut Cookies (page 233)

Handful of pumpkin seeds

SUNDAY

Breakfast

Baked beans on wholemeal toast with low-fat spread

Grapefruit juice

Lunch

Greek Cheese and Spinach Pie (page 228)

Side salad with olive oil French dressing

Plum Crumble (page 231) with Greek yoghurt

Evening

Roast Mushroom and Tofu Sandwich (page 206)

Snack

Fruit fromage frais

a few dried apricot halves

5 almonds

A-Z OF CHILD HEALTH & DIET

This section of the book is where you will find all the information you need to know about particular topics related to your children and their diet. The subjects range from particular foods (e.g. 'bread') and types of foods (e.g. 'junk food') to health topics (e.g. 'eczema') and well-being (e.g. 'sexual development').

To simplify things I have presented everything in alphabetical order so that you needn't consult the index in order to use this section. If there is any subject you want to know about, simply look here first. Each subject lists references if further information is available elsewhere in the book, and provides links to related topics.

Each listed food begins with its nutritional breakdown. I have only listed relevant details – hence, for example, if you find there is no figure given for saturated fat, that is because there is none

(or virtually none) in that food. The same applies to total fat, cholesterol, protein, carbohydrate, sugar, fibre and sodium. The vitamins and minerals listed are those that are found in good or excellent quantities in that food. Other vitamins and minerals may be present in smaller quantities.

In the nutrient listings and tables throughout this chapter a number of abbreviations have been used, most of which are self-evident, e.g. 'tot carbs' for total carbohydrates, 'sat fat' for saturated fat, 'chol' for cholesterol and 'prot' for protein. Minerals have been cited using several abbreviations depending upon the size of the table, these are: 'calc' or 'ca' for calcium; 'fe' for iron; 'iod' for iodine; 'mag' or mg' for magnesium; 'pot' for potassium; 'sel' for selenium, 'sod' for sodium and 'zn' for zinc. Where nutrient figures are not available I have indicated this with 'n/k' to denote 'not known'.

ACNE

The UK Institute of Child Health says that up to 85% of young people between the ages of 12 and 25 suffer from acne – oily patches of skin with red lumps or spots and black- or white-heads. Boys and girls are equally affected, with the peak age being around 17. The face, back and chest are the areas normally affected.

Acne is caused by over-production of oil in the sebaceous glands, which are affected by the sex hormones, which are, in turn, most active during puberty and young adulthood. This surplus oil blocks the pores and prevents the skin's normal 'waste disposal' system from working properly. Waste matter then accumulates beneath the skin as a 'plug' in the blocked pore, and a characteristic spot appears, made worse by bacteria. If left untreated, acne can cause scarring.

The causes: Research has found that over 80% of cases of acne are caused by genetic composition, and that other factors including diet had little or no effect. There is no reliable research showing that diet is a major influence on acne, or that chocolate or other fatty foods, sugar or 'junk foods' can cause acne.

What can be done: There is plenty of circumstantial evidence that young people with acne find an impressive improvement in its severity if they spend time outdoors in sunshine. It is thought that sunlight reduces inflammation. However, sunblock should, of course, be worn and sunburn avoided. Exercise may also help, though the evidence for this is less clear.

Girls may find that their acne 'breaks out' in the days before a period, and stress may possibly make it worse in both sexes. Keeping the skin clean can help control acne and it is also important to keep the hands clean, and to avoid touching the face or picking at spots.

Mild-to-moderate acne can be contained by using a cream containing benzoyl peroxide, while more severe acne usually responds well to low-dose antibiotics, which may need to be taken over months or longer. See your doctor for further advice.

Despite the lack of evidence for diet being a factor in acne, it is nevertheless a good idea to encourage any child to eat a varied diet, including plenty of fresh fruit and vegetables, especially those rich in carotenoids, such as carrots, mangoes, dark leafy greens and broccoli. These nutrients are linked to skin health and can also offer limited protection against sun damage.

> If antibiotics are prescribed, see also: Illness, feeding during p138 for information on 'probiotics'.

ACRYLAMIDE

Acrylamide is a chemical considered to be potentially cancer-causing which first came to public attention in 2002, when a Swedish study found very high levels in certain foods – notably crisps, chips, crackers and breakfast cereals, and to a lesser extent in breads. The chemical appears to be produced mainly in starchy foods which are fried, baked, grilled or roast at high temperatures, as raw or boiled foods have negligible amounts.

Previous studies on animals found that acrylamide is a potential carcinogen and may impair male fertility. There is evidence that high levels of exposure can cause nerve damage in humans, while the evidence for its causing human cancer is slighter and, indeed, one study published in the *British Journal of Cancer* in January 2003 found that there wasn't a link – though the researchers admitted that the study was small.

We currently don't know all the answers and won't until a lot more research has been done. Meanwhile, the UK Food Standards Agency says: 'People shouldn't change their diet… continue to eat a healthy, balanced diet, including plenty of fruit and vegetables'. The USA Food and Drug Administration has advised that the acceptable daily intake of acrylamide is 12 mcg (micrograms) per person per day (see the box opposite). The World Health Organization has given the following advice:
• Food should not be cooked for too long or at too high a temperature. Though all foods should be cooked thoroughly to destroy food-borne pathogens, particularly meat and meat products.
• People should moderate their consumption of fried and fatty foods.

ACRYLAMIDE IN FOODS

(Adapted from figures provided by the USA Food and Drug Administration and the World Health Organization)

FOOD	ACRYLAMIDE MCG PER AVERAGE SERVING
Boiled potatoes	0
Tortilla chips	5
Honeynut breakfast cereal	6
French fries (fast food), cooked	59–82
Potato crisps	25
Savoury crackers	21
Bread	2.5

My own advice is for you to limit your child's intake of the foods that appear to be likeliest to contain high levels of acrylamide and which also offer no particular benefits to health in large amounts. These are 'junk foods' such as crisps, chips and any baked goods which are high in fat and/or sugar and low in vitamins or minerals. Try to serve boiled and mashed potatoes more often as you cut back on chips. Don't serve food which is actually charred – e.g. burnt toast or blackened barbecued or grilled foods.

As breakfast cereals and bread are both traditionally regarded as a staple part of most children's healthy diets, the best advice is to continue serving them in reasonable quantities until all the current research can give a definitive answer on acrylamide and health. Including plenty of fresh fruits and vegetables in the diet is also important as these are linked with a reduction in the risk of several types of cancer.

See also: Junk Food pp140–3.

Further information:

www.who.int/fsf/Acrylamide/

www.ifst.org/acrylmd.htm

www.cfsan.fda.gov/~dms/acryfaq.html

ADDITIVES
see Food Additives

ADHD (ATTENTION DEFICIT HYPERACTIVITY DISORDER)

Other names, and other related names, for this disorder in children include hyperactivity, HKD (hyperkinetic disorder) and ADD (attention deficit disorder). To simplify matters, we'll use the umbrella term 'hyperactivity' here.

Hyperactivity is diagnosed, according to the Royal College of Physicians (RCP), as 'developmentally inappropriate levels' of inattention and difficulty in concentrating, excessive and/or disorganized levels of activity and impulsive behaviour. These symptoms should have persisted for at least 6 months, first start in children before the age of 6 or 7, must be present in more than one setting (e.g. at home and at school), must cause significant functional impairment and not be better accounted for by other disorders (e.g. depression or schizophrenia).

Prevalence of hyperactivity has been estimated by different bodies at between 1% and 17% of school age children in the UK. Recent official Department of Health figures say that 1 in 20 children aged between 6 and 16 have ADHD, while the figure in the USA is higher. Boys are 4 times more likely to have hyperactivity than girls.

If you think your child may be hyperactive, you should take him or her to see your doctor. There is some evidence, however, that diet can play a role. Much attention is focused on the role of food additives. A study by the University of Surrey in 2002 found that, in some children, some food chemicals could cause reactions within 30 minutes. Another study by the UK's Asthma and Allergy Research Centre (AARC) in 2002 found, in a study of 3-year-olds, that 'significant changes in children's hyperactive behaviour could be produced by the removal of colourings and additives from their diet'.

In a one-month trial of 3-year-olds, for two weeks they drank juice dosed with 20mg of artificial colourings (E102, E110, E122, E124) and with 45mg of E211, the preservative sodium benzoate. Parents kept a record of their behaviour. In the last two weeks the juice contained no additives. When the results were analyzed it was found that the impact of the additives on the children's hyperactive behaviour indicated substantial effects which were detectable by parents.

> Children with hyperactivity have been found to be more thirsty than other children, and to have a higher incidence of eczema, asthma and other allergies.

The UK's Hyperactive Children's Support Group recommends the Feingold Diet, a way of eating devised by a US doctor that is said to improve hyperactivity. It eliminates artificial food colourings, flavourings and preservatives, and other foods – including a long list of fruits. However, the American Pediatric Society says that studies have shown that the Feingold Diet fails to control hyperactivity and infer that some children benefit (from a special diet) because of the extra parental attention this involves.

While the RCP says that, on the current evidence, it is not possible to recommend diets which restrict or eliminate refined sugar and artificial additives for children with ADHD/ HKD. Neither do they support the idea that supplementation with minerals such as zinc, iron or magnesium will help treat hyperactivity.

On the positive side, there is convincing evidence that supplementation with long-chain omega-3 essential fatty acids does help some children. The RCP says that this may be true particularly of children with low levels of the essential fats. Another theory is that the brain may have trouble converting the essential polyunsaturated fats into the very-long-chain polyunsaturates, for instance DHA and EPA found in oily fish.

The UK Institute of Child Health says that modifying the diet might help, and that up to half of those children affected by hyperactivity can be helped by behavioural therapy alone.

> See also: Behavioural Problems pp78–9, Dyslexia and Dyspraxia pp103–5, Food Additives pp114–17, Junk Food pp140–3, Appendix 3 pp252–3 for support group contacts.

ALCOHOL

Alcohol consumption amongst older children and teenagers is probably a lot higher than most parents realise, as statistics from Alcohol Concern UK, shown in box opposite, indicate.

No parent can afford to be complacent about whether or not their child is drinking alcohol. Stress, peer pressure, a desire to overcome social inhibitions, the typical teenage need to experiment and to rebel – these are all reasons why children try alcohol. Research from the National Addiction Centre shows that by the age of 13 or 14, 65% of children who drink have begun to consume alcohol without their parents' knowledge.

The problems: Alcohol Concern reports that 'intoxication is more dangerous for children than adults, as they experience coma at lower blood alcohol levels and can develop hypoglycaemia, hypothermia and breathing difficulties. For young people, who come in all shapes and sizes and whose bodies may still be developing, risk-free drinking does not exist.'

Alcohol intake has been shown to affect school performance and encourage crime and accidents. Taken regularly over a period of time, alcohol can cause many health problems in later years. Although there is a small benefit in moderate alcohol intake for some adults (for example, the antioxidant content of wine can be helpful for older men in preventing heart disease), in children and teenagers the drawbacks undoubtedly outweigh any benefits. People who drink regularly in their teens are more likely to drink heavily as adults.

What you can do: Lead by example – *Child Development* magazine reports that youngsters who have a close relationship with their mothers are least likely to drink. Alcohol Concern says that children who drink are twice as likely to have heavily drinking parents, while, interestingly enough, teetotal parents also produce higher numbers of children who drink.

In some countries, such as France and Italy, older children consume small amounts of wine at family meals and this is accepted as normal. Perhaps allowing occasional moderate consumption in the home, plus close watchful monitoring, are the keys.

ALLERGIES
see Food Allergies

ANAEMIA

Anaemia is a lack of haemoglobin, which carries oxygen around the bloodstream. The major cause of anaemia in childhood is iron deficiency, which is usually due to too little of the mineral in the diet. About 50% of teenage girls have iron intakes below the recommended levels. Girls around puberty and/or with heavy periods are particularly at risk of iron-deficiency anaemia.

The symptoms: a pale colour, tiredness, lethargy, headaches, dizziness and – when the anaemia is severe – a shortness of breath. If the anaemia isn't treated, there may be mental and physical developmental impairment.

What to do: If you think your child may be anaemic, take him or her to the doctor who will probably do a blood test. If lack of iron in the diet is the cause, the doctor may prescribe supplements and/or a diet high in iron-rich foods, such as red meat, dark leafy green vegetables, pulses, whole grains, dried fruits and seeds. Iron is better absorbed if eaten with a good source of vitamin C, e.g. citrus fruit or juice, or red peppers.

See also: Appendix 1 pp240–9 for sources of iron and vitamin C.

ANAPHYLACTIC SHOCK
see Food Allergies

ANOREXIA NERVOSA
see Eating Disorders

ANXIETY
see Nervousness and Anxiety

ANTIOXIDANTS

'Antioxidant' is a term sometimes used to describe a range of vitamins, minerals and plant chemicals the benefits of which include, among others, the ability to 'mop up' free radicals within the body and thus help prevent the signs of disease and ageing. Free radicals are particles produced in the body as a result of normal living. However, in certain circumstances – for example, when people are ill, under stress, smoke or take a great deal of physical activity, or when they get old – the production of free radicals increases and it is thought that a surfeit of free radicals is linked with increased risk of diseases including cancers and coronary heart disease. The damaging effects of free radicals can be counteracted by the antioxidants, which in effect neutralize them.

Healthy children are not at as great a risk from free radicals as are the ill or elderly, but nevertheless should be encouraged to eat foods rich in the antioxidant vitamins, minerals and plant compounds regularly as part of an overall healthy diet.

THE MOST IMPORTANT ANTIOXIDANTS:

• **Vitamins:** A, C, E and Beta-carotene
• **Minerals:** Zinc and Selenium
• **Plant chemicals:** the Flavonoid group

See also: Convalescence pp96–7, Minerals pp148–9, Phytochemicals p160, Vitamins pp194–6, Appendix 1 pp240–9 for recommended intakes and sources of antioxidants.

APPETITE LOSS

In the short term, almost all children, just like adults, will go through periods of having a small or poor appetite. This can be because they are ill or perhaps because they are experiencing negative emotions – such as worry, fear, and stress.

Eating less than is normal, or appropriate, for a few days – or even weeks – is no great cause for worry, especially if you know the cause. Try to deal with the cause and the appetite problems should resolve. Check that your child isn't filling up between meals on fatty, sugar items or drinks, which would dull the appetite for mealtimes.

Long-term poor appetite – or 'restrictive eating' as it is sometimes known – is when a child eats smaller than average portions for her or his age, or may not want to eat as often as other children, or at normal mealtimes, resulting in fewer calories than average being consumed. This will usually result in the child being thinner than average and can, if severe, restrict growth and normal development.

Who suffers and why? Poor appetite is most common in pre-school and primary-school age children, but is sometimes found in adolescents. Children who are 'slow feeders' when young seem to be more likely to have a poor appetite later on, and to generally be less interested in food.

While worrying, poor appetite doesn't necessarily signify the onset of a serious eating disorder, such as anorexia nervosa.

What to do? Take your child to see the doctor to ensure that he or she is healthy and a suitable weight. If this is the case then nothing more needs to be done. Trying to force, persuade or encourage the child to eat bigger portions – or to eat more frequently – makes no difference, and may make matters worse. Simply attempt, without any comment or discussion, to provide your child with foods that offer a high level of vitamins, minerals, and protein, even in small portions, rather than letting the child fill up on sweets, fizzy drinks or crisps, which contain few. This will help ensure he or she meets the recommended levels of nutrients.

If the doctor feels that the child's growth is being restricted or health impaired, then he or she will discuss the options with you.

The good news is that, in the long term, poor eaters do usually find their appetite improves. They may stay slim and become slim adults, but this need not be linked to poor health – indeed, a moderately low Body Mass Index (BMI, see Appendix 2 pp250–1) is linked to better health than a high one.

See also: 'Feeding Problems Aged 1–4' pp26–7, 'Eating Problems' pp59–60 and pp13, 21–4, 33–8, 53–6 for nutritional requirements at each age, Convalescence pp96–7, Eating Disorders pp105–7, Fussy Eating and Food Refusal pp131–2, Illness, feeding during p138, Underweight pp190–1, Appendix 2 pp250–1 for Growth Charts.

APPLES

Nutrient content per average dessert apple:

Cals	**50**	(of which) sugars	**12g**
Tot fat	**trace**	Fibre	**1.8g**
Prot	**0.4g**	Vits	**C**
Tot carbs	**12g**	Mins	**potassium, boron**

Compared with many other fruits, apples are a good but not excellent source of vitamin C, the content of which can vary considerable, depending on how long they have been in storage before being bought, and on storage conditions at home.

Apples have been found to help lower blood cholesterol and improve lung function, probably due to their high content of the phytochemical quercetin, and of another plant compound, catechin, both of which are members of the flavonoid group. One large Finnish study of 10,000 people over 28 years found that those who had a high intake of quercetin also had less risk of contracting diabetes, prostate cancer and other illnesses.

Apples contain the mineral boron, which helps to prevent calcium loss and may help to build good bone structure. Cooking apples have a similar nutrient profile to dessert apples.

See also: Asthma p76, Fruit pp129–30, Vitamins pp194–6, Appendix 1 pp246–7 for further information on flavonoids.

ARTIFICIAL SWEETENERS

Several artificial sweeteners are licensed for use in foods and drinks throughout the world – for instance, aspartame, acesulfame-K and saccharin. These sweeteners are virtually calorie-free and are mainly used in drinks and sweet foods aimed at people who want to lose weight or cut down on sugar in the diet for other reasons. They come in tablet, liquid or granular form, as sweeteners to replace sugar used in cooking or at the table, but the largest percentage of use by far is in commercial foods and drinks.

As, research shows, children of all ages are drinking more and more fizzy drinks, squashes and sweetened juice-type products, many of which use artificial sweeteners instead of sugar, it is likely that intake of these sweeteners is cumulatively high in many children. A research project by the UK Food Commission showed that if drinks were sweetened with cyclamates, the average child would consume 40% more than recommended levels.

Although, as I write, the sweetener cyclamate (E952 or cyclamic acid) is still in use in the UK and other countries, the EU is considering lowering the maximum amount of this sweetener per litre permitted to a level which would force manufacturers to abandon its use. The UK Food Standards Agency issued a warning in May 2003 that young children should not drink more than 3 beakers (about 180ml) of dilutable soft drinks or squashes containing cyclamate per day, as this could lead to children aged 1½-4½ taking in more than the acceptable daily intake.

The popular sweetener aspartame (brand name Nutrasweet) shouldn't be used by children with a phenylketonuria (PKU) metabolic defect (a rare inherited condition) as it contains the amino acid phenylalanine which needs to be restricted in PKU sufferers. Research from America also showed that, in animals, aspartame hinders production of serotonin in the brain, a lack of which is linked to depression and binge eating.

So is there a use for artificial sweeteners? Even for obese children, the benefits do seem to be doubtful. One research study showed that people who have a high intake of artificial sweeteners actually consume more calories in their diet than those who don't. Other researchers believe that artificial sweeteners encourage a 'sweet tooth' in the young. Perhaps most importantly, the long-term effects of consuming large quantities of artificial sweeteners are as yet unknown.

There are other sweeteners that contain fewer calories than sugar but which are not actually 'artificial'. Sorbitol, for example, is a cousin of sugar – it is a polyol alcohol which is absorbed less rapidly into the bloodstream than sugar and is thus sometimes used in diabetic products. Mannitol and xylitol are two other polyol sweeteners. All these products do still contain about two-thirds the amount of calories of sugar and thus are only of limited use in reducing the calorie content of foods in which they are used. Regular use of xylitol has been shown to help prevent tooth decay, but it is best used for this purpose as a chewing gum. Xylitol gum may be purchased from pharmacies or health food shops.

My advice: Choose water, semi-skimmed milk or diluted fruit juice as the drinks of choice for children rather than artificially sweetened OR sugary products. Provide a balanced diet, high in fresh and nutritionally sound foods, which will automatically then be low or moderate in artificially sweetened products.

See also: Drinks pp103–4, Junk Food pp140–3, Sugar and Sweeteners pp182–5.

PRODUCTS WHICH OFTEN CONTAIN ARTIFICIAL SWEETENERS:

- Diet drinks
- Squashes (even if not labelled 'low-calorie' or 'diet' – check the label)
- Juice 'drinks' (as opposed to 100% juices)
- Flavoured mineral waters
- Low-calorie or 'diet' yoghurts and fromage frais
- Low-calorie desserts
- Reduced-calorie or 'diet' sauces and salad dressings
- Ice creams

ASTHMA

Asthma is a disease of the airways that carry air into and out from the lungs. These tubes become sensitive and inflamed and, when an asthma attack is triggered, the airways swell making it hard to breathe. In severe cases asthma can be life-threatening.

Rates of asthma in the UK have doubled in the past ten years, and now 1 in 5 children are affected, making it the most common long-term childhood illness. The causes of this epidemic may be varied, but diet certainly seems to play a significant role.

At an international asthma conference in Edinburgh in 2002 it was claimed that diet is the biggest factor contributing to increased asthma in wealthier countries, where there is a move away from natural towards fast foods. Studies indicate that a diet rich in fruit, vegetables and perhaps oily fish, which tends to be anti-inflammatory, can help prevent or minimize the condition.

Research in recent years has shown a link between low fruit consumption and poor lung function. The American Thoracic Society found that regular intake of apples and tomatoes is linked with lower incidence of wheezing and improved lung capacity, and the National Asthma Campaign (NAC) says that regular intake of fresh fruit can protect against asthma and other lung diseases.

Omega-3 fish oil is known to have anti-inflammatory properties which may ease asthmatic symptoms, and there is evidence that low magnesium intake is associated with higher prevalence of asthma.

There is less research linking particular foods with increased risk of asthma, but one Australian study in 2001 found that it could be linked to high intake of omega-6 fats found in many vegetable and seed oils (e.g. corn, sunflower and safflower) and trans fats in commercially manufactured foods. Findings strengthened by a study at Manchester University reported in March 2003, which found that the only dietary difference between a group of asthmatic children and non-asthmatic children was that the asthmatic group had more polyunsaturated fat in their diets. Omega-6 oils tend to be pro-inflammatory. However this doesn't appear to apply to the very long-chain omega-6s (highly unsaturated fatty acids) which may actually be beneficial.

For women planning a new pregnancy, taking antibiotics in pregnancy may increase the risk of the child developing asthma, as may smoking and a shortfall of vitamins C and E, while intake of oily fish and fish oils, rapeseed oil and soya bean oil have been linked with a reduction of wheezing in babies. The Scottish Intercollegiate Guidelines Network (SIGN) reports a significant protective effect of breast-feeding against the development of asthma.

Lastly, the SIGN also recommends weight reduction in obese children with asthma to improve asthma control.

The NAC says that food and drink are *not* common triggers for people with asthma, although food allergies can produce symptoms which can resemble an asthma attack. Some of the most common foods to produce such a reaction are dairy produce, shellfish, products containing food additives called sulphites (E numbers 220–227) and tartrazine (E102), and wheat – but a variety of other foods may cause asthmatic symptoms in susceptible individuals.

See also: Eczema pp107–8, Fats and Oils pp110–12, Food Allergies pp117–18, Obesity pp152–5.

AUTISM

Research by Scottish biochemist Dr Gordon Bell published in 2001 found that two-thirds of autistic children have a deficiency in the omega-3 fatty acids, and those who were fed fish oils made significant improvement – for example, their concentration and sleep patterns improved. It was also found that children with Asperger's syndrome, a condition related to autism, had low blood levels of omega-3s.

See also: Behavioural Problems pp78-9, Fats and Oils pp110–12, Fish pp113–14.

BABY RUSKS
see Biscuits

BACON

Nutrient content per 2 thin slices of grilled lean back bacon (about 50g)

Cals	146	Fibre		0g
Tot fat	9.5g	Vits		B group
Sat fat	3.7g	Mins	zinc, potassium	
Chol	35mg	Sodium		
Prot	15g	content		1,120mg
Tot carbs	0g			

Lean bacon is not one of the higher-fat meats and, because of its high protein content and rich source of most B vitamins and zinc, is a valuable food for many children. The fatty cuts, such as streaky or middle, are much higher in fat and lower in protein.

Bacon has a very high sodium content, though you can sometimes buy reduced-salt packs. Bacon, gammon and hams may also contain nitrites, chemicals used to cure meats and prevent growth of the bacteria which cause botulism. Nitrites may turn into nitrosamines in the digestive system, which may be carcinogenic. Cured meats must contain added vitamin C, which blocks the production of nitrosamines. Both smoked and burnt bacon may be carcinogenic so avoid giving these to children. Lean gammon has a similar nutrient profile to bacon.

See also: Grilled Food p135, Meat p145, Pork p161, Salt pp171–4, Smoked Foods p177.

BANANAS

Nutrient content per medium banana:

Cals	95	(of which) sugars		21g
Tot fat	0.3g	Fibre		1.1g
Prot	1.2g	Vits		B6, C
Tot carbs	23g	Mins		potassium

Bananas are one of the best sources of potassium, which helps to regulate body fluids. They also contain a type of dietary fibre known as fructo-oligosaccharides (FOS). This can help to promote healthy bacteria in the gut and may be useful for children who suffer from frequent stomach upsets and constipation. Bananas are easily digested and popular with most children. They are one of the few fruits to have a reasonable starch content, allowing for a slower release of energy – the majority of the carbohydrate content of most fruits is in the form of fruit sugars.

See also: Carbohydrates pp87–8, Constipation p96, Dietary Fibre pp101–2, Fruit pp129–30.

BEANS, BAKED

Nutrient content per 200g serving:

Cals	162	Fibre		7g
Tot fat	1.2g	Vits		Beta-carotene,
Sat fat	trace			folate
Prot	9.6g	Mins		magnesium,
Tot carbs	30g			potassium, iron
(of which) sugars	11.6g	Sodium		1,060mg

Beans in tomato sauce contain a range of important nutrients for children – they provide iron, magnesium and fibre, all of which are in shortfall in many young diets, as well as being a good low-fat source of protein. What's more, most children enjoy baked beans and this makes them even more valuable for parents.

On the negative side, they are high in sodium and sugar – but the reduced-salt and -sugar versions, which are widely obtainable, contain both in reasonably small quantity.

Baked beans are also a good source of the phytochemical lycopene.

See also: Phytochemicals p160, Protein pp165–6, Pulses pp166–8, Salt pp171–4, Appendix 1 p247 for sources of lycopene.

BEANS, DRIED
see Pulses

BEANS, GREEN

Nutrient content per 80g portion:

Cals	20	(of which) sugars	1.8g
Tot fat	0.4g	Fibre	1.7g
Sat fat	trace	Vits	Beta-carotene,
Prot	1.5g		folate, C
Tot carbs	2.5g	Mins	potassium

Green beans are a useful vegetable for children, especially if cut into small segments, as they are higher in fibre than many other vegetables. French beans and runner beans have similar nutritional value to green beans.

BEDWETTING

Bedwetting, or enuresis, is a common problem in young children and can persist well into the primary school years. Dietary factors are rarely the main cause but, obviously, if your child is prone, it is worth managing their levels of hydration by providing plenty to drink during the day rather than giving a lot to drink in the hour or two before bedtime. A supper meal (or tea followed by a supper snack at bedtime) rich in carbohydrates may also help prevent bedwetting, as the carbohydrates (such as bread, potatoes or a scone) literally 'mop up' liquid and diminish the need to go to the toilet. Avoid natural diuretic foods in the evening – these include celery, melon, asparagus, citrus fruits, watercress.

There is some research to indicate that bedwetting is more common in obese children.

If your child begins to wet the bed after having been dry, and especially if he or she begins to drink a lot more than previously, take him or her to the doctor, who should consider doing a test for diabetes.

See also: Carbohydrates pp87–8, Diabetes p101, Obesity pp152–5.

BEEF

Nutrient content per 100g for lean raw beef (per Quarterpounder grilled burger, in brackets):

Cals	125 (255)	Prot	22g (21g)
Tot fat	4g (19g)	Vits	B group (same)
Sat fat	1.7g (8.5g)	Mins	potassium, zinc,
Chol	60mg (60mg)		iron (same)

Lean beef is an excellent source of protein, B vitamins and minerals, particularly iron, and is lower in fat and saturated fat than you might think. Always go for lean cuts, or, if using fattier cuts for casseroles and so on, pre-cook the dish, leave to cool in the fridge and remove the fat from the top before reheating until piping-hot to serve.

The children's perennial favourite, beefburger, can be much fattier, especially those bought from takeouts, because fatty cuts of minced beef may be used. If choosing burgers from the supermarket, go for those described as 'extra-quality' or 'extra-lean' and grill them thoroughly to remove excess fat. Better still, make your own from top-quality lean minced steak.

See also: BSE pp84–5, Food Poisoning pp122–3, Food Safety pp123–6, Sausages pp175–6, Takeaways pp186–8, Home-made Burgers recipe p225.

BEHAVIOURAL PROBLEMS

Can diet influence children's mood and behaviour? ADHD, depression, dyslexia and dyspraxia, nerves and anxiety are all discussed elsewhere in this A–Z section. But several other, or related, behavioural problems, such as mood swings, irritability and even delinquency, have been linked with diet.

FOOD ADDITIVES

There is some research to indicate that food colourings (E numbers and others) and, to a lesser extent, other additives, such as preservatives and flavourings, may cause behavioural changes or problems in children. The Isle of Wight research is detailed in the ADHD feature and further details appear under Food Additives in this section.

More recently, one large primary school in the UK which banned additives in school meals found children better behaved at school, and the parents said that the children slept better at night. However, numerous professional bodies and government departments say that the scientific evidence for a link between behaviour and additives is slight.

My advice? Because many of the additive-rich foods and drinks are also those low in nutritional value, a diet which limits these items is worth a try.

SUGAR

Many people believe that sugar and sugary foods are the cause of behaviour disruption, but this is widely disputed. There is no real proof that sugar disrupts behaviour, and people have been eating sugar for hundreds of years without problems.

However, there is some scientific rationale behind the sugar/bad behaviour theory. If a child eats a diet high in sugar, this may cause blood glucose levels to rise quickly, giving a 'high', which can make a child excitable. Then, as insulin is released, the levels may plummet and the child may feel unusually drowsy and perhaps unable to concentrate. Then, to stop the levels falling further, adrenaline may be released in the body, which can increase irritability. This pattern depends on what else the child has eaten, etc., but in theory 'sugar overload' behaviour is possible.

My advice? Again, as sugar is a nutrient-poor food, limiting its use won't cause any problems in your child's diet and so it is worth a try. If you do offer sugary foods or drinks, let your child have them as part of a nutritious meal to limit any side-effects by keeping blood sugar levels more even.

It is also worth pointing out that although the brain needs sugar (glucose) to function properly, the body converts foods into sugar as necessary; actual sugar isn't required for blood glucose to be made.

NUTRITION AND DELINQUENCY

In 2002, the *British Journal of Psychiatry* published the results of a study into the effect of diet on juvenile offenders. This study found that violent offences fell by almost 40% amongst the youngsters who took

supplements of vitamins, minerals and fatty acids. While the International Society for the Study of Fatty Acids and Lipids (ISSFAL) found in a trial of school children that those who had higher levels of the long-chain omega-3s, DHA and EPA, in their bodies had lower scores for both violent aggressive behaviour and anger. However, this same study found that very-long-chain omega-6 acid actually increased anger and aggression. So it seems that it is the omega-3 fatty acids which effect positive changes in behaviour and other problems such as ADHD, rather than the omega-6s.

These studies reinforce the notion that a good well-balanced diet is important for proper brain functioning, which is, of course, where 'behaviour' begins. If, on the other hand, your child's diet contains an optimum amount of vitamins, minerals and fatty acids, it is unlikely that giving him or her even more will effect any further improvement.

EATING AS A FAMILY

One recent Spanish study indicates that children from families who rarely eat meals together suffer from more psychological problems than those who do. Try to eat as a family, as often as you can, and make mealtimes enjoyable and relaxed.

DEHYDRATION

Children sometimes don't drink enough hydrating fluids, especially when they are at school, and this can result in lethargy, lack of concentration and irritability. Try to ensure that your child's school has a facility for drinking water available all the time and when children are busy or out and about, encourage them to take a bottled water drink with them.

EXERCISE

Exercise may be as important as diet in improving children's behaviour. A recent experiment has found that with at least half an hour a day of sports, primary school children are quicker to settle down in class, more enthusiastic and less disruptive.

See also: 'The School Day' pp40–4, ADHD pp71–2, Brain Power pp81–2, Drinks pp103–4, Dyslexia and Dyspraxia pp103–5, Fats and Oils pp110–12, Food Additives pp114–17, Food Allergies pp117–19, Sugar and Sweeteners pp182–5.

BERRY FRUITS

Nutrient content of strawberries per 100g portion

Cals	27	Fibre	1.1g
Prot	0.8g	Vits	C
Tot carbs (all sugars)	6g		

All berry fruits are low in calories and have a good vitamin C content. Most are a good source of dietary fibre and are high in natural sugars. Most are also a good source of ellagic acid, which is both anti-cancer and a strong antioxidant. Blueberries (1st), blackberries (2nd) and strawberries (5th) are all in the 'Top Five' foods ranked on the ORAC scale, which measures antioxidant activity in foods. Raspberries have a similar nutrient profile to strawberries but have a higher fibre content (2.5g per 100g) and are a good source of folate.

Most children enjoy berries. Try serving them with Greek yoghurt or natural fromage frais, which contain less fat than whipped or double cream, or blend into drinks or purée and stir into natural yoghurt.

See also: Antioxidants p73, Drinks recipes pp238–9

BISCUITS

Nutrient content per biscuit

Chocolate digestive		Rich Tea	
Cals	75	Cals	35
Tot fat	4g	Tot fat	1.4g
Sat fat	2g	Sat fat	0.7g
Chol	10mg	Chol	2mg
Prot	1.2g	Prot	0.5g
Tot carbs	12g	Tot carbs	5.5g
(of which) sugars	5g	(of which) sugars	1.5g
Fibre	0.4g	Fibre	0.1g
Sod	68mg	Sod	32mg

Sweet and semi-sweet biscuits are, basically, fat, sugar and flour, with a variety of added ingredients and/or flavourings. The fat may be at least partially trans fat and/or saturated fat, both of which are the less-healthy types of fat. Commercially made biscuits tend to be low on vitamins and minerals, and devoid of phytochemicals. They are also usually low on fibre and some have a higher sodium content than you might think.

If you like to give your child biscuits, then consider making them yourself so that you can use good-quality ingredients, such as wholemeal flour, oils, nuts, seeds and dried fruits. Otherwise, you can often find good-quality biscuits from local markets or specialist grocery shops. Consider offering less sugary options sometimes – e.g. rice cakes or bread. Cereal bars are not necessarily a better option as they can be very high in sugar and sodium.

Baby rusks sometimes contain added sugar – check the label. Sugar content in any snack which is chewed or nibbled over periods of time can contribute to tooth decay. One UK Government survey found that 11% of children who ate biscuits more than once a day were found to have dental caries, as opposed to just 1% of children who ate them less frequently.

See also: Fats and Oils pp110–12, Salt pp171–4, Sugar and Sweeteners pp182–5, Teeth and Gums pp189–90.

BONE HEALTH

Bones continue to grow and develop their density and strength until around the age of 30, after which bone density slowly begins to decline. About 45% of bone mass is built up in adolescence, and by the late teens the bones usually stop growing in length, thus deciding your child's final height.

A good bone structure helps minimize symptoms of osteoporosis in later life and reduces the risk of fractures. Although regular weight-bearing exercise (e.g. running around) is important to maximize bone density, diet is a major factor in bone development.

Bone consists of collagen plus minerals, mostly calcium and phosphate. Calcium is a major component of bone and a growing child's diet needs to be adequate in calcium-rich foods, such as dairy produce and dark leafy green vegetables.

CALCIUM HELPERS

Dietary calcium is not always well-absorbed by the body – 70% or more of it may be excreted in urine. As well as ensuring adequate intake, it is therefore important to help absorption as much as possible.

Vitamin D is needed to help calcium absorption and vitamin D deficiency can cause rickets. Calcium works with magnesium to form bone, so an adequate magnesium intake is also needed.

Essential fatty acids – such as fish and plant oils – are thought to play a role in helping calcium metabolism, and absorption of calcium from leafy green vegetables also seems to be better than that from dairy produce. A diet generally high in fruit and vegetables seems to favour calcium retention. Research has found a link between optimum vitamin E intake and bone density, while zinc is another important mineral to help build bone.

CALCIUM ROBBERS

Similarly, certain foods and drinks decrease mineral absorption or increase excretion. A diet high in protein, especially animal protein, can increase calcium excretion. Caffeine, found mainly in coffee, cola drinks, tea and chocolate, seems to cause small but significant increases in calcium excretion. And a diet high in salt also increases the excretion of calcium in urine.

Perhaps the crucial factor for children is that a diet high in phosphates appears to limit calcium absorption. Carbonated drinks, soft drinks and processed foods can all contain high levels of phosphates, and their consumption by children has increased considerably over the past few years. One study published in 2001 found that teenage girls who drink fizzy drinks are three times more likely to suffer bone fractures than those who don't.

Alcohol and cigarette smoking can both reduce the absorption of calcium. In girls, lack of periods can affect bone density, and anorexia or low body weight also have a bearing. If your child has any kind of restrictive or special diet (e.g. vegan), it is important that you ensure adequate intake of the nutrients vital for bone-building.

See also: Alcohol pp72–3, Caffeine p85, Carbonated Drinks pp88–9, Drinks pp103–4, Eating Disorders pp105–7, Processed Foods pp164–5, Appendix 1 pp243–4 for sources of calcium.

BRAIN POWER

There has been much research over the past years to indicate that children's diet has a great influence over their brain power.

In a variety of trials, children who eat an optimum range of nutrients have shown improved IQ, concentration and memory. In 1999, the *Journal of Alternative and Complementary Medicine* analysed all the controlled trials on diet and intelligence and summarized that 'poor dietary habits (in children) may lead to impaired intelligence. Low-dose vitamin-mineral supplementation may restore the cognitive abilities… however there is also evidence that supplementation has no measurable effect on the intelligence of well-nourished children.' In other words, if your child already has optimum intake of all the nutrients, then further supplementation won't achieve anything.

Most trials have focussed on multi-nutrients, but some individual vitamins and minerals seem particularly important. In one trial published in the *British Journal of Nutrition*, vitamin C status was linked with IQ in boys. Iron deficiency can reduce the IQ of adolescents by up to 10 points, affecting not only cognitive ability and psychomotor skills but also behaviour, while replenishing iron stores can reverse these trends. A trial in Holland in 2000 found that children lacking in vitamin B12 were less able to reason and solve problems than children.

IS FISH REALLY BRAIN FOOD?

One important area of research is in the link between intelligence and very long-chain fatty acids. Most research has focussed on the omega-3 oils, DHA and EPA, which are provided by oily fish in the diet, and can also be made from the long-chain omega-3 fatty acid alpha-linolenic acid. DHA and other long-chain fats make up approximately 60% of the brain's material, so it is not really surprising that from the baby in the womb through to adulthood, a diet which contains plenty of these essential fats appears to boost brain power. One trial in County Durham in 2002 showed that learning abilities could be boosted by two years over a 12-week period in some children given long-chain omega-3 and omega-6 supplements.

Because our consumption of fish, especially oily fish, has decreased significantly it seems that these very long-chain essential fats are often missing in our children's diets.

OTHER FACTORS

There is some evidence that food additives may have an effect on children's ability to concentrate. The Food Commission found in 2002 that behaviour in 3-year-olds was affected by certain E numbers and a common preservative, and when one large primary school banned all artificial additives from school menus it reported that the children became calmer and more able to knuckle down to their work. Caffeine-containing fizzy drinks have also been linked with concentration problems at school, since a diet high in caffeine-rich items causes children to sleep less well at night and become sleepy during the day.

A lack of water or other hydrating fluids can also induce lethargy and lack of concentration, so aim to ensure school children take plenty of water or diluted juice to drink during the day – one small bottle is not sufficient. Regular exercise has also been shown to boost brain function, enhancing mood, concentration and memory.

BLOOD SUGAR LEVELS

There is plenty of evidence to show that children's academic work improves when they receive regular nutritious meals. Children who skip meals or who aren't given a good breakfast may have low blood sugar levels, which has a knock-on effect on the brain, as it uses sugars supplied in the blood as its source of energy. All types of thinking use up the brain's energy supplies more quickly than was previously realized.

A significant proportion of school children never have a breakfast, yet this meal can improve educational performance, memory, concentration and problem-solving abilities. It is particularly important because of the long time-gap since the last meal.

See also: ADHD pp71–2, Behavioural Problems pp78–9, Caffeine p85, Drinks pp103–4, Dyslexia and Dyspraxia pp103–5, Fats and Oils pp110–12, Fish pp113–14, Food Additives pp114–17, Appendix 1 pp240–9 for sources of B vitamins and essential fats.

BREAD

Nutrient content per 50g portion (2 small slices)

White		Wholemeal	
Cals	118	Cals	108
Tot fat	1g	Tot fat	1.2g
Sat fat	trace	Sat fat	trace
Prot	4.2g	Prot	4.5g
Tot carbs	25	Tot carbs	21g
(of which) sugars	1.3g	(of which) sugars	1g
Fibre	0.7g	Fibre	3g
Vits	B1, B3	Vits	B1, B3, folate
Mins	calcium	Mins	mag, iron, sel
Sodium	260mg	Sodium	275mg

Bread is the major source of starchy carbohydrates in the Western diet and most is made from wheat grain. White bread contains up to 80% of the whole wheat grain but no outer layer (bran) or seed (germ). Because of this it contains less fibre than whole-grain bread, and would contain less vitamins and minerals but in the UK B vitamins, calcium and iron are added to the refined white flour to give it a better nutritional profile, although the iron content is still lower than that for wholemeal bread.

Both white, whole-grain and brown breads (which contain 85–90% of the whole grain) are nutritious foods for children, as are the range of breads made from flours other than wheat – e.g. dark or light rye breads, corn bread and so on. Most breads are low in fat, although some – like croissants and garlic bread – are not.

Most bread contains moderately high amounts of sodium, as it tends to taste very bland unless a reasonable amount of salt is added. This will only be a problem if your child eats more than average amounts of bread and has a lot of other high-salt foods in his or her diet.

Mass-produced bread usually contain more additives than you might imagine – bleaching agents, preservatives, GM-soya bean flour, and colourings such as caramel. To avoid these you will need to buy organic or traditional loaves.

A small proportion of children are allergic to, or intolerant of, one or more of the constituents of bread. Children who are allergic to the gluten in wheat, rye, barley or oats have coeliac disease and should follow a special gluten-free diet. Other children may be intolerant of the yeast in bread, and you therefore need to buy or make yeast-free loaves. Soda bread is free from yeast, as are some – but not all – flatbreads. A few children are intolerant of wheat but not rye, barley or other grains. This is not the same as a gluten allergy. If you think your child may have an allergy or intolerance, see your doctor.

See also: Carbohydrates pp87–8, Coeliac Disease p94, Food Allergies pp117–19, Grains p132.

BREAKFAST CEREALS

Breakfast cereals are the most popular breakfast-time food and make a considerable contribution to the carbohydrate intake of UK and USA children. Their nutritional value varies tremendously, partly because they may be made from wheat, oats, rice, corn or rye, and also because manufacturers may add any number of ingredients to make the dozens of different cereal varieties – although some cereals have virtually nothing added.

BREAKFAST CEREALS – NUTRIENT CONTENT OF SELECTED PRODUCTS

Cereal per 30g portion unless otherwise stated	Cals	Tot fat (g)	Sat fat (g)	Protein (g)	Tot carbs (g)	Sugars (g)	Fibre (g)	Vits*	Mins*	Sodium (mg)
Corn flakes	108	trace	—	2.5	26	2.5	0.3	1	1	333
Fruit 'n' Fibre	105	1.4	0.7	2.7	22	7.3	2.0	1	1	210
Muesli, luxury 50g portion	185	3.9	0.8	5.3	34	7.8	3.8	2	2	23
Porridge oats (dry weight)	113	2.8	0.5	3.4	20	trace	2.1	3	3	3
Special K	113	trace	trace	4.6	25	5.2	0.6	1	1	253
Sugar-coated Rice Crispies	107	trace	trace	1.8	26	3	0.3	1	1	0.2
Wholewheat biscuits, 2	130	1.0	trace	4.4	25	1.8	3	4	4	100

*Vitamin and mineral content as follows:

Code no.	Vitamins (good source of)	Minerals (good source of)
1	B group, folate, D	iron
2	B3, E	—
3	—	—
4	B1, B2, B3	iron

Children tend to go for what many parents consider to be the least healthy cereals – those with a lot of added sugar, such as sugar-coated varieties, or with added fat, e.g. with chocolate pieces, or with both a lot of added fat and sugar, e.g. baked into 'clusters' or 'crisps'. In general, cereals are becoming more and more 'added-value', that is, manufacturers are adding an ever-greater variety of items to the basic product to suit what they perceive as children's tastes. A few years back a breakfast cereal was daring if it had a few sultanas in it – now you can find chocolate chips, chocolate flakes, sweets and every type of nut and fruit combination. And, if this isn't enough to tempt the kids, there are often free toys and games in the packs. If you must choose a cereal with added items in it, good-quality nuts and dried fruits such as raisins, apricots and peaches are all nutritious.

The plainer cereals that are low in fat and additives, and often reasonably high in fibre, are often less popular choices for children – though many do enjoy the wheat biscuits and instant porridge.

There is some evidence that cereals can help protect again some forms of cancer and diseases of the bowel. Whole-grain cereals will certainly make a valuable contribution to a child's insoluble fibre intake and help prevent constipation. Cereals which are not made from whole grains – e.g. corn flakes, rice crispies and many other mass-produced cereals – have added vitamins and minerals (e.g. those coded 1 in the table on page 83).

On the minus side, as well as the often high levels of added sugar and fat in some cereals, others may be reasonably high in added salt. A typical 30g bowl of corn flakes, for example, contains 333mg of sodium (832mg salt), which represents 42% of a 3-year-old child's recommended maximum daily intake. This may be fine if his or her diet is generally moderate in salt, but it is easy to see how a child's daily salt intake mounts up.

The verdict: when choosing breakfast cereals try to avoid or restrict those high in added sugar, fat and salt. Read the labels and also bear in mind that porridge oats and oat-based muesli are lower on the Glycaemic Index (see Obesity) than processed wheat, corn and rice cereals and should therefore keep your child's blood sugar levels even for longer – quite an important consideration on a school

morning, if not every morning. A glass of orange juice or a vitamin C-rich fruit chopped into any cereal will increase the nutritional profile and ensure better absorption of the iron in the cereal.

See also: Food Labelling pp119–22, Obesity pp152–5.

BSE

The disease of cattle, bovine spongiform encephalopathy, better known as BSE and sometimes as 'mad cow disease', has been at the heart of one of the major food scares in the UK, Europe and other parts of the world in recent years. BSE is thought to be passed on through infected feed, and attacks the brain and central nervous system of adult cattle causing death, and the consensus of opinion is that eating BSE-infected meat can cause a disease in humans called variant-Creutzfeldt-Jakob-Disease (vCJD).

Incidence of deaths from vCJD reached its peak in the UK in 2000, according to Department of Health statistics, while levels of BSE in UK cattle have dropped from approximately 45,000 in 1992 to less than 900 in 2002. Despite this, the EU still places the UK as a 'top risk' country at level 4.

Since the discovery of the BSE-vCJD link, the UK has introduced strict controls to reduce the risk of humans eating infected beef, but the risk cannot be completely eliminated. For example, BSE doesn't appear in cattle under age 30 months, and so it is now illegal to sell cattle for consumption over this age (the so-called 'Over Thirty Months' or OTM rule). As the brain and nervous system is most likely to carry BSE, by law these must be removed. There is also a ban on using certain types of mechanically recovered meat in food products. And lastly, since 1996 there has been a ban on feeding farm animals, including cattle, feed derived from the meat or bones of animals.

LOOPHOLES

Much of the meat on sale in the UK is imported, and imported meat does not have the same restrictions as UK meat. For example, the 'Over

Thirty Months' rule doesn't apply to imported meat products, such as sausages and pies, and the ban on animal feed for farm animals doesn't apply to countries outside the EU either. In addition, countries thought to be at low risk of BSE are completely exempt from the OTM rule, such as Argentina and Australia.

PROTECTING YOUR FAMILY

If you are worried about BSE but still want to eat beef, here are a few safeguards that may help minimize the risk as much as possible:
• Buy from the UK.
• Buy organic beef – organic herds have never been fed animal feed.
• Buy local beef from a known source – a good family butcher will be able to tell you not only what herd his beef came from, but also even describe the animal.
• Avoid the cheaper commercially-produced meat products, sausages, burgers and pies, especially from outside the EU – better to make your own burgers or buy good-quality specialist sausages now commonly available in supermarkets.

For further information on the current situation regarding BSE, vCJD etc., contact the UK Food Standards Agency on 020 7276 8000.

See also: Beef p78, Food Safety pp123–6, Lamb p143–4, Meat p145.

BULIMIA

see Eating Disorders

BURGERS

see Beef

CAFFEINE

Caffeine is a strong central nervous system stimulant, present in many drinks and foods – including coffee, tea, chocolate, cocoa and cola drinks. Moderate caffeine intake increases the

CAFFEINE CONTENT OF SELECTED FOODS AND DRINKS (APPROXIMATE)

Strong brewed fresh coffee (e.g. after dinner) 225ml	350mg
Single espresso	100mg
Average cafetière coffee, 225ml	200mg
Instant coffee, average strength, 225ml	76mg
Cappuccino, 225mg	100mg
Latte, 225mg	75mg
Decaffeinated instant, 225mg	5mg
Black tea, average strength, 225ml	50mg
Green tea, 225ml	50mg
Cola or diet cola, one 330ml can	30–55mg
7-up, one 330ml can	0mg
Chocolate, average 50g	10–50mg

metabolic rate and alertness, but high intake can cause 'jitters', anxiety, palpitations and insomnia. Caffeine is also a diuretic, meaning that drinks with a high caffeine content (see table above) can actually be dehydrating.

For children, too much caffeine may not be a good idea as there is research to show that young people who consume a lot of caffeine suffer from insomnia followed by sleepiness and lack of concentration at school. Children with hyperactive tendencies should probably avoid caffeine altogether. Caffeine intake has also been shown to increase calcium excretion, which could affect vital bone-building in the teenage years. In one USA study, teenage girls with high consumption of carbonated drinks were found to suffer 300% more fractures than others. It may also affect absorption or excretion of other important minerals, including iron, and so caffeine-containing drinks shouldn't be consumed with a meal.

If your teenager insists on drinking caffeine-containing drinks, try to persuade them to choose those that contain lower amounts. The consensus of expert opinion is that in adults, 250mg of caffeine a day is moderate – however, because children are usually smaller, I would advise no more than 50-100mg a day for kids and teenagers.

See also: Bone Health pp80–1.

CAKES

Most children enjoy cakes and bakery items, and for those who are slim, expend a lot of energy or who have trouble eating enough calories, a slice of cake can be a good idea. However, many types of cake are high in total fat, saturated or trans fats, sugar and calories, so for many children a certain amount of restraint needs to be exercised in how much cake you give them.

Mass-produced commercial cakes may also contain a long list of additives (just check out the label!) and may be high in salt (sodium). If you have the time, and your children enjoy cake, it is worth batch-baking some cakes and tea breads. All those in the recipe section have a better nutritional profile than most supermarket-shelf cakes and will freeze. It is quite easy to improve the nutrients in cake – for example, by using wholemeal flour instead of white for added B vitamins and fibre, by using good-quality oils or fats, by using honey or fruit purée instead of sugar, and by adding items such as dried fruits, nuts, seeds and wheatgerm.

See also: Carbohydrates pp87–8, Fats and Oils pp110–12, Salt pp171–4, Recipes pp232–5.

CANCER

According to the UK Institute of Child Health, 1 in 600 children up to the age of 15 get cancer, but approximately 70% are cured. Children tend to get different types of cancer from adults.

CANCER PREVENTION

Bacup (www.cancerbacup.org.uk), the UK's leading cancer information service, has general guidelines on the type of healthy diet which may help to prevent some forms of cancer. These can be summarized as keeping to a reasonable body weight, eating less fat, sugar and salt, and eating vegetables, fruit and grains. The diets outlined in Section 1 of this book are basic healthy diets for children similar to these guidelines (with differences appropriate to different ages).

There has been little research specifically about childhood cancer and diet – indeed, the British Nutrition Foundation says that the extent to which diet influences childhood cancer is unknown – but a prudent diet in childhood may certainly improve your child's chances of avoiding cancer later in life. In 2003, the UK's Social and Public Health Sciences Unit published interesting research which investigated dietary records of a large group of adults taken back in the 1930s, when they were children, and comparing them with those adults' health today. This revealed that the higher the fruit consumption during childhood, the less likely the risk of developing cancer as an adult. Also, a research study for the World Health Organization reported in March 2003 that 10% of all cancer cases in the developed world could be the result of people not eating enough fruit and vegetables. The clearest evidence of a link, they say, is for stomach and lung cancers.

As a significant number of children eat less than the recommended amounts of fruits and vegetables, encouraging your child to eat more is a positive way of helping them to good long-term health.

SPECIAL DIETS

Some carers of cancer sufferers – or sufferers themselves – feel that they should follow a special or restrictive diet (for example, drinking large quantities of carrot juice, or eliminating all meat from the diet) to try to effect a cure. Bacup summarizes the research on special diets and cancer thus: 'There is no scientific evidence that these diets cause cancer to shrink, increase a person's chances of survival or cure the disease. Some are expensive, some cause a lot of weight loss. Some may even be harmful. They can also be unpleasant to eat and time-consuming to prepare. Most doctors recommend a well-balanced diet and one that you enjoy …'

The famous Bristol Cancer Help Centre in the UK (www.bristolcancerhelp.org) doesn't offer restrictive diets – including the Gerson Diet, macrobiotic or naturopath diets, or juice or fasting diets – to its patients, but it does advocate avoiding red meat and dairy produce, saturated fat, smoked and cured foods, refined sugar, processed foods, caffeine, sweet fizzy drinks and excess alcohol.

If your child has cancer you should always discuss appropriate diet with his or her specialist and also modify any diet to suit your child's own preferences. Cancer treatments may leave a child feeling poorly, sick and perhaps with a poor appetite, so this all needs to be taken into consideration. If your child needs to be built up and has a reasonable appetite, the tips for dealing with an underweight child may be appropriate.

SUPPLEMENTS

Sometimes large doses of vitamins or supplements are recommended as a cure for cancer, but Bacup says, 'There is no scientific evidence that large doses of vitamin supplements are of any value. Indeed, it can be harmful to take excessive amounts, especially of vitamins A, D and beta-carotene, which the body can convert to vitamin A. Indeed, several trials have found that large doses of beta-carotene increased the risk of cancer…'

See also: Convalescence pp96–7, Illness, feeding during p138, Underweight pp190–1.

CANNED FOOD

Canned foods store easily with no need for refrigeration, will keep for long periods of time and are generally inexpensive. Although sales of canned food in the UK are increasing, cans come with a very bad press – and indeed, certain tinned foods (perhaps including ready-meals, pies and processed meats in a can) may be nutritionally poor. Some can, however, be a useful and nutritionally sound addition to the family larder. Here are some cans to consider:

• **Tinned pulses** such as red kidney beans, black eye beans, cannellini beans, butter beans, chickpeas and brown and led lentils. Go for those canned in water. These are ideal for quick meals – especially when you forgot to soak the dried versions. They are nutritionally similar to reconstituted dried pulses.
• **Canned fruits and vegetables** will have lost a proportion of their vitamins C and B group, but are still useful as an occasional standby. Vegetables canned

in brine are higher in salt than is a good idea for more than very occasional use, so choose those canned in water. Fruits canned in syrup are high in sugar – if you do have to use them, drain the syrup off – it is much better to go for fruits canned in juice.
• **Canned rice pudding and custard** are good dessert standbys. For many children it is better to opt for the low-fat versions of these. Serve with fruit for a balanced dessert.
• **Pulse and/or vegetable soups**. Some canned soups may be too high in sodium (salt) to make a regular part of a child's diet but a lentil or mixed vegetable soup served with bread makes a quick lunch for occasional use. If sodium is listed on the label, try to choose a soup which contains less than 0.2g sodium per half can (approx 250ml) serving.

Canned whole or chopped tomatoes are a storecupboard must, as are baked beans, both of which are rich in the antioxidant lycopene. Canned carrots are rich in the antioxidant beta-carotene, which is better absorbed in canned or cooked carrots than in raw ones.

In general, try to avoid cans that you know to be coated on the inside, as in tests in 2001, over half of coated cans leached bisphenol-A, a chemical which is oestrogenic. Bottling is a similar process to canning, so most of these comments also apply to bottled or jarred fruits, veg and so on. Glass is often considered to be a very safe packaging medium as it doesn't leach anything into the food.

See also: Antioxidants p73, Beans, Baked p77, Processed Foods pp164–5, Salt p171–4.

CARBOHYDRATES

Carbohydrate is one of the 'macronutrients' (major nutrients), along with fat, protein and alcohol. This means that it supplies energy (kilocalories, commonly known as calories) in the diet, at 3.75 calories per gram of carbohydrate. Indeed, carbohydrates are the main source of energy for most people, including children, at around 50% of the total calorie content of the diet.

The UK National Diet and Nutrition Survey (NDNS) of young people aged 4-18 (2000) found that carbs provided just over 51% of energy for children on average. There are two main types of carbohydrate – starches and sugars. Of total carbohydrates, starch contributed 55% of intake and sugars the remainder.

For good health, it is important that much of a child's carbohydrate intake is in the form of starches rather than too much sugar – especially what is sometimes known as 'non-milk extrinsic sugars' – i.e. those added to food in cooking or preparation, or at table. Currently, UK children eat too much of this extrinsic sugar. The Department of Health recommends that they should form a maximum of 11% of the total calorie intake, but the NDNS survey found that for both boys and girls they contributed over 16%. The other two categories of sugars in the diet are 'intrinsic sugars' – i.e. those found as a natural part of the plant, e.g. in fruits – and milk sugars, found as a natural element of milk.

The main source of starches in a child's diet are grain foods (such as bread, cereals, pasta, rice and couscous) and also root vegetables, such as potatoes, and pulses like kidney beans or baked beans. Most fruits don't contain starch, the exception being bananas, while most vegetables contain small or moderate amounts of starch.

The natural starchy plant-based foods are sometimes called 'complex carbohydrates'. Refining these carbs – e.g. as in white bread, white rice, white pasta and in baked goods – removes some of the fibre and nutrients from the plant and may alter its Glycaemic Index and its effect upon the blood sugars, although these refined foods are still an important part of most children's diets and may indeed be more suitable than unrefined starches for some – e.g. very young children, children with a poor appetite and/or those who are underweight.

The simplest way to ensure that your child eats plenty of starchy carbohydrates without too much added fat or sugar, is to restrict his or her intake of cakes, biscuits, pies and pastries, fried foods such as chips and crisps, and some of the sugary and/or fatty breakfast cereals.

See also: Biscuits p80, Bread pp82–3, Cakes p86, Dietary Fibre pp101–2, Grains p132, Obesity pp152–5 for information on the Glycaemic Index, Pasta p157, Potatoes pp161–2, Sugar and Sweeteners pp182–5.

CARBONATED DRINKS

Carbonated ('fizzy') drinks represent about a half of the total soft drinks market. In the US, the average teenage boy drinks 530ml of 'fizzy' drinks a day, equivalent to nearly two cans of cola or lemonade. Consumption has risen steadily since the 'fifties – by approximately 8–10 times – and young children are consuming more. One report found that a fifth of those aged 7–10 drink nearly 10 cans a week.

Carbonated drinks contain carbonated water, either sugar or artificial sweeteners ('diet' versions), colourings, flavourings, preservatives and some form of acid, which is needed to balance out the sweetness. A 330ml can of typical carbonated cherry drink contains approximately 95 calories and 25g (5 teaspoons) of sugar. They contain no useful nutrients, unless you count sugar as a form of energy – but recent research indicates that the high intake of sugary drinks is a significant contributory factor towards the growing incidence of overweight and obesity in children.

There is also concern over regular use of these drinks (and other sweet drinks, e.g. squash and fruit juice) leading to tooth decay. Apart from the sugar, they contain acids which can spoil tooth enamel if left in contact over time – e.g., if a child is allowed to sip a can or drink over a long period and this behaviour is repeated regularly.

Carbonated drinks – and squashes – are also a source of a variety of artificial additives, such as E number colourings, flavourings and preservatives. There is some evidence that these can cause hyperactive behaviour (or ADHD) in some children and may be a source of food allergy.

There is also a link between high consumption of carbonated drinks and a reduction in bone strength.

Research published in the *American Journal of Clinical Nutrition* in 2001 found that teenage girls who regularly drink carbonates are three times more likely to suffer fractures than those who don't. One likely culprit seems to be caffeine in cola drinks, which appears to increase calcium excretion in the urine. However, other studies have found that there is a link between reduced bone health and all types of carbonated drinks. The Creighton University Osteoporosis Research Center in the USA concludes that the main cause of calcium loss is the lack of bone-building nutrients in carbonated drinks. Youngsters who drink a lot of carbonated drinks may then have less calcium-rich milk in their diets (and may have a generally poorer diet). Other experts feel that there may be a link between the drinks' high phosphorous content, as this may damage bone strength by altering the mineral balance in the body.

In view of these potential negatives, it is surprising that research has found that 80% of carbonated drinks are bought by parents and consumed by children in the home, and just as surprising that most schools now sell these drinks via vending machines, while few provide good-quality drinking water.

See also: ADHD pp71–2, Behavioural Problems pp78–9, Bone Health pp80–1, Caffeine p85, Drinks pp103–4, Food Additives pp114–17, Food Allergies pp117–19.

CARROTS

Nutrient content per 100g portion:

Cals	35	Fibre	2.4g
Prot	0.6g	Vits	**Beta-carotene**
Tot carbs	8g		**(converts to vitamin A)**
(of which) sugars	7.4g	Sodium	25mg

Carrots are one of the most important vegetables to provide the carotenoid group of plant compounds in the diet. These antioxidants have been linked with improved lung function and the health of the eyes, skin and immune system. Diets which include plenty of carotenoid-rich vegetables have been linked to a reduced risk of some cancers in adults.

The body's absorption of the Beta-carotene content is improved if the carrots are cooked, and also when eaten with a little fat, so serve carrots with a dash of olive oil or small knob of butter, or with a small amount of oily dressing in a salad or as part of a stir-fry.

An excess of carrots – and, therefore, carotenoids – may turn the skin orange, but this, unlike high intakes of vitamin A, isn't dangerous. If carrot intake is reduced, the skin colour returns to normal.

See also: Phytochemicals p160, Vegetables pp191–4.

CHEESE

Most types of cheese are an important source of calcium for bone development and health in children and, to a lesser extent, protein, as well as some B vitamins and vitamin A, but they can also be high in fat, saturated fat and salt. The chart here shows nutrients in selected cheeses. Cheese aimed at children – like triangles of soft cheese spread and cheese slices – tend to be very high in sodium.

In general, full-fat hard cheeses, such as Cheddar and Stilton, are high in fat and sodium, but also high in calcium and protein, while full-fat soft cheeses, such as cream cheese (and also mascarpone, which has a very similar nutritional profile), are high in fat but contain less calcium and protein. Low-fat soft cheeses contain reasonable amounts of protein, but are low in calcium and vitamins compared with hard cheeses, so don't always choose these for preference.

Cheese contains no starch; its carbohydrate content is all milk sugars. When serving cheese to children, you need to weigh its positives (calcium, protein, vitamins) against its fat and sodium (salt) content. At least some of the time, try to choose the medium-fat cheeses such as Brie, mozzarella and feta, which contain good amounts of calcium and protein without too much of the fat.

For vegetarian children, you need to choose cheese without rennet in it – these days there is a wide range of rennet-free cheeses, both hard and

CHEESE – NUTRIENT CONTENT PER 50G PORTION OR AS STATED

	Cals	Tot Fat	Sat Fat	Chol	Prot	Tot carbs	Sugar	Vits	Mins	Sodium
Brie	160	13	8.2g	50mg	9.6g	trace	trace	A, B2, B12	calc	350mg
Cheddar	206	17	10.7g	50mg	13g	trace	trace	A, B2, B12	calc	335mg
Cheddar, half-fat	130	7.5g	4.7g	22mg	16g	trace	trace	B2, B12	calc	335mg
Cheese spread	138	11g	7g	33mg	6.8g	2.2g	2.2g	A, B12	calc	530mg
Cottage cheese	50	2g	1.2g	7mg	7g	1g	1g	B12	—	190mg
Cream cheese, full-fat	220	24g	15g	48mg	1.5g	trace	trace	A, B12	—	150mg
Danish blue	174	15g	9.5g	38mg	10g	trace	trace	A, B12	calc	630mg
Edam	167	13g	8g	40mg	13g	trace	trace	B3	calc, iod	510mg
Feta	125	10g	6.2g	35mg	7.8g	0.8g	0.8g	B12	calc	720mg
Fromage frais, 8%-fat	56	3.5g	2g	13mg	3.4g	2.8g	2.8g	A, B2, B12	t/c	trace
Mozzarella (ball-type)	145	11g	7g	33mg	13g	trace	trace	A, B12	calc	250mg
Parmesan 10g/1 tbsp	45	3.3g	2g	10mg	4g	trace	trace	B2, B12	calc	109mg
Processed cheese, 1 slice	66	5g	3g	17mg	4.2g	0.2g	0.2g	B12	—	264mg
Soft cheese, low-fat	98	7.5g	5g	n/k	6g	1.5g	1.5g	B12	—	165mg
Stilton	206	18g	11g	53mg	11g	trace	trace	A, B2, B12	calc, iod	465mg

soft, which will be labelled as such. For children with a cows'-milk intolerance, there are several cheeses available made from ewes' or goats' milk. Hard cheese, which contains an enzyme called tyramine, seems to cause migraine in some children – if this is the case, the soft cheeses, which don't contain tyramine, may not have this effect.

Avoid giving soft mould-ripened cheese, such as Brie and Camembert, as well as blue cheeses, to babies and infants under 12 months old as these may cause food poisoning. Avoid giving cheese of all types to babies under 6 months old.

See also: Fats and Oils pp110–12, Salt pp171–4.

CHICKEN
see Poultry

CHIPS

The basic ingredient of chips – or 'french fries' as they are known in the USA – is potato, a healthy high-carbohydrate food that forms a staple part of many Western diets.

The reason that chips are often thought of as less than healthy food is that they may be very high in calories, fat and/or saturated fat, and lately they have been linked with high acrylamide levels, discussed on pages 70–1. However, they can be a good source of fibre, potassium, and vitamin C, and some B vitamins.

Here we look at the different kinds of chip you or your child may consider eating, and weigh up the pros and cons of each type.

If you're cooking home-made chips fried in vegetable oil, by using recently-harvested potatoes they may be a good source of vitamin C. Frying retains the water-soluble vitamins and thus chips may be a better source of vitamin C and B vitamins than boiled potatoes. Fried potato chips can soak up a great deal of fat and if eaten regularly may give your child a diet too high in fat. If you use lard to fry the chips in, this will be high in saturated fat. The calorie content of standard home-made chips is also quite high (see the table below) and if a child eats a lot this may contribute to overweight or obesity.

To make your home-made chips healthier, choose a good-quality oil. Oils with a very high content of polyunsaturates tend to oxidize easily when used for cooking at high temperatures (causing free radicals to be produced, which have been linked with cancer) and so it is best to choose one with a good balance of mono- and polyunsaturates, such as rapeseed oil or groundnut oil. On the other hand, you can't use an oil really high in monounsaturates, such as olive oil, for deep-frying as its smoking point is too low. Don't use the same oil too many times and store cooking oil in dark, cool conditions. Both these precautions will help avoid exposure to oxidation.

Cook chips only once – don't refry them as they will soak up yet more fat – and serve them immediately to retain most vitamin C. It is important to keep the oil at the right temperature – if it is, or becomes, too cool (often because too big a batch of chips is added at one time), the potato absorbs much more oil. Also don't keep cut chips soaking in water before cooking them as the water-soluble vitamins B and C will leach out.

 Don't overcook any chips. Overcooking increases the acrylamide content, a chemical thought to be potentially cancer-causing. Indeed any dark brown/burnt edges are potentially carcinogenic.

COMPARING CHIPS

The nutritional profile, and in particular fat content, of the types of chips found in supermarkets and at fast food outlets varies considerably, according to the size of chip and cooking process involved.

Home-made chips/baked: For chips with less fat and calories than standard chips and less prone to oxidation, use the Potato Wedges recipe on page 220. This uses large wedges of potato, lightly brushed with olive oil and then baked in the oven.

Ready-made chips for frying: These should have a similar nutritional profile to good-quality home-made chips. Follow the tips for frying home-made chips, in particular choose large chips, as the smaller the chips, the more fat they absorb as the surface area is larger. Avoid crinkle cuts, for the same reason.

Ready-made oven chips: Commercial oven chips come in all shapes and sizes, with the fat already impregnated in the chip, so that all you have to do is bake them. They taste as good as deep-fried chips and do contain a little less fat than standard fried chips (see the table below). Go for the larger ones and straight-cuts, which will contain less total fat than small ones or crinkle cuts.

Microwave chips: Although they are thin-cut, they usually come in fairly small portions and have few, if any, additions, so they are a reasonable bet. However, of late, you can buy bigger portions which have additives to help them crisp up.

Speciality chips: Manufacturers in recent years have found ways to make 'new' varieties of chips to tempt taste buds. Batter coatings and special waffle shapes are two examples. Speciality varieties tend to be higher in fat and calories than other chips.

Burger bar chips: These are normally cut very thinly and so absorb a lot of fat. However, most burger chains have altered their cooking fats in recent years so that they are healthier – for example, they contain less of the artery-damaging trans fats.

Chip shop chips: These may be some of the highest-calorie, highest-fat chips you can buy.

CHIP VARIETIES – NUTRIENT CONTENT PER 100G			
	Cals	Tot Fat	Sat Fat
Home-made, medium-cut, fried in oil	189	6.7g	0.9g
Chip shop, fried in lard	239	12.4g	6.8g
Burger bar chips, average	265	11.5g	2.5g
Oven chips, average straight-cut	162	4.2g	1.8g
Microwave chips	189	8.5g	2.3g

Portions are usually very large compared with burger bar or home-served portions. The chips are often fried for a second time just to warm them up, so contain more fat than those fried only once. The fat can be hard or blended vegetable oils or other oils and may be oxidized if used too often (busy chip shops can't change their oil as often as is ideal).

THE VERDICT

Good-quality chips, cooked using the tips above, can be a reasonably healthy addition to a meal, at least some of the time. Avoid serving them too frequently, especially if your child tends to be overweight. Currently the problem of acrylamide in chips is under investigation and, meanwhile, it may be prudent to limit their intake for this reason too.

See also: Acrylamide pp70–1, Fats and Oils pp110–12, Fried Foods p128, Junk Food pp140–3, Obesity pp152–5, Potatoes pp161–2, Takeaways pp186–8.

CHOCOLATE

Chocolate is high in fat, saturated fat, sugars and calories. It is a reasonable source of some minerals and plain (or dark) chocolate can be a good source of antioxidant flavonols. The higher the percentage of cocoa solids the more antioxidants the chocolate should contain. Milk chocolate, which tends to contain only 20% of cocoa solids, is quite low in antioxidants and white chocolate contains little if

any. The antioxidant effect of chocolate has been shown to have beneficial effects on the heart and circulation. 40g chocolate has been shown to have the same effect as one glass of red wine.

Cocoa beans also contain other ingredients which may help to give chocolate its irresistible qualities. These are caffeine and theobromine, a stimulant. However, a child would need to eat quite a lot of dark chocolate for there to be much effect.

Chocolate bars and selections marketed to children are rarely high in flavonols, and are often little more than a chocolate coating surrounding high-sugar confectionery.

See also: Caffeine p85, Confectionery p95, Junk Food pp140–3, Sugar and Sweeteners pp182–5.

CHOLESTEROL

Although blood cholesterol levels have for a long time appeared to be an adult concern, in recent years more and more Western children are showing signs of high cholesterol and early heart disease.

Cholesterol is mostly made in the liver and is transported in the blood by two proteins – low-density lipoprotein (LDL) and high-density lipoprotein (HDL). LDL cholesterol is known as 'bad' cholesterol because it can be deposited on the blood vessel walls, forming 'plaques' which may lead to narrowing of the arteries, increasing the risk of strokes, heart attacks and cardiovascular disease. HDL is known as

CHOCOLATE – NUTRIENTS PER 100G										
	Cals	Tot Fat	Sat Fat	Chol	Prot	Tot Carbs	Sugar	Vits	Mins	Sodium
Milk chocolate	529	30.3g	17.8g	30g	8.4g	59.4g	56.5g	—	calc, pot	120mg
Plain chocolate	525	29.2g	16.9g	9mg	4.7g	64.8g	59.5g	—	mag, iron	11mg
White chocolate	529	30.9g	18.2g	n/k	8.0g	58.3g	58.3g	—	calc, pot	110mg

the 'good' cholesterol because it actually helps to transport excess LDL cholesterol back to the liver.

A high intake of saturated and trans fats is thought more of a risk factor for high LDL cholesterol levels and heart disease than is actual cholesterol in the diet, although people diagnosed with high LDL levels and/or other risk factors for heart disease are usually advised to follow a low-cholesterol diet. High-cholesterol foods include liver and other offal foods, eggs, fatty meat, dairy produce and shellfish, as well as manufactured foods including those items.

Children in the UK and USA eat more saturated and trans fats and have higher cholesterol levels than those in many other countries. By following a healthy balanced diet, low in saturated and trans fats and high in fruit and vegetables, from a young age (such as the sample diet plans in Section I of this book) children can significantly reduce their risk of heart and circulatory problems later in life.

> In a study of American children between the ages of 10 and 15, 7% were found to have early signs of arterial disease.

A suitable diet is even more important for a child with a parent who has high blood cholesterol levels and/or has had heart or circulatory disease. A simple blood cholesterol test carried out through your doctor can easily reveal whether the child has raised LDL levels. If the answer is 'yes', a more strictly modified diet may be advised, with intake of saturated and trans fats and dietary cholesterol reduced as low as possible.

Factors that can help to maintain a healthy blood cholesterol profile and reduce the risk of heart disease:
• avoiding obesity and taking regular aerobic exercise
• eating a diet high in soluble fibre, including plenty of soya beans and other pulses
• eating sufficient omega-3 oils
• eating sufficient antioxidants (found mainly in fruits and vegetables).

See also: Dietary Fibre pp101–2, Fats and Oils pp110–12, Heart Health p135–6.

CITRUS FRUITS

Fresh citrus fruits are all good sources of vitamin C and phytochemicals, particularly flavonones, which are powerful antioxidants that have been shown to protect against heart disease, lung disease and some cancers.

Grapefruit contains different flavonones from oranges, which give it its characteristic bitter taste and have similar health-protecting properties. Lemons contain limonone, a phytochemical which,

CITRUS FRUIT – NUTRIENT CONTENT PER PIECE OF FRUIT OR AS STATED							
	Cals	Protein	Total carbs	(of which) Sugars	Fibre	Vits	Mins
Grapefruit, half	25	0.6g	5.4g	5.4g	1g	C, folate	—
Lemon, juice, 20ml (of 1 lemon)	2	trace	trace	trace	—	C	—
Orange, medium	60	1.8g	14g	14g	2.7g	C	pot
Satsuma or tangerine, medium	25	0.5g	5.4g	5.4g	0.8g	—	—

again, can help protect against heart disease and cancer. Oranges and lemons are also good sources of pectin, a soluble fibre that has a cholesterol-lowering effect.

You get more of the vital plant chemicals if you eat the fruit, including the pith, rather than just the juice. If giving freshly made citrus juices to your children, it is better to use a blender and make a smoothie, rather than an extractor which leaves all the pith and solids behind.

See also: Drinks pp103–4, Fruit pp129–30, Juices pp139–40, Phytochemicals p160.

COELIAC DISEASE

This disease is an inflammatory condition of the digestive system, caused by an inability to tolerate gluten, the protein found in wheat and rye grains, and similar proteins in barley and oats. Exposure to gluten damages the lining of the small intestine and this prevents the absorption of nutrients. Children who have coeliac disease may have weight loss or failure to grow, and there are usually other symptoms, such as diarrhoea, bloating, vomiting. The lack of absorption of iron can lead to anaemia and lack of calcium absorption can cause osteoporosis.

It seems that coeliac disease is often hereditary. First symptoms usually appear whenever gluten-containing grains are introduced into the diet – however, symptoms may appear at any age and sometimes coeliac disease can go unnoticed for years.

The only 'cure' at the moment is to avoid gluten-containing products for the rest of the sufferer's life. The intestines will gradually repair themselves, the symptoms will disappear and health and growth should return to normal. If you suspect your child may have coeliac disease, it is important to take him or her to see your doctor, who will get proper tests carried out and then refer you for further advice.

Avoiding gluten-containing foods is not easy; it can be present in very many commercially manufactured foods as well as the more obvious foods, such as bread, cereals, cakes, biscuits and pasta. It is best to join a coeliac or gluten intolerance society who are likely to produce an up-to-date list of gluten-free foods.

See also: Anaemia p73, Appendix 3 pp252–3 for contact details for organisations associated with coeliac disease.

COFFEE

The effects of caffeine have already been discussed, but coffee does contain other ingredients that can have an effect on health. The coffee beans contain fatty chemicals called kahwol and cafestol which have been shown to raise LDL cholesterol levels in the blood. The actual amount of these depends upon the type of coffee and how it is made. Cafetière, Turkish and percolated coffee all contain high levels, as the chemicals are not filtered out using these methods, while filtered coffee, instant coffee and espresso all contain low levels.

Coffee also contains stimulants called theobromines, that have powerful effects on the heart and have been shown to raise blood pressure. Decaffeinated coffee still contains theobromines, kahwol and cafestol, and has a similar effect on blood LDL cholesterol levels, according to a USA National Institutes of Health study, and can also raise blood pressure, a study at the University of Zurich in 2000 found. However, as the caffeine content of decaf is very low, the side-effects of caffeine intake aren't present – for example, it doesn't hinder the absorption of vitamins and minerals.

There is no specific research on the effect of coffee on children or teens, but it may be assumed that consumption has a similar effect on them as it does on adults. For coffee-loving youngsters, my advice is to choose weak instant, filtered or espresso, have no more than 2–3 cups a day, and never have caffeinated coffee with, or directly after, a meal or in the evening as it may disrupt your sleep. Don't count coffee towards your daily fluid intake – and drink plenty of water.

See also: Caffeine p85, Cholesterol pp92–3.

COLA

See Caffeine, Carbonated Drinks

COLDS AND COUGHS

Childhood colds, coughs and infections are very common and normal, but their frequency, severity and/or duration may be influenced through diet. Colds, coughs and flu are caused by a viral infection and the infection is usually caught through contact with someone who already has it. It is hard to avoid this, but it is easier for a child to catch infections if his or her immune system is weakened. The immune system can be strengthened, at least partially, by means of the right diet:

• Include in the diet plenty of foods rich in Vitamin C – fresh fruits, salads and vegetables, and fruit juices. A low-dose supplement (250mg/day with bioflavonoids) at the first sign of a cold may help minimize the symptoms and should be stopped as soon as the cold is over.

• Include plenty of zinc-rich foods in the diet – e.g. lean red meat, nuts, seeds, wheatgerm, Quorn, All Bran, shellfish. You can buy vitamin C supplements that include zinc in the formula.

• For older children who don't mind strong flavours, ginger, chilli and garlic are all said to help fight off infection and act as decongestants. Use them in spicy soups, curries or stir-fries.

• Persuade your child to drink plenty of fluids, such as water, diluted juices and hot water with honey and lemon. Honey is an antiseptic and can also be used on bread or in desserts and with fruit.

• There is some evidence that dairy produce may increase production of mucus. However, as dairy foods are so important for most children because of their calcium and protein content, and because many items in this group are so easy to eat when unwell (e.g. milk drinks, custard, milk puddings, ice cream), it may be unwise to cut down on this group of foods too much while your child is ill.

See also: Convalescence pp96–7, Illness, feeding during p138.

COLIC

Colic is a fairly common disorder in babies and is characterized by a great deal of crying and distress, caused by abdominal cramps and discomfort. This often occurs at a similar time each day, often in the early evening, and some experts say that it occurs more frequently in bottle-fed babies. Most cases of colic are over by the time the baby is 4–5 months old.

There is no definitive cause of colic that we yet know, although it is possible that it is caused, at least in some babies, by intolerance of one or more foods in the mother's diet (if she is breast-feeding) – e.g. cows' milk, wheat, nuts, eggs or seafood. It may also be caused by normal baby formula milk. If you suspect that your baby's colic is caused by cows'-milk formula, see your doctor, who should refer you to a dietitian, who may change the baby to a different type of formula (e.g. soya formula).

There has also been recent research at the Miami Children's Hospital USA showing that the type of fruit juice a mother gives her baby could affect colic. In the study, 'colicky' babies aged between 4 and 6 months found it most difficult to digest apple juice, while white grape juice was one of the most well tolerated. This could be linked to sorbitol (a natural non-absorbable sugar alcohol) – the apple juice contained sorbitol while the grape juice didn't.

Some parents have reported improvement in colic symptoms if the baby is given the herb fennel (available as a drink at chemists), but as far as I know there is no scientific evidence of this.

The Institute of Child Health recommends that breast-feeding mothers of colicky babies avoid citrus fruits and very sweet fruits, which may cause diarrhoea in the baby and exacerbate the stomach problems. For more information about colic and coping with it by non-dietary means, see your doctor.

CONFECTIONERY

Many children's sweets are little more than sugar flavoured and coloured with artificial additives. Children who spend a lot of time chewing or sucking sweets will increase their chances of tooth decay.

Toffee and chewy-type sweets are particularly poor in this respect, as they cling to the teeth and gums.

Few sweets contain any decent nutrients. Liquorice contains a laxative substance and a range of minerals, including iron, magnesium and calcium, but high intake of liquorice can be dangerous. Toffee is one of the few sweets with a reasonably high fat content, at 18g per 100g, and 428 calories. Most other sweets contain around 328 calories per 100g and just a trace of fat.

Tips for helping prevent tooth decay:
• Let a child eat sweets at the finish of a meal or as part of a meal, rather than in isolation. Other components of the meal can limit the damage.
• If feasible, get a child to clean their teeth half an hour or so after a confectionery snack. Otherwise, encourage them to eat a carrot stick, or similar, to help saliva flow which will, in turn, help to remove the sugary deposits that cling to the teeth.
• It is better for a child's teeth to eat all his or her sweets at once rather than chewing regularly throughout the day.

See also: Food Additives pp114–17, Sugar and Sweeteners pp182–5, Teeth and Gums pp189–90.

CONSTIPATION

A common problem in childhood, constipation occurs when stools are dry and hard and can't be passed without difficulty. Once a child has been constipated this may set up a 'vicious circle', because he or she is frightened to go to the toilet.

It is wise to check with your doctor that the child's constipation isn't caused by any medical complaint. If the answer is 'no', a suitable diet high in soluble and insoluble fibre and fluids should almost certainly be able to cure the problem, although in the short term laxatives suitable for a child may be needed to get everything going again.

Each of the following measures will help:
• At least 5 portions of fruit and vegetables a day. Prunes are well known for their laxative effect – they contain a compound called isatin, as well as sorbitol, another laxative. Other high-sorbitol fruits include plums, pears, cherries and apples. Rhubarb is another

natural laxative and citrus fruits – especially oranges – seem to be too. Pulses and dried fruits are particularly high in total fibre and soluble fibre. Chillies and other spices seem to help move the bowels.
• Whole-grain cereal products rather than refined (white). Brown rice, wholemeal bread and whole-grain pasta contain more fibre than refined versions.
• At least 8 glasses of water a day, evenly spaced out. The fibre can't do its work in bulking and softening the stools without enough fluid.
• Rose-hip syrup, olive oil and black strap molasses can all be given in a daily dose while the child has constipation.
• Regular exercise. Exercise helps to stimulate the digestive system and bowels – many children don't get enough exercise.

In the long term, it is unwise to simply keep on giving your child laxatives, as the bowels can come to rely on these.

See also: Dietary Fibre p101–2, Fruit p129–30, Vegetables pp191–4.

CONVALESCENCE

When a child who has been ill is returning to normal health their appetite may return in full force, which is the body's way of making sure energy and nutrients are replaced. If this is the case, serve your child slightly bigger portions than normal and give plenty of healthy between-meal snacks, such as bananas, milk drinks, nuts and seeds (if old enough), and milk puddings.

If, however, during convalescence the appetite hasn't returned to normal, feed small portions as frequently as possible, going for foods which most appeal to your child and which are easy to eat and digest (see the box opposite).

Offer plenty of vitamin-C rich fruits between meals, such as berry and citrus fruits. If the child has been on antibiotics, feed plenty of foods rich in oligosaccharides (found in soluble fibre), such as onions or Jerusalem artichokes. These act as prebiotics, stimulating the growth of healthy bacteria in the digestive system; tablets that do this are also available.

Perhaps the most important thing is to find out what the child feels he or she would like to eat, and work round that. Preparing a highly nutritious meal that the child won't eat will have you both feeling bad.

Make sure the child always has a drink of water by the bed. Once children are feeling better, they soon make up any lost weight and regain energy.

CONVENIENCE FOODS

see Junk Food, Processed Food, Ready Meals, Takeaways

COURGETTES

Nutrient content per 100g (medium courgette):

Cals	18	(of which) sugars	1.7g
Tot fat	0.4g	Fibre	0.9g
Sat fat	trace	Vits	Beta-carotene, folate
Prot	1.8g		
Tot carbs	1.8g	Mins	pot, mag, iron

Courgettes – special types of marrow and part of the squash family – contain lower levels of nutrients than some other vegetables but nevertheless contain enough of those shown above to make a reasonable contribution to the diet. The carotenes in courgettes – which have an antioxidant action – are better absorbed if the courgettes are served with a little fat. You could serve them grilled and tossed in a mild olive oil and lemon dressing as a side dish, or stir-fry them in groundnut oil with sliced tomatoes, which will add to the carotenoid content.

CREAM

Virtually all of the calories in cream are from fat, and around 62% of this is saturated fat, so if you are watching your child's calorie, fat and saturated fat intake, cream is a good item to limit. However, as an occasional treat with fresh fruit salad or as a dessert topping after a low-fat meal, it is an enjoyable luxury. Cream is a good source of the fat-soluble vitamin A, but contains little in the way of minerals or other nutrients.

CREAM – NUTRIENT CONTENT PER 50ML PORTION			
	Cals	Tot Fat	Sat Fat
Single cream	99	9.6g	6g
Double cream	225	24g	15g
Whipping cream	187	20g	12.4g
Crème fraîche	190	20g	13.2g

Lower-fat alternatives to cream for more frequent use include Greek yoghurt and fromage frais. Greek yoghurt is a particularly good substitute for cream when cooking, as fromage frais tends to curdle.

See also: Dairy Produce p98, Yoghurt and Fromage Frais p197.

CRISPS

see Snacks

CUCUMBER

Nutrient content per average 50g serving cucumber:

Cals	5	(of which) sugars	0.7g
Prot	0.3g	Fibre	0.3g
Tot carbs	0.7g		

Cucumber is 96.4% water and thus contains few calories or nutrients, except for a moderate amount of potassium and carotenoids. It is a diuretic vegetable – increasing the flow of urine, and is a useful way to bulk up a salad for a low-calorie meal.

DAIRY ALTERNATIVES

For vegan children or those who are allergic to dairy produce, soya milk, yoghurt and ice cream make good alternatives. Soya is a good low-fat source of protein but soya 'dairy' produce contains little calcium, unless labelled as 'calcium-enriched'. Some children who are allergic to cows' milk can tolerate goats' milk. Unweaned babies who can't tolerate cows'-milk formula and are not being breast fed may be given soya milk formula – discuss this with your doctor or midwife.

See also: 'The Vegetarian Child' pp19 and 39–40, Milk pp146–7 and Yoghurt p197 for nutritional values of soya 'dairy' products.

DAIRY PRODUCE

Dairy produce – cows' milk, cream, yoghurt and cheese – varies in its nutritional profile according to the product and how it is made. Milk, yoghurt and hard cheese are good sources of calcium and protein, but hard cheeses are high in fat and saturated fat, and full-cream milk is also fairly high in fat. Cream cheeses and cream are very high in fat and saturated fat, and

low in protein and calcium. Low-fat cheeses, like cottage cheese and fromage frais, are reasonable sources of protein but quite low in calcium. Hard and blue cheeses are high in sodium.

Children under the age of 5, who need higher levels of fat in the diet than older children and adults, can be given full-fat dairy produce. Older children can be served more moderate-fat dairy produce, such as semi-skimmed milk and mozzarella and Brie cheeses. To cut saturated fat in the diet further, whole-milk yoghurt or 8%-fat fromage frais can be substituted for cream.

For children who are overweight, skimmed milk, low-fat yoghurt and low-fat fromage frais can be used much of the time, while small quantities of high-calcium full-fat dairy produce, such as Cheddar cheese, should be used to increase the total calcium intake.

Most dairy produce is a good source of fat-soluble vitamin A and some B vitamins, but vitamin A is lost in the low-fat varieties. Children who don't eat dairy produce can substitute soya products and should ensure they get enough calcium in the diet.

See also: Cheese pp89–90, Cream p97, Milk pp146–7, Yoghurt and Fromage Frais p197.

DEHYDRATION

Many children don't drink enough fluids to ensure that they are properly hydrated. Active children can easily become dehydrated, especially in hot weather or when doing sports or other aerobic exercise. They tend to get dehydrated more quickly than adults as they are smaller, sweat less and often don't pay attention to feelings of thirst.

Signs of dehydration include:
• dark yellow urine (which is very pale in colour when a child is fully hydrated)
• thirst
• headache

When dehydration is more severe:
• reduced concentration
• child displays a tendency to become easily fatigued and exercise feels harder.

Children should drink 6-8 (200ml) glasses of water, or equivalent, a day under normal circumstances. If they are exercising, they need around 500ml of fluid per hour to replace that lost in sweat. After exercise they should drink until they no longer feel thirsty and then have another 200ml on top of that.

What to drink: For normal rehydration, water is fine and has the added benefit of being calorie- and artificial-additive-free.

For children doing competitive sports or serious exercise or training lasting less than 90 minutes, a hypotonic drink may be called for. These are drinks which contain minimal amounts of carbohydrate and are absorbed into the body even more quickly than water for fast rehydration. There are several branded hypotonic drinks, or you can make one up by adding a tablespoon or two of orange juice to 500ml water.

Very sugary drinks are not generally the best way of rehydrating children who are not involved in prolonged intense sport. The British Nutrition Foundation says that increasing the carbohydrate content of drinks will increase the amount of fuel that can be supplied (i.e. calories – which might be a good idea for children in long football matches or long-distance runs, etc.) but will tend to decrease the rate at which water can be made available. 'Where provision of water is the first priority, carbohydrate content should be low' it says.

After intense exercise – or during exercise lasting more than 90 minutes – where both fluid and body minerals (electrolytes) have been lost, these need to be replaced and then an isotonic drink – which contains a higher concentration of carbohydrate (up to 8g per 100ml) as well as sodium – could be the answer.

See also: Carbonated Drinks pp88–9, Drinks pp103–4, Juices pp139–40, Water p196.

DELINQUENCY
see Behavioural Problems

DESSERTS

Few parents seem to make desserts or puddings these days. Instead, sales of individual desserts and ready-made puddings have soared in recent years.

Not all desserts are 'bad news', health- or calorie-wise, for children. Those based on fruit are perhaps the best addition to a meal, providing both vitamin C and dietary fibre as well as a potential range of other nutrients and phytochemicals. Many desserts also contain reasonable amounts of potassium.

If a simple portion of fresh fruit doesn't tempt your child, stewed and puréed fruits (or, occasionally, fruits canned in water or juice) served with yoghurt, fromage frais, low-fat rice pudding or low-fat custard are an excellent idea as the dairy produce adds calcium and protein to the pudding, while being low in saturated fat. Full-fat rice pudding or custard both contain more fat. In winter, oven-cooked fruits, such as bananas baked in their skins, baked apples, whole peeled pears casseroled in water and juice, or a dried fruit compote, are other good ideas. Nuts and seeds are healthy additions to dessert for children over 5, providing essential fats as well as vitamins and minerals. Sprinkle them over the top of fruit and other desserts or incorporate into recipes. The Recipe Section contains several ideas for healthy child-friendly desserts.

The more indulgent desserts, such as sponges, tarts, pies, cheesecakes, mousses and cream desserts like tiramisu and the now-ubiquitous sticky toffee pudding, are of more dubious nutritional value as they are mostly very high in fat, sugars and calories, with few vitamins or minerals. They may be of use in supplying calories to a child who needs to put on weight or perhaps during convalescence, but should otherwise be an occasional pudding only. Meringue is fat-free and quite low in calories, though high in sugar, while pancakes made with skimmed milk are another reasonable option, also supplying calcium. Both of these can be served with fruit coulis and sliced fresh fruit, such as strawberries or peaches, to make a low-fat dessert.

Commercially made desserts and puddings vary tremendously in their ingredients and nutritional value. Some may be high in artificial food additives, especially those sold at ambient temperature (not chilled or frozen) with a long shelf-life. Many are very high in sugar and most are high in fat, saturated fat and/or trans fats. However, portions may be quite small.

Most supermarkets and other food retail outlets sell individually portioned 'healthy' desserts containing fewer calories – and less fat – than other equivalent desserts. These will probably contain artificial sweeteners and possibly bulking agents, and the list of additives is usually long. They are sometimes also an unexpected source of sodium.

You can also buy reduced-fat, reduced-sugar ice cream, which can be served with fresh or tinned fruit or fruit coulis rather than with ready-made chocolate or other high-sugar sauces or syrups.

See also: Artificial Sweeteners p75, Convalescence pp96–7, Fats and Oils pp110–12, Food Additives pp114–17, Fruit pp129–30, Sugar and Sweeteners pp182–5, Weight Gain p191, Desserts and Bakes recipes pp230–5.

PUDDINGS AND DESSERTS – NUTRIENT CONTENT ALL PER 100G PORTION UNLESS OTHERWISE STATED

	Cals	Tot Fat	Sat Fat	Chol	Prot	Tot Carbs	Sugars	Fibre	Vits	Mins	Sodium
Apple pie, single crust	186	7.9g	2.9g	11mg	2g	28.7g	15.6g	2g	E	pot, iron	120mg
Cheesecake, fruit-topped	240	10.6g	5.6g	60mg	5.7g	33g	22g	1g	—	calc	160mg
Chocolate mousse	140	5.5g	3.4g	30mg	5.4g	20g	17.5g	—	E	mag iron	67mg
Custard, full-fat	117	4.5g	3.8g	16mg	3.7g	16.5g	11.4g	—	—	calc	81mg
Custard, low-fat	79	trace	trace	2mg	3.8g	16.8g	11.6g	—	—	calc	81mg
Meringue nest, 1	58	trace	trace	—	0.6g	13.9g	13.9g	—	—	—	trace
Rice pudding, full-fat	90	2.5g	1.6g	9mg	3.4g	14g	8.2g	trace	—	calc	50mg
Sponge pudding	340	16.3g	5.1g	92mg	5.8g	45g	26g	1.2g	A, D, E	iron	310mg
Trifle, fruit	160	6.3g	3.1g	44mg	3.6g	22.3g	16.8g	trace	—	pot	53mg

NOTE: See individual entries for values for other desserts including yoghurts, fromage frais and ice creams. See individual labels for values for commercial desserts.

DIABETES

Diabetes – or diabetes mellitus, to give it its full name – is a disease caused by insufficiency of the hormone insulin, which regulates blood glucose levels and helps the glucose to be utilized by the body. When insulin is lacking or unable to function properly, blood sugar levels rise and this can be very dangerous. Untreated diabetes can damage the organs, including the heart and kidneys.

There are two types of diabetes. Type 1 (insulin-dependent/IDDM) more commonly occurs in children and young adults, and while there is no cure the condition is managed with regular insulin injections. Type 2 (non-insulin dependent/ NIDDM) diabetes is on the increase across the Western world. Experts believe this is because of our Western diet, increasing incidence of obesity and lack of exercise. Weight gain and lack of activity appear to produce what is known as 'insulin resistance', meaning that although the body produces insulin, it isn't sufficient – because of the amount of fatty tissue – and there is reduced sensitivity to the insulin that is produced.

Children suffering from diabetes will display some or all of the following signs:
• Increased thirst
• Frequent urination
• Excessive tiredness
• Possible blurred vision
• Possible skin problems

Maintaining a reasonable body weight and taking regular exercise are the main ways to control or avoid NIDDM. Diet should be healthy and balanced, low in total fat and sugars. Meals should be regular and high-sugar snacks should be avoided as they tend to make the blood sugar levels fluctuate. A diet containing plenty of foods low on the Glycaemic Index can help maintain even blood sugar levels.

RISE OF TYPE 2 DIABETES

A few decades ago it was called 'mid-life onset' diabetes and was virtually unheard of in children and young people. Now it is not uncommon for teenagers to get Type 2 diabetes and the first signs of the disease are present even in children as young as 4.

All children with either type of diabetes should be monitored by their doctor and given personal lifestyle and dietary advice. In Type 2 diabetes, research shows that, with careful diet and activity, insulin sensitivity can be restored to a large extent.

How to avoid type 2 diabetes? Apart from watching weight and taking enough exercise, research shows that a general healthy diet including plenty of fruit and vegetables, vitamin E and oily fish or fish oil capsules, can help to prevent insulin resistance.

See also: Obesity pp152–5 for more information on the Glycaemic Index and health issues associated with obesity.

DIETARY FIBRE

The more scientific name for dietary fibre is non-starch polysaccharides (NSPs). These NSPs consist of parts of the plant cell walls, such as cellulose and pectin, which are not easily absorbed within the digestive system but are nevertheless an important element of the diet.

NSPs are divided into insoluble fibre and soluble fibre. Insoluble fibre consists mainly of cellulose and is found in all plant matter. It adds bulk to stools, speeds the passage of food through the digestive system and is linked with prevention of bowel cancer, constipation, diverticulitis and irritable bowel syndrome. Whole grains are a good source of insoluble fibre.

Soluble fibre – pectins, beta-blucans, arabinose and others – is found in highest quantities in fruits, pulses, oats, barley and rye. Soluble fibre is particularly linked with reducing LDL blood cholesterol levels and in controlling blood sugar levels. It slows the emptying of the stomach and thus can help prevent hunger and can be useful for weight control. It adds softness to the stools.

DIETARY FIBRE AND CHILDREN

Very young children don't need a lot of dietary fibre as their stomachs and appetites are small and they may not intake enough calories if given a high-fibre diet. From school age onwards, however, a diet containing adequate fibre is important.

> It is very important to drink enough fluids with a high-fibre diet as the fluid mixes with the fibre and waste matter to produce bulkier stools. Without sufficient water, the fibre cannot do its job properly, and increasing fibre in the diet without enough fluid intake can lead to constipation.

Although there is no recommended minimum fibre intake for children in the UK, by the time they are 18 young people should be getting at least 18g of fibre a day, according to the Department of Health. According to the American Health Foundation, as a general rule a child's fibre intake should equal his or her age plus 5g a day, up to a maximum of that age plus 10g – i.e. a 10-year-old should eat between 15g and 20g fibre a day.

For children prone to overweight, fibre is particularly important as high-fibre foods promote chewing and take longer to eat. They help the child to feel full more quickly during a meal and help prevent hunger returning too quickly after a meal.

Only plant foods contain fibre – meat, fish, dairy produce and eggs contain none. In general, pulses, whole grains, fruit and dried fruit are the best sources of fibre. Children should get their fibre naturally from food, rather than having it added in the form of bran or supplements. Raw bran can inhibit the absorption of minerals, including calcium and iron, both of which can easily be in shortfall in the diet.

There is currently no standard for labelling of fibre. Some countries – mainly USA – use the Association of Official Analytical Chemists (AOAC) system which includes various types of non-starch polysaccharides that aren't included in the other main system used, Englyst, the UK standard. Manufacturers are now tending to favour AOAC, as it often increases the total fibre content, but it is debatable whether these NSPs are useful to health. The fibre content of foods listed in this book are the Englyst method amounts.

See also: Carbohydrates pp87–8, Constipation p96.

DRIED FRUITS

Dried fruits are a concentrated source of sugars, which is why they can be high in calories, and many are high in fibre. Although they have lost all their vitamin C in the drying process, they are an excellent source of potassium, most are a good source of iron and all contain some calcium – figs being a fairly rich source. Some dried fruits, especially figs and prunes, have a laxative effect. Prunes (dried plums) are rich in the antioxidant ferulic acid and other anti-cancer phytochemicals.

Dried fruits count towards the 'five a day' portions of fruit and vegetables although only one

DRIED FRUITS – NUTRIENT CONTENT PER 50G (DRY WEIGHT) SERVING

	Cals	Tot fat	Protein	Tot carbs	Sugars	Fibre	Vits	Mins
Apricots	80	trace	2g	18g	18g	3g	B-carotene	pot, iron
Currants	135	trace	1g	34g	34g	1g	—	pot
Figs	114	0.8g	1.8g	27g	27g	3.8g	—	pot, iron, calc
Prunes, stoned	71	trace	1.3g	17g	17g	2.8g	—	pot, iron
Sultanas	138	trace	1.4g	35g	35g	1g	—	pot, iron

portion a day should count. They make a good alternative to sweets and a pleasant high-energy between-meal snack.

They can be added to rice and pasta salads, as well as coleslaw and other salads. They can easily be reconstituted by simmering in water or juice (no added sugar needed), and then make a good addition, hot or cold, to breakfast yoghurt, or as a hot winter pudding with custard or Greek yoghurt. If you purée prunes after simmering, they can be used in cakes and bakes to add bulk and sweetness instead of some of the fat and sugar.

Many dried fruits, especially of the 'no-need-to-soak' variety, contain preservatives such as sulphur. If your child eats dried fruit regularly it may be worth buying organic, which is preservative-free – the fruit is a less vivid colour but the taste is excellent. Ochratoxin A is a chemical produced naturally by moulds which grow on vine fruits, such as currants and sultanas, and which may cause kidney disease or cancer in high concentrations. The UK government has set upper limits for safety and although in a recent survey 2% of produce tested was higher than the legal limit, the levels of ochratoxin A contamination are reducing year on year.

DRINKS

See table on p104 for a comparison of the nutritional content of selected drinks.

DYSLEXIA AND DYSPRAXIA

Dyslexia is a disorder in which the sufferer has specific problems in learning to read and write in relation to general ability or IQ. Problems with arithmetic and reading music are also common.

Dyspraxia is a disorder in which the sufferer has difficulty with physical co-ordination, clumsiness, hand-eye co-ordination and tasks such as shoelace tying or getting dressed. There may also be difficulty with organization, poor memory and temper tantrums.

EATING TIPS FOR CHILDREN WITH DYSPRAXIA

The Dyspraxia Foundation UK has the following food-related tips for helping children to live with their dyspraxia:
- Let the child sit down to eat where possible.
- Use a damp towel under plates to stop them moving.
- Don't fill cups too full.
- Use a flexible straw with a drink to prevent spilling

Both are linked with ADHD and autism. Up to 50% of children with dyslexia or dyspraxia may also have ADHD and, in fact, the boundaries between these conditions are unclear.

There is some convincing research to indicate that both dyslexia and dyspraxia may be improved in some children by supplementation with highly unsaturated fatty acids, particularly the fish oils DHA and EPA and possibly with GLA (evening primrose oil). One of the leading researchers into dyslexia and related disorders and nutrition, Dr Alexandra Richardson (Dyslexia Research Fellow at Mansfield College, University of Oxford), has found that deficiencies or imbalances of these may contribute to both the predisposition and the developmental expression of dyslexia and dyspraxia, as well as ADHD and autism.

After one trial involving 120 dyspraxic school children in Durham, Dr Richardson said, 'Our research has already shown a clear link between diet and some of the behavioural and learning problems associated with dyslexia, dyspraxia and ADHD. Certain key fatty acids are crucial in shaping brain development and function, but they have been disappearing from many modern diets. These fatty acids matter to everyone, but they seem particularly crucial for individuals predisposed to these kinds of specific learning difficulties.'

The British Dyslexia Association gives a cautious nod to this link, saying that, 'there is no pill that makes learning to read easy. However, nutritional vulnerability or deficiencies may affect concentration and behaviour, therefore they affect learning indirectly. Research suggests that some dyslexics lack a natural production of some essential nutritional ingredients.'

Some typical signs of fatty acid deficiency, (apart from any actual diagnosis of dyslexia or dyspraxia) are thirst, frequent urination, rough or dry skin (particularly on the upper sections of the arms and legs), dry hair, a tendency towards allergies, eczema and hay fever, light sensitivity and sleep problems.

Although the body can, in theory, manufacture the highly unsaturated fatty acids itself, lifestyle factors can prevent this from happening and supplements may be necessary. Diets high in saturated fats and trans fat can 'block' the conversion of certain essential fats into the longer-chain highly unsaturated fats. Zinc deficiency and a diet high in coffee can also do the same. The conversion can also be hindered in people with diabetes and allergic conditions, as well as children under stress.

Dr Richardson suggests that supplementing with fish oils containing EPA and DHA (but not high doses of cod liver oil, which contain potentially harmful levels of vitamin A) and, possibly, evening

DRINKS FOR CHILDREN – A COMPARISON

Drink	Advantages	Disadvantages
Carbonated drinks and squashes	Moderate or high in calories which may be useful for supplying energy to children in some circumstances.	Most contain a range of artificial additives High in sugar and/or artificial sweeteners. Linked with obesity in young people and may contribute to behavioural problems.
Diet carbonated drinks and squashes	Virtually calorie-free which might be an advantage in weight control although this is a subject of debate.	High in artificial sweeteners and a range of additives.
Energy drinks and sports drinks	May be useful for highly active children to maintain blood sugar levels or for supplying calories to children with poor appetite	High in calories; usually high in sugar; may contain additives such as caffeine and guarana, which may not be suitable for children. May contribute to tooth decay.
Fruit juices and smoothies	Popular drink; may be high in vitamin C and other vitamins and minerals; natural.	May contribute to tooth decay; high in calories.
Milk	One of the major sources of calcium in the diets of Western children. Rich in some B vits.	Contains fat and saturated fat, which are both too high in many school-children's diets. Skimmed milk is a good compromise for kids aged 5 plus. Some children are intolerant of milk.
Yoghurt drinks	Contain calcium and other vitamins and minerals; may contain probiotics.	May be high in sugar and some contain artificial additives.

NOTE: For more information on each category of drink, see individual entries, e.g. Juice, Milk.

primrose oil, is not harmful and therefore worth trying. She suggests that the balance in most cases should be in favour of the fish oil EPA (500mg/day) which seems to have the strongest link with dyslexia. GLA (50mg/day) may be added, which – even if it does not help with dyslexia and related disorders – can help with the 'linked' symptoms, such as dry skin and allergies.

See also: ADHD pp71–2, Autism p76, Behavioural Problems pp78–9, Diabetes p101, Eczema pp107–8, Fats and Oils p110–12, Food Allergies p117–19, Appendix 1 pp248–9 for best sources of essential fats.

E NUMBERS
see Food Additives

EATING DISORDERS

The eating disorders anorexia nervosa and bulimia nervosa typically occur in adolescence, although more cases are being seen in younger children. Only about 10% of cases occur in boys. It is estimated (*Lancet*, Feb 2003) that 0.7% of teenage girls are affected by anorexia and 1-2% of 16-year-old girls are affected by bulimia. Although anorexia and bulimia are separate disorders, there is often some crossover and both are characterized by the fact that sufferers judge their self-worth largely by their shape, their weight and their ability to control these. This becomes more important that other factors in life – e.g. family, friends, hobbies, studies.

ANOREXIA NERVOSA
A typical anorexic gradually reduces the amount of food she eats until she is eating very little and loses weight accordingly. Anorexics typically always feel they are fat even when they are very thin, and often have a real fear of eating, although they may be unusually interested in food – for example, preparing food for others. They can be extremely

determined in their avoidance of food. If left untreated, anorexia can cause many health problems, including heart muscle degradation, lack of periods, malnutrition, osteoporosis and, in a minority of cases, death.

Symptoms of anorexia: It is very important for parents or carers to spot signs of anorexic behaviour early as it can become entrenched. Apart from weight loss, there are several other signs that may indicate that a child may be – or on the way to becoming – anorexic:

• Ritualized or fussy eating habits – eating very tiny forkfuls, or eating only a certain food at a certain time. Cutting out food groups – e.g. wheat or all carbs, dairy foods, or all animal produce. Fatty foods may be vigorously avoided.

• Secrecy about food and lying about what she or he has eaten. Does she or he skip meals with the family, saying they have already eaten? If she or he takes a packed lunch to school, do they eat it (ask her or his friends)? Do you ever find food thrown away – say, in their bedroom bin?

• Low self-esteem and a tendency to become more isolated are quite common.

• Increase in the amount of physical activity that she or he does. Many anorexics do a great deal of exercise, to try to burn off any calories that they have eaten. They may also seem hyperactive.

• Feeling the cold and wearing many layers of baggy clothes, both to keep warm and to disguise weight loss. Cold hands and feet.

• Irritability, lack of concentration, anxiety or depression.

• Lack of periods.

BULIMIA NERVOSA
Bulimia is more common than anorexia, and often harder to spot because the sufferer may not lose weight and can appear to eat normally. Bulimia is characterized by periods of fasting, or low-calorie intake, followed by periods of over-eating (bingeing), often on high-carbohydrate foods, such as chocolate, bread, cakes, pastries, or on high-fat foods, such as cheese or butter, and purging – vomiting and/or the use of laxatives. (Some anorexics occasionally binge and purge too, and about a quarter of bulimics have also been anorexic.)

Symptoms of bulimia: Bulimics are often clever at hiding the condition – eating normally at the table and then purging later. Several symptoms may be similar to anorexia – for example, periods of ritualized eating, depression or irritability, being secretive about food. Also watch out for:

• Drinking a lot of water – this makes it easier for them to vomit.

• Evidence of laxative tablets and/or diuretic tablets.

• Shortage of money – bulimics can spend a lot of money on their binge foods.

• Food disappearing in the house.

• Empty wrappers or food containers in her bedroom or hidden.

• Fluctuations in their weight – with periods of starving and then overeating, weight can vary considerably.

In the long term, bulimia can result in erosion of tooth enamel and/or mouth ulcers – the dentist may be able to spot this and tell you. Other physical symptoms will eventually occur – including, perhaps, gum disease, sore throat, digestive problems and fatigue.

Female bulimics tend to binge more preceding a period, when the hormones fluctuate, and a sensible diet containing plenty of low Glycaemic Index foods (see Obesity p152–5) can help to minimize this urge.

RISK FACTORS FOR DEVELOPMENT OF ANOREXIA AND BULIMIA

The consensus of opinion is that there are several factors that may result in a child being more likely to become anorexic or bulimic.

• Genetic predisposition and/or a family link. US studies have found that women are 12 times more likely to be anorexic and 4 times more likely to be bulimic if their mother or sister is a sufferer. Scientists have identified two actual genes linked to a higher risk of developing anorexia.

• There is more incidence of anorexia and bulimia reported in children from higher social classes and in white children.

• Sufferers are often described as 'perfectionists' or 'high achievers' and it seems that many feel a great need to 'be good' and/or live up to high family standards.

• There is higher incidence in families where there is a lot of parental conflict and/or the child has little emotional contact with parents.

• Critical comments from family or friends about size or shape can trigger dieting that may sometimes lead to anorexia, especially when coupled with other social, peer or environmental pressures to be slim. One Finnish study found that 1 in 3 adolescent girls of normal weight thought that they were overweight.

• There is no proven link between young children who are 'picky eaters' and those who later become anorexic or bulimic. Most small children with fussy eating habits become schoolchildren and teenagers with normal eating habits.

> **!** Young children should never be allowed to go on 'diets', weigh themselves frequently or see a parent becoming obsessive about food or weight control, all of which could help to bring on an eating disorder.

WHAT TO DO IF YOU THINK YOUR CHILD MAY HAVE AN EATING DISORDER

It is important to watch your child carefully and act quickly if you think they might be suffering from anorexia or bulimia. Research shows that when an eating disorder is short-lived (and/or starts young), it may be self-limiting or require only brief treatment. Many cases of anorexia and bulimia go unnoticed until very late (if at all, in the case of bulimia), because parents are often just too busy to see the signs.

You must always seek your doctor's advice and, as necessary, referral to specialists, when anorexia or bulimia are suspected. One of the most successful treatments for bulimia is cognitive behaviour therapy and this has been described as 'the treatment of choice'. In anorexia, the first stage is to help the sufferer to realize that there is a problem and that they need help. The second stage is to restore them to an acceptable weight. The third is to give psychological treatment in order to help them overcome their negative or obsessive feelings about their shape, size, weight, eating habits and other psychological problems that may have triggered the anorexia in the first place.

REDUCING THE RISK OF ANOREXIA AND BULIMIA

It is undoubtedly easier to help your child avoid an eating disorder than it is to 'cure' it once it is entrenched. Although some of the risk factors outlined above are not things you can change, others most definitely are.

A relaxed and happy family atmosphere may help a great deal, and it is important for parents not to encourage the idea that being ultra-slim is good or desirable, nor to encourage faddy eating habits, particularly by example.

For teenagers, many of whom already have low self-esteem issues, it is vital to help make them feel proud of their looks but not obsessive about them – encouraging the idea that other things such as friendship, and fulfilment of talent, for example, are more important than whether or not they are a size 8. Girls coming into puberty and developing breasts need plenty of encouragement and reassurance about their new shape.

If a child or teen is genuinely overweight, and is not suffering from an eating disorder, then it is legitimate for them to try to lose weight. However, you should work closely with your child and encourage them to follow a programme of healthy eating that ensures gradual weight reduction, as outlined in Section 1.

See also: 'Eating Problems' pp59–60, Appetite Loss p74, Fussy Eating and Food Refusal pp131–2, Obesity pp152–5, Appendix 3 pp252–3 for organisations to contact for more information on eating disorders and their treatment.

ECZEMA

Also known as atopic eczema, or dermatitis, eczema affects up to one-fifth of all children (often by the time they are only a year old), but 60–70% are clear of the disease by the time they are 16.

Eczema is an inflammatory skin condition that causes hot, dry and itchy skin which may break and even bleed. It is linked with asthma and other allergic conditions, and is common in children with dyslexia and related disorders. It is thought to be an allergic condition in which the immune system overreacts, producing IgG antibodies. Genetic predisposition is thought to be an important factor.

Several environmental factors are thought to trigger eczema, including house dust mites, pollen, air pollution, pets and others. Sometimes it may be a symptom of food allergy – it is thought that about 10% of cases are caused by food allergy or intolerance, and this is more likely in babies.

The most likely food allergens linked to atopic eczema are cows' milk, eggs, citrus fruits, chocolate, food colourings, and peanuts and peanut (groundnut) oil. It has been found that what women eat during pregnancy may affect the likelihood of their child developing eczema after birth.

IF YOU ARE PREGNANT...

Research seems to show that much can be done while your baby is still in the womb to minimize his or her chances of getting atopic eczema and other allergies.
• Eat foods rich in vitamin E. Research at Aberdeen Royal Infirmary showed that mothers with the lowest levels of vitamin E had more allergen-sensitive children.
• Avoid eating the foods that most commonly produce allergic reactions in children (see list above).
• One large Finnish trial published in the *Lancet* in 2001 showed that women given the probiotic supplement lactobacillus GG while pregnant had children 50% less likely to have atopic eczema at age 2, so it may be worth taking a daily probiotic.

If your child has eczema you should see your doctor, and if you feel that a food allergy may be triggering it, you should mention it to the doctor, who should arrange for your child to have tests done by a dermatologist. If this proves to be the case, it will be necessary to avoid the trigger foods.

There is some evidence that supplementation with long-chain essential fatty acids can help minimize the symptoms of eczema. Omega-3s, such

E

as those found in oily fish (DHA and EPA), and to a lesser extent the long-chain omega-3 GLA (evening primrose oil) have been shown to help a significant percentage of people in tests. These EFAs probably work because they have an anti-inflammatory effect. Supplements of 1,000mg a day of omega-3s and 300mg GLA are worth a try as they won't do any harm, but effects may not show for several weeks. In order for these fatty acids to be given a chance to work, the overall diet of the child needs to be moderately low in saturated and trans fats, which will otherwise block their work. It is also worth ensuring that the child has optimum levels of vitamins A, C, and E in their diet – these are all important for healthy skin and can help healing.

See also: Food Allergies pp117–19.

EGGS

Nutrient content per medium egg:

Cals	85	Prot	7.2g
Tot fat	6g	Vits	B2, B3, B12,
Sat fat	2g		folate, A, D, E
Chol	217mg	Mins	iron, zinc

Eggs are a good source of a range of vitamins and protein – the minerals they contain aren't well absorbed, so encourage your child to eat or drink a food rich in vitamin C rich with an egg meal or snack to help absorption. Eggs are higher in fat than you might imagine – over 50% of their total calories are fat calories, and over 20% is saturated. They are also high in cholesterol.

If your child likes eggs, they can be included in the diet several times a week. The UK Food Standards Agency doesn't offer an upper limit on how many eggs a week should be given to children,

The USA Nurses Health Study has shown that eating an egg a day in adolescence is linked with an 18% reduction in the risk of getting breast cancer later in life.

Eggs can be a cause of food poisoning. Salmonella in eggs is still present in the UK, so cook eggs thoroughly and avoid those with cracked shells, dirty eggs and those that are very stale. Raw or partially cooked eggs should not be given to babies or toddlers.

Use the following guidelines if serving eggs:
• 6 months or under – no egg at all.
• 6–9 months – you can give hard-cooked egg yolk, but avoid egg white and undercooked egg yolk.
• 9–12 months – you can give well-cooked egg white as well now. Avoid all raw or undercooked egg.
• Young children – the UK Food Standards Agency says that raw or partially cooked eggs should not be given to babies OR toddlers. My advice is that to be on the safe side this should also apply to ANY under-school-age children.

but my advice is that you can serve up to 5–6 a week for older children.

The shell colour of eggs doesn't make any difference to the nutritional value of the egg. The colour of the yolk is also not an indication of nutrients. A deep yellow yolk may be caused by the laying hens having been fed a diet including the food colorant canthaxanthin (E161g), high levels of which may have negative side-effects. Organic egg yolks are often quite pale.

See also: Food Additives pp114–17, Food Poisoning pp122–3, Food Safety pp123–6.

EPILEPSY

Two recent research trials in the USA and UK have found that a very-high-fat, very-low-carbohydrate diet appears dramatically to cut the number of seizures in epilepsy in children. About 50% of children on the UK trial who stuck to the diet over

3 months saw a 50% reduction in the number of fits they had, while in America, a larger trial found that over 6 years, 35% were completely cured and again, half showed a 50% reduction in the frequency of seizures. The UK trial continues and is being partly conducted by the Great Ormond Street Hospital in London.

EXOTIC FRUITS

So-called because they come from faraway places and/or are less familiar to our children in the UK, exotic fruits are to be found more and more frequently at the supermarket, particularly the ubiquitous kiwi fruit and melons.

Like many fruits, most exotic fruits are high in fruit sugars (fructose) and low in fat and saturated fat, and some contain good amounts of vitamin C, beta-carotene, potassium and fibre.

All contain a range of phytochemicals which may help prevent disease or have other health benefits. For example, guava, mango, orange-fleshed melon, papaya and passion fruit all contain high levels of carotenoids (not just beta-carotene), which are strong antioxidants. Mango and papaya also contain excellent amounts of vitamin E, another antioxidant.

Kiwi fruit is rich in chlorophyll, which inhibits cancerous cell growth, while pineapple contains the enzyme bromelain, which may be anti-inflammatory. Some children may be allergic to some exotic fruits, particularly mango.

See also: Antioxidants p73, Fruit pp129–30, Phytochemicals p160.

EXOTIC FRUITS – NUTRIENT CONTENT PER 100G EDIBLE FRUIT

	Cals	Tot fat	Protein	Tot carbs	Sugars	Fibre	Vit C	B-carotene	Pot
Guava	26	0.5g	0.8g	5g	4.9g	3.7g	230mg	435µg	230mg
Kiwi fruit	49	0.5g	1.1g	10.6g	10.3g	1.9g	59mg	40µg	290mg
Lychee	58	trace	0.9g	14.3g	14.3g	0.7g	8mg	0µg	75mg
Mango	57	trace	0.7g	14.1g	13.8g	2.6g	37mg	696µg	180mg
Melon, cantaloupe (orange-fleshed)	19	trace	0.6g	4.2g	4.2g	1g	26mg	1,765µg	210mg
Melon, honeydew (pale flesh)	28	trace	0.6g	6.6g	6.6g	0.6g	9mg	48µg	210mg
Passion fruit	36	0.4g	2.6g	5.8g	5.8g	3.3g	23mg	750µg	200mg
Papaya (paw paw)	36	trace	0.5g	8.8g	8.8g	2.2g	60mg	810µg	200mg
Pineapple	41	trace	0.4g	10.1g	10.1g	1.2g	12mg	18µg	160mg

EYE HEALTH

You can help to maintain your child's eye health and good sight by ensuring that the diet contains adequate amounts of certain vitamins, minerals and plant chemicals. There is a definite link between eyesight and the carotenoid group – the compounds found in greatest quantities in vegetables and fruits coloured orange, red, yellow and dark green. Two carotenoids in particular, lutein and zeaxanthin, can help with detailed vision and long-term eye health. Kale, Cos lettuce, spinach and other leafy greens are particularly good sources. Carrots are one of the foods that contain highest levels of the beta-carotenes to help night vision.

The carotenoids are also antioxidants, as are vitamin C and E. These antioxidants can help to maintain eye health and protect against eye problems such as conjunctivitis. Zinc can also help boost the immune system and fight eye infections.

Sometimes children complain of dry gritty eyes, which may sometimes look red. A diet high in essential fats may help. These symptoms may also be a sign of a deficiency in some of the vitamin B group. For good eye health, it is also important for a child to get adequate and regular sleep.

See also: Antioxidants p73, Carrots p89, Fats and Oils pp110–12, Insomnia pp138–9, Appendix 1 pp240–6 for sources of vitamins and minerals.

FAST FOOD
see Junk Food, Ready Meals, Takeaways

FATIGUE
see Lethargy

FATS AND OILS

Up to the age of 5, a child's diet should contain around 40% fat – after that, although there are no specific recommendations for children in the UK, a maximum total fat intake of 35% of calories is the population recommendation. Other bodies (USA and World Health Organization for example) recommended 30% as a better target.

All fat contains 9 calories per gram, and, as such, is the greatest energy provider in the diet, since protein contains only 4 calories per gram, carbohydrate 3.75 calories per gram and alcohol 7 calories per gram. As such, it is wise to limit the fat content of the diet to between 30% and 35% as a simple way to prevent obesity, as any surplus fat in the diet which isn't needed for energy is easily stored as body fat.

However, all children need some fat in their diets. Fat is the source of the fat-soluble vitamins A, D, E and K, and the polyunsaturated fats group contains the essential fatty acids, which are vital for health. The 2000 National Diet and Nutrition Survey of Young People Aged 4–18 (UK) shows that children are eating about the right amount of total fat – or a little too much, depending on which criteria you use.

Fats (or fatty acids, as they are properly known) can be divided into three main groups: saturated fats, monounsaturated fats and polyunsaturated fats.

Saturated fats: Saturated fats tend to be hard at room temperature. A high intake is linked with increased risk of heart and circulatory diseases, as saturates appear to encourage the formation of LDL cholesterol plaques in the arteries, and the consensus of opinion is that it is prudent to begin restricting the amount of these fats in the diet early in life. Saturated fats are found in greatest quantity in animal fats – e.g. fatty cuts of meat, suet, butter, lard, full-fat cheeses, cream, and products made with these.

A diet high in saturated fat can also block the work of the long-chain polyunsaturated fats (see page 112). The survey shows that children are eating more than the recommended level of saturated fat (10% of total energy intake) by about 50%.

Monounsaturated fats: These fats tend to be liquid at room temperature and partially solid when refrigerated. Found in highest quantities in olive oil, rapeseed and groundnut oil, avocados and nuts, they are, however, present in moderate amounts in most fat-containing foods. These fats are linked with lower incidence of heart disease.

FAT CONTENT IN GRAMS OF SELECTED FOODS PER 100G

Food	Tot Fat	Sat Fat	Mono Fat	Poly Fat	of which omega-6 (N6)	omega-3 (N3)	Trans
Beef, lean, raw	4.3	1.74	1.76	0.2	0.17	0.07	0.14
Lamb, leg, raw	12.3	5.36	4.05	0.63	0.47	0.27	0.93
Pork, lean, raw	4.0	1.36	1.50	0.69	0.61	0.09	0.02
Chicken breast, raw	1.1	0.31	0.48	0.22	0.18	0.04	0.01
Chicken, casseroled, including skin	9.7	2.6	4.37	1.9	1.58	0.34	0.13
Salmon, canned	7.8	1.38	3.29	2.24	0.27	1.85	0
Tuna, canned in oil, drained	9	1.43	2.13	4.32	3.29	1.22	0.23
Egg	11.2	3.15	4.31	1.68	1.61	0.08	0.12
Cheddar cheese	32.7	19.25	7.14	0.77	0.99	0.28	2.10
Processed cheese slices	23	14.32	5.56	0.48	0.63	0.2	1.13
Double cream	53.7	33.4	12.33	1.49	1.34	0.48	1.83
Greek yoghurt	10.2	6.75	2.35	0.25	0.23	0.05	0.21
Butter	82.2	52.1	18.48	2.27	1.41	0.68	2.87
Soft margarine, not polyunsaturated	80	23.38	31.13	12.08	9.76	2.68	8.87
Hard margarine	84.4	37.07	19.92	8.62	8.33	1.29	15.03
Olive oil	99.9	14.30	73	8.20	7.50	0.70	trace
Peanuts, plain	46	8.66	22.03	13.1	12.75	0.35	0
Shortcrust pastry	28.5	11.4	11	3.97	3.24	0.83	1.07
Pizza, cheese and tomato	7.5	3.06	2.22	1.23	1.1	0.24	0.24
Crisps, ready-salted, plain	34.2	14.04	13.51	4.97	n/k	n/k	n/k
Custard creams	20.7	11.03	5.48	1.64	1.28	0.57	2.03
Ring doughnuts	22.4	5.81	8.62	5.76	5.46	0.62	1.1
Sponge cake, buttercream-filled	16.7	7.39	5.15	2.52	2.3	0.31	0.51
Cheesecake, fruit topped	12.3	7.54	3.28	0.49	0.42	0.09	0.23
Custard, ready-made	2.9	1.89	0.69	0.06	0.05	0.01	0.07
Milk chocolate	30.7	18.06	9.45	1.11	1.02	0.09	0.38

Polyunsaturated fats: These fats are liquid at room temperature and when cold, and are contained in high amounts in many seed, grain and nut oils. They can be divided into two groups – the omega-6s (N6s) and omega-3s (N3s). At the head of each of these groups are the two essential fatty acids, linoleic acid (N6) and alpha-linolenic acid (N3), which everyone needs in their diets, albeit in small amounts.

Polyunsaturates tend to lower the 'bad' LDL blood cholesterol levels, but they may also have negative attributes. Polyunsaturated oils easily oxidize, for example when used in cooking at high temperatures, and this oxidization produces high levels of free radicals in the body (see Antioxidants page 73). A high intake of polyunsaturates also increases the need for vitamin E in the diet. To minimise oxidization, polyunsaturated oils should always be stored in cool, dark conditions, used up quickly and not reused for cooking. Oils with a higher monounsaturated content are more suitable for cooking at high temperatures.

The levels of total polyunsaturates in children's diets in the survey are in line with UK Department of Health recommendations, but many experts on dietary fat and nutrition now feel that the balance between the two types of polyunsaturated fat – omega-6s and omega-3s – may be crucial for health.

The bulk of children's polyunsaturated fat intake currently comes in the form of the omega-6s (N6s) with only a little as omega-3s (N3s). The consensus of opinion amongst many experts, including the British Nutrition Foundation, is that the ratio of N3s to N6s should increase, and the amount of what are called the long-chain N3s (or sometimes, highly unsaturated fatty acids), EPA and DHA (found in oily fish) should also increase – these are linked with protection against heart disease. A diet low in saturated fat can also help the work of the long-chain polyunsaturates, optimum intake of which has been linked with helping to prevent, cure or minimize a number of aliments and problems, such as attention deficit hyperactivity disorder (ADHD) and other behavioural problems, asthma, autism, dyslexia and dyspraxia, eczema, food allergies – and can even help boost brainpower.

Trans Fats: Trans, or hydrogenated, fats are polyunsaturated fats which are hardened during food processing so that they will be solid at room temperatures, for example in the production of hard margarines, biscuits and cakes. Research to date appears to show that trans fats no longer have the benefits of polyunsaturated fats and may even be more damaging to health than saturated fats. Currently, the UK DoH says that the daily upper intake of trans fats should be 5g or 2% of total energy intake, although other experts feel that this is too high. The National Diet and Nutrition Survey didn't examine trans fat intake, but children who eat a lot of processed foods are probably getting a lot more in their diets than is recommended.

BEWARE! As manufacturers are not currently obliged to reveal the trans fat content in their foods, these fats may be disguised on nutrition labels within total fats or even within polyunsaturated totals. You can tell if a product contains trans fats, however, by reading the ingredients label, where they are usually listed as 'hydrogenated fats'. The higher up the list this comes, the more trans fats the product contains.

The chart on p111 breaks down the fat content of a variety of high-fat foods. More detailed information on the essential fatty acid (omega-3 and omega-6) content of selected foods, including their long-chain fatty acid content, appears in Appendix 1 pp248–9. The total and saturated fat content of many other foods (e.g. bread) is listed in their individual entries in this A–Z.

See also: ADHD pp71–2, Antioxidants p73, Asthma p76, Behavioural Problems pp78–9, Brain Power pp81–2, Dyslexia and Dyspraxia pp103–5, Eczema pp107–8, Food Allergies pp117–19, Obesity pp152–5, Appendix 1 pp248–9 for sources of essential fats.

FEVER

Fever in a child is a symptom of infection, and not an illness in itself, characterized by a high temperature and, usually, flushing. Call your doctor if your child has a high fever. A child with fever should drink plenty of fluids – preferably cool – and is unlikely to want to eat much while the fever is high.

See also: Convalescence pp96–7, Illness, feeding during p138.

FIBRE
see Dietary Fibre

FISH

Cod and other white fish (which has a similar nutritional profile to that for cod given in the table below) are good sources of low-fat protein, B vitamins and minerals.

Oily fish, such as salmon, herrings, mackerel, pilchards and- to a slightly lesser extent – fresh tuna, is much higher in fat but still low in saturated fat and high in the long-chain omega-3 (N3) oils EPA and DHA, linked with a whole range of health benefits, such as protection from heart disease, alleviation of asthma and eczema – and even improvements in children's behaviour and performance at school.

Children should eat one portion of oily fish a week to get enough omega-3s in their diet, plus at least one portion of white fish. The UK Food Standards Agency doesn't advise eating more oily fish than this as, sadly, much of the oily fish in the sea is contaminated with dioxins and other by-products of industry. They, and the US Department of Agriculture, also advise children under the age of 16 not to eat marlin, swordfish or shark, as these may contain higher-than-recommended levels of mercury. For the same reason, none of these three should be eaten by pregnant or breast-feeding women, or women intending to become pregnant, and such women are also advised to eat fresh tuna only once a week, and no more than 2 medium cans of tuna a week.

Smoked fish, such as kippers, may be potentially carcinogenic (cancer-causing), so consumption of this too should be limited. There have been some recent concerns by consumer groups over levels of contaminants, antibiotic residues, and food colourings in farmed salmon.

Shellfish is low in fat and high in protein, vitamins and minerals, but prawns, in particular, are very high

FISH – NUTRIENT CONTENT PER 100G RAW FILLET UNLESS OTHERWISE STATED

	Cals	Tot fat	Sat fat	Chol	Prot	Carbs	Vits	Mins	Sodium
Cod	80	0.7g	trace	—	18g	—	B3, B12	iod, sel, pot	77mg
Fish fingers, 2 average	100	4.5g	1.5g	17mg	7g	8.5g	B3, B12	iod, sel, pot	190mg
Fish portion in batter, baked	276	16.2g	7.5g	n/k	16.5g	16.1g	B3, B12	iod, sel	500mg
Prawns, peeled	100	1g	0.2g	280mg	23g	—	B3, B12, E	pot, mag, zinc, sel, iod	1,590mg
Salmon	180	11g	1g	50mg	20g	—	B group, D, E	pot, sel, iod	98mg
Tuna, fresh	136	4.6g	1g	28mg	24g	—	B3, B6, B12, D	pot, sel, iod	47mg
Tuna, canned in brine	99	0.6g	trace	51mg	23.5g	—	B3, B6, B12, D	pot, sel	320mg

in sodium, and shellfish is one of the foods most likely to provoke allergic reaction in children.

WHEN TO START CHILDREN ON FISH:
• Babies under 6 months old shouldn't be given fish at all.
• From 6–9 months – you can offer white fish, such as coley and cod, but no oily fish.
• From 9–12 months – try offering small amounts of oily fish, such as tuna.
• After 1 year, a variety of fish can be offered, but remember that no children under 16 should be fed swordfish, marlin or shark.

> • For small children, flake all fish carefully and make sure there are no bones in it.
> • If there may be bones in fish, warn older children to look out for them.
> • Make sure all fish is fresh.
> • Go carefully when offering small children shellfish. Make sure it is really fresh and well cooked, and remember that this is a common allergen.
> • Don't give children raw fish.

See also: Fats and Oils pp110–12, Food Safety pp123–6, Appendix 1 pp240–9 for more information on the nutritional content of different fish.

FIZZY DRINKS
see Carbonated Drinks

FOOD ADDITIVES

The majority of foods and drinks manufactured with sales to or for children in mind contain additives, most of which add nothing to the nutritional profile of the food and, indeed, there is often a long list of these additions – preservatives, colorants, flavourings, flavour enhancers and many more.

A survey of 350 foods specifically aimed at children in 2002, backed by the Food Commission, found that they contained 1,800 additives – an average of 5 per item. Sadly, there is also a strong link between additives and food with a poor nutritional profile. In another survey reported in the *Food Magazine* in October 2001, it was shown that up to 87% of foods containing additives are also high in the exact nutrients that many children need to eat less of – total fat, saturated fat, sugar and/or sodium (salt).

The Food Commission – a highly respected UK non-profit organization which campaigns for safe and wholesome food (see Appendix 3 page 253 for contact details) – believes that the implication is that, 'additives are being used to sell just those foods of which children should be eating less.' In theory, additives are only allowed in foods according to European Union law if there is a 'technological need' for them – but one virtual loophole allows 'organoleptic qualities' to be improved. This means that the sensual quality of the food may be enhanced by their addition and this includes the colour (bright-red or orange added to drinks, for example, to make the drinking experience 'more attractive' for children).

What are additives and why are they in food? Answers to these questions can be found in the chart on page 116, which describes the types of additive that regulations allow to be in our children's food, what they do, their E numbers, and in what foods they are mainly used.

A WORD ABOUT FLAVOURINGS...
Artificial food flavourings make up a huge amount of the total of 2.25 kilos in weight each year that, on average most of us eat in additives. However, currently the flavouring category of additives is being evaluated by the EU, which hopes that by 2004 there will be a 'positive list of permitted flavouring substances'.

This means that currently most flavouring ingredients do not have E numbers and manufacturers don't even have to list all their names on food labels. In the USA, the Food and Drug Administration allows manufacturers simply to list 'artificial strawberry flavouring', for example, when that 'flavouring' may contain, according to Eric Schlosser in his well-researched book *Fast Food Nation* (see Appendix 3 page 253), 48 different chemical ingredients.

ADDITIVES AND HEALTH

Are additives harmful to children's health? Across the EU – and in the USA, Australia and other countries – there are regulations governing the use of additives, so that the authorities consider them safe to consume in the amounts present in our foods. The UK Food Standards Agency, says, for example, 'Giving an additive an E number means that it has passed safety tests and has been approved for use... EU legislation requires most additives to be labelled clearly in the list of ingredients either by name or by an E number. It is illegal in the UK to put anything into food that will injure health.'

Indeed, even the American Academy of Pediatrics endorses the idea that approved additives are safe for children. 'Properly used, they allow us to enjoy a wide variety of wholesome foods in every season. The great majority of additives allowed by the (US) Food and Drug Administration are foods or normal ingredients in foods.' Some of the benefits of additives are listed below. Many lovers of fresh and natural food would agree that the list makes sad reading.

SOME BENEFITS OF ADDITIVES
• Help prevent the product going rancid, mouldy or from spoiling.
• Enhance flavour, colour, texture or appearance.
• Keep consistency in manufactured foods.
• Help the manufacturing process.

It is true that some additives are 'normal ingredients in foods' – for example, the antioxidants used to stop fats going rancid may be vitamin C (ascorbic acid) and vitamin E (alpha-tocopherol) – on the other hand, they may be BHA, BHT, or one or more of several other definitely non-natural additives. Other 'additives' include salt, sugar and its many variants, such as glucose and corn syrup.

Nevertheless a high percentage of additives are NOT normally found in food, nor are they natural. And one of the main problems is that – with the increasing reliance on highly processed, fast foods, ready foods and convenience meals for our children – the long-term cumulative effect of these high intakes of additives is still unknown. 'Safe levels' of additives are worked out by a scientific research team who find that XXmg of a certain additive in a can of drink is OK – based on the assumption that an adult or child averages only XX amount of that type of drink in a day. What they can't work out is how many other processed items that contain the same additive will also be consumed.

There is already plenty of research to show that additives may, indeed, be linked with health problems in our children. In other parts of this book you will find that additives may cause or exacerbate ADHD, behavioural problems, allergies and asthma. In one survey, a diet free from additives seemed to help children work better at school (see Brain Power pages 81–2). The box here shows the additives which seem most likely to provoke a reaction in some children. All these additives are legal and declared safe!

Sometimes additives which are thought to be safe are later found not to be – for example, in 2003 the EU curtailed the use of the colorant canthaxanthin (E161g), widely used in farmed salmon and egg production, because high intake is linked with eyesight problems.

THE FOLLOWING FOOD ADDITIVES HAVE CAUSED THE MOST REPORTED PROBLEMS IN CHILDREN:

 Colours:
   Tartrazine (E102)
   Sunset yellow (E110)
   Carmoisine (E122)
   Ponceau 4R (E124)

Preservatives:
   Sodium benzoate (E211)
   Other benzoates (E210–219)
   Sulphides (E220–228)
   Nitrates and nitrites (E249–E252)

Flavour enhancers:
   Monosodium glutamate and
   other glutamates (E621–623)

Antioxidants:
   E310–312, E320, E321

ADDITIVES IN FOODS

Additive category	Why manufacturers use them	E numbers	Used in
Colours	Make the product look more attractive or more like the natural counterpart; restore colour lost in processing	E100–180	Soft drinks, desserts, cakes, sweets, snacks, crisps, very many products
Flavourings	Add flavour to a bland product; add aroma	see above	As colours – used very widely in processed foods and drinks
Flavour enhancers	Improve flavour in processed foods (e.g., monosodium glutamate)	E620–640	See Flavourings, also Takeaways pages 186–8
Preservatives	Prolong product life; prevent bacteria that may cause food poisoning	E200–285, E1105	Processed meats, ambient products (those stored at room temperature), dried fruits, many products
Sweeteners (intense artificial sweeteners and bulking agents)	Add sweetness, make more palatable, add bulk, reduce energy content	e.g. E420, E421 E953–959	Drinks, desserts, yoghurts, many products
Emulsifiers, stabilisers, thickeners.	Prevent separation, enhance texture	E322–495	Desserts, soups, sauces, shakes, and more
Antioxidants	Prevent fatty food going rancid	E300–321	Fats, fat-containing foods
Others	Flour improvers, bleaches, processing aids, glazes and others	E500–578, E901–914, E920–926, E999–1518	Wide range of processed foods

WAYS TO HELP YOUR CHILDREN AVOID ADDITIVES

While many children consume additives without any noticeable side-effects, and while, indeed, legal additives in moderate quantities may be safe enough, it is nevertheless true that the long-term cumulative effect is unknown, and it is also true that most of the food additives add nothing of benefit to our children's diets. As we have seen, they are also linked with poor food quality. Therefore it may be wise to try to cut back on additives in your child's diet, and if you would like to do this, here are some simple strategies:

• Go for natural unprocessed foods as much as possible. In this case, follow all the food safety tips, as additive-free foods will always have a shorter shelf-life. Especially, make sure these are fresh, store them in optimal conditions and always use by the 'best before' date.

• Try to do more home cooking – additives are rarely needed in home-cooked food.

• When buying convenience foods, go for quality and choose frozen or canned foods to cut down on preservative content.

• Avoid foods known often to contain high levels of additives, particularly colourings, which seem to be more likely to affect children – such as brightly coloured soft drinks, sweets and confectionery, packet desserts, processed cakes and biscuits, for example.

• If a food or drink looks too brightly coloured to be true – it probably is. Even meat may have been colour-enhanced to make it look more attractive. Nitrites are present in many preserved meats, such as bacon, and these not only help to prevent bacteria but can also make the meat appear more red.

• Read the labels – the longer the list of E numbers or chemical-sounding ingredients, the more additives that product contains.

See also: ADHD pp71–2, Artificial Sweeteners p75, Asthma p76, Bacon p77 for more information on nitrites, Behavioural Problems pp78–9, Food Allergies pp117–9, Food Labelling pp119–22, Junk Food pp140–3, Processed Foods pp164–5, Ready Meals p168.

FOOD ALLERGIES

Food allergies and food intolerance seem to be on the increase across the world and children are at a much higher risk of having or developing an allergy or intolerance than adults. About 5% of children under the age of 4 have a food allergy, as opposed to only 1–2% of adults.

FOOD ALLERGY

True food allergy is an adverse – and often immediate – reaction to a food or drink, caused by an overreaction by the body's immune system to something in that food or drink. A true allergy can be confirmed by testing. Typical reactions are: swollen lips, itchy mouth, hives, vomiting, diarrhoea, stomach ache, itchy rash (eczema), coughing or wheezing, runny nose, headache.

The most common foods which produce an allergic reaction in children are: cows' milk, peanuts (groundnuts), other nuts, eggs, soya milk and soya products, wheat, sesame seeds, fish and shellfish. However, many other foods may cause allergy. There is some evidence that some food additives can also cause allergic reactions.

Peanut allergy or other nut allergy is one of the most common – and fastest-growing – of allergies in children and it is one of the few allergies that is usually life-long. Research published in the *New England Journal of Medicine* in 2003 found that peanut allergy may be caused by the use of baby and child skin creams containing peanut oil and there is even some evidence that peanut allergy may be caused by consuming soya milk or formula (both soya and peanuts are members of the legume family). Once a nut allergy is diagnosed, the only 'cure' is to avoid nuts and nut traces throughout life.

Many food allergies are, however, outgrown by the time a child is of school age, or if not, by the teens, although some allergies are never outgrown.

Coeliac disease is an allergy to gluten in grains and this is dealt with in its own section.

FOOD INTOLERANCE

Food intolerance is perhaps less serious, and less easy to diagnose. It is a non-allergic reaction to food, not involving the immune system, with less predictable outcomes and the symptoms may be milder. Intolerance may be caused by a defect in how the body processes food, but there are likely to be other explanations.

One well-known form of food intolerance is lactose intolerance – sufferers lack a special enzyme (lactase) in the body which breaks down the sugars (lactose) in milk and dairy products, causing bloating, discomfort and diarrhoea, and, possibly, failure to thrive or grow properly. Some children who are lactose intolerant may be able to take goats' milk and, sometimes, hard cheeses; others can take skimmed milk but not full-fat milk, while others use soya products instead. Lactose intolerance varies in the strength of its symptoms and may go undiagnosed. It is often outgrown.

If you think your child might have a food allergy or intolerance: The only course of action is to take him or her to your doctor and get the right tests done, and then to see the dietitian for professional advice. Although some nutritionists recommend trying to pinpoint allergies or intolerance with exclusion diets, these are not easy to carry out and the results may be confusing. Childhood allergies can be hard to diagnose and cope with – get professional help!

If you know your child has a food allergy: A child who has already had an immediate reaction to a particular food should not eat that food again or even, in some cases, come into contact with that

food. A subsequent reaction could be more serious than the first one (see the box on Anaphylactic Shock below). You should be given antidote medication – antihistamine and adrenaline – which should be with the child at all times in case of emergency.

WHAT CAN BE DONE TO PREVENT ALLERGY AND INTOLERANCE?

Children who have one or more parents with food allergies, asthma or eczema, are more at risk, so there is a genetic influence. Breast-feeding may offer protection against allergy, but for 'atopic' women – those who themselves have allergy, asthma or eczema – it is advisable during pregnancy to avoid eating the foods most likely to cause allergy, such as peanuts, as this can sensitize the baby in the womb, and they should also avoid these foods while breast-feeding.

Babies and small children from atopic families should also not be given the known allergenic foods when they are small. Indeed, certain foods should be avoided by all infants. For more information on food allergy in infants and pre-school children, see 'Allergies and Infants' pages 16–17.

Although at some time in the future you may be able to get your child immunized against particular food allergies, as yet there is no cure for allergies and intolerance except to avoid the offending food(s). It is therefore important to read food labels carefully and to get good advice on feeding your child a proper balanced diet while excluding the problem food(s).

For many allergic children, a balanced diet isn't a problem, as the allergen food may be something that isn't a common ingredient of the diet anyway (e.g. shellfish or sesame seeds). However, excluding such foods as wheat, milk and milk products, soya and nuts from a diet can be difficult as these are either staple foods, or present in very many manufactured foods under various guises. Nut and soya allergy sufferers probably have the hardest time, as nut traces may be present in many foods and soya is a 'hidden ingredient' of very many processed foods. See Nuts pages 151–2 and Soya page 180 for lists of foods in which these items may be present.

The UK Food Standards Agency is currently strengthening the food labelling rules to help

ANAPHYLACTIC SHOCK

A severe and life-threatening allergic reaction to a food (or a sting or drug) which can occur after ingesting or even touching that food. Histamine and other chemicals are immediately produced in the body, the blood vessels widen and the blood pressure drops. Symptoms include red weals, rash or hives, wheezing and shortness of breath due to the airways being constricted, and swelling of the tongue and/or throat.

This is a medical emergency and the antidote medication should be given immediately and a doctor or ambulance summoned. For further information contact the Anaphylaxis Campaign (see Appendix 3 page 252 for details).

MMR AND EGGS

The MMR (combined measles, mumps and rubella) vaccine is egg-based and if a child has a known allergy to eggs the vaccine should be given in a hospital setting, or discuss the issue with your doctor.

sufferers recognize the foods they should avoid. Eating out and takeaway foods can be another problem, and the FSA is currently taking measures to raise awareness of the problem amongst caterers. Supermarkets and food manufacturers will normally provide lists of foods containing particular ingredients so that these can be avoided, while further help can be obtained from the British Allergy Foundation.

Scientists are developing injections which may help to prevent anaphylactic shock in peanut allergy sufferers, and genetic engineers are trying to develop a strain of peanut that doesn't trigger an allergic reaction.

See also: 'Allergies and Infants' pp16–17 and 'Peanuts and Food Allergies' p23, Asthma p76, Coeliac Disease p94, Eczema pp107–8, Food Additives pp114–117, Food Labelling pp119–22, Milk pp146–7, Nuts pp151–2, Soya p180, Appendix 3 pp252–3 for the addresses of relevant organisations.

FOOD LABELLING

Reading food labels, particularly those on products aimed at children, is something of a minefield. The information you want is usually there – but it may take some interpreting.

THE BANNER LABEL (FRONT OF PACK)

This is the manufacturer's shop window and he will do his best to sell this product to you – or your child – by how it looks and what it says. Although in the UK the Food Safety Act 1990 made it an offence to 'falsely describe a food or to mislead as to its nature, substance or quality', there is still room for manoeuvre. Here are the main things to watch out for:

Drink descriptions: A carton with a large photo of oranges on the front may not be orange juice at all. Watch out for 'juice drink' (usually in small print) – a juice drink need contain only 10% real juice and will usually have a high content of sugar or sweeteners, colourings and flavourings. 'Pure fruit juices' that may be kept in the chilled counter are usually made from concentrated juices with origin unspecified – not at all fresh!

Flavour descriptions: A dessert described as, for example, cherry-flavoured probably contains no real cherry or cherry derivative at all. Flavours such as these are nearly always artificially made. Even descriptions like 'with REAL cherries!' can be misleading – the 'real cherry' content may in fact be very small.

Hidden ingredients: Another problem is that there may be ingredients in a product which aren't immediately apparent from the front of pack. For example, who would think that a chicken stock cube might actually contain beef? Well some do! There are hundreds of other instances of this. Vegetarians, in particular, need to be wary of items such as gelatine in yoghurts or animal rennet in cheeses – look out for products with a symbol indicating 'suitable for vegetarians'.

Meat descriptions: Meat products, such as sausages, burgers and pies, can contain not just the meat flesh, but also rind, skin, sinew and gristle and, in some cases, mechanically recovered meat. Cheaper meat products are likely to contain less 'real' meat and more rubbish. A lot of meat also contains a significant percentage of water – pumped in for no particularly good reason, as far as I can see, except to bulk up the weight. Frozen fish (such as prawns) also contains a great deal of water. New EU rules coming into force in 2003 will ensure manufacturers give more information about the type of meat their products contain – for example, meat fat, skin and connective tissue will need to be listed separately in the ingredients from the lean flesh meat, and the presence of mechanically recovered meat will also have to be revealed.

Percentage of ingredients: If a carton has a tempting photo of, say, a chicken pie sliced open to reveal lots of succulent-looking large chunks of chicken, you may think that the pie does, indeed, contain a lot of chicken. However, labelling laws allow that the actual chicken content may be small – check the ingredients list to see how far down the list the chicken actually comes (See 'The Ingredients List' page 122).

Health claims and inferences: Many products give the impression that they are somehow healthier than other, similar, products – often by their name and/or the way the pack is illustrated, and/or by words such as 'natural' or 'wholesome',

PACKAGING NUTRIENT CLAIMS

In order to claim	The product should contain ...
FAT	
Fat-free	Less than 0.15g fat per 100g
Low-fat*	Less than 5g fat per 100g
Reduced-fat	25% less fat than the standard product
XX% fat-free (e.g. 99% fat-free)	FSA advises that this claim should not be made as it is confusing
Low in saturates	Less than 3g saturates per 100g
SUGAR	
Sugar-free	Less than 0.2g per 100g
Low-sugar	Less than 3g per 100g
Reduced-sugar	Contains at least 25% less sugar than the standard product
FIBRE	
Increased	At least 25% more fibre than the standard product and more than 3g fibre per 100g or per serving
Source of	More than 3g fibre per 100g or per serving
High in or rich source of	More than 6g fibre per 100g or per serving
SODIUM	
Sodium-free	Less than 5mg per 100g
Low-sodium	Less than 40mg per 100g or per serving
Reduced-sodium	25% less sodium than the standard product
ENERGY (CALORIES)	
Reduced-calorie	At least 25% fewer calories than the standard product
Low-calorie	No more than 40 calories per 100g product

*Excludes low-fat spread which can contain up to 40% fat.

and/or by banners saying 'reduced-fat' or 'reduced-sugar' or so on. Fat-reduced products may not be all that low in fat at all, and may also contain just as many calories as their ordinary counterparts (because other ingredients, such as sugar, are increased). Reduced-sugar items may be high in artificial sweeteners.

Also watch out for claims such as 'free from artificial colourings' – a look at the ingredients list may well reveal that the product is NOT free from artificial preservatives, flavourings, and so on!

To claim that a product is high in, or a rich source of, certain vitamins or minerals, it has to contain at least 50% of a day's recommended intake of that vitamin or mineral in a single serving.

The 'low in fat' scam: One often-used ploy to make a product appear very low in fat when really it isn't, is to use the 'xx% fat' claim. Let's say a chipped potato product is bannered as containing 'only 5% fat'. This means that 5% of the weight of the chips – i.e., 5 grams per 100g of chips – is fat. This doesn't mean that only 5% of the total calories in the chips are fat calories. Why? Because chips – and all other foods – have a high water content, which is calorie-free. Thus 5%-fat chips, which are about 60% water, will, in fact, have a fat content of about 28% of total calories. Not high, but not very low either!

To work out the true fat content of a product, you need to look at the Nutrition Panel (see right) and do this sum: multiply the total grams of fat in 100g by 9 – this is because each gram of fat contains 9 calories. This gives you the number of fat calories in 100g. Now divide this by the total calories per 100g and then percentage it. You will probably need a calculator!

> **Example using a product that is bannered '10% fat'**
> • *The product contains 10g of fat per 100g and 175 calories per 100g.*
> • *It therefore contains 90 (10 x 9) calories of fat per 100g.*
> • *Using a calculator, divide 90 by 175 and then key in %.*
> • *The resulting figure is the true fat percentage of the product, which is, in this instance, a whopping 51.4%!*

Not all nutrition panels give content per portion, but if they do, you can work out the fat content per portion in the same way.

The box opposite gives the UK Food Standards Agency's guidelines for nutritional claims on packs – but these are only guidelines, not law.

THE NUTRITION PANEL

The labelling laws in the EU are currently undergoing review but, at the moment, unless a food makes a nutrition or health claim on its pack, it doesn't have to carry a nutrition panel at all. If there is a claim for either calorie content or amount of protein or carbohydrate or fat, it must have a Nutrition Panel listing the amount of each of these nutrients per 100g or product. If other claims are made (e.g., 'high in fibre' or 'low in saturated fat') then a more detailed Nutrition Panel is required.

When reading a nutrition panel, watch out for:
• The 100g problem – although some packs list nutrients per serving, many others don't, and you then have to look at the total weight of the product, perhaps find a 'number of servings'

IS THIS FOOD RICH/LOW IN...?

The at-a-glance guide to whether a food contains a lot or a little of the main nutrients comes from the Food Standards Agency (FSA), UK.

Per Serving	This is a lot...	This is a little...
Total Fat	20g or more	3g or less
Sat Fat	5g or more	1g or less
Sugars	10g or more	2g or less
Fibre	3g or more	0.5g or less
Sodium	0.5g or more	0.1g or less

Remember these figures are meant for all the population – children who eat small portions would need to scale the figures down accordingly.

recommendation on the pack, and work out what the actual nutrient content for a portion may be. All very time-consuming!

• Sodium – when a pack lists the sodium content of a food, remember that sodium isn't the same as salt. You need to multiply sodium content by 2.5 to get the salt content (see Salt pages 171–4).

• Dry weights and reconstituted weights – if buying, say, a pack of dry instant dessert mix, the nutrients listed may be for the dry weight – not for the reconstituted weight.

THE INGREDIENTS LIST

Ingredients are listed in percentage of content by weight, starting with the greatest, i.e. the first ingredient listed will be that with the highest content, the last ingredient listed will be the smallest.

• E numbers should be included in this list but are allowed to be listed by their actual names (e.g. tartrazine rather than E102). Ingredients of flavourings don't have to be listed individually.

• Additives used in an ingredient forming a small part of the recipe (e.g. the sulphur dioxide used to preserve dried fruits in a currant cake) needn't be listed.

• Sugars come in several different forms, look out for: sucrose (proper name for sugar), glucose, glucose syrup, maltose, lactose, dextrose, hydrolized starch, honey, treacle, syrup and concentrated fruit juices.

• Trans fats are usually listed as hydrogenated fats or hardened fats.

See also: Food Poisoning pp122–3 and Food Safety pp123–6 for information on 'use-by dates', Nuts pp151–2 for information on the labelling of products which may contain nuts or nut traces.

FOOD POISONING

When people were interviewed for a Food Standards Agency survey in the UK in 2002, 12% claimed that they had suffered food poisoning in the previous 12 months. Food poisoning is more dangerous in children, as well as the elderly and the sick, whose immune systems may be weaker than the average adult.

The main causes of food poisoning are five different types of bacteria (although fungi and viruses may also occasionally be to blame) as per the table opposite. Even small amounts of bacteria present in food can grow to harmful levels in the right environment – warm, moist conditions. Poor food hygiene and management can also help spread the harmful bugs. All the tips described in the subsequent entry on Food Safety can significantly reduce your chances of anyone in your family getting food poisoning.

Detecting food poisoning in children: Since the bacteria that cause most food poisoning enter the body via the digestive system, most of the symptoms will be centred on this area. After a contaminated food has been eaten, symptoms may take hours – or even days – to appear, though a few hours is probably most usual. First symptoms are often feelings of nausea followed by vomiting and generally feeling unwell. This is often followed by abdominal cramps and diarrhoea. There may also be fever.

What to do: Many types of food poisoning bug are resistant to antibiotics and most cases simply clear up by themselves. However, if you are worried about your child, the symptoms last longer than a couple of days, or there is blood in the stools, then take him or her to see the doctor.

There is little point trying to feed the child while they are feeling, or being, sick but it is important to rehydrate them. You can buy oral rehydration solution from the chemist, or make your own by adding a pinch (⅓ teaspoon) salt and 1 teaspoon of sugar to 250ml water. As the child recovers, you can gradually start offering easily digested, plain foods, such as mashed banana, mashed potato or whatever the child asks for – they usually have a good instinct for what they will be able to eat.

If you think the food poisoning was caused by food eaten outside the home, you should report the incident to your local environmental health service (details can be obtained from the Food Standards Agency).

See also: Convalescence pp96-7, Food Safety pp123-6, Illness, feeding during p138, Appendix 3 p253 for contact details for the Food Standards Agency.

BACTERIA LINKED TO FOOD POISONING

The bug	How common?	Most likely occurring in	Tips
Campylobacter	Responsible for about half of all UK cases of food poisoning	Poultry, red meat, unpasteurized milk, untreated water	Commonly no vomiting, but abdominal pain and diarrhoea may be severe
Clostridium Perfringens	Responsible for only a small fraction of food poisoning cases	Meat, poultry and very many other foods especially those kept warm and insufficiently reheated	Spores produced by the bacteria can survive cooking and reheating – reheated foods need to be piping hot
E Coli 0157	Causes an increasing amount of poisoning with a very low infective dose	Undercooked minced beef, raw milk	Can be very dangerous – diarrhoea with blood is typical
Listeria Monocytogenes	Uncommon in healthy adults; responsible for small fraction of food poisoning cases	Can be present in dangerously high numbers in soft mould-ripened cheeses and pâtés. Can also occur in pre-packed salads and hams	Listeria can thrive at fridge temperatures and is particularly dangerous for pregnant women, small children, the ill and the elderly
Salmonella	This group of bugs is the second largest cause of food poisoning in the UK	Meat, poultry, eggs, unpasteurized milk	Easily spread by contact, grows easily at room temperature. Raw or undercooked eggs and animal products particularly vulnerable

FOOD SAFETY

To minimize the risk of food poisoning in your family, sensible food management, kitchen practice and good hygiene are all very important. We also look at the long-term implications of food standards considerations, such as pesticide residues and genetically modified foods in our children's diets.

BUYING AND STORING FOOD

Food safety begins with buying food that is as fresh as possible, and of good quality. When shopping, check 'sell by'/'use by' dates and buy those that are as far away from the current date as possible. Check and make sure eggs aren't cracked and try to buy those that have only recently been laid as this reduces any potential salmonella build-up. In shops where meat and fish is sold unpacked, avoid anything with a noticeable odour. Avoid minced meat which doesn't look red. If doing a big shop, try to purchase meats, fish, frozen foods last so that they remain cool, pack them in cool-bags (vital in the summer months) and get them home quickly.

• Unpack food as soon as you get home and put it away, starting with any frozen foods. Then put away all fresh meat, fish, fruit and vegetables (with the

exception of potatoes) in the fridge (or freeze them, carefully wrapped and labelled, if appropriate). To avoid cross-contamination, don't store raw meats above cooked meats, and always store raw meat in a sealable container. Keep all raw foods away from all cooked foods. Make sure everything is well wrapped, bagged or sealed in a container. Always wash your hands after handling raw foods.
• Store eggs in the fridge – they only need an hour or two out of the fridge for recipes that require them at room temperature.
• When freezing foods, keep like types together. Vegetables are best blanched before freezing.
• Make sure your fridges and freezers are at the correct temperature.
• Keep perishable goods, such as flours, grains, pastas and rice, in tightly lidded containers in a cool dry place.
• Use up food in date order.
• Discard any badly dented cans or tins.
• Keep all fridges and food cupboards regularly cleaned.

FOOD PREPARATION AND EQUIPMENT
• Check the 'use by' date on food and discard if out of date, even by just one day.
• Wash your hands thoroughly before beginning food preparation and after every visit to the toilet or after doing any other job – such as emptying the bin or changing baby's nappy – while preparing and cooking food.
• Wash salads and fruit to be eaten raw.
• Defrost all food thoroughly before cooking, unless the label says otherwise. It is particularly important to defrost chicken and minced meat properly.
• Use a separate chopping board for preparing raw meat and another for other raw foods. Use a different board for preparing food which will be eaten without any further cooking.
• After preparing raw foods, clean knives or other utensils thoroughly, wash the chopping board and work surface thoroughly and always wash your hands. Wash the taps, which you will probably have touched. Use very hot water and detergent to clean everything. Dry your hands thoroughly on a clean paper towel before continuing to prepare other food. Don't dry your hands on your apron or the tea towel.

• Once raw food is prepared, don't leave it hanging around in the kitchen for long before cooking it. If cooking is to be delayed, put in a container, cover and put it in the fridge.

COOKING
• Cook all meat thoroughly for children – especially make sure that chicken is cooked all the way through, with no pink juice or flesh, and make sure that burgers, sausages and other minced meat products are cooked all the way through. Proper cooking kills many bugs including salmonella and campylobacter.
• To test that meat is cooked through, use a clean skewer through the thickest part to check the juices run clear, and wash it after every use.
• Make sure that fish and shellfish are well cooked.
• Make sure that eggs are well cooked for all young children and sick children.
• Before serving any composite dish, make sure it is cooked right through into the middle and is piping-hot.
• When heating up (or cooking) a ready-made dish, follow the pack instructions, but also make sure yourself that it is fully heated or cooked until it is piping-hot all the way through.

STORING COOKED FOOD AND LEFTOVERS AND REHEATING
• Once food is cooked, if it isn't to be eaten straight away, it should be cooled as quickly as possible and put in a sealed container in the fridge within 2 hours.
• An over-full fridge will not be as efficient, and may not store food at a low enough temperature.
• Don't keep cooked foods in the fridge for more than a day – either use them or discard them. Pasta and rice salads and dishes containing fish or shellfish are probably best discarded if not eaten straight away.
• Leftovers should also be refrigerated immediately after the meal is finished, but don't save leftovers from people's plates.
• Reheat cooked food thoroughly until it is piping-hot. If microwaving food to reheat, make sure it is piping-hot all the way through.
• If any food doesn't smell or look right – discard it rather than take a risk.

EATING OUT

Over 70% of people who get food poisoning believe that it was caused by a food eaten outside the home. Indeed, the huge rise in fast food, café and takeaway eating is one often-cited cause of the rise in food poisoning cases. Before eating while taking the family out and about, check the following points about where you intend to eat:

• It looks clean and tidy. Particularly check it has clean tables and floor and that dirty plates, etc., are cleared away quickly. Check that the eating utensils, crockery, etc., are properly clean with no lipstick or food traces.
• Check that any waiters/serving staff/cooks/chefs that you see have clean uniform and aprons. Try to check their fingernails and hands, and that hair is short or tied back and/or kept under a cap or hat.
• Check if the toilets and rest room areas are clean.
• Make sure raw foods aren't displayed anywhere near cooked foods.
• Make sure that ready-to-eat salads, cooked meats and sandwiches, and all other ready-to-eat food is well covered to avoid insects and is kept in a suitably chilled environment.
• If food that is supposed to be served hot is not, don't eat it.
• If it is not properly cooked, don't eat it. Check that your children's food is properly cooked – don't rely on them to tell you.
• Look for hygiene certificates on the walls.

BARBECUES

All children love a barbecue, but you need to obey some safety precautions in order to keep the food safe. The biggest risk to children's health is from undercooked meat and from cross-contamination (allowing raw meats or utensils or hands that have touched raw meats to come into contact with food that is to be eaten without cooking, or that is already cooked). Food left hanging around outdoors in heat is another danger.

Avoiding undercooked meat:
• Make sure the barbecue is properly hot before starting to cook – the coals should be glowing with a powdery grey surface; they could take half an hour to reach this stage after lighting.
• Make sure all frozen food is thoroughly defrosted before barbecuing.
• Pre-cook chicken portions (in an oven preheated to 180°C/gas 4 for 25 minutes) before putting them on the barbecue, as it is otherwise hard to ensure that they are cooked right through – often the outside can become charred while the inside is still raw. You could also use this method for large sausages and any pork meat.
• Turn food regularly and move it around the grilling area to make sure that everything gets cooked evenly.
• Before serving, check that the centre of all cooked meats is piping-hot and cooked through.
• Discard all barbecued leftovers unless they have been taken into the house, cooled and refrigerated immediately after cooking.

Avoiding cross-contamination:
• Always keep raw meat and cooked meat on separate plates.
• Don't put cooked meat on a plate that has been used for raw meat.
• Don't allow raw meat to come into contact with food that isn't to be cooked – e.g. burger buns or salad.
• Don't put raw meat next to cooked or partially cooked meat on the barbecue.
• Keep separate utensils for raw and cooked foods.
• If possible, have different people in charge of the non-cook foods, such as burger buns and salads. Otherwise, wash hands between handling raw meat and serving non-cook foods.

Other tips:
• Keep prepared salads and sauces in a cool place – and covered – in the house until just before you serve them, to avoid bacteria build-up and contamination by insects or animals.
• Don't serve children home-made mayonnaise which has raw eggs in it.
• Try to have a table set aside outdoors, but which is in the shade, for salads, breads, drinks, etc.
• Don't bring out any desserts until after the main barbecue has been eaten – particularly ones which contain cream.

- Keep as much food as possible in chiller bags or boxes before cooking.

PICNICS
- Avoid salads and sandwiches containing meat, fish or pâtés; avoid meat pies and pasties.
- Take food in cool-boxes or bags and don't unpack it until just before it is time to eat.
- Take antiseptic hand wipes to use before eating. Children playing in fields and parks can easily pick up bugs and such that may contaminate the food that they handle.

FOOD STANDARDS

In the long term, can the way our modern food is produced harm our children? We look here at the most contentious issues.

RESIDUES IN FOOD

The type of intensive or factory farming which has been carried out across the Western world for many years now has brought up some pertinent safety considerations, not least of which are worries about the contamination of our food with pesticides or herbicides in plants and growth hormones and antibiotics in animals.

Of course, government agriculture departments across the world all have strict regulations governing the use of these items, and all also do regular testing of foods to ensure that these are being obeyed. Sadly, a significant percentage of some foods do seem to be flouting the laws.

For example, in the UK, pesticide levels are regularly tested in a range of vegetables, and a small percentage of items, such as lettuce and carrots, are normally found to contain levels over the legal limit.

Safe plant foods: As we are being urged to eat more fruits and vegetables – virtually all of which have been grown with the help of pesticides, herbicides and a variety of chemical fertilisers and may then have been treated with other chemicals to prolong 'freshness' or storage time (for

exceptions in organic farming methods, see Organic Foods pages 156–7) – a real concern is that even if residue levels are acceptable in individual items, the cumulative effect, if our children eat a lot of fruit and veg, may be more of a problem. One US expert in neurological disease (Dr Andrew Grandinetti, University of Hawaii) claimed recently that unwashed or peeled fruits and fruit juice pose an increased risk of Parkinson's disease because of the high levels of residues they contain.

The truth is that nobody really knows the long-term effects of eating a diet containing these residues. Until we do know, it may be prudent to choose to grow or buy organic produce, or, at least, the organic versions of the more vulnerable plant foods, which are:
- Those imported from countries outside the EU, whose growing methods are harder to trace and whose laws may be less strict than ours.
- Leafy vegetables – e.g. cabbage and lettuce. Vegetables with a lot of surface area, like these, are likely to contain higher overall residue levels.
- Carrots – residue levels in carrots tend to be higher than in many other vegetables.
- Produce made from grains such as wheat. Grains, being small, like lettuce will tend to absorb higher levels of residue. They are also a food staple, so our children's intake is normally high.
- Fruits and vegetables which aren't peeled. Peeling can remove a percentage of the residues – but for health reasons many parents encourage their children to eat peel, skins, and so on. Washing can also help to remove a small amount of residue.

Safe animal and dairy foods: Factory or intensive farming of our beef, pigs, poultry, eggs and dairy herds – and even of our fish – means that much of the animal produce on sale in our supermarkets contains traces of residues in their feeds and possibly traces of growth hormones used to promote faster or larger growth, and possibly traces of antibiotics used to contain disease and also to improve growth rates. What animals eat will also show up in their milk, flesh and organs. Again, there is little research showing the long-term effect of regularly eating these foods on our children's health. If you prefer to minimize his or her intake of these residues, here are some tips:

- Buy organic meat, eggs and dairy produce – and/or from a local source.
- Avoid imported produce; overseas standards on production are sometimes less stringent than our own.
- Buy lean meat and cut fat off meat when you see it – toxins tend to accumulate in fat, not lean, flesh.
- Lamb is generally reared in a more natural way than any other of our meats.
- Genuinely wild game, such as wild duck, is 'organic'. But pheasants are usually reared with the help of antibiotics.
- Avoid factory-farmed fish, such as salmon or trout, which may contain antibiotic residues as well as being artificially colour-enhanced. If possible, try to buy fish caught by traditional methods in deep waters (see below).

Heavy metals and industrial waste:
Nutritionally, fish is very good for our children. We are urged to get them to eat a portion of oily fish and a portion of white fish every week. Sadly, this advice is tempered because much of the fish caught today is contaminated with mercury, dioxins or PCBs, by-products of industry which are dumped at sea or arrive there via our rivers.

White fish, which has a very low fat content, contains much less contamination by dioxins and PCBs than oily fish, as these toxins are stored in the liver and fatty tissue rather than in lean flesh. Thus, although oily fish is good, more than one portion a week is not good as it could increase intake (especially in smaller people, such as children) beyond safe levels.

However, several large non-oily fish have been found to have high levels of mercury contamination, and the UK Food Standards Agency has issued advice that pregnant women, women hoping to become pregnant or breast-feeding, and children under 16, should avoid shark, marlin and swordfish. Tuna should also be avoided before and during pregnancy and during breast-feeding.

GENETICALLY MODIFIED FOODS AND INGREDIENTS:

As yet, no one really knows what the long-term effects of consuming genetically-altered foods or ingredients might be. The food scientists and multinational companies who produce this food – and indeed, to a lesser extent, the current UK Government – seem to believe that arguments against genetically modified foods are based on ethics, morals, ignorance or fear of the unknown rather than actual scientific evidence that they can be harmful to health or environment.

There is not the room here to debate the topic, but the fact is, that many people prefer to buy food that they know to be GM-free and this is surely an undebatable right. If you want your family to avoid GM products, the box below provides tips which may help you to minimize the risk. It isn't possible to eliminate it entirely, as in April 2000, the EU set a legal 'tolerance level' for GM in foods of 1%. This means that if a food contains less than 1% GM ingredients, it can be declared 'GM-free' and/or need not be labelled as containing genetically modified ingredients.

Also, some products are given exempt status even if the GM ingredient is present in amounts larger than 1%. These include animal feed, oils from GM crops, lecithin and modified starches (the last two being ingredients typically added in many manufactured food processes).

AVOIDING GM FOODS

- Avoid foods containing soya as an ingredient. Avoiding processed foods is the only practical way to do this, as about 70% of all processed foods contain soya in one form or another. Approximately half of the world's soya crop is now genetically modified beans, which tend to be mixed with non-GM beans before being distributed.
- Avoid foods containing maize (corn) – much of the world's maize crop is now also GM.
- Read labels carefully. When a GM content meets the legal requirements explained above, it will have to say so on the label. Much tomato purée contains modified tomatoes.
- Buy organic – genetic modification is not allowed in foods produced to the UK Soil Association organic standard.

See also: Organic Food pp156–7.

FRIED FOODS

Fried food has a poor profile and gets a very bad press. Its reputation as a greasy and inferior product has led to more and more parents turning away from the deep-fat fryer. Indeed, frying chips, battered fish and other items in a large vat of dubious-quality fat is something that perhaps we can all afford to live without. Oven chips – and all those other baked goods that taste like fried – mean that you really don't need a fryer in your home any more. If you choose to deep-fry, however, it is important to fry at the correct, constant temperature and never to overfill the pan with food as the oil temperature then drops too far and the food absorbs oil.

For parents watching their children's total fat intake and calorie intake, there are other alternatives to deep-frying that are just as pleasing to children's taste buds, if not more so.

Shallow-frying and alternatives: Food still absorbs a significant proportion of fat when it is shallow-fried, so reserve this method for occasional rather than nightly use. And, again, use good-quality groundnut or rapeseed oil. For a buttery flavour, a very tiny knob of butter can be added to the oil. Most children enjoy a 'real' fried egg with some oven chips, and an average fried egg contains about 30 extra calories' worth of fat (about 3–4g), but a lot of foods that were traditionally shallow-fried can be dry-fried or griddled with virtually no extra fat. Many of these foods – e.g. bacon, sausages, burgers – are high in their own fat anyway. For dry-frying or griddling, all you need to do is lightly brush the griddle or a non-stick frying pan with oil and then add the food and cook it on moderate heat until the food's own fat begins to melt and run out. You can then turn the heat up higher to cook the food thoroughly.

Grilling may be an even healthier option as it is so easy to discard the fat that runs from the grid into the pan after the food is cooked. Sausages also bake very well – 200°C/gas 6 for around 25 minutes for large ones. Fish fingers taste better grilled than fried and children often prefer bacon when it has been grilled. Home-made potato wedges brushed with a little olive oil make a tasty alternative to fried chips or oven chips.

Stir-frying is an ideal method for cooking a variety of vegetables – not only do children often prefer the taste, but the oil helps many of the vital phytochemicals to be more readily absorbed in the body, and also helps to retain the water-soluble vitamin C and B group. With a good-quality pan, only a small amount of oil needs to be used. For vegetables that absorb a lot of fat – e.g. aubergines, mushrooms – don't keep adding more fat. A little stock or water is better – or turn the heat down, cover with a lid and the moisture in the vegetables will do the job itself.

See also: Acrylamide pp70–1, Chips pp90–2, Fats and Oils pp110–12, Junk Food pp140–3, Phytochemicals p160, Snacks pp178–9, Takeaways pp186–8, Vegetables pp191–4, Potato Wedges p220 for an alternative recipe for oven chips.

If you are using a deep-fat fryer, the oil will be prone to oxidation, which can be dangerous to health and possibly carcinogenic. To prevent oxidation, you should change the oil in the pan very regularly, and use oils with only a medium polyunsaturated fat content, such as groundnut or rapeseed oil, avoiding oils with a very high polyunsaturated content, such as safflower or corn oil, and blended vegetable oils. Store your cooking oil in the fridge, which also helps prevent oxidation.

FROZEN FOOD

Well-frozen food should be as nutritious as fresh food – and can be even more so. To ensure you make the most of frozen foods and don't compromise on safety, there are a few guidelines you should follow. Don't freeze any food which is past its sell-by date or stale. Frozen foods should be eaten within weeks (baked goods, fish, shellfish) or months (vegetables, meat) and discarded if they look dry or discoloured. Defrost foods well before cooking, unless the label says you can cook from frozen, and cook thoroughly. Don't refreeze frozen food that has thawed – although you can refreeze frozen food which you have cooked, e.g., if you use defrosted minced meat to make a lasagne, you can then freeze the cooked lasagne).

When buying, make sure that foods are properly frozen – avoid packs of vegetables (e.g peas) in large lumps as this means they may have thawed and refrozen. When taking frozen foods home, always use a cool box.

> Good-quality vegetables that have been frozen within hours of picking and then properly stored at home, probably contain a lot more vitamin C than vegetables bought from a corner shop that have been stored for several days (or longer) and then kept in sunlight – both warmth and light deplete the vitamin C content of foods.

See also: Food Poisoning pp122–3, Food Safety pp123–6

FRUIT

All children would benefit from eating two to three portions of fruit a day, according to several reports into diet and health. One large UK study of adults who ate fruit regularly as children showed that they had less incidence of cancer in adulthood, and the World Health Organization report that 10% of cancers in the developed world could be the result of people not eating enough fruit and vegetables. Fruit intake is also linked with less risk of other types of disease. Yet, according to the 2000 survey into the diets of British schoolchildren, an average of only 39% regularly consume fruit, and 1 in 5 have no fruit at all.

Details of individual fruits and their nutrient profiles appear in their own entries (e.g. Apples) and see the 'See also' box at the end of this entry; this page contains more general information about fruit in your child's diet.

Nutrients in fruit: Most fruits are very low in fat, low in protein, low in calories and low in starch – the exception being bananas, which do have a significant starch content. Most fruits are quite high in fibre and many are high in soluble fibre. Fruits are also a major source of phytochemicals – special plant chemicals which many experts believe may make a large contribution to their health benefits. Fruits are also often rich in the antioxidant vitamin C, and in folate and potassium.

The calorie content of fruit comes mostly from fruit sugars (correctly called fructose). The sugar found in fruit is described as intrinsic sugar – which means that it is a natural part of the plant structure. This type of sugar, like other sugars, is associated with risk of tooth decay – but it is fruit juice that seems to pose more of a potential risk to teeth than whole fruits, as juice tends to be in contact with teeth and gums for longer periods than a fruit portion.

TIPS ON FRUIT

• Remember that children should have 5 portions of fruit and vegetables a day. A breakdown of 2 of fruit and 3 of vegetables is about right, but there is no need to stick to this to the letter.
• To benefit from maximum vitamin C, eat fruit really fresh and always store it in the fridge. When it is cut, fruit immediately starts to lose its vitamin C, so only cut fruit for children immediately before they are going to eat it.
• Try to offer a wide variety of different fruits to your child for maximum nutritional benefit.
• When making fruit salad, put slices of apple and pear into the serving bowl one-quarter filled with an acidic juice (e.g. orange, pineapple) to stop the fruits from going brown (oxidizing). Top up with water to serve.
• Children who don't like chewing big lumps of fruit will almost always enjoy fruit smoothies to drink, and fruit purées or coulis poured over ice cream, yoghurt, custard and so on.
• Many children love cooked fruit. Bake cooking apples (core and fill with dried fruit and brown sugar mix, then circle the skin horizontally with a knife and place in an ovenproof dish with 1.5cm water in the bottom, bake for 40 minutes or until puffed up and tender all the way through), or peel, cut and cook them in a tablespoon or two of water in a saucepan until broken down. Slice and poach pears in fruit juice, or bake bananas whole in their skins until blackened and serve with Greek yoghurt.

Cooked fruit loses some of its vitamin C but still retains the rest of the nutrients.

• Use fresh fruit as part of a salad platter for lunch – slices of apple go very well with cheese or ham, while oranges, mango or satsumas go well with cooked chicken.

• Some children are allergic to certain fruits – strawberries are one of the more frequent culprits and can produce symptoms such as a rash. Citrus fruits also sometimes cause a problem. However,

many children grow out of fruit allergies by the time they are in their teens.

See also: 'What is a Serving?' p24, 'The Food Pyramid' pp35–8, 'Serving Sizes for Teenagers' p56, Berry Fruits p80, Citrus Fruits pp93–4, Exotic Fruits p109, Food Allergies pp117–19, Juices pp139–40, Pastry p158, Phytochemicals p160, Teeth and Gums pp189–90, Vegetables pp191–4, Appendix 1 pp240–7 for full fruit sources of vitamins, minerals and phytochemicals.

FIVE A DAY: WHAT IS A PORTION?

This list is based on the UK Department of Health's guide to portions, which will apply to older children and teenagers as well as adults.

Fruit	This gives one portion
Apple, medium banana, pear, orange	1 fruit
Plums, fresh apricots and similar medium fruits*	2 fruits
Grapefruit, avocado, mango	½ a fruit
Melon	1 average slice
Pineapple Fruit salad or tinned fruit in juice	2 rings 3 tablespoons
Stewed fruit	3 tablespoons
Grapes, cherries, berries	1 good handful
Dried fruits	1 tablespoon
Fruit juice or fruit smoothie	1 × 150ml glass**
Fruit in a pie filling	(see note *** below)

* Fruits in between the size of a plum and an apple – e.g. satsuma or kiwi fruit – can be considered as a full portion for small children, while older children may be able to eat two.
** Only one glass of fruit juice a day can count towards the 'five a day' recommendation, no matter how much is consumed.
*** If a portion of fruit pie or tart contains the equivalent of a portion of fruit as listed above (e.g. 3 tablespoons stewed fruit or 2 plums) then it can count as a portion. But beware, as many manufactured fruit pies don't contain this much.

FUSSY EATING AND FOOD REFUSAL

Although fussy eating is common in pre-school children – to the point where the Royal College of Physicians (RCP) describes it as, for many, a stage of normal development – in older children eating problems can be a great worry for parents. Loss of appetite and eating disorders, such as anorexia and bulimia, are discussed elsewhere in this A–Z section; here we look at other categories of eating problems that can beset school age children.

Selective eating: When a child will eat only certain foods – often quite a small range – this is termed selective eating, or extreme food faddiness. There is no particular pattern to the types of food that a child will eat – it could be only bread, jam and ice cream, or only chips, crisps and tomato ketchup – and there is a great unwillingness to try new foods. Other children will eat only 'baby foods' with a very soft or sloppy texture (this is called 'inappropriate texture of food for age'). The child eats the foods he or she has selected quite happily and there are no emotional problems.

In the short term this may not be a huge health concern but, if it goes on for a long time, it may be. A very narrow range of foods can cause nutritional problems and if the foods selected are high in sugar, that may cause problems with teeth and gums. Underweight, surprisingly, is not necessarily a problem.

If you are worried, or the problem seems to have gone on for a long time or the child seems to have restricted growth, it is wise to see your doctor, who can examine your child for health problems and may refer you as a family to a specialist in eating problems. However, the peak age for selective eating is in the primary school years, and many children do gradually accept a wider range of foods and, eventually, eat a normal range. Experts say that trying to force the child to eat new foods, or showing extreme concern or negative emotions just makes matters worse.

Food refusal: According to the RCP, this differs from selective eating in that it is often associated with emotional problems such as worry or unhappiness, and/or food is only refused when in certain situations (e.g. at school). Once the child's worries have been identified and dealt with, the food refusal tends to go away, but your should see your doctor as professional help may be needed to help the child with his or her problems.

The RCP also defines another category similar to food refusal – food avoidance emotional disorder. This seems to occur when there is a chronic or acute distress in the child's life – the child may be depressed, sad, withdrawn and disinterested in food, and his or her refusal to eat may result in weight loss, although the condition isn't the same as anorexia nervosa, as the child often wishes he or she could eat. Professional help should be sought for this disorder.

Food phobia: This may occur when a child has had a particularly bad experience of eating a food. For example, he or she may have eaten something that caused choking or induced sickness. He or she may have fears about the texture or taste or odour of food, or have difficulty in swallowing. The phobia results in the child refusing food, or certain foods, or certain textures of food, for example. True food phobia needs professional treatment (cognitive therapy is often used) and you should see your doctor as a starting point.

Most cases of fussy eating and food refusal do get sorted out in time, with professional help as necessary. Often there is no way of telling who will get problems and who won't, but the Royal College of Physicians suggests that the following children are more likely to suffer with an eating problem:

• If they had an unpleasant, abnormal or slow early feeding experience
• If they had a low birth weight
• If they are delayed in their development
• If they develop eating problems early on in life
• If they have a history of being sick

Source: Eating Problems in Children – Information for Parents, by Claudine Fox and Carol Joughin (Gaskell, 2002)

See also: 'Feeding Problems Aged 1–4' pp26–8, Appetite Loss p74, Eating Disorders pp105–7, Teeth and Gums pp189–90, Underweight pp190–1, Appendix 2 pp250–1 for Growth Charts.

GLUTEN

see Coeliac Disease

GRAINS

Grains in their natural state are a good source of starchy 'complex' carbohyrate and fibre, most are a good source of minerals and some a good source of B vitamins. They also mostly contain reasonable amounts of protein. Cereals are linked with protection from bowel and other cancers and from diverticulitis, and can also help to prevent constipation. Barley, rye and oats are a good source of soluble fibre to help prevent heart disease, and they also contain phytochemicals which have anti-cancer effects.

Refined grains – such as pearl barley and white rice – contain much less fibre, vitamins and minerals than whole grains. Wheat (and couscous, which is made from wheat), bulghar wheat, rye, barley and oats are not suitable for children with a gluten intolerance, but corn and rice are – another substitute for flours containing gluten is soya flour.

See also: Bread p82–3, Carbohydrates pp87–8, Coeliac Disease p94, Dietary Fibre pp101–2, Food Allergies pp117–19, Pasta p157, Phytochemicals p160.

GRAINS – NUTRIENT CONTENT PER 100G (DRY WEIGHT)*

	Cals	Tot Fat	Sat Fat	Protein	Tot Carbs	Sugars	Fibre	Vits	Mins	Sodium
Wheat, whole**	310	2.2g	0.3g	12.7g	63.9g	2.1g	9g	B1, B3, B6	mag, sel, zn	3mg
Barley, pearl	350	1.8 g	trace	8g	84g	—	6g	—	—	trace
Barley, pot	302	2g	trace	10.6g	64g	1.8g	14.5g	B3, B6	fe	trace
Couscous***	350	1.8g	trace	10.6g	78g	—	2g	—	—	trace
Oats	376	9.3g	1.7g	11.3g	67g	trace	7g	—	fe, mag, zn	trace
Rye, whole	335	2g	0.3g	8.2g	76g	trace	11.7g	E	mag, fe, zn	trace
Corn	354	0.7g	trace	0.6g	92g	trace	0.1g	—	—	52mg
Rice, brown	357	2.8g	0.7g	6.7g	81.3g	1.3g	1.9g	B1, B3	mag, zn	3mg
Rice, white	359	0.5g	trace	7.4g	80g	trace	0.4g	—	—	trace

* Similar values apply to flours made from these grains.
** Bulghar wheat (cracked wheat) has similar values.
*** Instant-type couscous – traditional couscous, available in health-food shops and which needs cooking contains higher levels of fibre, vitamins and minerals.

GRAPES

Nutrient content per 100g:

Cals	60	Fibre	0.7g
Tot Fat	trace	Vit C	3mg
Tot Carbs	15.4g	Pot	210mg
Sugars	15.4g		

Grapes are higher in sugars – and, therefore, calories – than many fruits and contain less vitamin C and fibre than others. However, red grapes are rich in phytochemicals from the polyphenol group called resveratrol, which seems to be linked to protection against heart disease and stroke. Grapes make a useful sweet snack or lunch-box addition for children – pick seedless kinds.

See also: Fruit pp129–30, Juices pp139–40, Phytochemicals p160.

GREENS

Leafy vegetables – the cabbage or cruciferous family, as well as broccoli and cauliflower which are flower heads – are a very important group of foods with several health benefits. This is why so many of us were told as children to 'eat up your greens'. Now we are still asking our kids to eat them up – and they are still, by and large, trying to avoid doing so.

The reason that many greens have such a strong flavour – the cause of so much hatred amongst the young – is that they are full of extraordinary plant compounds (phytochemicals) and are a particularly rich source of several minerals. They also contain good-to-excellent amounts of vitamin C, folate, carotenes and fibre. The table overleaf lists the exact content of several of the important nutrients – as you can see, they do vary tremendously.

In addition to the above nutrients, leafy greens are also a reasonably good source of iron, and its absorption is helped by vitamin C. Luckily, most greens come with their own good vitamin C content. Spinach is rich in calcium and is also high in iron, but because of its oxalic acid content, these

minerals aren't easily absorbed. The dark outer leaves of greens contain much more carotenoids than the paler leaves and hearts, and fat increases the absorption of carotenoids.

I haven't listed their fat content as almost all greens contain less than 1g of fat per 100g and only a trace of saturates. The only exceptions are Brussels sprouts, which contain 1.4g fat/100g. They are all cholesterol free. Neither have I listed protein content – only sprouts, white cabbage, broccoli and cauliflower contain more than 1g protein per 100g. The carbohydrate content of greens is mainly in the form of sugars (with only a trace of starch in most), but as these vegetables are so low in calories, the sugar content is very low also (e.g. cabbage 4g/100g and kale 1.3g/100g).

Try to serve your children several portions of greens a week as part of their 'five a day'.

GOOD SOURCES OF:

VITAMIN C:
sprouts
kale
spring greens

FOLATE:
spinach
kale
sprouts

CAROTENOIDS:
kale
Savoy cabbage
spring greens
spinach

POTASSIUM:
all leafy greens

CALCIUM:
kale
pak choi
spring greens

MAGNESIUM:
kale
broccoli

Phytochemicals in greens: Greens contain a range of plant chemicals which can protect your children's health. Here are a few of those that have been discovered to date:
• Broccoli and cauliflower contain glucosinolates – broccoli has one called sulphoraphane – which inhibit cancer cells, help stop cancer from developing.
• Kale, spring greens and spinach are very high in the carotenoids lutein and zeaxanthin, which help keep eyes healthy and maintain good eyesight. Kale,

GREENS – NUTRIENT CONTENT PER 100G PORTION (RAW)

	Cals	Fibre	Vit C	Folate	Carotene	Potassium	Calcium	Magnesium
Broccoli	33	2.6g	87mg	90µg	575µg	370mg	56mg	22mg
Brussels sprouts	42	4.1g	115mg	135µg	215µg	450mg	26mg	8mg
Cauliflower	34	1.8g	43mg	66µg	50µg	380mg	21mg	17mg
Kale	33	3.1g	110mg	120µg	3145µg	450mg	130mg	34mg
Pak choi/ bok choi	12	1.6g	27mg	40µg	n/k	238mg	80mg	n/k
Red cabbage	21	2.5g	57mg	21µg	n/k	206mg	51mg	15mg
Savoy cabbage	27	3.1g	20mg	40µg	1150µg	270mg	52mg	8mg
Spinach	25	2.1g	26mg	114µg	3535µg	500mg	170mg	54mg
Spring greens	33	3.4g	180mg	92µg	8295µg	370mg	210mg	19mg
White cabbage	27	2.1g	35mg	34µg	9µg	240mg	49mg	6mg

which also contains high levels of glucosinolates (see broccoli above), contains the highest overall levels of antioxidants of all vegetables, as measured on the ORAC scale.

• Brussels sprouts get their strong taste from sinigrin – a chemical which can destroy pre-cancerous cells in the body.

• Cabbage contains indoles – a member of the glucosinolates family – which seem to block cancer-causing agents.

• The high levels of antioxidants in all greens may also help to protect against heart disease and several other diseases.

TIPS FOR GETTING CHILDREN TO EAT GREENS

• Don't overcook them – soggy boiled greens don't taste nice or feel nice in the mouth and, what is more, they lose a great deal of their vitamin and mineral content into the cooking water. Steam greens over a pan of water for just a few minutes until just tender and serve immediately.

• Chop or shred greens and use them along with vegetables, meat and pulses in soups and stews.

• Cooking with a little fat or oil helps the beneficial compounds be absorbed by the body and children usually prefer the taste – so stir-fry in groundnut or olive oil to serve as a vegetable side dish, stir-fry with meat or fish as a main meal. Children also enjoy baked vegetables – bake them drizzled with a little olive oil and seasoning. If you give greens as part of a meal that contains fat (e.g. greens with Sunday roast) this also serves the same purpose.

• Use greens in salads – white cabbage in a coleslaw, red cabbage in a winter salad with carrot and beansprouts; pak choi or Chinese leaves (similar nutritional profile) instead of lettuce.

A recent survey revealed that Brussels sprouts are children's most-hated vegetables – over 40% of youngsters said that they can't stand them.

See also: Antioxidants p73, Minerals pp148–9, Phytochemicals p160, Vitamins pp194–6, Appendix 1 pp240–9 for a full list of sources of nutrients and essential fats.

GRILLED FOOD

Grilling is a good way to reduce the fat content of a variety of meats – such as lamb chops, pork chops, bacon, gammon, sausages and burgers – compared with frying. When grilling or barbecuing, however, care should be taken not to overcook or burn the food. When lean meat (beef, lamb, pork, chicken and even fish) is cooked at high temperatures, the proteins in the meat react to form hydrocarbons which have been linked with increased risk of stomach and other cancers. Also, when barbecuing over coals or wood, aromatic amines in the smoke may also be cancer-causing.

To minimize the risk from grilled or barbecued foods, keep the cooking heat moderate only (don't cook over coals until they are greyish and glowing). Precook large pieces of meat and just finish off on the barbecue. Throw overdone or burnt portions away, serve with plenty of salad or vegetables and follow with fruit, all of which contain antioxidants to mop up the dangerous chemicals that may be in the grilled food.

> Take special care when grilling foods for children that the meat or fish is thoroughly cooked all the way through and no pink flesh remains – undercooked burgers and chicken are particularly dangerous.

See also: Food Safety pp123–6, Fried Foods p128.

HAY FEVER

It is quite common for children to suffer from seasonal allergic rhinitis, as hay fever is properly called. This allergic reaction to airborne pollens from trees and grass, when high levels of histamine are released in the body, may start as early as March (tree pollen) and continue until mid-summer. Symptoms are sneezing, runny nose, streaming eyes and, perhaps, headache, itching and inflammation of the nasal passages.

There are some trials to show that a daily supplement of 500mg vitamin C can help to reduce the severity of hay fever by reducing the levels of histamine. There is also evidence that a group of phytochemicals called bioflavonoids – found in citrus fruits, onions, apples and many fruits and vegetables – can act as natural antihistamines. So a balanced diet high in fruit and vegetables seems the best line of approach to help hay fever sufferers.

See also: Asthma p76, Food Allergies pp117–19, Phytochemicals p160.

HEALTH FOODS

The term 'health food' means different things to different people. To some, health food is everything that is sold in a 'health-food shop'; to others, it means organic food; to many, it is simply fresh unrefined natural foods; to some people, food supplements and herbal remedies; to others, it means food that is well-balanced nutritionally.

In fact, there is no real or legal definition of the words 'health food' and really no such thing. There is a healthy diet, which varies somewhat from individual to individual, and there are nutrient-rich foods, which may be rich in a few, or some, or very many, of all the nutrients we need for good health or body maintenance.

'Healthy eating' is sensible eating with a wide variety of different good-quality foods. And what is good quality? Fresh food, grown in a responsible way and stored to retain maximum nutrients. If cooked or processed, add that it should be cooked and/or processed in a responsible way to retain maximum natural nutrients and minimize unnecessary artificial or other additives.

HEART HEALTH

Children as young as primary school age are beginning to show early signs of, or risk factors for, heart disease – high levels of the less desirable fats in the bloodstream, obesity, and so on. Experts believe that it is never too early to start protecting the body against cardiovascular diseases and it is comprehensively documented that a well-balanced diet – including plenty of fruit and vegetables, whole grains, pulses and fish, as well as nuts and seeds, and possibly other items such as olive oil and garlic – can all help in this quest. The diet should also be low in saturated fats and trans fats, low in sodium and a child should not be allowed to become obese. The diet plans and recipes in this book will help you to achieve this.

> **!** **For children whose close family members (e.g. parents and/ or grandparents) have cardiovascular problems, including high blood pressure or high cholesterol, it is particularly important to lead a lifestyle which minimizes the risks – and to get regular check-ups via your doctor.**

See also: 'Weight Control' p28 and pp57–8, 'Weight Problems' p48, Fats and Oils pp110–12, Obesity pp152–5, Appendix 3 pp252–3 for contact details of relevant organisations.

HERBS AND SPICES

Herbs and spices all contain a range of vitamins, minerals and, importantly, phytochemicals which can offer a range of health benefits, including protection from cancers and heart disease. One research study found that, even used in small amounts, herbs and spices still have powerful benefits.

For example, chives contain similar compounds to other members of the onion family, which can help protect the heart; thyme is a powerful antioxidant, and parsley is a good diuretic. Chillies contain compounds that can help relieve pain, cumin helps digestion and cinnamon is said to help treat colds. The yellow spice turmeric seems to have anti-cancer effects, while ginger is very good at calming nausea and flatulence, and may help joint pains.

Many children take readily to both herbs and spices if they are introduced in small amounts, e.g. a little chopped chive sprinkled over a bowl of soup, or flat-leaf parsley as part of a salad, or fresh chilli in a chilli con carne.

See also: Antioxidants p73, Phytochemicals p160, Recipes section pp198–239 for more ideas on using herbs and spices in children's food.

HONEY

Nutrient content per 25g:

Cals	72	(of which) sugars	19g
Tot carbs	19g		

Honey has a higher water content than sugar and therefore contains slightly fewer calories, but it is also less sweet. Honey contains no fat and only a trace of protein, and although it does contain vitamins and minerals they are present in such small amounts that they hardly contribute to the amounts needed in the diet. However, good-quality honey does have one very special property – it is a proven antibacterial and has been shown to heal even stubborn wounds. It may also help heal mouth ulcers if applied direct to the ulcer, may help ease sore throats if bacteria are the cause of the problem (sometimes sore throats are viral, and honey doesn't improve viral infections). In older people, honey has also been shown to help heal stomach ulcers caused by Helicobacter pylori.

However, any old pot of bargain-basement honey from the supermarket shelf won't necessarily do the trick. Research has mostly been carried out using

> **!** **Honey is best not given to children under one year old as it may occasionally cause infant botulism, a form of food poisoning. However, honey is a good antiseptic and is worth including in the diet of older toddlers, especially honey of good quality.**

manuka honey, a pure honey from New Zealand and Australia. Although this honey is fairly easy to find in the shops, it is likely that other pure honeys, which haven't been through too much processing, will also have an antibacterial effect. Look for honeys made by bees who frequent only single types of flower, and look for pure honeycomb honey.

Experts haven't pinpointed the x-factor in honey which gives it such special healing powers, but Dr Rose Cooper, a leading honey researcher, says she believes that 'an unknown ingredient is at work' and it is likely that the magic ingredient or ingredients are similar to the phytochemicals found in plants.

See also: Phytochemicals p160.

HUNGER

If a child complains of hunger it is usually a quite natural mechanism which ensures that he or she gets something to eat. Children quickly become ravenous if they spend a lot of time outdoors or playing sport, and can eat quite amazing amounts for their size. If your child is of about average weight or underweight, gets plenty of exercise and seems permanently hungry – keep feeding him or her, but offer good-quality foods that will provide a more sustained blood sugar level, not sugary snacks or too many crisps (see the information on foods with a high, medium and low Glycaemic Index in the entry on Obesity pp152–5). Older teenagers in particular need more calories than at any other time in their lives, and girls during puberty also often need more. Children who are sedentary for much of the time and take little exercise, but still seem to be very hungry and tend to snack while watching TV and so on, may be eating from habit, boredom or comfort. You need to consider helping them to change their lifestyle and then the snacking habit should become less of a problem.

If your child is overweight or obese and gets very hungry, you need to be careful not to encourage unnecessary intake of calories, particularly those in the form of sweets, sugary drinks and snacks. These foods and drinks don't satisfy hunger for long –

better to give your child an apple, an oat cracker with a small piece of cheese or some other foods low on the Glycaemic Index.

Children who have been unwell and are beginning to recover often develop a short-term big appetite, which is the body's way of replenishing the body fat that may have been lost. Lastly, very occasionally a big appetite can be a sign of disease, so if you have eliminated all the other suggestions here and can't explain your child's appetite – see your doctor, who should carry out any necessary tests.

See also: Convalescence pp96–7, Obesity pp152–5, Underweight pp190–1.

HYPERACTIVITY
see ADHD

ICE CREAM

Small portions of ice cream are a reasonable dessert and a favourite treat for a hot summer's day. Although they contain little in the way of useful nutrients – apart from a little calcium – individual ices aimed at children are often fairly small – a choc ice being a good example – and therefore aren't all that high in fat or sugar proportionally.

However, typical 'designer' ice creams from an ice cream parlour usually contain a whopping amount of calories, fat and sugar, so reserve larger fancy ices for very occasional indulgence.

Useful cooling alternatives are ice lollies and sorbets which contain no fat but are high in sugars. Home-made ice lollies using real fruit juice are easy to do and have a higher juice content than most commercial lollies. If you use orange juice or blackcurrant juice, the lolly will be a good source of vitamin C. Make sure children clean their teeth soon after sucking on lollies or ices. Reduced-calorie ice creams are worth considering if you have an overweight child, but the saving in calories isn't huge.

See also: Teeth and Gums pp189–90.

ILLNESS, Feeding During

When children have a short-term illness, such as a cold or chesty cough, they often eat less than usual. Obviously part of the reason is that being ill makes you less inclined to feel hungry. Also, sense of smell may be affected, and this sense has a large bearing upon how well the taste buds work, which in turn affects appetite. During the inactivity of illness, less calories are burnt up in any case, so eating less is a natural follow-on from that.

Taking all those factors into account, the best course of action is to give the child small fairly frequent portions of food, and, as far as is sensible, give him or her what he or she feels like most, although endless sweets are probably not a good idea. Plenty of easy-to-eat fruit, such as seedless grapes, banana, seedless satsumas and slices of peach or pineapple should all be well received. The vitamin C and plant chemicals in these fruits may help boost the immune system and speed recovery. Ice cream, Greek yoghurt and custard are all good ways to get some calcium and calories into the diet as well as soothing a sore throat.

Don't worry too much if they can't eat much in the way of savoury food – bowls of puréed soup and sandwiches, or even just bread and butter, may be all that can be managed. Make soup yourself and it is surprising how many nutrients can be crammed into one bowlful. You could grate a little cheese on top to add more protein and calcium.

Don't be too ready to offer bland flavours – sometimes the taste buds need something a little more lively. For potent savoury flavour, try Marmite which, though too high in salt for frequent use, is truly powerful and a good source of B vitamins. Avoid foods very high in fat, which may cause nausea, and avoid large chunks of anything or any foods which are hard to chew or swallow.

If the appetite really has gone in the short term – don't worry. Just provide plenty of fluids, such as water, diluted juices, milk, lemon and honey (which has antibiotic properties) in hot water, for example, so that the child doesn't get dehydrated.

For long-term illness it is best to consult a dietitian who knows your child's case (ask your doctor to refer you to one) and will give suitable advice on diet.

PROBIOTICS

If children are taking antibiotics for illness, these can destroy the good bacteria in the digestive system as well as those that are causing the symptoms. To re-colonize the gut, offer your child bio yoghurt, containing bacteria such as acidophilus and bifidus, or you can buy probiotic capsules (store them in the fridge). Research shows that probiotics can help to minimize the symptoms of both respiratory infections and diarrhoea.

See also: Convalescence pp96–7, Honey pp136–7, Appendix I pp240–7 for sources of vitamin B, vitamin C, calcium and other nutrients.

INSOMNIA

Occasionally most children have a bad night's sleep and this is nothing to worry about – they tend to sleep for longer the next night. If insomnia persists for more than a couple of nights and is bad enough to cause the child to feel overtired during the day, check that there is nothing worrying him or her – anxiety is one of the most common causes of sleeplessness for all ages, even for quite young children.

Make sure that the bed is comfortable and that the room is not too hot. Lack of exercise can cause poor sleep, so ensure that your child gets outside every day, if possible. Exercise helps relaxation and releases endorphins which have a calming effect. A warm bath before bedtime is also a good idea.

Diet can have a considerable effect on sleep, so use the following tips to help your child get a good night's sleep:
• Make sure that the child's evening meal is rich in complex carbohydrates – e.g. rice, potatoes, pasta, bread. These stimulate the production of serotonin, a chemical that has a relaxing effect on the brain. The whole-grain carbohydrates (brown basmati rice, whole-wheat pasta, whole-grain bread) tend to

keep the blood sugar levels even for longer as they are lower on the Glycaemic Index (see Obesity pages 152–5) than many highly refined carbs, and thus may prevent night hunger, which can keep children awake, especially those who have their tea/supper early. If you serve supper more than three hours before a child goes to bed, a bedtime snack is appropriate (see suggestions below).

• A few protein foods are rich in the amino acid tryptophan, which helps production of serotonin. Turkey and milk both contain tryptophan and, surprisingly, bananas are another good source, although their protein content is not high.

• Calcium is also a relaxant and a sleep-promoter, so a calcium-rich drink or snack before bedtime is a good idea. Milk is, in fact, a perfect night-time drink, as it contains carbohydrate, tryptophan and calcium, as well as B vitamins which help tryptophan to convert to serotonin. Warm milk tends to be more soothing and comforting than cold milk, though both will do the trick.

GOOD BEDTIME SNACKS TO HELP SLEEP:

• Digestive biscuit or oatcake with hot milk.
• Banana sandwich on whole-grain bread.
• Pot of whole-milk yoghurt with banana chopped in.

WHAT TO AVOID TO ENSURE A GOOD NIGHT'S SLEEP:

• Anything containing caffeine during the evening – tea, coffee, cola drinks, chocolate – as caffeine is a stimulant.
• Hard cheese: a significant number of people find that they sleep badly if they eat cheese too near to bedtime – it often seems to produce bad dreams.
• High-protein, low-carb meal: steak and salad, for example, is a high-protein, low-carb meal. These tend to be stimulating rather than calming.
• A large meal just before bedtime. This can cause the digestive system to go into overdrive and disrupt sleep. A better pattern is a main meal no later than two hours before bed, or high tea about 3 hours before bed, followed by a small bedtime snack.

See also: Nerves and Anxiety p150.

JUICES

Fruit juices contain some minerals, and citrus and berry or blackcurrant varieties are reasonable sources of vitamin C. High intake of fruit juice is, however, linked with dental problems, and paediatricians recommend that children drink juices through a straw to help protect teeth from contact with the juice. As most juices – except tomato – are high in calories, they are best used diluted with water and drunk with a meal. Indeed, there is evidence from the USA that children under the age of five who have easy access to fruit juice are three times more likely to be overweight. High intake of juice can also cause diarrhoea and flatulence.

Juices contain some of the special plant chemicals present in the original fruit – although the pith, peel and fibre are all lost and there is a lot to be said for encouraging children to eat whole fruits rather than drink juice. Try giving your child vegetable juice instead of fruit juice some of the time – vegetable juices aren't associated with tooth decay and are low in calories, but also contain the valuable chemicals, vitamins and minerals of fruit. Also consider buying organic juice, as pesticide and herbicide residues in juices from apples and other fruits may be high enough to be linked with a long-term risk of Parkinson's disease, researchers have found.

However, whether you buy long-life juices (UHT) or freshly squeezed juice, it doesn't make a great deal of difference to the juice's nutritional profile. Researchers found that long-life juices contained, on average, just as many nutrients and plant chemicals as fresh ones.

The American Academy of Pediatrics issued a policy statement in 2001 about the use of fruit juice for children. They concluded that fruit juice offers no benefits for infants younger than 6 months and no benefits over whole fruits for children over 6 months, and therefore children should be encouraged to eat whole fruits rather than fruit juice. They also found that excessive consumption may be associated with diarrhoea, flatulence and abdominal distension, and also with tooth decay and overweight as outlined above. In addition, they made the recommendations in the box overleaf.

JUICE – NUTRIENT CONTENT PER 100ML					
	Cals	Total carbs	Sugars	Vitamin C	Minerals
Apple	38	9.9g	9.9g	14mg	110mg pot
Pineapple	41	10.5g	10.5g	11mg	6mg mag, 53mg pot
Orange	36	8.8g	8.8g	39mg	8mg mag, 150mg pot
Tomato	14	3g	3g	8mg	230mg pot, 10mg mag 230mg sod

- Infants should not be given juice at bedtime
- Intake of fruit juice should be limited to 170ml a day for children aged 1–6 and to 325ml or two servings a day for children aged 7–18
- Infants, children and adolescents should not drink unpasteurized juice
Source: The American Academy of Pediatrics, 2001

See also: Apples p74, Bananas p77, Berry Fruits p80, Citrus Fruits pp93–94, Exotic Fruits p109, Fruit p129–30, Grapes p133, Pears p159, Stone Fruits p181, Teeth and Gums p189–90, Appendix 1 pp246–7 for a list of phytochemicals and their best sources.

JUNK FOOD

The Collins English Dictionary definition of junk food is 'food that is low in nutritional value'. This is a good starting point, but something of a simplification. Strictly speaking, 'nutritional value' refers to the amount of essential nutrients a food contains (fat, carbohydrates, protein, vitamins, minerals and so on). And, although there are a few 'junk' foods which certainly don't contain any essential nutrients (for example, many carbonated soft drinks), many foods that are typically described as 'junk' do contain a variety of nutrients that are necessary for health (for example, beefburgers have protein, iron, and B vitamins).

So not all perceived junk food is all bad – or as bad as it could be – but neither is all food that is marketed as 'good' or 'healthy' as good or healthy as it could be. The food industry has huge powers of persuasion; the ability to make you think something is good even when logic says it isn't. Their clever marketing teams can almost always come up with something good to say about even the most nutritionally defunct 'food' you could imagine. Fizzy sugary additive-rich calorific tooth-unfriendly drink? Ah – it's got added vitamin C, and it helps prevent dehydration.

Sadly, many of the processed foods offered in the shops today have a nutritional profile almost the complete opposite of what health departments throughout the Western World advise is 'good for us'. As the UK Food Standards Agency says, 'We should only be eating small amounts of foods containing fat and sugar'. In the USA, the Food and Nutrition Service says that only 2% of young people meet all the recommended guidelines in what they eat, and they lay a lot of the blame on the food manufacturers. 'Compared with home-prepared foods, food made outside the home contains more of the nutrients that Americans over-consume, such as fat and saturated fat, and less of those that they under-consume, such as calcium, fibre, and iron.'

RATING JUNK FOODS

Because it is not easy to decide what food/drink is good, what is acceptable, what is barely acceptable and what is probably unacceptable, here I aim to help you decide by offering a set of ten straightforward criteria. These are based on two premises – the first of which is that 'junk' food contains *too much* of the nutrients that we are told by international health departments and by nutritional scientists are not good for us in excess.

The first five on my list – excess calories, fat, saturated fat, sugar and sodium – come into this category. These are the 'big bad five'. While many people realize which foods are high in fat, often added sugars and sodium are harder to spot. According to figures published by the National Health and Medical Research Council of Australia, 75% of sodium and 73% of sugar in our diets comes from that added in food processing.

Then I add a sixth category, to which governments pay little attention but which, according to a growing amount of evidence, seems to be a pertinent addition to the list – non-essential additives, items such as flavourings, colourings, high levels of preservatives, and so on.

The four final criteria are based on whether or not a potential junk food makes a significant contribution to your child's intake of items that, research shows, many children fall short on – fruits, vegetables, dietary fibre and certain vitamins and minerals. However well a food may score on the first six criteria, if it doesn't add something positive to the diet in these respects, it may not be 'high junk', but is not a particularly useful food for over-regular consumption either.

First we look at the ten criteria in a little more detail, and then the table on page 142 shows you a selection of 20 perceived 'junk' foods, analysed and scored using these criteria. The higher the score the more compatible this item may be with the word 'junk'.

High calorie contribution: As we have seen in the sections in this book on obesity, many children are now officially classed as overweight or obese, and should reduce their calorie intake and take more exercise. Although for children who are underweight a high calorie contribution may be a plus factor, research shows that many overweight children are the highest consumers of junk food. Foods which offer a high ratio of calories to nutritional benefit are the particular high-calorie foods to limit. Many typical junk foods come in larger-than-average servings, which is another pitfall to look out for. A food/drink receives a 'bullet' in the table overleaf if it would be likely to make a significant contribution to excess calorie intake if consumed regularly.

High in total fat: Because fat is very calorie dense, at 9 calories per gram, foods containing a high proportion of fat tend to be high in calories (see the previous criterion). Hardly surprising then that research shows that it is a high-fat diet which most contributes to obesity. Although pre-school children should have more dietary fat than older children, it is important to limit total fat intake to around 30–35% in schoolchildren and to try to ensure that a high proportion of total fat is in the form of polyunsaturated or monounsaturated fats. A food that scores badly in this section is likely to be high in total fat and low in the 'good' fats. Criteria for high fat (and saturated fat) content appear in Fats and Oils pp110–12.

High in saturated or trans fats: Of all the different types of fat, it is saturated fats and trans fats that are most linked with health problems, including cardiovascular diseases, a growing problem in the young. Foods high in saturates and trans fats score a bullet in this section.

High in sugars: A high-sugar diet is linked with obesity, dental caries and possible nutrient deficiencies. The US Department of Agriculture Center for Nutrition Policy reports that 59% of high sugar consumers also consume too many calories and that high sugar consumers eat significantly less fruit, vegetables, milk and grains than others. As the UK Department of Health has set maximum non-milk extrinsic sugar intake at 60g a day, foods that contain more than 10g sugar in a portion will score a point in this section.

High in sodium: Many snack foods and fast foods are high in sodium. A high sodium intake is linked with high blood pressure and cardiovascular disease. The UK government is currently proposing to limit sodium intake for children aged 7–10 to 2g a day (equivalent to 5g salt). Main meal items containing

JUNK FOODS – A COMPARISON

	Cals	Total fat	Sat fat	Sugars	Sodium	Additives	Fruit	Veg	Fibre	Nutrients	Score
Beefburger in bap, ¼ lb		★	★		★	★	★	★	★		7
French fries, average	★	★					★	★	★		5
Crisps, cheese and onion, standard pack	★	★	★		★	★	★	★	★	★	9
Cola, regular size takeaway	★			★		★	★	★	★	★	7
Chocolate, milk, 50g bar	★	★	★	★			★	★	★	★	8
Sweets, 50g	★			★		★	★	★	★	★	7
Pork pie, 140g individual	★	★	★		★		★	★	★		7
Pizza, margarita, half a two-serving pizza	★	★	★		★			★			5
Chicken nuggets, 6		★	★		★	★	★	★	★		7
Salted peanuts, 50g	★	★	★		★		★	★			7
Strawberry milkshake, regular size	★	★	★	★		★	★	★	★		8
Cookies, choc chip, 2		★	★	★	★		★	★	★	★	8
Frosted breakfast cereal, 30g serving			★	★		★	★	★			5
Ice cream, vanilla, 100ml serving	★	★	★	★			★	★	★		7
Instant noodle snack, chow mein variety, 90g pack	★	★	★		★	★	★	★			7
Rich fruit cake, 50g slice	★			★				★			3
Iced bun, 65g	★	★	★	★		★	★	★	★	★	9
Jam doughnut, average, 1	★	★	★	★			★	★	★	★	8
Apple pie, 110g plus custard 100ml	★	★	★	★				★			5
Strawberry Cornetto	★	★	★	★		★	★	★	★	★	9

J

more than 0.6g sodium a day or snack or breakfast foods containing more than 0.4g sodium a day and therefore likely to contribute to raising children's sodium intake to over this level, will score a point in this section. Children younger than 7 need to try to eat even less salt. Note – sodium isn't the same as salt. When checking food labels, note that 1g of salt is equivalent to 0.4g sodium, and that 1g sodium equals 2.5g salt.

Additives: Foods that contain artificial colourants and flavourings, such as brightly coloured sweets or drinks, are likely to be low in nutrients. Artificial ingredients tend to be added by manufacturers to enhance what would otherwise be a poorly flavoured unappetising-looking product. There is also new scientific evidence to show that additives *can* contribute to hyperactive behaviour in children, and in the longer-term we don't know the whole story. In my opinion and that of many experts, it is worth limiting your child's intake of such additives. Foods with a high additive content score a point in this section.

Fruit content low: A regular intake of fruit is important for children. Fruit intake is linked with reduced risk of asthma, nutrient deficiencies and many other problems. Children who eat a diet high in junk foods tend to eat low amounts of fruit.

Vegetables content low: A regular intake of vegetables is important for children. See 'Fruit content low' above.

Fibre content low: Small children don't need a lot of dietary fibre, but as children get older they do need to increase their fibre intake to help prevent constipation and to regulate blood sugars. Fibre also helps children to feel full and may stop them over-consuming calories, and may help prevent diseases such as CHD (coronary heart disease). Many junk food items are low in insoluble and soluble fibre. Main meal foods with a fibre content less than 3g/portion and other foods with less than 1.5g/portion receive a bullet for being low in dietary fibre.

Low in essential nutrients: While not every food should be expected to provide a complete range of nutrients, everything that children eat should ideally provide at least some essential nutrients. Key nutrients for children include protein, calcium, iron, vitamin C, and omega-3 essential fatty acids. A food that provides none of these gets a bullet.

See also: Beef p78, Chips pp90–2, Fats and Oils pp110–12, Fizzy Drinks p114, Food Additives pp114–17, Processed Food pp164–5, Salt pp171–4, Takeaways pp186–8.

KIWI FRUIT
see Exotic Fruits

LACTOSE INTOLERANCE
see Feeding Your Child: 'Weaning and the Pre-school Years', Food Allergies, Milk

LAMB

NUTRIENT CONTENT PER 100G			
	Cals	Tot Fat	Prot
Lean lamb fillet	153	8g	20.2g
Lamb mince	196	13.3g	19g
Lamb chop, lean and fat	277	22g	26.5g
Leg, roast (no skin)	203	9.4g	29.7g
Shoulder, roast	298	22.1g	24.7g

Lean cuts of lamb – such as leg or fillet or steaks – are high in protein and reasonably low in fat and saturated fat, particularly when cooked so that some more of the fat runs out and is discarded – say roasted on a trivet or grilled. The fattier cuts, such as shoulder of lamb, lamb chops and some lamb mince, however, are just about the fattiest meat you can buy. The lamb mince figures above, from *The Composition of Foods*, are averages only and the researchers found that mince varied in its fat content per 100g from 8.1g for very lean minced lamb up to 22.8g for the cheaper minces.

Because of lamb's good B vitamin and mineral content, it can make a welcome addition to a child's diet – but my advice is to go for the leaner cuts

L

(e.g. leg, not shoulder, steaks not chops), buy best-quality lean mince and, if using lamb in stews and casseroles, cook it then refrigerate, remove the layer of fat that solidifies on the top and then reheat to piping hot before serving.

Recently there has been concern that BSE may be present in sheep as some sheep ate the same feed that gave cattle BSE in the UK. As I write, the Food Standards Agency hasn't issued any advice against the consumption of lamb or other sheep products. Until more is known, however, it is wise to avoid feeding the family sausages in casing made from sheep's intestines (about 15% of sausages sold in the UK), and mutton (meat from sheep over 1 year old). More up-to-date information can be found at www.foodstandards.gov.uk.

See also: BSE pp84–5, Fats and Oils pp110–12, Meat p145.

LETHARGY

Most children go through bouts of lethargy and, by the teenage years, they can seem permanently exhausted and needing twelve hours sleep a night just to function! This is partly caused by the huge amount of growth that children have to do. There really are 'growth spurts' which occur after relatively long periods when they don't seem to grow a lot.

If your child seems unduly lethargic for more than the odd day, or without an obvious cause – such as insomnia, lack of sleep, anxiety, growth spurt, boredom or having done a great deal of physical or other tiring activity – it would be worth getting him or her checked out by your doctor. Problems such as anaemia or other illnesses can cause fatigue, as can any illness lasting more than a few days. Some food allergies can also be the culprit, or clinical depression could be the cause. Girls who are having their periods can become very tired in the few days before the period starts. ME (chronic fatigue syndrome) is not unusual in adolescence and, as the name suggests, can cause long-term severe fatigue.

A poor diet and lifestyle can certainly make matters worse and a good one can help. Try out the tips given below for a few weeks and you may see a real difference in your child – though these tips should not be tried at the expense of seeing your doctor.

TIPS TO HELP BEAT YOUR CHILD'S FATIGUE

• Encourage him or her to take regular daily exercise (e.g., a half-hour cycle ride, walk or roller skating) in the fresh air – this can produce better results than going to bed, by oxygenating the system and helping to lift depression.

• Discourage the use of lots of caffeine-rich drinks, e.g. cola and coffee, or alcohol, which may cause long-term fatigue.

• Discourage too many highly refined carbohydrates (such as white bread, biscuits, cakes, sweets) in the diet, particularly during the day, as these can produce feelings of lethargy and 'head weariness' – they tend to have a soporific effect. Eaten alone, they can also cause low blood sugar levels, which can lead to feelings of tiredness.

• The ideal lunch is one that contains good amounts of lean protein with a little unrefined carb, a little fat and plenty of fresh fruit/salad/vegetables. Save high-carb meals for the evening, when the soporific effect may be beneficial and aid sleep, but even so try to ensure they are not too highly refined as there are higher levels of beneficial vitamins and minerals in unrefined carbs.

• Offer regular nutritious meals and try to prevent older children from dieting. Crash-type diets led to low blood sugar.

• Sometimes children who follow a faddy diet, or vegetarians or vegans, may not be getting sufficient iron or B vitamins in the diet, a lack of both of which can cause fatigue.

• A generally healthy diet, containing sufficient of all the vitamins and minerals, and enough protein, complex carbohydrate and fat, should help avoid chronic fatigue and lethargy.

• Long periods in front of the TV or computer, combined with lack of circulating air in a sitting room or bedroom can contribute to fatigue.

See also: Anaemia p73 , Carbohydrates pp87–8. Food Allergies pp117–19, Insomnia pp138–9 Nerves and Anxiety p150, Appendix 2 pp250–1 for Growth Charts.

LIVER

Nutrients per 100g fried lambs' liver:

Cals	237	Prot	30g
Tot fat	12.9g	Vits	A, B group
Sat fat	3.5g	Mins	iron, zinc, selenium
Chol	400mg		

Liver and all other offal meats, such as kidneys, is very high in a range of vitamins and minerals and is a good source of protein. Liver is moderately high in fat, but kidneys are leaner if you remove the fat which encases them. However, offal is high in cholesterol and so anyone following a low-cholesterol diet should avoid it.

Liver is very high in vitamin A (19,700µg per 100g, which is nearly three times the recommended upper regular intake of 7,500µg for women and 9,000µg for men). Large amounts of vitamin A are toxic and can cause birth defects in children, so liver should be avoided during pregnancy.

> For children, regular daily intakes of vitamin A shouldn't exceed 900µg under the age of 1; 1,800µg between 1 and 3 years old; 3,000µg from 4 to 6 years old; 4,500µg from 6 to 12 years old and 6,000µg for adolescents. Therefore it is best not to give anything more than tiny amounts of liver to small children once a week, and moderate portions no more than once a week to older children.

See also: Appendix 1 pp240–6 for other sources of vitamin A, iron, etc.

MEAT

Meat is the major source of what is sometimes called 'first-class' protein in most Western children's diets. This means that it contains all the essential amino acids (the 'building blocks' of complete protein) that we need. Dairy produce contains complete protein, but most plant sources of protein – e.g. most pulses, and the protein in grains, nuts and seeds – only contain a proportion of these eight amino acids and so vegetarians need to 'mix and match' their protein sources to get all eight necessary for growth, repair and health.

Meat is also a good source of B vitamins (important for growth, nervous system, digestion and usage of food, and body maintenance) and minerals especially iron and zinc as well as selenium.

Many people feel that meat is not 'healthy' as it contains high levels of fat and saturated fat. If you choose lean cuts, however, beef, pork and even lamb can be low or moderate in both. Some 'new meats', such as venison and ostrich, are very low in fat indeed. The fat in fattier cuts of meat can be reduced by sensible cooking – such as grilling until the fat runs off, or casseroling then allowing to cool and removing the fat from the top. You can also purchase cooks' brushes which soak up liquid fat from the top of dishes.

See also: Bacon p77, Beef p 78, BSE pp84–5, Fats and Oils pp110–12, Food Poisoning pp122–3, Food Safety pp123–6, Lamb p143–4, Liver p145, Pork p161, Poultry and Game pp162–5, Protein pp165–6, Sausages pp175–6, Appendix 1 pp240–7 for a full list of vitamin and mineral sources.

MICROWAVES

Although there has been much speculation over the years that using microwave ovens may cause health problems – from reduced immune function to cancer to blood disorders – there is, as yet, no proof of this, and the UK Government has not found any cause for alarm.

Microwaves work by generating electromagnetic energy (microwaves) via a magnetron inside the oven. These waves agitate the water molecules in food (all food contains a high percentage of water) and this vibration causes the food to heat up and cook.

Some experts feel that microwave cooking is actually healthier than some other methods, as more of the water-soluble vitamins B and C may be retained and foods such as fish or chicken can be cooked without any added fat.

For family cooking, microwave ovens tend not to be practical as they can't cook large amounts at a time. However, if you do use the microwave to reheat food or cook for your children, below are some government guidelines on safety precautions. Utmost care should be taken to heat foods right through until piping hot, especially if a food has been defrosted, to prevent food poisoning.

It is best not to heat infant's formula milk in the microwave as it is very easy to overheat – use a jug of warm water instead.

MICROWAVE SAFETY GUIDELINES

- Follow manufacturers' instructions.
- Follow instructions on food packaging.
- Use the right microwave oven equipment (e.g. containers). Anything with metal in it or on it is not suitable – use glass, paper or microwaveable plastics.
- Defrost food thoroughly before cooking or according to food packaging instructions.
- Cook thick pieces of food for longer than thin pieces of food. Place thick pieces towards the outside of a dish or plate and thin ones in the centre.
- Stir food during the cooking process to avoid hot and cold spots.
- Before serving, ensure food is piping hot throughout.
- Allow food to stand for a few minutes before eating.
- Keep the oven clean.

MILK

Milk is a good source of calcium (in fact, it is the main source of calcium in many Western children's diets), which is linked with prevention of heart disease, osteoporosis and colon cancer. It also contains some B vitamins, is one of the few major sources of iodine and is a reasonable source of protein. Full-fat milk is also a good source of the fat-soluble vitamin A. The proportion of saturates in milk fat is quite high, but if you want to watch your child's overall fat intake, semi-skimmed milk is a good compromise as it contains just over 4g of fat in an average 250ml glass, and only 2.75g saturates.

MILK – NUTRIENT CONTENT PER 100ML

	Tot Fat	Tot Carbs	Vits
Whole milk	3.9g	4.5g	B2, B12
Semi-skimmed milk	1.7g	4.7g	B2, B12
Skimmed milk	0.2g	4.4g	B2, B12
Goats' milk	3.7g	4.4g	A, B2, B12
Soya milk, unsweetened*	1.6g	0.5g	B2, E

* Calcium-fortified soya milk contains 89mg calcium/100ml.

Cows' milk shouldn't be given to children under the age of 6 months, and not as a drink until after 1 year old, and neither should ordinary unmodified goats' or other types of milk. Until aged 1, a formula should be given if not breast-feeding, although from 6 to 12 months small amounts of milk can be given within foods (e.g. custard, cheese sauce). Whole milk should be given to children under the age of 2, semi-skimmed milk can be given between 2 and 5, and skimmed milk may be given after 5.

COWS'-MILK PROTEIN (CMP) ALLERGY

Quite a significant proportion of small children (about 2% of infants) are allergic to cows'-milk protein (CMP) and this allergy is often outgrown by the age of 3 to 5. In fact, one report says that 50% recover by the time they are 1-year-old, up to 75% by 2 and up to 90% by 3.

CMP allergy symptoms may include sickness and diarrhoea, eczema, wheezing, coughing and a runny nose. Symptoms usually occur within a week to a month of first exposure to cows'-milk formula. Children with CMP allergy need to avoid all cows'-milk protein and products containing it or

M

derivatives (see below) and infants usually take a casein or whey hydrolysate milk formula instead, which is often the best option as many children with CMP are also allergic to soya formula and may also have a reaction to modified goats'- or sheep's-milk proteins.

CMP – READING THE LABELS

Once a child is diagnosed, all cows'-milk protein needs to be excluded from the diet. This includes several products that aren't immediately recognisable as such. Obviously all cows' milk needs to be excluded, as well as products made from cows' milk which contain protein – e.g. butter, cheese, yoghurt. Less obvious sources are those containing, or that may contain, casein or whey (see box below). Look out for these terms on labels: caseinate, caseinate salts, sodium caseinate, whey protein, whey sugar, whey syrup, hydrolysed whey.

If your child has CMP allergy, or you suspect it, you should see your doctor, who should refer you to a dietitian for further advice. The dietitian will be able to supply a comprehensive list of foods free of cows'-milk protein.

FOODS WITH 'HIDDEN' CMP PROTEIN

- Soya cheese, vegetarian cheese
- Margarine and low-fat spreads
- Some breads
- Biscuits
- Sausages
- Rusks
- Non-milk-fat ice cream
- Muesli and other breakfast cereals
- Fish fingers and fish in batter
…and possibly many other products

LACTOSE INTOLERANCE

Lactose intolerance is allergy to the milk sugars (lactose) rather than the protein, and is a result of the absence of the lactase enzyme which digests the lactose. This causes bloating, stomach ache and other uncomfortable symptoms, and is more common in Asian, Indian, Afro-Caribbean, and middle Eastern populations, who traditionally didn't drink cows' milk. It is also more common in older

children of these races, affecting only about 5% of children under 4 but 33% at age 13. About 2% of the total UK population has lactose intolerance.

Avoiding lactose is not easy as it is used widely in the food industry and may even be present in crisps and sausages. Ironically, several dairy products are not lactose-rich. Hard cheeses contain very little and bio yoghurt may also be tolerated because the fermentation makes them easy to digest. Again, your dietitian can help by suggesting a suitable balanced diet for a lactose-intolerant child and by providing lists of foods that can be eaten and of which should be avoided. In recent years it has been found that tolerance to lactose can be improved by gradually introducing very tiny amounts of lactose-containing foods, such as cows' milk, into the diet. Some experts find this treatment controversial, but it does seem to work for many. However it should be tried only with the help of a qualified dietitian.

MILK SAFETY

There has also been controversy in the last few years about the possibility that our milk is contaminated with antibiotics, pesticide residues, hormones that have been fed to cows to increase their yield (BST) and so on. A bacterium (*Mycobacterium avium* subsp. *paratuberculosis* or MAP) which has been linked to Crohn's Disease (a human disease of the bowel) has been found in 1.8% of UK pasteurized milk samples and the food poisoning bug E coli was also found in a few samples. There is even speculation that BSE may be passed to humans in cows' milk. At present there are no official guidelines to consumers on avoiding these potential problems. However, low-fat milk contains fewer residues than whole milk because the toxins are stored in the fat. Also, organic milk will not contain BST, the yield hormone, and should be free from pesticide residues. The ultra-heat-treated (UHT) milk tested contained no MAP, and pasteurized skimmed milk contained lower levels than semi-skimmed or whole milk.

See also: 'Successful Weaning' pp11–12, 'Allergies and Infants' pp16–17, Dairy Produce p98, Food Allergies pp117–19, Food Poisoning pp122–3, Food Safety pp123–6, Pulses pp166–8.

M

MINERALS

Fifteen different minerals are essential in the human diet: calcium, iron, zinc, selenium, magnesium, potassium, iodine, chromium, sodium, phosphorous, copper, fluoride, manganese, cobalt and sulphur. The three main functions of minerals are: in body structure – e.g. calcium is a major component of bone; to control the balance of body fluids; and to regulate all the body functions such as the nervous system and the blood supply. Adequate amounts of minerals are vital for child growth, development and health.

Minerals are present in almost all foods and drinks – even water – but the modern diet may be deficient in several of those listed above, such as iron, selenium and magnesium. Minerals are best absorbed as a natural part of food/drink rather than as supplements – and several factors hinder or improve their absorption. Several of the minerals are very unlikely to be deficient in the body as they are so widely present and/or are needed in very small quantities. An excess of minerals in the diet isn't wise either, as they can be toxic in large amounts.

The table opposite lists the minerals that may be in short supply in the diet, with their functions, main sources (all sources not listed) and recommended daily amounts for children – sodium is dealt with in the A-Z entry on Salt pages 171–4.

There are no UK RDAs (recommended daily amounts) for the mineral chromium, but this mineral is important as it helps to promote correct insulin response (diabetes) and blood sugar levels. Meat, offal, eggs, seafood, cheese, whole grains, vegetables and nuts are good sources of chromium. A diet high in refined foods and sugars may stimulate excretion of chromium.

Fluoride is another essential mineral, but again there are no UK RDAs and deficiency is unlikely. In areas where tap water is fluoridated, high intakes may lead to mottling of the teeth, but water fluoridation has decreased incidence of tooth decay by 50%. Teenagers obtain most of their fluoride intake from water, soft drinks and tea.

See also: Diabetes p101, Salt p171–4, Appendix 1 pp243–6 for a full list of mineral sources.

MINERALS THAT MAY BE IN SHORT SUPPL

Mineral	What it does
Calcium (Ca)	major constituent of bones and teeth; vital to ensure peak bone mass; helps control muscle/heart function and nervous system.
Iron (Fe)	carries oxygen through the bloodstream; boosts immune system and helps healing.
Zinc (Zn)	essential for growth, development and fertility; antioxidant, boosts immune system, helps wound healing.
Selenium (Se)	powerful antioxidant protecting against heart disease and cancer; normal growth, fertility and metabolism.
Magnesium (Mg)	component of bone, works with calcium; releases energy from food and helps nutrient absorption; regulates body functions; helps heart health.
Potassium (K)	works in conjunction with sodium to regulate body fluid; regulates cell and heart function and blood pressure.
Iodine (I)	essential for the functioning of the thyroid gland to maintain correct body metabolism and cholesterol levels, regulates oxygen uptake and other vital body functions. During pregnancy vital for development of the nervous system of the foetus.

Deficiency can cause	Found in	Notes	Recommended daily amounts
ickets, poor bone structure, later steoporosis; heart problems.	dairy produce, dark leafy green vegetables, fortified white bread.	absorption helped by vitamin D and essential fatty acids. Absorption hindered by phytates in insoluble fibre (e.g. wheat bran) and by oxalates in spinach, rhubarb, beetroot, chocolate and by tannin in tea and compounds in coffee.	0–12months 525mg; 1–3 350mg; 4–6 450mg; 7–10 550mg; males 11–18 1000mg; females 11–18 800mg.
naemia, tiredness, weakness.	red meat, dark leafy greens, pulses, whole grains, seeds, offal, nuts, dried fruit, fortified cereals.	absorption is helped by vitamin C in the same meal; hindered by phytates, oxalates, tannin and coffee (see Calcium). Excess iron can cause stomach upsets, constipation, kidney damage.	0–3months 1.7mg; 4–6 months 4.3mg; 7–12 months 7.8mg; 1–3 years 6.9mg; 4–6 years 6.1mg; 7–10 years 8.7mg; males 11–18 11.3mg; females 11–18 14.8mg.
etarded growth/sexual levelopment; poor immunity to isease and infection.	meat, dairy produce, offal, seeds, shellfish, nuts.	absorption hindered – as calcium and iron. Vegans may need to take special care to ensure adequate intake. Diet very high in zinc may inhibit copper absorption.	0–6 months 4mg; 7 months–3 years 5mg; 4–6 years 6.5mg; 7–10 years 7mg; 11–14 years 9mg; males 15–18 years 9.5mg; females 15–18 years 7mg.
ncreased risk of cancer and heart lisease, linked with miscarriage and rthritis.	nuts, offal, pulses, fish, seeds, meat.	levels in foods vary tremendously depending on levels in the soil where plant foods grow or where animals graze. Levels in the UK soil may be low. Toxic in excess; upper limit for adults is set at 450µg a day.	0–3 months 10µg; 4–6 months 13µg; 7–12 months 10µg; 1–3 years 15µg; 4–6 years 20µg; 7–10 years 30µg 11–14 years 45µg; males 15–18 70µg; females 15–18 60µg.
eart problems, muscle weakness, ramp, appetite loss.	whole grains, nuts, seeds, leafy greens, hard tap water.	less than half of dietary magnesium is absorbed; absorption may be hindered by a diet rich in sweet foods.	0–3 months 55mg; 4–6 months 60mg; 7–9 months 75mg; 10–12 months 80mg; 1–3 years 85mg; 4–6 years 120mg; 7–10 years 200mg; 11–14 years 280mg; 15–18 years 300mg.
aised blood pressure; heart problems.	fruits and vegetables, pulses, nuts.	high sodium (salt) intake increases body's need for potassium. Diuretics and laxatives increase excretion.	0–3 months 800mg; 4–6 months 850mg; 7–12 months 700mg; 1–3 years 800mg; 4–6 years 1,100mg; 7–10 years 2,000mg; 11–14 years 3,100mg; 15–18 years 3,500mg.
goitre, malfunctions of the thyroid gland, including underactive thyroid which can lead to slowing of metabolic rate, weight gain, coldness, constipation.	milk, seafood, seaweed.	foods from the brassica family (e.g. cabbage), sweet potatoes, corn and lima beans inhibit absorption of iodine. Almost half the populations of Europe have been found to be deficient in iodine.	0–3 months 50µg; 4–12 months 60µg; 1–3 years 70µg; 4–6 years 100µg; 7–10 years 110µg; 11–14 years 130µg; 15–18 years 140µg.

M

MUSCLE DEVELOPMENT

In order to build optimum lean tissue (muscle) in their bodies, children need a diet that contains adequate protein, minerals – including magnesium – and adequate calories. If enough calories aren't provided for the child's energy needs, the body will use its stored glycogen (glucose stores), then its stored body fat and then its lean tissue for energy. Children also need to take adequate exercise in order to convert dietary protein into muscle.

MUSHROOMS

Nutrients per 100g:

Cals	*13*	(of which) sugars	*0.2g*
Tot fat	*0.5g*	Fibre	*1.1g*
Sat fat	*0.1g*	Vits	*B2, B3, folate*
Prot	*1.8g*	Mins	*pot, sel*
Tot carbs	*0.4g*		

Exotic and dark-gilled mushrooms (e.g. shiitake) may contain various types of phytochemical, including lentinan, which may help to fight cancers, increase immunity and fight bacterial infections.

See also: Phytochemicals p160.

NERVES AND ANXIETY

Most children go through periods of feeling anxious or nervous and can suffer stress through life events such as exams, moving home or having friendship or school problems. If an anxious child has trouble sleeping, this will exacerbate the problem.

A diet rich in the vitamin B group, and the minerals calcium and magnesium is known to help the nervous system to cope – calcium has been called nature's tranquillizer. Prolonged stress depletes the body of the water-soluble B and C vitamins, so it might be wise to ensure that an anxious or stressed child has a diet rich in these (or you could consider providing a supplement). Short-term anxiety can be eased a little with a high-carbohydrate meal or snack, such as pasta, baked potato or a sandwich. Carbohydrate foods are known to have a soporific effect. Exercise also helps to calm the nerves by releasing endorphins.

A child who is stressed out or worried may lose his or her appetite but it is counterproductive to try to force a child to eat at such times. Indeed, stress can produce feelings of nausea and the child may even be sick if forced to eat.

TIPS FOR FEEDING AN ANXIOUS CHILD
• Offer very small portions of foods that are normally favourites.
• Avoid anything too rich – e.g. chocolate cake, fatty meats, cheese sauces.
• Provide food in as relaxed an atmosphere as possible: music – even upbeat – can ease nerves. If eating as a family, try to ensure the conversation is light and chatty.
• Research shows that people eat more if there is a variety of different foods available to choose from, so go for buffet-style meals and let the child pick what they want.
• Serve a meal after the child has taken exercise – preferably outdoors.
• Don't worry too much, appetite usually returns before long. However, if the child is stressed or anxious for more than a few days you need to try to resolve the problems causing this and, if necessary, see your doctor.

THE FAMILY THAT EATS TOGETHER...
One Spanish study has found that families who don't eat meals together produce children with more psychological problems than families who do.

See also: Appetite Loss p74, Eating Disorders pp105–7, Fussy Eating and Food Refusal pp131–2, Insomnia pp138–9, Supplements pp185–6.

NUTRIENTS

'Nutrients' is the term used to describe the various components of what we eat and drink that will make a contribution to our nutritional intake. These nutrients are the macronutrients – carbohydrate, fat, protein and alcohol, which provide the calorie content of our diets; and the micronutrients – the vitamins, minerals, and other compounds which the body needs in small amounts. Dietary fibre isn't a nutrient as such, but is necessary for body function and, of course, we also need water.

See also: Minerals pp148–9, Vitamins pp194–6, Appendix I pp240–9 for sources of all micronutrients.

NUTS

Nuts are extremely high in fat (for example, 90% of the calories in Brazils are fat calories) but most nuts are fairly low in saturated fat and high in mono-unsaturates, with the exception of walnuts, which are high in polyunsaturates and contain good amounts of the omega-3 fats as alpha-linolenic acid. In other words, they contain the 'healthy' fats. The exception is the coconut, which is very high in a saturated fat called lauric acid and other saturates.

Nuts are also a good source of protein and fibre, but one of their main benefits is that they are packed with a selection of vitamins and minerals. Almonds, hazelnuts and pecans are some of the best food sources of antioxidant vitamin E, and almonds, cashews, hazelnuts and walnuts contain good amounts of folate. Almonds are a very good source of calcium – a handful contains about a quarter of a teenage girl's daily needs – while Brazils, hazelnuts and walnuts also contain very good amounts.

Iron and zinc are present in good amounts in most nuts, but cashews and pecans are particularly high in zinc. Brazils are unique amongst nuts in their very high content of the antioxidant mineral selenium – the figure below is an average – sometimes they contain as much as 690mg per 100g.

Walnuts are a good source of the phytochemical ellagic acid, also found in many fruits. Several research projects have linked regular nut intake with protection from heart disease and some cancers – possibly because of their high antioxidant content. More than

NUTS – NUTRIENTS PER 100G, SHELLED WEIGHT, RAW*

	Almond	Brazil	Cashew	Coconut	Hazel	Pecan	Walnut
Calories	612	682	574	604	650	689	688
Total fat	55.8g	68.2g	48g	62g	63.5g	70g	68.5g
Saturated fat	4.4g	16.4g	9.6g	53.4g	4.7g	5.7g	5.6g
Protein	21g	14g	17.8g	5.6g	14g	9.2g	14.7g
Total carbs	6.9g	3g	18.2g	6.4g	6g	5.8g	3.3g
Sugars	4.2g	2.4g	4.6g	6.4g	4g	4.3g	2.6g
Fibre	7.4g	4.3g	3.2g	13.7g	6.5g	4.7g	3.5g
Vitamin E	24mg	7.2mg	1.3mg	1.3mg	25mg	44.3mg	3.8mg
Folate	48µg	21µg	68µg	9µg	72µg	39µg	66µg
Calcium	240mg	170mg	35mg	23mg	140mg	61mg	94mg
Iron	3mg	2.5mg	6.2mg	3.6mg	3.2mg	2.2mg	2.9mg
Magnesium	270mg	410mg	250mg	90mg	160mg	130mg	160mg
Selenium	2µg	254µg	34µg	12µg	2µg	12µg	3µg
Zinc	3.2mg	4.2mg	5.7mg	1mg	2mg	5.3mg	2.7mg

*For peanuts, see Peanuts pp158–9, for salted nuts see Snacks pp178–9, for pine nuts see Seeds p177.

one trial has showed that a diet high in nuts significantly reduces LDL cholesterol in the blood. So it may be wise to give children small packs of fresh nuts to snack on rather than crisps or sweets. However, nuts need to be bought unbroken and stored in cool dark conditions to retain their nutrients. Nut oils are good in dressings and should also be kept in cool dark conditions.

> **FOODS THAT MAY CONTAIN NUTS:**
>
> • Chocolates • Sweets • Toffee
> • Biscuits • Cakes • Desserts
> • Baked goods
> …any foods produced in a factory which also makes foods containing nuts

Nut allergies and choking: Nuts shouldn't, though, be given to small children, as they can easily choke on them – avoid nuts until the age of 5 although nut butters can be given earlier. Although peanut allergy is quite common in children, some children are allergic to other nuts. The box above lists foods that are likely to contain nuts, but a high number of processed foods may have a 'may contain nuts/nut traces' on the label as a precaution. Supermarkets and food manufacturers should be able to supply a list of their products which definitely don't contain nuts or nut traces if you ask.

See also: 'Allergies and Infants' pp16–17, 'Peanuts and Food Allergies' p23, Antioxidants p73, Fats and Oils pp110–12, Food Allergies p117–9, Peanuts pp158–9, Phytochemicals p160, Seeds p177, Snacks p178, Appendix 3 pp252–3 for contact details of relevant organisations.

OBESITY

Overweight and obesity are ever-increasing problems for children and adolescents in the Western world. Specific advice for each particular age group appears in the different parts of Feeding Your Child. Here we look at general strategies for preventing or, as necessary, reversing overweight in children.

What causes obesity?: Weight balance is maintained by matching the amount of energy (kilocalories/joules) that a person consumes in the form of food and drink, with the amount of energy that he or she expends (burns up) in the process of living and, in the case of children, growing and developing. If a child takes in more energy than he or she expends in living, then the surplus calories will be stored as body fat. The more out of kilter the energy balance is, and the more body fat is stored, the more the child gradually becomes overweight and then obese. (This can also work in reverse, see Underweight pages 190–1.) To find out whether or not your child is overweight or obese, consult the Growth Charts in Appendix 2 pages 250–1.

Why does it matter?: Children come quite naturally in all different shapes and sizes, and there is much variation in what is classed as 'normal weight'. A skinny child and a slightly plump child can both be healthy. If a child is classed as clinically overweight, however, this gives him or her an increased risk of becoming obese in the years ahead, and both clinical overweight and obesity are linked with a variety of health problems – not just when the child reaches adulthood, but often sooner.

Experts believe that childhood obesity is a main cause of increasing incidence of signs of heart disease and diabetes in children. And an overweight child has a much greater chance of becoming an overweight adult, which is linked with not only heart disease and diabetes, but also with some cancers, arthritis, stroke and several other serious health problems.

So how can overweight be prevented?: There are two ways to keep a child from gaining too much weight which should complement each other. The first is making sure that he or she takes enough regular exercise/activity. This burns calories, speeds up the metabolic rate, builds lean tissue (muscle) – which is more metabolically active than other body tissue – and also helps keep the child healthy.

Some experts believe that lack of exercise is a main factor in the increase in obesity in our children. TVs, computers, lack of organized sport at school, transport to school rather than walking or cycling – all combine to produce a sedentary lifestyle for our children. This means that they need fewer calories in

N

Obesity has increased by over 60% in the Western world in the last 10 years. If we don't tackle the problem in our youngsters, within 50 years it is estimated that over 90% of the population in the USA and UK will be clinically overweight. 'We have produced the most obese generation of children in our history' says the US Surgeon General. In the UK, one major report says that 'overweight in children is a serious public health problem'.

day-to-day living than they used to, say, 50 years ago. But they are not taking in fewer calories.

So the second way to prevent overweight and obesity in children is to make their calorie intake match their calorie needs. The healthy Eating Plans in Section 1 for the different age groups are a good starting point. They all contain a balance of carbohydrates, fat and protein, and are low on sugar and other foods that are high in calories but low in nutrients.

TIPS ON PREVENTING YOUR CHILD FROM BECOMING OBESE

Research shows that children who become overweight tend to eat higher amounts of sugar and fat, and drink more sugary drinks, than children who don't become overweight. The following tips will help to ensure that your child gets a healthy well-balanced diet without excessive calories:

• Restrict intake of sugary sweets, drinks and snacks, such as packet cakes and biscuits, to very occasional use. Fresh fruit is the best between-meal snack. Fruit teabreads or crumpets contain less fat and calories than many other baked goods.

• Restrict intake of snacks high in fat, particularly highly-processed snacks, such as crisps.

• Try to serve more fruit-based desserts (e.g. fruit salad, fruit kebabs, baked apple – see Recipes) rather than high-fat/high-sugar ready-made desserts.

• Try to get your child to drink bottled water or semi-skimmed milk rather than high-sugar drinks or full-fat milk shakes – this can save hundreds of calories.

• Cook with less fat at home. This will help the whole family reduce their fat intake.

• Try to limit visits to the burger bar or fish and chip shop. Much fast food is very high in fat and calories.

• Try to match portion sizes to your child's appetite and needs. It is better that a child feels he or she

can ask for more food if still hungry at the end of the meal, rather than piling the plate high – research shows that people (including children) tend to eat what is on their plate, even if full.

And if your child is already overweight...: Most experts feel that if a child is still growing in height, the best course of action is to try to maintain the current weight and, as the child grows taller, he or she will literally grow into correct weight. This still means exercising some control over their calorie intake so that he or she doesn't put on more weight.

If a child is obese, you should visit your doctor, who will put you in touch with a dietitian to organize a suitable eating plan, as it is unlikely that your child will slim down naturally without intervention.

Puppy fat: Some parents feel that an adolescent who is overweight may simply be suffering from 'puppy fat' – natural chubbiness that occurs at puberty and will disappear of its own accord. Although it is true that a number of children do put on weight at puberty, it is a false assumption that the weight will always disappear.

Body image: During the teens, many children take an increased interest in their body image and many, often girls, worry about their size even if they are not overweight. It is important to stay relaxed and to give your child positive feedback and encouragement, whatever their size, in order to build their self-esteem.

Even if the child is clinically overweight, they should not be made to feel they are on a 'strict diet'. Don't weigh children frequently or fret and fuss about their size or try to bully them into dieting, or make it obvious that the meal they are receiving is a special 'slimmer's' meal, especially in front of others. Children can become very downcast, depressed and self-conscious, and the parent may not always realize how bad they are feeling. It is not uncommon for adolescents who think they are overweight, or who are made to feel bad about their size by peers or family, to develop an eating disorder.

The hungry child: If an overweight child has his or her calorie intake reduced too drastically or too suddenly, he or she will probably feel both hungry and resentful. A list of healthy, appealing and hunger-reducing snacks appears in the Snacks feature on pages 178–9 and here are some tips.

• Choose snacks from foods low on the Glycaemic Index (see box below). This is an index used by dietitians to measure how long carbohydrate foods take to be absorbed into the bloodstream once they are eaten. A food that takes a short time (e.g. glucose, sugar) has a high GI rating, while one that takes a long time (e.g. pulses, apple) has a low GI rating. The Index measures only carbohydrate foods, but both fat and protein take a long time to be absorbed into the bloodstream and, when eaten with a high-GI food, have the effect of lowering its GI rating. Low-GI foods will help keep hunger at bay, medium low- or medium-GI foods are reasonably good, but high-GI foods – unless eaten as part of a meal containing fat, protein and/or low-GI carbs – will soon have the child feeling hungry again.

• Feed little and often.

• Encourage the child to eat slowly and chew carefully.

• Provide plenty of high-fibre foods, which often take longer to eat than highly-refined foods (compare eating an apple with having a glass of apple juice). Most high-fibre foods also take longer to be digested.

• Give plenty of low-calorie drinks (e.g. water) with a meal; this also helps a feeling of fullness.

THE TRAFFIC LIGHT SYSTEM

If you want a less formalized way to help your child eat fewer calories than the eating plans in Section 1, you could try the established 'traffic light' system. This categorizes foods into either Red for 'stop', Amber for 'proceed with caution' or Green for 'go'.

This way neither you nor the child needs to be worried about calorie-counting and, as long as you give him or her plenty of foods from the Green section, they needn't have a meagre plateful. As you look through the list, the categories may seem obvious, but if you stick to the rules the system really will help you control your child's weight.

NOTE: Suitable for children over the age of 5 who are overweight.

Green for Go – eat as much as you like:
• Fruit – fresh, frozen or canned in water or juice.
• Vegetables – fresh, frozen or canned in water including plainly cooked potatoes.
• Fresh salad items.
• Whole grains; whole-wheat pasta; pulses.
• Whole-grain breads, good-quality white bread and breakfast cereals.
• Dried apricots and prunes.
• Fish and shellfish.
• Lean poultry and lean red meat.
• Natural yoghurt and fromage frais; skimmed or semi-skimmed milk, low- or medium-fat cheeses.
• Quorn, tofu.

Amber for Proceed with Caution – eat in moderate portions or occasionally:
• Refined grain products (e.g. crisped rice breakfast cereal).
• Eggs, full-fat cheese, full-fat milk.
• Olive oil, groundnut oil, rapeseed oil.
• Nuts and seeds, low-fat spread, reduced-fat salad dressings.
• Fruit juice.
• Oven chips, roast potatoes, mashed potatoes.
• Low-fat custard, low-fat rice pudding.

THE GLYCAEMIC INDEX

Low-GI foods:
all pulses (e.g. baked beans, butter beans, chickpeas) and foods made from them (e.g. hummus); whole-wheat pasta; whole-rye grain; barley; apples, peaches, cherries, grapefruit, plums, oranges, pears, dried apricots; most green vegetables, avocados, onions, peppers, tomatoes, yoghurt, milk, nuts.

Medium-low- or medium-GI foods:
sweetcorn, peas, root vegetables except mashed and baked potatoes; carrots; white pasta, oats, popcorn, noodles; dark rye bread; pitta; bulghar wheat; white and brown basmati rice; slightly underripe bananas, grapes, dates, figs, kiwi fruit.

High-GI foods: glucose, sugar, honey, sweets, lollies, pineapples, raisins, melon, ripe bananas; baked or mashed potatoes; non-basmati brown and white rice; wholemeal and white bread; couscous; cornflakes and similar cereals.

Red for Stop and Think – avoid or eat in very tiny amounts or very occasionally:

• Confectionery.
• Cakes, biscuits, pastry, puddings.
• Butter, lard, margarine, cream.
• Crisps, salted nuts and other savoury salted snacks.
• Deep-fried foods, battered foods.
• Fatty cuts of meat.
• Sugary squashes and soft fizzy drinks. (Before offering 'diet' versions see Food Additives pages 114–7 and Artificial Sweeteners page 75.)
• Takeaway meals, such as fish and chips, pizza, Indian, Chinese, fried chicken. (See the Recipes section pages 211–29 for home-made versions of these, which are much healthier and lower in fat and calories.)

LOW-FAT FOODS – ANY USE?

When you go round the shops you will see dozens of products labelled 'reduced-fat' 'low-fat' or 'fat-free', and some of these are foods normally very high in fat. Is it worth buying these for your child?

Research seems to show that overall reduced-fat products don't actually help anyone to lose weight. This may be because, although the fat is reduced, the product may not be much lower in calories than a comparable high-fat version, as there may be extra sugar or other ingredients added. It may also be because when people buy reduced-fat reduced-calorie products they tend to eat more of them, or more of other foods instead.

You would be wiser to offer different types of foods to the high-fat snacks at least some of the time (e.g. fruit instead of cake) and/or reduce the amounts of high-fat food (e.g. a small bar of chocolate rather than a large one). Often, the taste/ texture/ satisfaction quotient of low-fat foods just doesn't

compare to their original counterparts. Exceptions may be low-fat spreads, which can save a lot of unnecessary fat in sandwiches, etc., and lower-fat salad dressings (e.g. diet salad cream or mayonnaise), as well as low-fat custard and rice puddings, both useful in a child's diet as quick puddings.

See also: Artificial Sweeteners p75, Eating Disorders pp105–7, Food Additives pp114–17, Hunger p137, Snacks pp178–9, Takeaways pp186–8, Underweight pp190–1, Appendix 2 pp250–1 for Growth Charts.

ONIONS

Onions, leeks and garlic are all from the same family and all contain phytochemicals called allylic sulphides which convert to allicin in the body and help to protect against heart disease, some cancers and infections such as colds and coughs. The members of the onion family are also all very low in fat. Children who aren't keen on normal onions or leeks often prefer the milder red onions, which are a good source of the phytochemical quercetin – frying them in oil rather than cooking in water helps to preserve this compound.

Garlic is a powerful antioxidant, rating third on the ORAC scale (Oxygen Radical Absorbance Capacity). Many children find the bulb too pungent, but if it is crushed and used in casseroles, stews, soups, minced meat dishes, curries and so on, the taste becomes mild. New-season's garlic is also milder than strong over-wintered garlic, and the plant chemicals it contains are more potent when the garlic is fresh.

ONION FAMILY – NUTRIENTS PER 100G RAW WEIGHT							
	Cals	Protein	Tot Carbs	Sugars	Fibre	Vitamins	Minerals
Onion	36	1.2g	7.9g	5.6g	1.4g	—	pot, calc
Leek	22	1.6g	2.9g	2.2g	2.2g	B-carotene, folate, C, E	pot, calc
NOTE: Figures for garlic are not available							

ORGANIC FOOD

Although the number of people buying organic food rose tremendously in the past decade, the majority of what we buy is still non-organic. In truth, if we all wanted an organic diet there wouldn't be enough of it to feed us all. So should you worry if you are feeding your children standard non-organic foods?

What is the difference between organic and non-organic produce? Organic produce is difficult to discuss as one entity, because it embraces so many different types of food now, from so many countries, produced in so many different growing conditions, soil types and climates, with varying degrees of care. Organic standards vary from country to country and much of the organic food that we eat in the UK is imported.

I am sure it is true to say that a lot of the 'organic' items on the supermarket shelves are not, in essence, a great deal better for you or any nicer to eat than a lot of other similar, non-organic products. And, sadly, I can't give you the definitive list of what to choose and what to ignore.

For most parents, cost is a major consideration, and organic foods range from between 20% and 70% more expensive than non-organic equivalents. So perhaps it makes sense to buy organic when it really might make the most difference to your child's diet.

NUTRITIONAL BENEFITS OF ORGANIC

Ethics and morals aside, the points to consider are nutritional benefits; taste and health benefits.

Vitamins and minerals. There have been several trials to show that fresh organic produce does sometimes contain higher levels of some vitamins and minerals than non-organic examples of the same food. This could be because organic food may be given longer to reach maturity or may be grown with more care on non-impoverished soil.

However, if organic fruit and vegetables are not stored well, or stored too long, they may also lose vital nutrients, such as vitamins B and C, before you can eat them. This is why it is important to buy your fresh produce, whether organic or not, from a shop where food is kept in cool, non-bright conditions

and turnover is high. As an example, avoid box schemes where your box of produce arrives after a day in a hot van looking decidedly wilted and sad.

It has also been shown that the water content of organically reared meats and poultry is much less than factory-farmed meat. This will mean that the meat should cook better, cut better and contain more nutrients than watery mass-market meats. B vitamins in meat will also leach away in the water that comes out of such meat when it is cooked.

Fat content. Ironically, many organic meats may contain higher levels of fat than factory meat, because traditional methods are more likely to be used, which results in fattier animals. If you choose the lower-fat ways to cook most of the time, this shouldn't be a problem. The exception is factory-farmed salmon, which becomes fattier than wild salmon because of its unnatural diet and lack of exercise.

Taste. Because proper organic food is grown in a more traditional way, it does often taste better than mass-produced food. Hastily matured food, whether it is lettuce, cucumbers, beef, salmon or chicken, doesn't have the chance to develop flavour as it should. The big food manufacturers will claim time after time that organic tastes no different. For once I cannot be objective, because I have tried both organic and non-organic versions of virtually all foods over several years, from many different sources, and I can say without doubt that a significant percentage of organic food does taste better. Often, the best-tasting organic food is that which I have sourced locally in my own area. There seems to be much less difference in imported organic produce and in processed organic foods. So if you have a choice, try to shop locally and find local produce.

The question of taste is only important because children may be more inclined to eat a healthy wholesome fresh diet – as opposed to a fast-food diet – if the food tastes good. And, of course, great-tasting food is a life-enhancer while insipid food is a depressant for adults and children alike.

Health benefits. The main reason that most people buy organic is that they want to avoid eating a wide variety of residues (e.g. pesticides, herbicides, fertilizers in plant foods, colourings and antibiotics in eggs) that may be present in mass-produced foods. These residues, if ingested in large amounts, could have potentially serious side-effects over the years. In the UK, only a very few chemicals are allowed in organic farming, while non-organic farming has a list of over 300 that can be used. Use of antibiotics, growth hormones and medicines is strictly limited, as is the use of non-organic feed to farm animals. Also, foods containing GM ingredients will not be certified as organic in the UK.

Governments in the Western world frequently test our food for what are considered safe levels of residues and usually only a small percentage of those tested prove to contain more than these levels. However, as we are being encouraged to eat more fruit and vegetables, we may get a cumulative intake that may be higher than is wise. Therefore, if you can afford to buy just some organic food, it may be sensible to invest the extra pennies in your fruits, salads and vegetables, particularly those that aren't going to be – or can't be – peeled. Peeling removes much of the residues, but along with the peel you will also be throwing away nutrients that may be concentrated in, or just under, the peel in many fruits and vegetables. Lettuces and leafy greens tend to retain more residues than other vegetables – also carrots. If not buying organic carrots, cut off the top 2cm and discard. Buy organic citrus fruits if you are going to use the peel (e.g. in marmalade or desserts) and if your children eat a lot of dried fruit, buy organic, which doesn't contain sulphur preservatives linked with allergy in some children.

Organic flour and bread are good choices, but remember that it is unlikely to keep as long as mass-market bread. Lastly, remember that more and more processed food manufacturers are jumping on the 'organic' bandwagon. Just because a pack says the contents are organic, it doesn't necessarily mean that the food inside is extra-specially good, or well made, or tasty. On the other hand – it may well be. I tried some of my son's organic tomato ketchup the other day and it really was the best I have ever tasted!

See also: Food Additives pp114–17, Food Standards pp126–7, Health Foods p135, Whole Foods pp196–7.

PAPAYA
see Exotic Fruits

PASTA

Pasta and noodles are rich in starchy carbohydrates. Wholewheat pasta contains much more fibre, B vitamins and minerals than does white pasta. Most Italian dried pasta is made without eggs, but fresh pasta and Chinese egg thread noodles do contain egg, making the fat content higher.

Children who suffer from a wheat allergy need to avoid products containing wheat, including wheat-based pasta – they should eat rice or gram flour in place of other types of carbohydrate foods.

See also: Carbohydrates pp87–8, Food Allergies pp117–19.

PASTA – NUTRIENTS PER 100G DRY WEIGHT									
	Cals	Tot Fat	Sat Fat	Protein	Tot Carbs	Sugars	Fibre	Vits	Mins
White pasta, all types	342	1.8g	trace	12g	74g	3.2g	3g	—	calc
Wholewheat pasta, all types	324	2.6g	0.4g	13.4g	66g	3.8g	8.4g	B2, B3	mag, iron
Egg noodles	391	8.2g	2.3g	12g	71.7g	1.9g	2.9g	B3	pot, calc, zinc

PASTRY

With the exception of filo, pastry is high in fat and calories. The fat content of filo will increase depending upon how much fat is added in the preparation process. Pastry made with wholemeal flour contains more vitamins and fibre than white flour pastry. Commercial pies and pastries tend to contain high amounts of trans fats. All pastry tends to contain a reasonable amount of sodium. Pies and pasties are normally very high-calorie, high-fat snacks or meals. If making pies at home, use just one crust to top the pie and make sure there is plenty of filling, to keep the calorie and fat content down.

See also: Cakes p86, Desserts pp99–100, Fats and Oils pp110–12, Meat p145, Ready Meals p168.

PEANUTS

Nutrients per 100g shelled weight fresh peanuts:

Cals	**563**	(of which) sugars	**6.2g**
Tot fat	**46g**	Fibre	**6.2g**
Sat fat	**8.7g**	Vits	**B1, B3, B6, folate, E**
Prot	**25.6g**	Mins	**pot, mag,**
Tot carbs	**12.5g**		**calc, iron, zinc**

Peanuts are not true tree nuts but ground nuts, by which name they, and the oil derived from them, are sometimes known. Peanuts contain a wide range of vitamins and minerals, and are particularly rich in potassium and magnesium. Like most nuts, they are very high in calories because of their high fat content, and so are best eaten in small portions, unless the child is underweight.

PASTRY PRODUCTS – NUTRIENT CONTENT PER 50G PORTION PASTRY OR AS STATED

	Cals	Tot Fat	Sat Fat	Chol	Protein	Tot Carbs	Sugars	Fibre	Vits	Mins	Sodium
Shortcrust	225	14g	4.3g	7mg	2.8g	23.4g	trace	1g	—	calc	200mg
Puff	186	12g	6g	15mg	6g	5.4g	1g	3g	—	—	167mg
Wholemeal	216	14.3g	4.4g	7mg	3.8g	19.3g	0.6g	2.7g	B3, E	calc, fe, zn	170mg
Filo	160	1.8g	0.2g	trace	4.4g	30g	0.6g	1.6g	—	calc	170mg
Quiche, egg/ cheese, 150g average slice	472	33g	15g	200mg	18.6g	25.6g	2.25g	1g	A, E	calc, mg, zn	550mg
Pork pie, 1 × 140g	525	38g	14.5g	75mg	14g	35g	trace	1.3g	B1,3,12	calc	910mg
Cornish pasty, 1 × 200g	535	32.6g	11.8g	66mg	13.4g	50g	1.8g	1.8g	B3, E	calc	800mg
Chicken and ham pie, individual 200g	576	35.4g	14g	64mg	18g	49.2g	3.2g	1.6g	B3	pot, calc	860mg

Peanuts are a good source of the phytochemical resveratrol which, research shows, helps to protect against heart disease and some cancers. Good-quality peanut butter has a similar nutrient and resveratrol profile to peanuts. Peanuts can be added to stir-fries, chopped and added to veggy burgers, sprinkled over salads and added to coleslaw.

Peanut allergy is significantly common in very young children, and can even be life-threatening. Groundnut oil can produce an allergic reaction in a small number of people with a peanut allergy; the oil may also be present in cosmetics.

Peanuts or peanut traces may be present in many commercial foods, including chocolates and all confectionery (e.g cakes, biscuits, desserts), and all processed foods made in factories that also handle peanuts, where contamination is a possibility. Supermarkets and food manufacturers should be able to provide you with a list of foods which definitely do not contain nuts or peanuts if you ask.

> ! Don't give peanuts to children under the age of 5 in case they have an undiagnosed peanut allergy. Whole nuts of any kind shouldn't be given to children under the age of 5 as there is a risk of choking.

See also: Food Allergies pp117–19, Minerals pp148–9, Nuts pp151–2, Phytochemicals p160, Snacks pp178–9, Spreads and Dips p180, Underweight pp190–1.

PEARS

Nutrients per average dessert pear (150g):

Cals	**60**	Fibre	**3.3g**
Prot	**0.5g**	Vits	**C (9mg)**
Tot carbs	**15g**	Mins	**pot (225mg)**
(of which) sugars	**15g**		

Pears are a fruit with a low allergy rating – i.e., children who tend to have allergies rarely have a reaction to pears. They are also a good source of the antioxidant plant chemical hydroxycinnamic acid, which has both antibacterial and anticancer action.

PEAS

Even if children don't care for most vegetables, they will usually eat peas – so it is lucky that these little legumes contain a very good range of nutrients. They are rich in vitamin C and some B vitamins, and have good amounts of potassium and calcium. Fresh peas are a good source of iron. All contain plenty of fibre. Mangetout peas are about twice as rich as ordinary peas in both vitamin C (54mg/100g) and calcium (44mg/100g), but poorer in B vitamins and potassium. Canned and/or processed peas lose some nutrients – they have very little vitamins C or B, but still have good amounts of minerals and fibre.

P

PEAS – NUTRIENTS PER 100G RAW

	Cals	Tot Fat	Sat Fat	Protein	Tot Carbs	Sugars	Fibre	Vits	Mins
Shelled frozen peas	66	0.9g	trace	5.7g	9.8g	2.6g	5g	B-carotene, B1, B3, folate, C	pot calc
Shelled fresh peas	83	1.5g	0.3g	6.9g	11.3g	2.3g	4.7g	B-carotene, B1, B3, folate, C	pot calc, iron
Mangetout peas	32	trace	trace	3.6g	4.2g	3.4g	2.3g	B-carotene, C	pot, calc

PEPPERS

Nutrients per 100g (medium sweet red pepper):

Cals	32	*(of which) sugars*	**6.1g**
Tot Fat	0.4g	*Fibre*	**1.6g**
Prot	1g	*Vits*	**Beta-carotene, B3, C**
Tot Carbs	6.4g	*Mins*	**pot**

Sweet peppers are a very useful vegetable for children as they are sweet and juicy (particularly the red, orange and yellow varieties) and can be used raw or cooked in very many dishes. Once cooked, they become sweeter and the high levels of beta-carotene that the red colours contain are better absorbed if cooked in a little oil. Sweet peppers are also very high in vitamin C. Red peppers contain a particular carotenoid antioxidant called beta-cryptoxanthin, with helps to prevent heart disease.

PERIODS AND PMS

When girls begin their periods it is common for them to suffer from period pains and other pre-menstrual symptoms, like tiredness, bloating and sugar cravings. These symptoms can be eased by following a healthy diet high in B vitamins (including B6), essential fats and vitamin E in the week before a period, and at any time. Extra calcium and magnesium may also help.

The diet, particularly in the pre-period days, needs to be low in salt, caffeine and refined carbohydrates (which encourage bloating and fluid retention), and intake of plain fluid (preferably water) needs to be kept high. Sugar cravings can be minimized by eating 'little and often', and choosing foods and snacks from items which have a low Glycaemic Index (see page 154). If periods are heavy, she may suffer from iron-deficiency (anaemia) and/or be very tired.

All PMS symptoms, including constipation, can also be eased by regular moderate exercise. A teenager who is missing her periods needs checking out by the doctor. Over-exercise, over-dieting or stress may be the cause, but there may be other medical reasons.

See also: Anaemia p73, Caffeine p85, Lethargy pp144, Salt pp171–4, Appendix 1 pp243–5 for sources of calcium and magnesium.

PESTICIDES
see Food Safety

PHYTOCHEMICALS

These are a range of hundreds of chemicals and compounds found in plant material – fruits, vegetables, grains, pulses, nuts and seeds. Many of them have antioxidant properties and are linked with reduced risk of heart disease, cancers and ill health. They may be even more important in the diet than vitamins and minerals (some of which also have an antioxidant effect), and many experts believe that this is why taking vitamin/mineral supplements is not a substitute for eating whole fruits, etc. Cooking doesn't necessarily destroy phytochemicals, in fact sometimes their absorption can be enhanced through cooking. Carotenoids, in particular, are better absorbed when cooked with oil.

See also: Antioxidants p73, Appendix 1 pp246–7 for a list of phytochemicals and their sources.

PIZZA

Nutrients per 200g slice of cheese and tomato pizza:

Cals	475	*(of which) sugars*	**4g**
Tot Fat	24g	*Fibre*	**2.8g**
Sat Fat	11g	*Vits*	**A, Beta-carotene,**
Chol	44mg		**B1, B2, B3, E**
Prot	18g	*Mins*	**calc, pot, iod, mag**
Tot carbs	50g	*Sodium*	**496mg**

Most children enjoy pizza and it does have its good points. The base and cheese are rich in calcium – a 200g slice contains about 460mg, which is a

P

significant proportion of a child's daily recommended intake. The tomato sauce contains beta-carotene and lycopene, the phytochemical that helps fight heart disease and cancer. They also contain a good range of other vitamins and minerals. However, most pizzas are very high in fat and saturates. If you make your own, you can reduce the fat content by using a lower-fat cheese, and put sliced vegetables on top instead of meat (see Traditional Pizza recipe page 212).

See also: Junk Food pp140–3, Phytochemicals p160, Ready Meals p168, Takeaways pp186–8.

POPCORN

see Snacks

PORK

Lean cuts of pork, such as leg and tenderloin fillets, are low in fat and an excellent source of protein, B vitamins and minerals. It is only if you choose fatty cuts that the fat content becomes high – so choose lean pork steaks or well-trimmed chops rather than leaving the fat on for the children, and if cooking a pork leg for Sunday roast try to give only tiny portions of crackling. If making gravy, skim the pan of most of the fat before doing so.

See also: Meat p145, Pastry p158, Sausages pp175–6

POTATOES

Potatoes are a starchy carbohydrate food, which also contains some protein, virtually no fat and a range of vitamins and minerals as well as fibre. They make an important contribution to most children's vitamin C intake and also provide energy. Roast and mashed potatoes can be almost as high in fat as chips, so if you need to watch the family's fat intake, go easy with the butter in your mash, and consider dry-roasting the potatoes by just brushing unpeeled potato chunks with olive oil to bake. This would bring the fat content per 100g down to around 2g. Use groundnut oil or light olive oil for roasting rather than blended vegetable oil or lard.

The skin is a good source of fibre and the flesh just under the skin contains much of the vitamin C, so try to use potatoes well scrubbed but unpeeled. New potatoes contain most vitamin C – indeed, potatoes that have been overwintered and then stored in a

PORK CUTS – NUTRIENTS PER ITEM AS STATED							
	Cals	Tot Fat	Sat Fat	Chol	Prot	Vits	Mins
Leg, lean, or tenderloin raw, 100g	123	4g	1.4g	63mg	21.8g	B group	pot, zinc, sel
Chop, 125g grilled, lean or fat	320	20g	7g	108mg	35g	B group	pot, zinc, sel
Pork crackling, 25g	137	11g	3.9g	26mg	9g	—	—
Pork spare ribs lean or fat, raw, 100g	93	6.4g	2.2g	n/k	8.8g	B group	pot, zinc, sel
For Pork Pie see Pastry p158, for Pork Sausages see Sausages p175–6.							

POTATOES – NUTRIENT CONTENT PER 100G OR AS STATED

	Cals	Tot Fat	Sat fat	Protein	Tot Carbs	Sugars	Fibre	Vits	Mins	Sodium
Boiled, old	72	trace	—	1.8g	17g	0.7g	1.2g	B3, C	pot	*
Boiled, new	75	0.3g	trace	1.5g	17.8g	1.3g	1g	C, folate	pot	*
Mashed, old, with butter, milk and seasoning	104	4.3g	2.8g	1.8g	15.5g	1g	1.1g	A, B3	pot	*
Roast, old, in corn oil	149	4.5g	0.6g	2.9g	26g	0.6g	1.8g	C, E, folate	pot, mg	*
Baked, 1 x 200g weight after baking	272	0.4g	trace	7.8g	63.5g	2.4g	5.4g	B3, B6, C, folate	pot, mg	24mg

*NOTE: Sodium content varies according to how much is added to cooking water. Potatoes contain around 7–11mg sodium/100g raw. Adding 1 tsp (5g) salt to the cooking water for 500g potatoes may add approx. 200mg sodium to each 100g cooked potatoes.

warm larder may contain very little vitamin C. Don't peel potatoes and then leave them soaking, as vitamin C will leach out. Cooking potatoes with a little oil or baking them loses less vitamin C than boiling. Avoid green skin or flesh as this contains toxins.

See also: Carbohydrates pp87–8, Chips p90–2, Fats and Oils pp110–12, Root Vegetables pp169–71.

POULTRY AND GAME

The lean meat from all poultry and game, (whether dark meat or light) is reasonably low in fat. But, if you eat chicken with its skin, or a duck portion with the layer of fat intact, then the dish can be as high, or higher, in fat than red meats.

Poultry and game is a good source of B vitamins and many minerals and an excellent source of protein. Poor-quality poultry is often laced with a great deal of added water and may even contain other meats, e.g pork, so try to buy good-quality meat.

Other game meats – venison and pheasant, for example – have a similar vitamin and mineral content, although venison is extremely low in fat (2.5g/100g) and pheasant is higher in fat than chicken (12g fat per 100g lean meat).

 Along with meat, eggs and unpasteurized milk, salmonella is most likely to occur in poultry. Cooking poultry all the way through, leaving no pink flesh, kills the salmonella bug and protects against poisoning.

See also: Food Poisoning pp122–3, Junk Food pp140–3, Meat p145, Protein pp165–6, Ready Meals p168, Takeaways pp186–8.

POULTRY AND GAME – NUTRIENTS PER ITEM AS STATED

	Cals	Tot Fat	Sat Fat	Chol	Protein	Vitamins	Minerals	Sodium
Chicken breast fillet, 100g	106	1.1g	0.3g	70mg	24g	B3, B6	pot, sel, zn	60mg
Chicken, roast, light and dark meat, average 100g	177	7.5g	2.9g	120mg	27.3g	B3, B6	pot, sel, zn	100mg
Chicken leg 1 x average portion, with skin, baked or grilled, 200g	472	34g	9.2	230mg	42g	B3, B6	pot, sel, zn	190mg
Chicken breast 1 x average portion, baked or grilled, skin removed, 150g	230	5.4g	3.1g	157mg	45g	B3, B6	pot, sel, zn	120mg
Chicken nuggets in breadcrumbs, 1 x average portion, baked, 100g	235	11.4g	3.5g	n/k	15.3g	B group	sel	300mg
Chicken burger, frozen ¼-pounder, baked/ grilled	285	15g	2g	n/k	16g	B group	sel	400mg
Chicken wings, Chinese-style, baked, 100g	274	16.6g	4.6g	120mg	27.4g	B3, B6	pot, calc, iron, sel	390mg
Turkey, stir-fry meat, raw, 100g	105	1.6g	0.5g	70mg	22.6g	B group	pot, sel	68mg
Turkey breast, roast, 100g	153	2g	0.7g	82mg	33.7g	B group	pot, sel	50mg
Duck, 1 leg portion, roast, skin on 150g cooked weight	425	38g	11g	100mg	20g	B group	pot, fe, zn, sel	90mg
Duck, lean meat only, 100g	137	6.5g	2g	110mg	20g	B group	pot, fe, zn, sel	110mg
Rabbit, meat only, 100g	137	5.5g	2g	53mg	22g	B3, B6, B12	pot, sel	67mg

PROCESSED FOODS

All food is processed in one form or another before you eat it – even cutting a lettuce from the garden could be described as processing it. However, what we usually mean by processed food is that which looks, or is, substantially different from its original ingredient(s).

Over the past 50 years, food processing has evolved from a few cans or bottles or jars of foods on the corner shop shelf among all the fresh and loose produce, into one of the largest industries in the world. There are several reasons for processing:

• To preserve food in a fit state to eat.

• To add value, interest and/or palatability to a basic product.

• To use up by-products: e.g. after skimming whole milk, manufacturers use the skimmed-off cream in desserts, etc.

Although food processing has given us much in the way of variety, interest and added options to our daily menus - and convenience in the form of all the long-life items that we can now buy - it does have some drawbacks, especially bearing in mind that it is the busy parent, juggling family and work,

who often turns to processed foods to provide simple, quick meals and snacks for the children.

Some processed foods are, indeed, a fine and nutritious part of a child's diet and few, if any, parents can say they rely wholly on fresh produce all the time. Items such as tinned tomatoes, tomato purée, tomato passata, pulses or fish canned in water, frozen foods and many items produced lovingly by small local kitchens may be a welcome addition to any child's diet.

Sadly, however, a significant proportion do have negatives. Processed foods in general are the first home of food additives, and research shows that many are high in fat, saturates, trans fats, salt or sugar. Canned fruits and vegetables may contain less vitamin C and B than fresh or frozen, and the vital plant chemicals may be missing from many products. Look at the box of comparisons below. At its worst, food processing strips the original food of all its nutrients and then adds a list of ingredients that are unhealthy and/or unnecessary to health, and/or artificial.

If you have to rely on a lot of cans, packs, jars and so on to feed your children, try to buy the best quality you can afford, read the labels and supplement them with plenty of fresh fruit, salads and vegetables. Also take a look at the recipes in the Recipes section, most of which are quick and easy to prepare.

COMPARISON OF FRESH FOODS AND THEIR PROCESSED COUNTERPARTS, ALL PER 100G

	Vitamins	Sodium	Additives
Fresh peas	C (24mg)	1mg	—
Processed tinned peas	trace	380mg	tartrazine, Green S (colours), sugar, salt
Farmhouse Cheddar cheese	A, B2, B12	723mg	—
Processed cheese slice	B12	1,390mg	E331, E341, salt, lactic acid, potassium sorbate, colourings
Fresh beef	B2, B3, B6, B12	54mg	—
Corned beef	B3, B12	860mg	sodium nitrite, salt, sugar
Potatoes, fresh	C (16mg)	11mg	—
Potato crisps	—	800mg	monosodium glutamate, salt, vegetable oil

See also: Artificial Sweeteners p75, Biscuits p80, Breakfast Cereals pp83–4, Carbonated Drinks pp88–9, Confectionery p95, Crisps p97, Desserts pp99–100, Drinks pp103–4, Food Additives pp114–17, Junk Food pp140–3, Ready Meals p168, Salt pp171–4, Snacks p178, Sugar pp182–5, Takeaways pp186–8, Yoghurt and Fromage Frais p197, Recipes pp198–239.

PROTEIN

Protein is essential in all children's diets to provide the 'building blocks' for body maintenance, repair and growth. Proteins are essential constituents of all cells and also regulate body processes and provide structure. The formation of the body's lean tissue (muscle and other non-fat and non-bone structures) is dependent upon regular adequate protein in the diet. While surplus protein can be converted into energy, neither carbohydrate nor fat – the two other major nutrients and energy suppliers – can be converted into protein.

Proteins in foods are formed from chains of amino acids and there are eight essential amino acids which the body must get from its food (plus a ninth, which is important in infancy but not needed afterwards). Some foods, mainly animal sources of protein, contain all eight of these amino acids and these are sometimes called 'complete proteins'. While others, mainly pulses and grains, contain only a few and are sometimes called 'incomplete proteins'; soya beans do contain all eight essential amino acids and are unique amongst pulses in this respect. As the amino acids work best when eaten together, children who eat little animal protein foods (e.g. vegetarians or vegans) can increase the quality of the plant protein foods by combining them within meals so that they form a 'complete protein'.

Some examples of this are:
* Combine a grain food with a pulse food: e.g., baked beans on toast; hummus and pitta bread; rice and beans.
* Combine a pulse with nuts/seeds: e.g., lentils and nuts in a carrot salad; sesame seeds with chickpeas in tahini.
* Any incomplete protein eaten with a complete protein: e.g., meat-free chilli sin carne made from red kidney beans topped with a little grated cheese; yoghurt with nuts and seeds.

Children need more protein than adults, proportionally, in their diets as they are growing in stature. Children's current intake, according to the UK survey of schoolchildren's diets, is about right at around 13% of total calories.

 Very high protein intakes (especially of animal protein) are linked with higher calcium excretion and the possibility of osteoporosis later in life, as well as possible kidney disease. A high protein intake is also linked with a high fat intake, as most sources of protein in children's diets are also potentially high in fat (e.g., dairy produce and meat). So don't be tempted to think that if adequate protein is vital, twice as much is even better – it isn't.

Good sources of protein are listed in the box below while amounts of protein in many individual foods are listed throughout the A–Z (e.g. see Beef page 78). Choose low-fat protein foods at least some of the time to help moderate your child's total fat and saturated fat intake.

SOURCES OF PROTEIN:

Very good sources of protein:
• Lean meat, poultry and game
• Fish and shellfish
• Eggs
• Cheese
• Quorn (mycoprotein)
• Peanuts (only for children aged 5 plus who are not allergic)

Good sources of protein:
• Milk, yoghurt and fromage frais
• Most nuts and seeds
• Pulses, especially soya and tofu

Reasonable sources of protein:
• Whole grains
• Potatoes

P

See also: 'Daily Nutritional Requirements' pp13, 22, 35 and 55 for recommended amounts of protein in children's diets, Beef p78, Dairy Produce p98, Eggs p108, Fish pp113–14, Meat p145, Nuts pp151–2, Pulses pp166–8, Seeds p177.

PULSES

Pulses are an extremely useful food group for all the family – they are high in both protein and carbohydrate, low or very low in fat and saturates, and high in fibre. Many are also good sources of some vitamins and excellent sources of minerals. They are low on the Glycaemic Index and so are useful for regulating blood sugar levels and preventing between-meal hunger (see Obesity page 154). They are also low-cost and very convenient as the canned versions contain a similar nutritional profile to the cooked dried beans (although potassium content may be lower and sodium content much higher, e.g., 3-400mg/100g if pulses canned in brine are used – so buy them canned in water).

Most pulses are a source of isoflavones and other phytochemical compounds of the phyto-oestrogen family. These may mimic the female hormone oestrogen. Soya beans are the richest source of these plant oestrogens (see opposite).

COOKING TIPS FOR PULSES

• If using dried beans, always soak them overnight or as recommended on the packet, change the soaking water before cooking and boil rapidly for 10 minutes or as instructed on the pack. This will destroy substances in the beans called lectins, which can cause symptoms similar to food poisoning if they are eaten undercooked. Lentils don't need fast boiling.
• Some people advise salting beans after cooking, as they feel cooking in salted water makes the beans tough. I have never noticed any difference.
• Use whole cooked pulses to replace some of the meat in casseroles, curries, pies, meat sauces and stews.
• Use pulses in vegetable soups to increase the mineral, fibre and calorie content – purée the soup for a fine, smooth texture.

• Cooked pulses can be added to winter salads – e.g. lentils with grated carrot, chickpeas with red peppers.
• Cooked pulses can be puréed with a little olive oil and lemon juice to make a spread, dip, paste or pâté (consistency depending upon how much oil or liquid you add).
• Tofu (beancurd) is a smooth lean protein made from soya beans which is very useful for vegans in stir-fries, soups, casseroles, etc. It comes in a variety of forms – e.g. silken, smoked, fried. TVP (textured vegetable protein) is suitable for use in dishes to replace chunks of meat or minced meat.

THE VERY SPECIAL SOYA BEAN

Soya beans are similar to the other pulses in most respects – however they do have a few major differences worth examining.
• They are a 'complete protein' – unlike most plant foods and pulses, they contain all eight essential amino acids that can form complete protein, so they are an important food for vegans and vegetarians – and, indeed, for families trying to cut down on their meat and dairy intake.
• They are relatively high in fat. Soya beans contain a high percentage of fats compared with other pulses, including not insignificant amounts of omega-3 oils.
• They are very high in isoflavones (see left). One isoflavone, called genistein, has been shown to lower LDL blood cholesterol. The US government has allowed a claim to appear on foods that eating 25g of soya protein a day as part of a low-saturated-fat diet can help reduce the risk of coronary heart disease. Other isoflavones in soya may help to maintain bone density and prevent osteoporosis, and may even provide protection against some forms of cancer.

There is much speculation – and research currently in progress – about a possible link between intake of soya in pregnancy, while breast-feeding and in infancy, and increased risk of male fertility problems later in life for the child. Much of the research done to date, which seems to indicate this may be the case, has been done on rats and mice.

PULSES – NUTRIENT CONTENT PER 100G COOKED WEIGHT OR AS STATED

	Cals	Tot fat	Sat Fat	Protein	Tot Carbs	Sugars	Fibre	Vits	Mins	Sodium
Baked beans in tomato sauce	84	0.6g	trace	5.2g	15.3g	5.9g	3.7g	B-carotene, folate	mg, pot, fe	530mg
Baked beans in tomato sauce, reduced-sugar, reduced-salt	73	0.6g	trace	5.4g	12.5g	2.8g	3.8g	B-carotene, folate	mg, pot, fe	330mg
Beansprouts, mung, raw	31	0.5g	trace	2.9g	4g	2.2g	1.5g	C, folate	fe	5mg
Black-eye Beans	116	0.7g	trace	8.8g	20g	1.1g	3.5g	folate	pot, mg, fe	5mg
Butter beans canned, drained	77	0.5g	trace	5.9g	13g	1.1g	4.6g	—	pot, mg, fe	420mg
Chickpeas	121	2.1g	trace	8.4g	18.2g	1g	4.3g	E	pot, ca, mg, fe	5mg
Chickpeas, canned, drained	115	2.9g	trace	7.2g	16g	0.4g	4.1g	E	ca, mg, fe	220mg
Hummus, 50g portion	94	6.3g	n/k	3.8g	6g	1g	1.2g	E	ca, mg	335mg
Lentils, green or brown	105	0.7g	trace	8.8g	16.9g	0.4g	3.8g	B6, folate	pot, mg, fe, zn, sel	3mg
Lentils, red	100	0.4g	trace	7.6g	17.5g	0.8g	1.9g	—	pot, fe	12mg
Red kidney beans	103	0.5g	trace	8.4g	17.4g	1g	6.7g	—	pot, ca, mg, fe	2mg
Soya beans	141	7.3g	0.9g	14g	5.1g	2.1g	6.1g	B6, E	pot, ca, mg, fe	1mg
Soya flour 100g	447	23.5g	2.9g	36.8g	23.5g	11.2g	11.2g	B1, B3, B6, E	pot, ca, mg, fe, zn	9mg
Soya mince, cooked	172	9.5g	0.9g	17.3g	4.5g	1.4g	1.8g	B group	mg, fe, sod	1.1mg
Tofu, steamed	73	4.2g	0.5g	8.1g	0.7g	0.3g	trace	E	ca	4mg

NOTE: for soya milk see Milk p146.

See also: 'Allergies and Infants' pp16–17 for information on soya allergy in infants, Fats and Oils pp110–12, Milk pp146–7, Obesity pp152–5, Phytochemicals p160, Protein pp165–6, Recipes for pulses pp200–2, 204–5, 209–10, 213, 215, 224, 237.

QUORN

Nutrient content per 100g:

Cals	92	*(of which) sugars*	0.8g
Tot fat	3.2g	Fibre	4.8g
Sat fat	0.6g	Vits	B1
Chol	0	Mins	cal, mag, zinc
Tot carbs	2g	Sodium	348mg

Quorn is a 'man-made' high-protein food based on 'mycoprotein', which is a relative of the mushroom family. Quorn contains no animal or dairy ingredients and is moderately low in fat (31% of its total calories are fat calories) and saturates. Quorn doesn't contain a wealth of vitamins and has a relatively high sodium content, but otherwise makes a good substitute for meat. Recent research, however, has shown it can cause asthma in susceptible individuals.

READY MEALS

Ready meals – mass-produced, pre-cooked meals that just require reheating – vary tremendously in their nutrient profile and while some are perfectly acceptable as an occasional meal for your child, others are less good. A significant number contain very little in the way of vegetables and few contain more than a trace of vitamin C. Fibre content is often low as ready meal manufacturers tend not to use whole grains for their carbohydrate element.

Salt content is not always very high, but can be – so this needs watching, bearing in mind that the recommended amounts of salt per day for children are less than that for adults. Some ready meals have an unacceptably high level of fat while many others contain around 30–35% of their calories as fat, which is not too bad. Again, some contain long lists of food additives.

A major problem for hungry active children – and especially teens – is that portion sizes of ready meals are often small and would not provide sufficient calories or possibly other nutrients (e.g. protein) for good health if consumed too regularly. Improve the nutritional status of ready meals by adding a side salad or some vegetables, or at least make sure that the meal is followed with some fruit. Also bear in mind that you get what you pay for, and that chilled meals are likely to be nicer and better nutritionally than frozen ones.

See also: Food Additives pp114–17, Junk Food pp140–3, Salt pp171–4, Takeaways pp186–8.

RHUBARB

Nutrient content per 100g:

Cals	7	Fibre	1.4g
Prot	0.9g	Vit C	6mg
Tot carbs	0.8g	Mins	pot, calc
(of which) sugars	0.8g		

Rhubarb is a very-low-calorie fruit that is, in fact, a vegetable – the stalks of a variety of the rheum plant. It is rich in calcium and contains iron, but ironically is high in oxalic acid, which hinders the absorption of these minerals.

Rhubarb is probably best known as a laxative – this is due to its content of anthraquinone gycosides. Because of this effect, go easy on portion sizes until you know how your child will react. Make sure to use only the pink stalks and cut off the green leaf end – the leaves are poisonous.

Stewed rhubarb is nice mixed with yoghurt or low-fat custard, while baking the stalks helps them retain their shape and gives a good flavour. Instead of adding large quantities of sugar, try adding a little fructose (available from supermarkets or chemists) and a little ground cinnamon, which acts as a sweetener and gives a nice flavour.

ROASTED FOOD

When roasting meat, for example for a Sunday joint, add a little water or stock at the base of the pan, then at the end of the cooking period skim off the fat before using the juices to make a vitamin B-rich gravy.

Roasted vegetables tossed in oil retain more vitamin C than boiled ones, and the carotenoids in red, orange and yellow vegetables, such as peppers, squash and carrots, become more easily absorbed by the body when brushed with a little oil.

Try not to overcook foods in the oven, as B and C vitamins are destroyed with prolonged heat, and burnt bits may be carcinogenic. Also, roasting at very high temperatures can cause a cancer-promoting reaction when meat or fish is cooked. However, when roasting make sure to cook poultry thoroughly to kill any salmonella bugs; and if serving stuffing, cook it separately in a dish or in small balls. In fact, it is wise to cook all meat to be served to children right through (and avoid pink bits) to prevent any possibility of food poisoning via other bugs such as E coli.

See also: Food Poisoning pp122–3, Grilled Food p135.

ROOT VEGETABLES

People often think of root vegetables as high in starchy carbohydrate and little else – in fact, only some roots, such as artichoke, parsnip, sweet potato and yams are high or moderately high in starch. Others, such as carrots, beetroot and swede, are moderately high in carbohydrate, but much of this is in the form of sugars.

The other popular misconception is that root vegetables are all very high in calories – as you can see from the table below, mostly they are not. Roots are all low-fat foods with only a trace of saturates, and some (especially parsnips, which are also the best source of fibre) contain good amounts of vitamins and minerals. Surprisingly, several are good sources of vitamin C – parsnips have 17mg/100g, swede 31mg/100g and sweet potato 23mg/100g. Beetroot is one of the best food sources of folate, but most of the folate is destroyed if the beets are pickled.

Orange-fleshed sweet potatoes are an excellent source of carotenoids and vitamins, while white-fleshed yams contain virtually none and are relatively low on all the micronutrients. Sweet

ROOT VEGETABLES – NUTRIENTS PER 100G

	Cals	Tot Fat	Protein	Tot carbs	Sugars	Fibre	Vits	Mins
Artichokes, Jerusalem	76	trace	1.6g	11g	1.6g	1.6g	—	pot, iron
Beetroot	36	trace	1.7g	7.6g	7g	1.9g	folate	pot
Parsnip	64	1.1g	1.8g	12.5g	5.7g	4.6g	B1, B3, folate, E, C	po, calc, mag
Swede	24	0.3g	0.7g	5g	4.9g	1.9g	B3, B6, C	pot, calc
Sweet potato, orange-fleshed	87	0.3g	1.2g	21.3g	5.7g	2.4g	B carotene, C	pot
Yam	114	0.3g	1.5g	28.2g	0.7g	1.3g	—	pot

potatoes have one other benefit compared with ordinary potatoes, they have a much lower rating on the Glycaemic Index (see Obesity page 154). Jerusalem artichokes are rich in fructo-oligosaccharides, which help build up 'good' bacteria in the gut – useful for children with digestive problems or constipation.

Ideally, root vegetables should be bought in season to maximize their nutrient content. Most children enjoy at least some of the root vegetables apart from potatoes. Carrots are almost always a favourite, while parsnip can have too strong a taste for some. Beetroot is very sweet, but not all children enjoy it swimming in vinegar. Below are some child-friendly and health tips for cooking and serving root vegetables.

TIPS FOR SERVING ROOT VEGETABLES TO CHILDREN

• Bake beets in their skins, then peel and slice them as a nice sweet vegetable; or parboil them and then grate into winter salads. Avoid pickling them as this destroys their important folate content.
• Cube a selection of root vegetables, toss them in oil and seasoning, and bake for about 50 minutes, turning halfway through. Great with the Sunday roast as a change from roast potatoes, or top with cheese sauce and breadcrumbs and brown under the grill for a winter supper.
• Thinly slice roots, toss them in olive oil, season, lay on a baking tray and bake, turning halfway through cooking time, until they are crisp and golden – makes a healthier option to commercial crisps.
• Cut roots into large crudités and bake as above, then use as finger foods with a savoury cheese or tomato dip.
• Peel, cube and steam roots until tender, then mash with equal parts potato for a change from basic mash; or mash two different roots together – carrot with parsnip is excellent.
• Bake sweet potatoes in their skins, or peel, cube and mash them, just like ordinary potatoes – they go very well with chicken and beef.

See also: Carrots p89, Phytochemicals p160, Potatoes pp161–2 and Vitamins pp194–6.

SALAD

Salad is perceived as 'healthy' and yet a small side salad of the children's favourite – a few shreds of iceberg with a couple of slices of cucumber and a small heap of mustard and cress – contains hardly any nutrients worth mentioning. As you can see from the table above, a whole punnet of mustard and cress is a good source of beta-carotene (about 500ug), folate (23ug) and vitamin C (13mg) – but the spoonful with which you may adorn a side salad or put into a sandwich contains only about a sixth of those amounts.

Because salad weighs so little, people need to eat a lot of it to make a real difference to the diet. Ironically, however, children rarely have the capacity – or the willingness – to eat a lot, and they seem to have a particular aversion to the stronger-tasting items, such as Cos lettuce, radicchio and watercress – a pity because it is these stronger-flavoured salad items that generally contain the highest amounts of vitamins, minerals and plant chemicals, while iceberg and other very pale lettuces are some of the poorest.

Leaves with shades of red (such as lollo rosso, radicchio, red mustard) contain anthocyanins and quercetin – both of which are strong antioxidants. Dark green leaves contain carotenoids, while the curly-leaved endive and radishes contain the anti-cancer phytochemical kaempferol. Watercress is an excellent source of calcium, iron and vitamin E, and contains phytochemicals from the isothiocyanate group which also have string antioxidant and anti-cancer properties.

Don't worry if you child can't eat a lot of salad at one time – little and often is the key for children, so try to make at least one portion of the 'five a day' fruit and vegetables a salad one. Here are some of the more nutritious salad items which I have found that children do often enjoy.
• Oak leaf lettuce – red-tinged dark leaves but with a milder, sweeter flavour than some other red salads.
• Lamb's lettuce – small rosettes of delicious mild dark green leaves which children can easily grow themselves in a tiny plot.
• Little Gem – almost as nutrient-rich as the Cos, another member of the same family, and with a

SALAD VEGETABLES – NUTRIENTS PER 100G OR AS STATED								
	Cals	Tot Fat	Protein	Tot Carbs	Sugars	Fibre	Vits	Mins
Celery	7	0.2g	0.5g	0.9g	0.9g	1.1g	—	pot, calc
Chicory	11	0.6g	0.5g	2.8g	0.7g	0.9g	—	pot
Lettuce, Cos	16	0.6g	1g	1.7g	1.7g	1g	B carotene, folate	pot, calc
Lettuce, iceberg	13	0.3g	0.7g	1.9g	1.9g	0.6g	folate	pot
Mustard and cress, 1 box	5	0.2g	0.6g	0.2g	0.2g	0.4g	B carotene, C	calc
Radish	12	0.2g	0.7g	1.9g	1.9g	0.9g	folate, C	pot
Watercress	22	1g	3g	0.4g	0.4g	1.5g	B carotene, C, E	pot, calc, iron

similar antioxidant profile, but because these lettuces are small they have greater child appeal. Serve the heart with some shredded outer leaves which contain most of the carotenoids.

• Greek cress – another easy-to-grow seed for a child's vegetable plot; it will grow large enough to harvest in 3–4 weeks, has a mild but interesting taste and contains plenty of nutrients.

Try to serve mixed salad that you have prepared yourself – research shows that ready-to-eat mixed salads from the supermarket, that come in modified-atmosphere packaging (where the salad is packed in a balance of gases to retain freshness and prevent browning), have a reduced content of vitamin C and phytochemicals in the leaves. Also try not to chop leaves until immediately before serving, as cutting also destroys the vitamin C (another minus point for the pre-packed varieties).

See also: Antioxidants p73, Carrots p89, Cucumber p98, Onions p155, Peppers p160, Phytochemicals p160, Tomatoes p190, Vegetables pp191–4, Vitamins pp194–6, Appendix 1 pp240–9 for sources of vitamins, minerals and phytochemicals.

SALT

Salt consists of 40% sodium and 60% chloride, two minerals which are present in small amounts in virtually all basic foods, including fruit and vegetables. We need a little sodium in our diets – it helps to balance our body fluids and is necessary for the proper functioning of our nerves and muscles – but a little IS all we need (see table 'Average Sodium Requirments' overleaf).

Salt has been used for centuries as a preservative and a flavour enhancer, but it is only in recent years that it has been used in relatively large amounts in the food manufacturing industry. Indeed, experts now estimate that 75% of all the salt that we consume comes from processed foods, while only 9% is added in cooking at home and 6% added at the table.

Health experts have been worried for some time about our high intake of salt. Adults eat around 9g salt a day (3.6g sodium), equivalent to nearly 2 teaspoons, although they need only 4g a day (1.6g sodium), and the children surveyed for the UK 2000 National Diet and Nutrition Survey were eating at least twice as much salt as they needed for health.

AVERAGE SODIUM REQUIREMENTS (MG/DAY) (DOH 1991)	
Note: 1 level teaspoon = 2g sodium, 1g = 1000mg	
Age	**Reference Nutrient Intake***
0–3 months	210mg
4–6 months	280mg
7–9 months	320mg
10–12 months	350mg
1–3 years	500mg
4–6 years	700mg
7–10 years	1200mg
11–18 years and adults	1600mg

*The amount of sodium that is sufficient for most people i.e. average minimums.

TARGET AVERAGE DAILY AMOUNT OF SALT IN THE DIET* (1G = 1000MG)	
Note: 1 level teaspoon = 5g salt (2g sodium)	
Age	
0–6 months	Less than 1g (equivalent to 400mg sodium)
7–12 months	1g
1–3 years	2g (equivalent to 800mg sodium)
4–6 years	3g (equivalent to 1.2g sodium)
7–10	5g (equivalent to 2g sodium)
11–14 years	6g (equivalent to 2.4g sodium)
over 14 years to adulthood	6g** (equivalent to 2.4g sodium)

* i.e. average maximums
** The World Health Organization has set targets at 5g a day for adults, but this recommendation is still in draft form. (Source: Department of Health/ UK Food Standards Agency UK Scientific Committee on Nutrition 'Salt')

In 2003 the UK Scientific Committee on Nutrition released its report on salt, which concluded that there is a direct association between high salt intake and high blood pressure, heart disease and stroke. The report affirms the recommendations for maximum daily intakes of salt for children (see box above right).

Other research indicates that a diet high in salt is linked with increased risk of asthma, osteoporosis, stomach cancer and fluid retention, and only small reductions in intake (for adults, 2g a day) are shown to have a significant effect on blood pressure.

WHAT ARE THE HIGH SODIUM (SALT) FOODS?

Very many processed foods have a high salt content – and they are not all those that you would necessarily think of, such as crisps and other savoury snacks. Breakfast cereals are a big source of dietary salt – one estimate is that cornflakes, weight for weight, have more salt in them than sea water. Much bread is high in salt, and so are most baked beans, even though they taste sweet. Takeaways and canned foods also frequently tend to be high in salt. Government guidelines suggest that all products with over 500mg sodium (1.25g salt) per 100g product are high in salt – and those are guidelines for adults. Almost all the products in this list opposite are over that level.

The list shows the hidden salt in many popular children's foods per average portion and per 100g – compare it with the amounts that children actually need in their daily diet, and with the maximum amounts recommended (see charts above). Values for a six-year-old child are shown as an example. The figures show that it would take only one average bag of crisps plus a slice of takeaway pizza, for example, or a bowl of cornflakes, plus six chicken nuggets for a six-year-old child to reach the daily recommended target maximum intake.

Foods or food groups often particularly high in sodium include: cereals, crackers, savoury snacks,

Food	Amount of sodium (salt) per average portion	Amount of sodium (salt) per 100g of product	% RNI (500mg) for 3-year-old (per portion)	% of daily target intake (800mg) for 3-year-old (per portion)
Salt, 1 level teaspoon	2g (5g)	40g (100g)	400%	250%
Savoury Snacks				
Ready-salted potato crisps (35g bag)	280mg (700mg)	800mg (2g)	56%	32.5%
Pretzels	860mg (2.15g)	1720mg (4.3g)	172%	107%
Twiglets	670mg(1.7g)	1340mg (3.3g)	134%	84%
Hula Hoops, salt and vinegar, 1 pack	342mg (855mg)	1070mg (2.7g)	68%	43%
Skips, 19g pack	285mg (712mg)	1500mg (3.75g)	57%	35.5%
Breakfast cereals (All portions 30g)				
Bran Flakes, Cheerios	240mg (600mg)	800mg (2g)	48%	30%
Cornflakes	300mg (750mg)	1000mg (2.5g)	60%	37.5%
Frosties, Fruit 'n Fibre	180mg (450mg)	600mg (1.5g)	36%	22.5%
Rice Krispies	195mg (490mg)	650mg (1.6g)	39%	24%
Miscellaneous				
Bread, premium white, sliced, 2 slices	360mg (900mg)	530mg (1.3g)	72%	45%
Baked beans, average, 200g	1060mg (2.6g)	530mg (1.3g)	212%	132.5%
Baked beans, low-salt, 200g	660mg (1.6g)	330mg (825mg)	132%	82.5%
Tomato soup, cream of, canned, 200ml	800mg (2g)	400mg (1g)	160%	100%
Corned beef, 100g portion	860mg (2.1g)	860mg (2.1g)	172%	107.5%
Pork chipolatas, 2, grilled	1080mg (2.7g)	1080mg (2.7g)	216%	135%
Sherbert sweets, 100g	1050mg (2.6g)	1050mg (2.6g)	210%	131%
Takeaways				
Chicken nuggets 6	510mg (1.3g)	510mg (1.3g)	102%	64%
Cheeseburger, standard, including bun, etc	780mg (1.95g)	678 (1.7g)	156%	97.5%
Pizza, cheese and tomato 200g slice	564mg (1.4g)	282mg (705mg)	113%	70.5%

tinned soups and vegetables canned in brine; fish canned in brine; stock cubes; bacon, dried packet soups and sauces; cook-in, stir-in or pour-over ready-made sauces; processed cheeses; smoked foods; soya sauce and some other bottled sauces. Butter and margarine can contain quite high levels too – about 75mg sodium for a 10g portion.

TIPS FOR REDUCING THE SODIUM CONTENT OF YOUR CHILD'S DIET

• Try not to encourage a taste for salt from the start. Children who are not used to very salty flavours find salty foods almost unpalatable.
• Research shows that if you reduce salt in the child's diet gradually over several weeks the taste buds alter and previously enjoyed foods seem far too salty.
• Check food labels for sodium content (see below).
• Stop adding salt to cooked vegetables and at table – this will save about 20% of your child's salt intake.
• Go for low-salt versions of favourite foods – e.g. baked beans, crisps, butter, bacon, ketchup. Every little saving does add up.
• Try to offer very low salt between-meal snacks – a significant percentage of children's salt intake is in the form of snacks.
• Try to buy fresh chilled ready meals and soups rather than long-life canned or dried ones, which often contain a lot more sodium.
• Offer few preserved and processed meats – e.g. sausages, frankfurters, burgers, corned beef – and more fresh meat.

SALT AND FOOD LABELS

• The nutrition panel may give sodium content per 100g, but bear in mind that this isn't necessarily the same as a portion.
• Remember that more than 500mg of sodium per 100g food is considered 'a lot'.
• If sodium per portion IS given (which some manufacturers do – and they are obliged to do so if they make a claim for salt content on the front of the pack), try to work out approximately what proportion of your child's maximum target intake for his or her age this will be (see the charts on page 172). For example, half a 400ml can of tomato soup

contains 800mg sodium, which is 100% of a 3-year-old's daily target intake.
• Remember not to confuse sodium and salt. Salt is 40% sodium, so 1g (1000mg) sodium equals 2.5g (2500mg) salt. Some manufacturers list salt content, not sodium content.
• If there is no sodium listed on the nutrition panel, check the ingredients list for sodium – the higher up the list it appears, the more sodium the product will contain.

See also: individual food listings (e.g. Cheese pp89–90) for sodium levels, Junk Food pp140–3, Ready Meals p168, Snacks pp178–9 Takeaways pp186–8.

SAUCES AND DRESSINGS

Mayonnaise, the similar Thousand-Island dressing, French dressing and salad cream are the only sauces/ relishes/ pickles with a high fat content. Mayonnaise is particularly high in fat so it is worth buying the reduced-fat varieties or mixing full-fat with equal parts yoghurt to reduce the calorie and fat content. Low-fat salad cream contains only 3.4g fat per 20ml serving.

The other sauces and relishes are high in sugar and, usually, salt – indeed, children who eat a lot of sauce may be getting a surprisingly high percentage of their day's maximum target intake from these products. For example, one 20ml portion of BBQ sauce contains over a quarter of the maximum target intake for a 6-year-old. Some are also high in additives – read the label. Tomato ketchup contains the carotenoid antioxidant lycopene in an easily absorbed form. I buy organic ketchup for my family as I know it won't contain genetically-modified tomatoes or pesticide residues – and it tastes excellent. Buy reduced-salt and -sugar versions of these sauces when you can find them.

See also: Antioxidants p73, Phytochemicals p160, Salt p171–4.

SAUCES AND DRESSINGS – NUTRIENTS PER 20ML SERVING

	Cals	Tot Fat	Sat Fat	Chol	Prot	Tot Carbs	Sugars	Fibre	Vits	Mins	Sodium
BBQ sauce	19	trace	trace	—	0.2g	4.7g	4.6g	0.1g	—	—	238mg
Burger relish	23	trace	trace	—	0.2g	5.5g	5g	0.1g	—	—	96mg
French dressing	92	9.9g	1.6g	—	trace	0.9g	0.9g	—	E	—	92mg
Mayonnaise	138	15g	2.3g	15mg	0.2g	0.3g	0.3g	—	A, E	—	90mg
Salad cream	70	6.2g	0.7g	8.5mg	0.3g	3.3g	3.3g	—	E	—	208mg
Soy sauce	8.6	—	—	—	0.6g	1.6g	1.5g	—			1.4g
Sweet pickle	28	trace	trace	—	0.1g	7.2g	6.8g	0.2g	—	—	322mg
Tomato ketchup	23	trace	trace	—	0.3g	5.7g	5.4g	0.2g	—	—	326mg

SAUSAGES – NUTRIENT CONTENT PER 100G

	Cals	Tot Fat	Sat Fat	Chol	Prot	Tot Carbs	Sugars	Fibre	Vits	Mins	Sodium
Beef sausage	278	19.5g	7.9g	42mg	13.3g	13.1g	1.4g	0.7g	B3 B12	ca, fe, zn	1200mg
Frankfurter	287	25.4g	9.2g	76mg	13.6g	1g	1g	trace	B1, B3 B12	fe, zn	920mg
Pork sausage	294	22g	8g	53mg	14.5g	9.8g	1.5g	0.7g	B3, B12	ca, fe, zn	1080mg
Salami	438	39.2g	14.6g	83mg	21g	trace	trace	trace	B1, B3, B6, B12	fe, zn	1800mg
Sausage rolls	383	27.6g	11.2g	n/k	9.9g	25.4g	0.9g	1g	n/k	n/k	600mg
Vegetarian	179	9.4g	2.3g	—	15g	9.2g	1.3g	2.6g	B1, B3	ca, mg, fe, zn	895mg

SAUSAGES

Most sausages are high in fat, but grilling them until the fat runs out will reduce their total fat and calorie content. Most are high or very high in salt, but can be a good source of B vitamins, iron and zinc. Most children enjoy vegetarian sausages for a change, which tend to be (but are not always) lower in fat and have good amounts of fibre. Some vegetarian sausage mixes, which you can buy in packets, are actually as high in fat as meat sausages.

You really do get what you pay for with sausages. Good-quality ones tend to contain more proper meat than cheap ones. Many supermarket 'pork' or 'beef' sausages are padded out with a lot of cereal, and all the bits of carcass (e.g. sinew, gristle, shin, tongue) that no one would normally want to eat, as well as 'mechanically recovered meat' (or MRM as it is known in the trade), and usually have a fair selection of additives – colorants, preservatives and so on.

A good read of the ingredients label will help you decide whether a sausage is worth feeding to your child or not – but until the EU laws are tightened up, it isn't always easy, and it may be worth paying that extra for premium brands, or local butcher's home-made varieties.

See also: Beef p78, Food Additives pp114–17, Food Labelling pp119– 22, Grilled Food p135, Meat p145, Pastry p158, Pork p161.

SEAFOOD

Most seafood is low in fat and calories, high in protein and a good source of some of the minerals that are harder to find in the average child's diet – zinc and selenium. On the minus side, some are high in cholesterol, especially prawns (but for healthy children this shouldn't be of concern), and in sodium. Peeled prawns have a whopping 1.59g of sodium per 100g, which is equivalent to 4g of salt – or nearly a teaspoonful, which is over the recommended levels for most children. Mixed with other seafood, such as squid (190mg sodium/100g) or mussels (360mg/100g), the total sodium content becomes lower. However, the occasional prawn sandwich or salad as part of a diet that is generally low in salt is fine. Canned or fresh dressed crab is a handy sandwich filler or salad component.

> **!** Shellfish shouldn't be given to small children as it is one of the food groups most likely to cause food allergies.
>
> **●** If buying fresh shellfish, make sure it really is fresh, and buy good-quality frozen produce. Take special care over storage, cleaning and preparation of all seafood to prevent any likelihood of food poisoning.

See also: Food Allergies pp117–19, Food Poisoning pp122–3, Salt pp171–4.

SEAFOOD – NUTRIENTS PER 100G									
	Cals	Tot Fat	Sat Fat	Chol	Prot	Tot Carbs	Vits	Mins	Sodium
Crabmeat, fresh	128	5.5g	0.7g	72mg	19.5g	trace	B2, B3	mg, fe, zn, sel	420mg
Crab, canned drained	77	0.5g	trace	72mg	18.1g	trace	B3	fe, zn	550mg
Crabsticks	68	0.4g	trace	39mg	10g	6.6g	—	zn	700mg
Prawns, peeled	99	0.9g	0.2g	280mg	22.6g	—	B12	ca, zn, sel	1590mg
Scampi (breaded prawns), fried in oil	237	13.6g	1.4g	110mg	9.4g	20.5g	B3, B12	ca, fe, sel	660mg

S

SEEDS – NUTRIENT CONTENT PER 25G AVERAGE SERVING										
	Cals	Tot Fat	Sat Fat	Protein	Tot Carbs	Sugars	Fibre	Vits	Mins	Sodium
Pine kernels	172	17g	1g	3.5g	1g	1g	0.5g	B1, B3, E	pot, mg, fe, zn	trace
Pumpkin seeds	142	11.2g	1.7g	6g	3.7g	0.5g	1.2g	B1, B3	mg, fe, zn	trace
Sesame seeds	150	14.5g	2g	4.5g	0.2g	trace	2g	B3, folate, E	ca, mg, fe, zn	5mg
Sunflower seeds	145	12g	1g	5g	4.6g	0.4g	1.5g	E, B3	pot, mg, fe, zn, sel	trace

SEEDS

Seeds can make a good contribution to a child's intake of minerals, including many minerals that are not found in quantity in a wide variety of foods – such as zinc and selenium. Though high in fat, it is mostly polyunsaturated and there are some of the important omega-3s present in most seeds.

Seeds can be used as between-meal snacks, on their own or included with nuts, sprinkled on breakfast cereal, chopped fruit or yoghurt, sprinkled into salads or used in home-made breads and bakes. Eating them raw preserves more of the nutrients. Store them in the fridge and eat within a few weeks to ensure the polyunsaturated oils don't oxidize.

Linseeds (flax seeds) are not widely available but can be bought at health shops and have the highest omega-3 content of all seeds at 3.5g per 25g. Tahini – sesame seed paste, commonly used in hummus – is a concentrated source of all the goodness of seeds.

 Seeds – particularly sesame seeds – may produce an allergic reaction in some children and should also not be given to very small children as there may be a risk of choking.

See also: 'Allergies and Infants' pp16–17, Fats and Oils pp110–12, Food Allergies pp117–19, Pulses pp166–8, Hummus recipe p205.

SEXUAL DEVELOPMENT

A healthy well-balanced diet will help to ensure optimum sexual development. During puberty, however, you may want to ensure your child has adequate zinc in the diet. This can be found in seafood, nuts, seeds and wholegrains.

See also: Appendix 1 p246 for sources of zinc.

SMOKED FOODS

There is evidence that a diet high in smoked foods may cause stomach and other cancers. One of the agents used in modern smoking processes is sodium nitrite, which can combine with the proteins in meat and fish to form potentially carcinogenic toxins. Serve smoked foods only occasionally and choose unsmoked bacon and fresh salmon, for example.

For the same reason, smoked flavourings in foods such as smoky bacon crisps and barbecue sauces may also be banned or severely curtailed in the EU.

See also: Bacon p77, Cancer pp86–7, Grilled Food p135.

S

SNACKS

There is no harm at all in children having one or two between-meal snacks a day. Indeed, snacks can help to keep blood sugar levels up and should help children to function better both mentally and physically, especially if they have a busy school workload or are very active. Snacks can also help provide adequate calorie intake for children who are underweight or have trouble facing large meals.

When the child is small and at home during the day, assuming you are there too, it's no hardship to provide snacks of bread, fruit, cheese and so on. Here we look at snacks that are bought every day by the million in bags and packs for eating 'on the run', and think of some healthier alternatives.

A glance at the table opposite will show you that many of the snacks foods most popular with our children are high in fat and/or saturated fat, sodium and calories. Most also contain a long list of food additives. The trick, as a parent, is to continue to provide your child with daily snacks while keeping their intake of the less-good elements as low as is practical and ensuring they don't consume more calories than they need.

Until the teens, the majority of snacks are bought for children by their parents. So first try to buy only what you really want your child to eat. Limit crisps and similar savoury mass-market snacks to a few times a week. Nuts can make an excellent part of an older child's diet, being rich in unsaturated fats, vitamins, minerals and fibre. When they are roasted and salted, however, they lose nutrients and gain a lot of sodium, so again I'd advise limiting these.

If older children have access at school to a kettle they may enjoy instant noodle or rice snack pots. These vary in fat content but usually contain a lot of sodium and food additives, with a low fibre content. They also tend to be satisfying only in the short-term, making them inadequate for a lunch, but too high in calories to regard as a between-meal choice.

HEALTHIER SNACKS FOR KIDS

Here are a few suggestions for snacks that can be dropped into your child's pocket or school bag:
• **Popcorn:** ready-made plain popcorn is a good alternative to crisps some of the time as it is very low in sodium. Or you can pop your own at home, which is very easy and will also lower the fat content. Popcorn will keep in a lidded container for a few days and you can bag it up as needed.
• **Fresh shelled nuts:** bag a mixture up yourself but don't give to children under five.
• **Dried fruit:** These now come in small pocket-friendly bags and, although they are quite high in sugars, they contain a good range of nutrients and are low in fat and sodium, as well as lower in calories than fatty savouries.
• **Nuts and raisins:** small packs of mixed unsalted nuts and raisins are ideal and easy to find in shops.
• **Home-made mixes:** I sometimes give my teenage son a bag made up from a variety of different shelled nuts, seeds and dried fruits (e.g. hazelnuts, pine nuts, sunflower seeds, chopped dried apricot and fig), and then just to prove I'm not completely heartless I throw in a handful of chocolate chips! Such a dense, nutrient-rich mixture is, though, low in saturates and sodium. Its other advantage is that because it is full of fibre and takes some chewing, it is much more satisfying than a bag of crisps which is gone in a few seconds.
• **Apples:** not all fresh fruit makes an ideal portable snack but small firm apples do.

See also: 'School Lunchtime' pp42–3 and 'Eating Plans' pp49–51 for snack ideas for lunch boxes, Dried Fruit pp102–3, Food Additives pp114–17, Nuts pp151–2, Recipes for snacks pp203–6, pp232–5 and 238–9.

FIVE-A-DAY...
Research shows that some kids have up to five bags of crisps a day – five bags *a week* might be more acceptable. The reduced-fat 'light' crisps are a little lower in fat but they save on fat and calories mainly because they come in smaller packs! Weight for weight, the sodium content is similar.

CEREAL BARS
Cereal bars may seem like a healthier option to crisps and confectionery, but on average they contain as much fat and sugar as confectionery and no micronutrients or fibre in significant amounts.

SNACKS – NUTRIENTS AS STATED

	Cals	Tot fat	Sat Fat	Chol	Prot	Tot carbs	Sugars	Fibre	Vits	Mins	Sodium
Crisps, salted, 35g bag	185	12g	5g	0	2g	18.6g	0.2g	1.8g	E, C	pot	280mg
Crisps, salted, reduced-fat 21g pack	95	4.5g	2g	0	1.4g	13.2g	0.3g	1.2g	B3	pot	152mg
Popcorn, plain, 30g bag	178	13.2g	1.3g	0	1.5g	2g	trace	n/k	E	—	1.5mg
Salted roasted peanuts, 50g bag	301	26.5g	4.7g	0	12.2g	3.5g	1.9g	3g	B3	mg	200mg
Peanuts and raisins, 50g bag	217	13g	2.5g	0	7.6g	18.7g	17g	2.2g	B3, folate, E	ca, mg fe, zn	14mg
Tortilla chips 50g bag	230	11.3g	2g	0	3.8g	30g	0.6g	3g	E	ca, mg	430mg
Corn snacks (e.g. Wotsits) 21g bag	110	6.7g	2.5g	0	1.5g	11.4g	1g	0.2g	E	—	237mg
Pot noodle 100g pot	365	11g	n/k	0	11.6g	58.8g	8.2g	n/k	—	ca, mg fe, zn	1310mg
Cereal chewy bar, 21g bar	90	3.4g	1g	0	1.5g	13.6g	6.9g	0.7g	—	—	23mg

SOUP

Soup is easy to eat, popular with children and can be very nutritious as a snack or complete meal. Yet many canned and packet soups are not nutrient-rich, don't contain enough calories for a child's needs as a meal, and can be very high in sodium.

For example, an average child's portion of canned tomato or chicken soup contains a whole day's maximum recommended amount of sodium for a child of 6. Instant packet soups usually contain even more sodium and lots of artificial food additives.

The best thing to do is batch-make and freeze your own soups, and the Recipe section includes several healthy, delicious and easy-to-cook soups. A compromise could be fresh soups from the chilled counter, which, though more expensive than either home-made or canned, usually have a reasonable nutrient profile. Go for vegetable and pulse varieties for vitamins, protein and fibre – soups containing cheese or milk will also add protein and calcium. Cheese grated on top and bread served alongside will turn a soup into a filling meal.

See also: Food Additives pp114–17, Recipes for soups pp200–3.

SOYA
see Pulses

SPREADS AND DIPS

Most children seem to adore something smooth and easy to eat in a sandwich, or on bread or toast, or with crackers or finger foods like carrots and celery sticks. Sweet spreads contain little in the way of nutrients except calories and sugar — even so-called fruit spreads are high in sugars because of their fruit sugar (fructose) content. Marmite (yeast extract), although rich in B vitamins, is very high in salt, while nut butters and meat spreads offer a variety of nutrients but are high in fat.

Hummus, made from chickpeas and tahini (sesame seed paste), can be used as a nutritious dip with crudités or pitta fingers, or as a filling for sandwiches. It is easy to make your own hummus by blending a can of drained chickpeas in an electric blender with the juice of a lemon, some olive oil, a tablespoon of tahini, a crushed clove of garlic (for older children) and some seasoning to taste. If it is too thick, thin it down with water rather than more oil to keep the fat content down.

Peanut butter can be warmed and mixed with fromage frais or even skimmed milk for another good dip idea. Try to buy peanut butter that doesn't contain added sugar – check the label. Ready-made taramasalata usually contains artificial colours and other additives, and is quite high in salt.

For a low-fat dip, consider half-fat Greek yoghurt blended with finely chopped cucumber, or low-fat fromage frais beaten with some low-fat soft cheese and finely chopped herbs.

See also: Recipes pp203–5 for spread and dip ideas.

SPREADS AND DIPS – NUTRIENTS PER 25G PORTION UNLESS OTHERWISE STATED

	Cals	Tot Fat	Sat Fat	Chol	Prot	Tot Carbs	Sugars	Fibre	Vits	Mins	Sodium
Jam or marmalade	65	—	—	—	trace	17g	17g	trace	—	—	7.5mg
Pear and apple spread	30	trace	—	—	0.2g	8g	7.7g	trace	—	—	2.5mg
Hummus	83	7.3g	0.9g	—	2g	2.3g	2.2g	3g	—	—	167mg
Liver pâté	79	7.2g	2g	42mg	3.3g	0.3g	0.2g	—	A, B12	fe	187mg
Marmite, 1 tsp	16	—	—	—	3.7g	0.3g	0.2g	—	B1, B2, B3, folate	—	382mg
Peanut butter	156	13g	2.9g	—	5.7g	3.3g	1.7g	1.4g	B3, E	pot, mg, zn	87mg
Taramasalata	126	13g	1g	6mg	0.8g	1g	—	—	B12	—	162mg
Tartex vegetarian pâté	54	4.5g	n/k	—	1.8g	1.5g	n/k	n/k	B group	—	n/k

S

STOMACH UPSET

'Mummy [or Daddy] – I've got tummy ache!' is a cry all parents are likely to hear many times and there could be numerous causes. If a child has persistent stomach ache or accompanying problems, such as fever, vomiting or diarrhoea, for more than a day or two, you should see your doctor.

STOMACH ACHE, NO OTHER SYMPTOMS:

If the child says they have stomach ache but you can find nothing else wrong, the cause could be psychological (doesn't want to go to school that day or is under stress). If this happens several times you may be able to link the problem to some particular occasion (e.g. sports at school). The child may not actually be making up the stomach pains as stress can cause physical symptoms.

Otherwise, try to find out whether the child has eaten something that could cause stomach pains. For example, too many apples or under-ripe bananas. Check also that the child isn't constipated.

STOMACH ACHE, OTHER SYMPTOMS:

With other symptoms such as a temperature, hot head, drowsiness, vomiting and/or diarrhoea, it could be food poisoning. It could also be food allergy. Any or all of these together could be symptoms of some other illness, in which case see your doctor. With constipation, the stomach ache should go away when the constipation is relieved.

A bloated, tight-looking stomach could simply be too much food in one session, e.g. from a kids' party. Stomach ache with bloating could, again, be food allergy. Bloating and pains can also be caused by too much sodium which retains fluid in the body, or by too much refined carbohydrate, which has a similar effect. Food allergy can also cause bloating. In older girls, stomach ache and bloating may be symptoms of pre-menstrual syndrome.

See also: Carbohydrates pp87–8, Constipation p96, Food Allergy pp117–19, Food Poisoning pp122–3, Periods and PMS p160, Salts pp171–4.

STONE FRUITS

Stone fruits are suitable for most children and rarely cause allergies, but stone them first before giving to small children – especially cherries. Nectarines and peaches are a good source of vitamin C, while most stone fruits contain good amounts of beta-carotene and other carotenoids. Cherries are a good source of the phytochemicals anthocyanins and ellagic acid, while plums are a very good source of phenolic compounds, all of which help to fight heart disease and some cancers.

See also: Phytochemicals p160.

STONE FRUITS – NUTRIENTS PER WHOLE FRUIT OR AS STATED

	Cals	Tot Fat	Prot	Tot Carbs	Sugars	Fibre	Vitamin C	Other Vits	Mins
Apricot, x1, 50g	15	trace	0.5g	3.6g	3.6g	0.8g	3mg	B-carotene	pot
Cherries, 50g	24	trace	0.5g	5.7g	5.7g	0.5g	6mg	—	pot
Nectarine, x1, 100g	40	trace	1.4g	9g	9g	1.2g	37mg	B-carotene	pot
Peach, x 1, 150g	50	trace	1.5g	11.4g	11.4g	2.2g	46mg	B-carotene	pot
Plum, x 1, 50g	18	trace	0.3g	4.4g	4.4g	0.8g	2mg	B-carotene	pot

SUGAR AND SWEETENERS

NUTRITIONAL VALUE OF SUGARS AND SWEETENERS

Sugar and the other sweetening foods contain no fat, cholesterol, starch or fibre. Only honey, syrup and treacle contain traces of protein. Their calorie content is all, or virtually all, in the form of sugars. Sugar itself contains no vitamins, and although there are some minerals present (e.g. potassium, calcium, magnesium), these are not present in large enough quantities to make any significant contribution to the diet. Syrup is similarly low in nutrients. Honey contains traces of some B vitamins as well as minerals, but again, not in enough quantity to make a difference to a child's dietary intake. (However, good-quality honey has excellent antiseptic properties and can be used to help heal wounds and treat sore throats, for example.)

Treacle is rich in some important minerals, such as calcium, magnesium and iron, and even quite small quantities of treacle contain good amounts - for example, a 15ml tablespoon will yield 82mg of calcium (15% of a 10-year-old's daily needs), 27mg magnesium (13.5%) and 3mg iron (34%).

Fructose is a sugar found in fruit and, although it contains about the same number of calories as ordinary sugar (sucrose), it is much sweeter, so approximately half the amount can be used to achieve the same sweetness as sugar. It is also absorbed into the bloodstream less rapidly than sucrose, and may help remove 'bad' LDL cholesterol from the blood. However, it may cause diarrhoea and have other side-effects if used too heavily.

As a carbohydrate, sugar contains approximately 4 calories a gram or 20 calories a teaspoonful. Honey contains only around 14 calories a teaspoonful, but is less sweet so more may need to be used.

SUGAR CONSUMPTION

The UK National Diet and Nutrition Survey of pre-school children found that over half of their carbohydrate intake was in the form of sugars rather than starches. Two-thirds of these sugars were in the form of non-milk extrinsic sugars (NMES), i.e. from

SUGAR AND SWEETENERS – NUTRIENTS PER 100G			
	Cals	Tot Carbs	Sodium
Sugar, white	394	105g	5mg
Sugar, brown	394	105g	5mg
Honey	288	76.4g	11mg
Golden syrup	298	79g	270mg
Black treacle	257	67.2g	180mg
Fructose (fruit sugar)	384	100g	n/k

items such as sweets and sugars added in food processing, rather than from milk or from natural foods such as fruits, vegetables, nuts, seeds and grains. Altogether nearly 20% of these children's total calorie intake was in the form of extrinsic sugars – nearly double the recommended amount of 10% of total diet. For older children (aged 4–18), the 2000 survey found that nearly 17% of their total diet is in the form of NMES. Research shows that across the Western world, approximately 75% of this sugar intake is from processed foods and drinks, rather than sugar added to foods at home.

SUGAR AND HEALTH

The reason that health departments of several countries set recommended targets of around 10% for NMES in our diets – and why the World Health Organization, in its 2003 report, suggests an upper limit of 10% of total energy for sugar in manufactured foods – is that there is plenty of convincing evidence that high sugar intake is not good for us or our children.

Sugar and weight: Research in the USA has shown that increased intake of sugary drinks is linked with increased weight and obesity in children, while other research shows that while children's total fat intake over the past 20 years has actually declined slightly, sugar intake is replacing those lost calories. (UK NDN survey 2000).

While a diet high in natural, starchy complex carbohydrates and intrinsic sugars (found within the structure of the food – e.g. in fruit) is linked with good health and ease of weight maintenance, a diet high in NMES is linked with obesity. It is foods such as chocolates, sweets, sugary desserts, cakes and biscuits, which are most likely to be eaten when children are not hungry. Such foods are often also high in fat and low in fibre and are very easy to eat. Cutting out these items and doing nothing else at all can result in slimming down an overweight child over time.

Sugar and oral health: High and/or regular consumption of NMES foods and drinks is linked with an increased risk of dental caries, gum disease and, in the case of certain drinks, with the erosion of tooth enamel.

Sugar and diabetes: A diet high in sugar can be a factor in promoting insulin resistance – a condition where insulin (a hormone that converts blood sugars into energy and has other roles) is produced by the body in ever-increasing amounts to deal with the sugars in the bloodstream. Eventually its action is weakened or its response is blunted so that, over time, more and more insulin is needed in order to clear the blood of sugars. Eventually this can lead to diabetes and is one of the five factors in the increasingly common Western complaint, Syndrome X.

Sugar and other nutrients: As we have seen, sugar contains little except calories. If a high-sugar diet is eaten at the expense of other more nutritious foods, it would be possible for a child to develop malnutrition, with shortfalls in protein, vitamins, minerals, fatty acids, for example… while possibly being overweight!

HOW MUCH SUGAR IS ALL RIGHT?

The table above right shows maximum amounts of NME sugar your child should eat per day at various ages, going by the 10% recommendation. However, some people, myself included, feel that 10% of total calories is still a lot and, if possible, you should aim for nearer 5%, especially if your child has a weight problem or any signs of insulin resistance.

Age	Boys max daily sugar intake	Girls max daily sugar intake
1–3 years	31g	29g
4–6 years	43g	39g
7–10 years	49g	43g
11–14 years	55g	46g
15–18 years	69g	53g

SUGAR IN SELECTED FOODS

Check the amounts of sugars in these foods against the chart above and you may be shocked by the sugar content. For example, one individual Mars Bar contains a whole day's sugar allowance for a 10-year-old girl!

Sweets and chocolate

50g bar of milk chocolate	28.5g
Mars Bar 65g	43g
Fudge, vanilla, 50g	40g
Sherbert sweets, 50g	47g

Drinks

Cola, 500ml bottle	55g
Orange juice, 200ml glass	17.6g
Fizzy orange drink, 500ml bottle	51.5g
Lucozade, 500ml bottle	71.5g
Fruit juice drink in 200ml carton	19.6g

Cakes

Individual (30g) iced French fancy	16g
100g slice of Black Forest gateau	17.4g
100g slice of chocolate fudge cake	44.5g
75g slice of jam and cream sponge	19g

Breakfast cereals

Coco Pops, 30g	12.6g
Crunchy Nut Cornflakes, 30g	11.3g
Ricicles, 30g	12.6g
Muesli cluster-type cereal, 50g	18g

…continued overleaf

Biscuits and bars, per item

Nutrigrain breakfast bar	12g
Milk chocolate digestive (round)	5.2g
Chocolate chip cookie	6.2g
Flapjack, average 60g	20.5g

Desserts

100ml serving of vanilla ice cream	18.7g
100ml serving of full-fat custard	12.8g
50g choc ice	10.2g
Cheesecake, 125g slice	31.2g
100g individual chocolate mousse	17.5g
100g slice of fruit pavlova	41g
100g canned rice pudding	8.7g

Miscellaneous

Low-fat fruit yoghurt, individual 125g	15.9g
Baked beans in tomato sauce, 200g serving	11.8g
Tomato ketchup, 20ml serving	5.5g

HOW TO CUT THE SUGAR IN YOUR CHILD'S DIET

• Always read the label! Sugar is contained in a great many processed foods – even ready-made salads, such as coleslaw, and breads contain sugars. Get in the habit of reading the labels and, if there is a nutrition panel, see how much sugar there is in a portion. As a rough guide, if the product contains more than one-fifth of your child's total daily maximum recommended intake (see the tables above and on page 183), then it contains a lot of sugar. Also check the ingredients list. All the following names are other names for sugar: glucose, dextrose, glucose syrup, lactose, maltose, treacle. And remember the higher up the list they come, the more there is in the product.

• Avoid giving your child too much fruit juice, as well as the more obvious sugary soft drinks. The sugar in juice doesn't count as 'intrinsic' as it does in whole fruit, and it is just as bad for children's teeth, and just as high in calories, as ordinary sugar. Offer water or very diluted juice instead.

• Try to get into the habit of giving children a low-sugar diet right from weaning. Small children

need more fat than adults, but they don't need a lot of sugar. Try to give them sweet tastes in natural products, such as fresh and dried fruits.

• If you make cakes and bakes at home, they are likely to contain a lot less sugar then commercial varieties. Try adding prune or apricot purée to cakes instead of a lot of sugar. Just simmer the dried fruits in a little water to cover until tender, let cool and purée in a blender, then tip the fruit into your recipe to replace an equal amount of sugar. This also works to replace fat (or replace half fat, half sugar).

• If buying any commercial foods which come in a reduced-sugar version, get them – you can save a lot of grams of sugar a day by doing this. But, in general, try to buy fewer of the ready-made, high-sugar products.

• Research shows that trying to ban your child from sweets and chocolate rarely works. Instead, either give a certain amount of pocket money for confectionery, and, when it is gone, be strong or allocate a time of day (say, straight after supper) when children can have a small amount of sweets.

WHY DO CHILDREN LOVE SUGAR?

Young children are thought to enjoy sweet tastes because breast milk is sweet. There are then two main schools of thought about why this liking for sweet things continues. Sugar may be if not actually addictive then perhaps difficult to resist because, one expert has found, eating sweet food causes the brain's levels of opiates to increase. These stimulate dopamine, which is a 'happy' chemical, like serotonin.

Other experts believe that a liking for sugar is a learned habit, like a taste for salt, with an added element of 'reward', i.e. sweet foods are often used as bribes, rewards for good behaviour, instant remedies for a cut or a disappointment, or treats for special occasions. They are thus linked in children's minds with something desirable or comforting.

And, of course, the shops are full of sugary foods and drinks, and items with 'hidden' sugar, which reinforces the message. Manufacturers love sugar because it is cheap and plentiful, and can make indifferent products appealing to children.

S

They should then wait half an hour before cleaning their teeth thoroughly.

• Choose low-sugar varieties of breakfast cereal and add a little sweetness, if necessary, with chopped fresh fruit or a little dried fruit.

• Reduce the sugar in your child's diet slowly. Research shows this is a better way, which has longer-lasting results than making them go 'cold turkey'. Children who are used to a low-sugar diet find sweet foods that other children enjoy, such as sweets, packet desserts and sugary drinks, much too sweet for their taste buds. It takes around 2 months to effect the change.

See also: Confectionery p95–6, Diabetes p101 Junk Food pp140–3, Obesity pp152–5, Teeth and Gums p189–90.

SUPPLEMENTS

As a general rule, food supplements in the form of pills, drops and so on shouldn't be necessary for healthy children following a normal balanced diet. If this is the case and you are considering supplements for a child for any reason, it is best to discuss the reasons why you think they are necessary with your doctor who will advise you and/or put you in touch with a dietitian.

Supplementing when you don't really know what you're doing is fraught with possible problems (see the box opposite) and may do more harm than good. What's more, if a supplement really is necessary, in the UK it should be provided for children free via the NHS, rather than paying what can be premium prices.

Some supplements that are most commonly given to children are:

• **Vitamin D for small children.** In the UK, the advice is that children up to 2 years of age should receive vitamin D supplements (in the UK those provided on the NHS also contain vitamins C and A), unless the professional adviser is confident that the child is receiving an adequate intake from the diet or the sun. In practice, deficiency is only likely if the child rarely gets

• There is a risk of overdosing on some supplements if the maximum recommended intake is overstepped (see Minerals pp148–9 and Vitamins pp194–6 for recommended dosages). Single doses of vitamin A of only 100mg can be harmful for children. High intakes of vitamin D can lead to failure to thrive in children. High doses of vitamin B6 can cause nerve problems, and high doses of vitamin C can cause diarrhoea. Excess zinc can hinder absorption of other minerals. And so on. If you are providing your child with any supplement, you must ensure that it is taken at the recommended dosage.

• Sometimes supplements can interfere with the action of prescription drugs. For example, calcium supplements can interact with some antibiotics; fish oils can react with Warfarin.

• Herbal supplements – such as echinacea or gingko biloba, for example – should not be given to children.

• The UK Food Standards Agency also advises against any supplements that contain chromium picolinate.

outdoors, or is given cows' milk rather than formula milk or breast milk before weaning.

• **Iron for girls during and after puberty.** A significant proportion of girls become iron-deficient once they start their periods, and if there are signs of anaemia your doctor will do a test and may prescribe iron tablets. Don't buy iron tablets yourself without getting your daughter checked out.

• **Multi-vitamins/ minerals** for children with eating problems or disorders and/or failure to thrive. Such children should be in the care of a physician anyway.

• **Supplements for vegans or children with special diets** who may run the risk of lack of nutrients in the diet – for example, iron, calcium and vitamin B12 may be deficient in vegan children.

In addition, children with ADHD, autism, eczema, asthma, learning difficulties or behavioural problems may benefit from supplements of omega-3 fish oils. As this is a fairly new area of medical research, your doctor may not suggest supplementing even if your child has one, or a combination, of these problems. There is no harm in giving your child a 100mg-a-day omega-3 supplement, especially if he or she doesn't eat fish or oily fish. The only contraindication is if a person is on Warfarin or other anti-blood clotting drugs, but this normally applies to older people.

See also: ADHD pp71–2, Asthma p76, Anaemia p73, Autism p76, Behavioural Problems pp78–9, Brain Power pp81–2, Eczema pp107–8, Minerals pp148–9, Phytochemicals p160, Vitamins pp194–6, Appendix 1 pp240–9 for sources of vitamins, minerals, phytochemicals and essential fats.

SWEETCORN

Nutrients per 100g:

Frozen kernels		Baby corn cobs	
Cals	85	Cals	24
Tot Fat	0.8g	Tot Fat	0.4g
Sat Fat	trace	Sat Fat	trace
Prot	2.5g	Prot	2.5g
Tot Carbs	17g	Tot Carbs	2.7g
Sugars	1.9g	Sugars	0.8g
Fibre	2.2g	Fibre	2g
Vits	C, folate	Vits	B-carotene, C, folate
Mins	pot	Mins	pot
Sod	trace	Sod	trace

Sweetcorn, like peas, is often a favourite of children because it is pretty to look at and tastes sweet. Corn contains good amounts of vitamin C, folate and carotenoids, and is a good source of the carotenoids zeaxanthin and lutein, which can help promote eye health.

Keep cooking times as short as possible to retain folate and vitamin C. Cooking with a little oil helps the carotenes to be absorbed – stir-fry baby corn or serve whole corn on the cob with a little butter

See also: Snacks pp178–9 for information on popcorn.

TAKEAWAYS

Although sales from some of the multinational burger chains seem to be on the decline, total sales of takeaways throughout the worlds are certainly not. A quarter of the US population visits a fast-food takeaway outlet every day, while in the UK we spend £1.4billion a year just on ethnic takeaways such as Chinese and Indian, while burgers, pizza and fried chicken account for another £2.5 billion. And much of the sales are to, or for, children. It is a rare child who doesn't have a takeaway burger, pizza, chicken korma or sweet-and-sour on a fairly regular basis and many have them several times a week.

The image of takeaways is one of high-calorie, high-fat foods that are 'bad for you'. But is this true? Well – it can be. Many of the dishes on offer have a high proportion of their calories as fat (e.g. a QuarterPounder with Cheese is 47% fat, a chicken burger (which sounds as if it should be low in fat) is about 41% fat and an average prawn and vegetable stir-fry is a whopping 50% fat even though its total calorie content is quite low) and very many are extremely high in sodium.

The chart opposite shows nutrient content of selected takeaways and lists the percentage each represents of a day's recommended intake for a 10-year-old girl of calories, fat, saturated fat and sodium. For younger children with lower calorie/ fat/ sodium needs, the meals will provide a higher percentage.

TAKEAWAY TYPES

There are, however, wise – or, at least, better – choices to be made. The problem is that it is not always easy working out which takeaways to choose. Some burger bar items can be much lower in fat and saturates than many items from Indian and Chinese takeaways, while side orders such as fries or drinks can contain more calories, fat and even sodium than you might imagine.

Burger bars: If you are of firm mind, you can provide a reasonably balanced meal for your child from most chain burger bars. You will see, for instance, that if your child were to have just a regular hamburger he or she would be having only

TAKEAWAYS

Nutrient values for some common takeaway meals. All values average.
* % rec intake is daily recommended intake for a 10-year-old girl
** % rec intake is daily maximum recommended intake for a 10-year-old girl
*** % recommended daily target for a 10-year-old

	Cals	% rec intake*	Tot Fat	% rec**	Sat Fat	% rec**	Sodium	% rec***
Chicken nuggets (6)	253	14.5%	15g	20%	3.4g	18%	300mg	15%
Chicken caesar salad	374	21.5%	25g	33%	4g	21%	960mg	48%
Chicken burger (incl. bun etc)	375	21.5%	17.2g	23%	3.3g	17.5%	800mg	40%
Chicken chow mein, 300g portion	440	25.3%	21.6g	28.8%	3.6g	19%	1398mg	70%
Chicken curry, 300g portion	435	25%	29.4g	39%	8.7g	46%	1068mg	53.5%
Chicken, fried, 2 pieces	415	21.4%	29g	39%	n/k	n/k	500mg	25%
Chicken or pork, sweet-and-sour, 300g portion	582	33.5%	30g	40%	3.9g	20.5%	777mg	39%
Chicken korma, 300g portion	660	38%	50g	67%	22g	116%	1700mg	85%
Doner kebab, in pitta bread with salad	765	44%	48.6g	65%	23.4g	123%	1650mg	82.5%
Egg fried rice, 250g	465	27%	12.5g	17%	1.8g	9.5%	1045mg	52%
Fish, fried in batter, 250g portion	617	35.5%	38.5g	51%	4g	21%	400mg	20%
Chips (fish shop), 250g small portion	600	34%	31g	41.5%	9g	47.5%	87.5mg	4.5%
French fries, regular	400	23%	16g	21.5%	2.8g	15%	844mg	42%
Hamburger, standard, in bun	255	15%	7.7g	10%	3.3	17%	500mg	25%
Milkshake, strawberry, large	512	29.5%	12.7g	7%	8.7g	46%	trace	trace
Pasta salad with chicken	265	15%	6.7g	9%	trace	trace	100mg	5%
Pizza margherita, whole individual average pizza	621	36%	20.5g	27%	7.7g	41%	617mg	31%
Prawn and vegetable stir-fry, 300g portion	250	14.5%	14g	9%	2g	11%	1608mg	80%
QuarterPounder with Cheese	515	29.5%	27g	36%	13.5g	70%	1100mg	55%

10% of recommended fat intake and 25% of sodium. Some bars now offer a choice of salad as a side dish, or fruit salad to follow. However, as there are only about 250 calories in an average burger, she might feel hungry leaving it just at that – certainly a small burger is not adequate for a 10-year-old child's lunch or evening meal, but add a portion of regular fries and a milkshake to the small burger and she has eaten 67.5% of her day's calories, 48.5% of her fat, 78% of her saturated fat and 67% of her sodium. Nevertheless, this might be all right if, for the rest of the day, she eats foods low in saturated fat and sodium to compensate.

At some large chains you can now get main-course salads, which is a move in the right direction – but beware, as these are not all necessarily low in fat or sodium, although the examples listed above are reasonable – and, of course, there is the benefit of at least a little vegetable in the dishes.

Most chains will supply you with a nutrition leaflet – or visit their websites for nutrition information. The food is standardized, so you can be sure the figures are reasonably accurate.

Pizzas: These vary tremendously in their fat, calorie and sodium content. A pizza with a thick base and a topping that contains plenty of tomato sauce, vegetables and a little Mozzarella cheese can make a balanced contribution to a child's nutrient intake. If the takeaway pizza is eaten at home, you could add a side salad. Large pizza houses will also supply you with nutrient details.

Fried chicken: Breaded, seasoned and deep-fried, takeaway chicken portions are high in fat, calories and sodium. A better bet would be a chicken fillet burger in a bun, sold for example at KFC - but adding mayonnaise lifts the fat content by 6.5g.

Chinese, Thai and Indian: Many choices are high in fat and sodium (or in the case of some Chinese meals, monosodium glutamate – which has been linked with adverse reactions in some people, although scientific evidence for this is thin). At the Chinese, go for stir-fried prawns, chicken with vegetables and plain noodles or boiled rice. At the Indian, tandoori chicken or a chicken or vegetable balti plus plain rice are reasonable choices. Thai

'sizzle' curries are good, but too hot for many children. Dishes containing a lot of cream or coconut cream will always be high in fat.

Fish and chips: Frying fish in batter means that the batter soaks up a lot of fat. Many fish and chip shops will twice-cook their fish and the chips too, so they get a double soaking. The fat may be oxidized if it is used too often, producing trans fats; sometimes lard is still used, which is very high in saturated fat. Most fish and chip portions (especially the chips) are very large – ask for a half portion for your child.

TAKEAWAY TIPS

• If your child is prone to weight gain, or is overweight, choose small or regular-size meals and side orders and drinks, not the large ones – even if they are on special offer. Take your own bottle of water for the child to drink rather than the milkshakes or juices.

• Choose burger/ chicken/ pizza takeaways where there is a choice of salad and fruit.

• Choose ethnic meals which contain vegetables.

• Go for good-quality takeout shops. Poor-quality imported meat and chicken may be sold at the cheaper, smaller bars. Chicken meat at takeouts has been shown to contain pig and cow matter, for example.

• Check out the cleanliness of the takeaway shop: Clean counters? Clean aprons? And so on.

• Limit takeaway meals to occasional visits rather than regular happenings.

• Make sure that your child's diet for the rest of the day counterbalanced what he or she has eaten for the takeaway. For example, if the takeaway meal was high in sodium, avoid high-salt items for the rest of the day. If it was very high in fat, choose lower-fat options for other meals and snacks that day.

• The golden rule for nutrition is 'balance and variety' – takeaways can fit into a child's diet as an occasional or even regular meal – if the bigger picture of the whole diet is good.

See also: 'Daily Nutritional Requirements' pp13, 22, 35 and 55 for nutritional recommendations for girls and boys of varying ages, Fats and Oils pp110–12, Salt pp171–4.

TEA

Tea – black, green or white – is an antioxidant and may help to protect against heart disease and other diseases. Its tannins and fluoride can also help protect teeth. However, tea does contain caffeine, a high intake of which is not a good idea for children, and tannins can hinder the absorption of minerals, including iron. Although tea is calorie-free, a mug made with whole milk and 2 spoonfuls of sugar is approximately 60 calories per cup. If your child enjoys tea, don't serve it with a meal and limit it to 2–3 weak cups a day.

See also: Antioxidants p73, Caffeine p85.

TEETH AND GUMS

TOOTH DECAY

About one in six children under school age has signs of tooth decay and this level rises to 45% by age 5, and 58% by the mid teens. Here we look at the dietary factors that can cause decay and erosion.

Sugar: When sugary foods or drinks are eaten, the bacteria in the mouth feed on the sugar. This produces acid which, if left in contact with the teeth for long, can cause the tooth enamel to dissolve and, eventually, cavities to form. Starches (e.g. bread and biscuits) can also be broken down by the mouth bacteria, and one report showed that sugars mixed with starches in the form of sweet biscuits showed the greatest link with decay.

Acid: Acids in foods and drinks, such as fizzy carbonated drinks which are high in phosphoric acid, fruit juice and children's yoghurts, can soften the enamel surface of the tooth, causing erosion.

WAYS TO KEEP YOUR CHILD'S TEETH AND GUMS HEALTHY:

• Brush teeth with fluoride children's paste as soon as teeth appear. Supervise twice-daily brushing at least until seven years of age. If the teeth aren't properly cleaned, plaque – largely made up of bacteria – can form at the gum margins and will, if not removed regularly, form tartar, a hard deposit

which can cause inflammation, bleeding and gum disease. The British Dental Association (BDA) says that children's teeth shouldn't be flossed.

• Offer water or milk to drink rather than soft drinks and juices. If acidic and/or sugary drinks are offered, give them at meal-times. Small children shouldn't be allowed to sip sweet drinks from drink cups or bottles over long periods nor be given such drinks at bedtime. Acidic drinks bathe the child's mouth in the acids which can destroy tooth enamel.

• After acidic or sugary drinks don't brush the teeth for at least 20–30 minutes, because the drink will soften the tooth enamel surface – immediate brushing could cause what the BDA call 'accelerated abrasion' or increased wear on the enamel.

• Restrict the amount of sugary foods in the diet and, when they are given, encourage your child to eat them in one go rather than chewing them over a period of time. Whole fruits contain both sugar and acids, but the BDA doesn't offer a recommendation on limiting their intake. Crunching on fresh fruit increases saliva in the mouth, which may cancel out some of the effects of the fruit acids. It is a good idea to get your child to rinse his or her mouth out with water after eating apples and other fruit.

• 'Sticky' foods containing sugar and/or starch – such as biscuits, toffee, chocolate – tend to cling to the teeth and may have the potential to cause more damage.

• Frozen ice lollies should be limited – when frozen, the acids which attack tooth enamel take longer to neutralize in the mouth.

• Frequent consumption of yoghurts and fromage frais can contribute to enamel erosion and tooth decay – the bacteria in the milk react with the lactose (milk sugar) to produce acids.

• Non-sugar chewing gum may help keep the gums healthy by stimulating the flow of saliva, which may wash away acids and sugars clinging to the teeth. Strong foods, such as Cheddar cheese, can also stimulate saliva production. Tannins and fluoride in tea can also help prevent tooth decay. Chewing gum should not be given to pre-school age children, however.

OTHER ORAL PROBLEMS

Ulcers: Although a high percentage of mouth ulcers have no obvious cause, there is some evidence that deficiency in vitamin B12, folate or iron may be a factor.

Bad breath: Good mouth hygiene usually prevents bad breath in children, but other causes could be illness (e.g. throat infection, bronchitis) or constipation. Unexplained bad breath that continues for more than a few days should be investigated by your doctor.

Bleeding gums: Frequent bleeding gums may be a sign of vitamin C deficiency.

TOMATOES

Nutrients per 100g tomatoes:

Cals	17	Tot carbs (sugars)	**3.1g**
Tot fat	**0.3g**	Fibre	**1g**
Sat fat	**trace**	Vits	**Beta-carotene, C, E**
Prot	**0.7g**	Mins	**pot**

All tomatoes are rich in lycopene, an antioxidant phytochemical which protects against heart disease and cancers and can also help to build strong bones. Canned tomatoes have a similar nutrient profile, though slightly lower in fibre and vitamin C (12mg per 100g, whereas fresh raw have 17mg); but on the plus side the lycopene in canned (and cooked) tomatoes is better absorbed than in fresh raw ones. As tomatoes also contain beta-carotene which converts to vitamin A in the body, vitamin C and E, (the 'ACE' group of antioxidant vitamins), they are real powerhouses of antioxidant ability.

Some children don't enjoy slices of tomato – and for much of the year commercial tomatoes are dry and tasteless – but do like cherry tomatoes, which can be served whole in a lunch-box or halved and mixed with spring onions or cucumber for a side salad.

Frying, grilling or roasting tomatoes enhances sweetness – most children will enjoy a serving of cooked tomatoes as a side vegetable or on toast. Fry in good-quality oil to increase vitamin E content.

Add canned or fresh chopped tomatoes to stews, casseroles, soups or curries to increase antioxidants. Tomato pastes, purées, passatas and juice are also all rich sources of antioxidants.

See also: Antioxidants p73, Phytochemicals p160, Appendix 1 pp240–7 for a full list of nutrient sources.

UNDERWEIGHT

All children differ, and averages are just that, so if your child falls under the average weight for his height/age but is still within the normal range, that is fine. If he or she is beneath the lowest band, take him or her to the doctor who will advise you if there could be a problem.

Being slim or 'skinny' is partly due to inherited genes – so if the parents are both naturally thin (or were as children), then it is likely that offspring will also be slim. Other children are more active than their friends, and thus burn off more energy (calories). If either of these is the case and your child seems strong, with a good bone structure and of reasonable height, slimness should not be a problem. Indeed, on balance it is probably better for a child to be slightly on the slim side than overweight.

Some children, however, have a smaller appetite than others, or an eating problem, and so take in fewer calories and can get thin that way. It is this group of children that has the most potential for possible problems. As we've seen throughout this book, growing children need a variety of nutrients in the right amounts in order to grow, build muscle and bone, and be healthy. If a child is taking in too few calories he or she is likely also to be taking in too few nutrients and thus may not be giving his or her body the chance to develop peak bone mass, as one example (see Bone Health pages 80–1). So for a child who is a poor eater, follow your doctor's advice.

Occasionally, children can fluctuate in their weight. For instance, if they are going through an illness/convalescence lasting several weeks they may lose weight. And weight gain throughout childhood is rarely steady – there are growth spurts and times when a child eats more, and eats less.

 Sometimes low weight can be an indication of an underlying condition (e.g. diabetes, Crohn's disease) – which is why it is important to see your doctor about very low weight or failure to thrive. Children who are thin because they have an eating disorder need professional help.

TIPS FOR WEIGHT GAIN

If your child needs to gain some weight, and you don't have a specific diet plan from your doctor or dietician, these tips will help:

• Follow a basic healthy diet plan for your child's age as described in the Eating Plans in Feeding Your Child, but add extra calories in the form of extra/larger snacks and calorific drinks. Children who need to gain weight often can't face large meals, so simply increasing portion sizes is rarely the answer – though it's fine do this if your child can eat more.

• Ideal snacks are nuts and seeds (for children over 5), dried fruits and handfuls of muesli.

• Although a diet very high in fat isn't recommended for any schoolchild, whether over- or underweight, as fat contains more calories per gram than other nutrients (9 calories a gram as opposed to 4 for protein and 3.75 for carbohydrate) it is useful to increase the amount of foods which contain higher amounts of the healthy polyunsaturated and monounsaturated fats in order to help a child put on weight. Ideal snacks are nuts and seeds (for children over 5) and handfuls of luxury muesli. These can also be added to soups, casseroles, salads and so on, to add calories. Oily fish are also much higher in calories than white fish, and contain more nutrients.

• Increasing the complex carbohydrate content of a child's diet may also help to put on weight – offer good-quality breads, muesli, oatcakes, tea breads and as snacks. Potatoes, pasta and rice are all fairly high in calories and can be mixed with, or drizzled with, olive oil or similar to increase the calorie content.

• Many children like savoury white sauces, such as cheese or parsley sauce – these are high in calcium and can be added to white fish, ham, pasta, roast vegetables, for example to increase the calorie value of a meal.

• Drinks can provide many calories and nutrients. Milk is ideal as it contains protein and calcium as well as calories – go for whole milk, or home-made milk shakes. At night-time, offer hot milk/hot chocolate/malted drink about half an hour before bed, then get the child to brush his or her teeth immediately before bed. Fortified milky drinks are available at the chemists and supermarkets, containing calories and a range of nutrients and tasting quite pleasant. Juices are also higher in calories than you would think (but their use has some drawbacks).

• Try to avoid giving a lot of extra sweets, chocolate and other sugary foods to help weight gain – they contain few nutrients and are not good for the teeth.

• Don't forget still to offer plenty of fruits and vegetables – although they don't usually contain a lot of calories, they are vital for health.

See also: 'Eating Plans' pp18–19, 28–31, 49–51 and 64–7, Appetite Loss p74, Convalescence pp96–7, Eating Disorder pp105–7, Illness, feeding during p138, Juices pp139–40, Milk pp146–7, Nuts pp151–2, Obesity pp152–5, Seeds p177, Teeth and Gums pp189–90, Appendix 2 pp250–1 for growth charts.

VEGETABLES

Most vegetables are very low in fat, don't contain a great deal of protein and are low or moderate in calories and starch. Almost all vegetables are a good source of dietary fibre, including soluble fibre. Vegetables contain a wide range of vitamins and minerals. Many are good sources of beta-carotene, vitamin C and folate and potassium, while some – especially leafy green vegetables – are good sources of calcium and iron.

Vegetables are also a major source of phytochemicals – natural plant chemicals that can have potent effects in protecting health. One last bonus is that few vegetables are common causes of food allergies in children.

Details of individual vegetables (e.g. Beans, Carrots) appear in their own entries; this entry contains more general information about vegetables in your child's diet, and doesn't include potatoes, which are classed as a carbohydrate food.

FIVE-A-DAY

Two to three portions of vegetables should go towards making up your child's daily 'five-a-day' intake of fruit and vegetables – and yet few children meet this target.

The 2000 survey of British schoolchildren's diets found that less than half met the 'five-a-day' target, less than half ate any raw or salad vegetables (excluding tomatoes and carrots) during the week they were surveyed, and only about a third ate any leafy green vegetables. In the USA, according to the Department of Agriculture, less than 15% of school-age children eat the recommended servings of vegetables.

Fresh, frozen or canned vegetables can count, as can cooked vegetables, as long as they make up a portion. Vegetables in commercial ready-made products can count towards your five-a-day as long as you know that they contain a portion – many manufacturers now include this information on the labels. Many manufactured vegetable soups and ready meals will contain vegetables that can count – but it is best to get as many of your child's vegetable intake as possible in the form of meals that you prepare yourself.

Try to vary your child's intake as much as possible; aim for at least one salad portion a day and for as wide a variety of different colours as possible. Remember: the advice is that your child should aim for *at least* five portions of fruit and vegetables a day – even more may be beneficial.

A note about pulses: Although pulses are not strictly vegetables, one portion a day can count towards a child's five-a-day – with some provisos. The UK Food Standards Agency (FSA) says, 'Beans and pulses can only make up one portion a day no matter how much you eat. And if beans and pulses are providing the protein in your meal, they won't count as a fruit or veg portion too. For example, you might eat egg and baked beans on toast, or chicken with lentil dhal. The egg and chicken provide protein in these meals so the beans and dhal can count as vegetable portions.' Whereas, if your child had a lentil dhal on rice as a main meal with no other protein, then the lentil dhal wouldn't count towards the five a day.

The FSA also says that baked beans in tomato sauce and canned pulses count as a pulse portion, but 'try to choose low-sugar, low-salt varieties of baked beans when you can, and choose pulses canned without added salt if possible'.

TIPS ON SERVING VEGETABLES TO CHILDREN

• There is little appeal or nutritional merit in overboiled vegetables – serve them steamed, baked, microwaved, sautéed or as part of composite dish in order to retain colour, texture, visual appeal and maximum vitamins.

• Children often find vegetable mixes more appetising than one large serving of a single vegetable, so mix and match when you can. Try purées of two vegetables (carrot and parsnip for example) or stir-fries (e.g. beans, carrot, sweetcorn and shredded cabbage).

• For children who don't like their leafy greens, purée them into soups, shred them into casseroles and add them to stir-fries.

• Chunks of vegetable cooked in the roasting pan under a meat joint are delicious – the meat juices drip down on to them and the fats from the meat help the carotenes in the vegetables to be absorbed.

• For reluctant vegetable eaters, vegetable soups are ideal, as they can be puréed and/or mixed with other flavours and textures – e.g. cheese, chicken.

• Adding vegetables to meat dishes increases the nutritional variety of the dish and reduces its total fat content (because you use less meat). For example:

— Finely chopped tomatoes, carrots, onion, celery or mushrooms are ideal to add to minced meat dishes, such as cottage pie, pasta sauce and chilli con carne.

— Chopped or shredded cabbage, swede, parsnips, peppers, broad beans or broccoli are ideal to add bulk and flavour to stews and casseroles.

— Small chunks of cauliflower, squash or aubergine, or whole spinach leaves, work well in curries and other spiced dishes.

— Add broccoli and sweetcorn to chicken stir-fries, mushrooms and Chinese leaves (e.g. pak choi) to beef stir-fries, mixed peppers to pork stir-fries.

— Mix suitable vegetables into rice dishes – for example petit pois, sweetcorn kernels or chopped spring onions.

• Aim for one salad a day for your child. Grate vegetables such as carrots, beet, onion or firm cabbage together in a dressing, or cut vegetables

WHAT IS A PORTION OF VEGETABLES?

This list is based on the UK Department of Health's guide to portions, which will apply to older children and teens as well as adults.

Vegetable	This gives one portion…
Aubergine	⅓ of a whole large fruit
Broad beans	3 tablespoons or 2 serving spoons
Beans, French or runner	4 tablespoons or 2–3 serving spoons
Bottled beetroot	3 whole baby beets or 7 slices
Broccoli	2 average spears (80g)
Brussels sprouts	8 sprouts
Cabbage	2 handfuls/ 3 tablespoons of sliced cabbage (80g)
Carrots, cooked	3 tablespoons/ 2 serving spoons sliced carrot
Carrots, raw, grated	⅓ of a cereal bowl
Cauliflower	8 small florets
Celery	3 stalks
Courgettes	½ large or 1 small
Cucumber	5cm piece
Curly kale	4 tablespooons or 2–3 serving spoons
Leeks	1 trimmed leek
Lettuce (mixed leaves)	1 cereal bowl
Mangetout or sugar snap	1 handful/ 70g
Mixed vegetables, frozen	3 tablespoons or 2 serving spoons
Mushrooms, button sliced	3–4 heaped tablespoons
Onion	1 medium onion
Parsnips	1 large
Peas	3 tablespoons or 2 serving spoons
Pepper, fresh	½ medium pepper
Pulses, cooked – e.g. lentils, cannellini beans, red kidney beans, including baked beans in tomato sauce	3 tablespoons or 2 serving spoons
Spinach, cooked	2 heaped tablespoons
Spinach, raw	1 cereal bowl
Spring greens, cooked	4 tablespoons or 2–3 serving spoons
Spring onion	8 onions
Swede, cooked, diced or mashed	3 tablespoons
Sweetcorn, baby cobs	6 cobs
Sweetcorn, frozen or canned	3 tablespoons or 2 serving spoons
Sweetcorn, on the cob	1 whole cob
Tomato, canned peeled plum	2 whole tomatoes
Tomato, fresh,	1 medium or 7 cherry
Tomato, sun-dried	4 pieces
Tomato or vegetable juice	1 × 150ml glass*

* Only one glass a day of vegetable or fruit juice can count towards the five.

NOTE: All tablespoons should be heaped. If using vegetables in composite dishes, two half portions of different vegetables count as a whole portion – e.g. in a stir-fry, 3 × baby sweetcorn cobs and half a cereal bowl of raw spinach would together count as one portion.

into batons and serve with a dip if your child dislikes the traditional 'lettuce and cucumber' salad. Don't slice, chop or grate vegetables until just before they are needed as they will lose vitamin C and the cut edges will 'oxidize'.

• Halved, scooped-out beef tomatoes, or large flat mushrooms can be filled with a meat or vegetarian mix and baked with a cheese and breadcrumb topping.

See also: 'What is a Serving?' p24, 'Serving Sizes for Children Aged 5–10' p38 and 'Serving Sizes for Teenagers' p56, Carbohydrates pp87–8, Dietary Fibre pp101–2, Food Allergies pp117–19, Fruit pp129–30, Minerals pp148–9, Phytochemicals p160, Vitamins pp194–6 – plus individual entries for vegetables, Appendix 1 pp240–9 for sources of nutrients.

VITAMINS

Vitamins are organic compounds present in minute quantities in the diet which are essential for bodily health and day-to-day functioning.

Vitamins B group and C are water-soluble, meaning that excess intake is excreted in the urine and also that they are leached out of foods when water is used in their preparation or cooking. These vitamins need to be taken on a regular basis as they cannot be stored in the body. Vitamins A, D, E and K are fat-soluble, meaning that they can be stored in the body and surplus is not excreted in the urine.

Each of the eleven vitamins has a different role to play in the body and deficiencies can cause all kinds of growth and health problems. To ensure that a child's diet contains recommended amounts of all the vitamins, a varied, balanced diet is required. If this is in place, there is little need for a parent to pore over vitamin charts, although it is useful to have a working knowledge of which foods are good sources of which vitamins. If a child eats only a small range of foods – as some do, especially when young – you can see which vitamins they may be lacking and discover alternative sources.

Vitamins, like minerals, are best absorbed in foods rather than as supplements. Here we look at the role of the various vitamins and list recommended amounts for children.

VITAMIN A (RETINOL) AND RETINOL EQUIVALENTS (ALPHA- AND BETA-CAROTENE)

What it does: Vision, healthy eyes, skin and growth.

Deficiency can cause: Poor night vision and eye problems and poor resistance to infection.

Found in: Retinol is found in liver, dairy produce, eggs and oily fish. Carotenes can be converted to vitamin A in the body, and they are found in red, orange, yellow and dark green fruits and vegetables. In addition, the carotenes are an important group of phytochemicals with antioxidant powers.

Notes: Excess vitamin A is toxic. It can be stored in the liver and can cause liver and bone damage, and other problems. Excess is linked with birth defects and so high vitamin-A intake should be avoided in pregnancy (no more than 3,300mcg/day). The DoH (UK) recommends that daily intake should not exceed 900mcg in infants; 1800mcg aged 1–3; 3000 aged 4–6; 4500mcg up to 12 and 6000mcg for adolescents. Beta-carotene is not toxic as excess is excreted, although intakes over about 30mg a day may colour the skin orange.

Recommended daily amounts (retinol): 0–12 months 350mcg; 1–3 years 400mcg; 4–6 years 500mcg; 7–10 years 500mcg; 11–14 years 600mcg; 15–18 (males) 700mcg; 15–18 (females) 600mcg.

VITAMIN B1 (THIAMIN)

What it does: Helps to release carbohydrate from foods and ensures supply of glucose to the brain and nerves.

Deficiency can cause: The disease beri beri.

Found in: Variety of foods, including pork, bacon and nuts.

Notes: Excess not harmful. As B vitamins are water-soluble they can be leached from food during prolonged simmering.

Recommended daily amounts: 0–9 months 0.2mg; 10–12 months 0.3mg; 1–3 years 0.5mg; 4–10 years 0.7mg; 11–14 years 0.9mg (males) 0.7mg (females); 15–18 years 1.1mg (males) 0.8mg (females).

VITAMIN B2 (RIBOFLAVIN)

What it does: Helps release fat and protein from the food that we eat and convert it for use as energy and lean tissue. Maintains healthy skin and mucous membrane.

Deficiency can cause: Eye and mouth problems.

Found in: Offal, fortified breakfast cereals, dairy produce.

Notes: Water-soluble vitamin; no upper safe limits.

Recommended daily amounts: 0–12 months 0.4mg; 1–3 years 0.6mg; 4–6 years 0.8mg; 7–10 years 1mg; 11–14 years 1.2mg (males) 1.1mg (females); 15–18 years 1.3mg (males) 1.1mg (females).

VITAMIN B3 (NIACIN)

What it does: Helps to release energy from food and requirement is related to the amount of energy expended.

Deficiency can cause: Pellagra, a sunburn-like skin complaint which is rare but can be fatal.

Found in: Yeast extract, liver, meat and fish.

Notes: Very high intakes (3g plus for adults, less for children) can cause liver and kidney damage, which is reversible if B3 intake is withdrawn.

Recommended daily amounts: 0–6 months 3mg; 7–9 months 4mg; 10–12 months 5mg; 1–3 years 8mg; 4–6 years 11mg; 7–10 years 12mg; 11–14 years 15mg (males) 12mg (females); 15–18 years 18mg (males) 14mg (females).

VITAMIN B6 (PYRIDOXINE)

What it does: Important player in the metabolization of protein and helps the body to manufacture vitamin B3 (niacin) from the amino acid tryptophan if necessary; helps blood health.

Deficiency can cause: With B12 and folate, B6 deficiency plays a part in causing high levels of the amino acid homocysteine in the blood, which is linked with heart disease.

Found in: Meats, fish, eggs, whole grains, fortified cereals, some vegetables.

Notes: May help to ease the symptoms of PMS, but high doses are inadvisable as they can cause nerve damage at levels over 50mg a day.

Recommended daily amounts: 0–6 months 0.2mg; 7–9 months 0.3mg; 10–12 months 0.4mg; 1–3 years 0.7mg; 4–6 years 0.9mg; 7–10 years 1mg; 11–14 years 1.2mg (males) 1mg (females); 15–18 years 1.5mg (males) 1.2mg (females).

VITAMIN B12

What it does: Necessary for the formation of blood cells and nerves.

Deficiency can cause: Pernicious anaemia, nerve damage, with B6 and folate can contribute to high blood homocysteine levels (see B6).

Found in: Meat, fish, animal produce, seaweed.

Notes: Vegans may need a supplement as B12 is only found in animal produce, apart from seaweed.

Recommended daily amounts: 0–6 months 0.3mcg; 6–12 months 0.4mcg; 1–3 years 0.5mcg; 4–6 years 0.8mcg; 7–10 years 1mcg; 11–14 1.2mcg; 15–18 1.5mcg.

FOLATE

What it does: Vital for formation of blood cells and infant development.

Deficiency can cause: Birth defects, such as spina bifida; megaloblastic anaemia, and with B6 and B12 deficiency can contribute to high blood homocysteine levels (see B6).

Found in: Offal, leafy greens, whole grains, nuts, pulses, fortified breakfast cereals.

Notes: Very high folate intake may hinder absorption of zinc. New research indicates that folate supplements in pregnancy can lower the chances of a child developing leukaemia.

Recommended daily amounts: 0–12 months 50 mcg; 1–3 years 70mcg; 4–6 years 100mcg; 7–10 years 150mcg; 11–18 years 200mcg.

VITAMIN C

What it does: Antioxidant vitamin helps boost immune system; builds healthy connective tissue, bones and teeth, helps wound and fracture healing, helps iron absorption.

Deficiency can cause: Bleeding gums, poor wound healing, low resistance to infection and, eventually, scurvy, which is nowadays very rare in Western society.

Found in: Fruits and vegetables.

Notes: Extra vitamin C may be needed when the body is under stress. This water-soluble vitamin needs to be taken regularly as the body cannot store it. High doses of vitamin C can produce a laxative effect and/or stomach irritation. Vitamin C is best taken in the form of real food rather than supplements. Many experts feel that the RDAs for vitamin C may be too low – certainly moderately higher intakes may be beneficial and 60–100mg a day may be a better target for schoolchildren.

V

Recommended daily intake: 0–12 months 25mg; 1–10 years 30mg; 11–14 years 35mg; 15–18 years 40mg.

VITAMIN D (CHOLECALCIFEROL)

What it does: Helps mineral absorption in the body and therefore vital for building bone.

Deficiency can cause: Rickets in children.

Found in: Eggs, oily fish, fortified breakfast cereals, fortified margarines, manufactured by sunlight on the body.

Notes: This fat-soluble vitamin is necessary in the diet in the early years of a child's life; later, sunlight normally provides enough for children. Excess vitamin D causes kidney damage and other problems.

Recommended daily amounts: 0–6 months 8.5mcg; 7–12 months 7mcg; 1–3 years 7mcg; 4 and over – no dietary need.

VITAMIN E (TOCOPHEROL)

What it does: Antioxidant vitamin which protects cell membranes and helps prevent plaque build up in the arteries; thins the blood and thus helps prevent heart disease; boost immune system and may protect against cancers; helps boost skin condition, healing and fertility. Also prevents polyunsaturated fats from oxidizing.

Deficiency can cause: Blood problems in premature infants, nerve problems in older children.

Found in: Leafy green vegetables, whole grains, nuts, seeds, butter, egg yolk, poultry, seafood.

Notes: Requirement for vitamin E is closely linked with intake of polyunsaturated oils – the higher the fat intake, the more vitamin E is required. Because of this the UK doesn't set RDAs for vitamin E, so the following figures are those set by the USA Department of Health; amounts are IUs (international units) where one IU is approximately equal to 1mg vitamin E.

Recommended daily intake: 0–6 months 3IU; 6–12 months 4IU; 1–3 years 6IU; 4–10 years 7IU; 11–18 years – males 10IU, females 8IU.

VITAMIN K

What it does: Essential for normal blood clotting.

Deficiency: Rare but may occur in cystic fibrosis or liver disease. Deficiency at birth can cause bleeding disorders.

Found in: Widespread, but green leafy vegetables are a major source.

Notes: Vitamin K can be synthesized in the body so no RDAs have been set. However some new born babies are deficient and so supplements are routinely given at birth.

See also: Antioxidants p73, Periods and PMS p160, Phytochemicals p160, Supplements pp185–6, Appendix 1 pp240–3 for sources of vitamins.

WATER

Infants who are being breast-fed or on formula milk don't need much in the way of extra fluids, but once they start on solids they will need to increase their fluid intake. Water is the ideal fluid to add to their milk allowance as it can make no contribution to tooth decay or over-consumption of calories.

Schoolchildren should drink about 6–8 glasses of fluid a day, more during hard exercise or hot weather. Regular water intake can help to prevent constipation and if you can get children used to drinking water at an early age rather than sugary and/or acidic soft drinks (including juice) this may be of long-term benefit both to their waistlines and their dental health.

See also: 'Drinks for Infants' p16, Caffeine p85, Carbonated Drinks pp88–9, Coffee p94, Constipation p96, Drinks pp103–4, Milk pp146–7, Tea p189, Teeth and Gums pp189–90.

WHEAT
see Grains

WHOLE FOODS

Whole foods is a term that has come to represent food which is in its natural, unadulterated form – e.g. whole grains, fresh fruits and vegetables, nuts, seeds and pulses. Some people may also interpret the phrase to cover food which is organic, but the term may have any variety of other meanings.

V

As a general rule, whole unprocessed or minimally processed foods should form a significant part of the older child's diet as they are likely to contain more vitamins, minerals and dietary fibre, and fewer of the not-so-good things, such as saturated fat, sugar and additives. They can also be more satisfying to hunger, take more chewing and can thus help prevent overweight, and children raised on a whole-food diet may have less of a taste for sugary, fatty snacks and sweets.

See also: Health Foods p135, Processed Foods pp164–5.

YOGHURT AND FROMAGE FRAIS

Yoghurt and fromage frais can be good sources of calcium for children, but full-fat varieties contain over half of their calories as fat, a significant amount of which is saturated. Many yoghurts aimed at children contain a good deal of added sugar or fruit sugars, and the speciality varieties containing items such as crunchy sweets, chocolate chips, etc., are not the healthy foods some parents perceive them to be. They may also contain several food additives and 'fruit flavours' are just that – flavourings not real fruit.

Go for natural yoghurt or fromage frais and add puréed fruits yourself, or drizzle honey over the top. Younger children can enjoy full-fat yoghurt, but as children's fat needs decline it is best to choose the lower-fat varieties. Bio yoghurts contain natural bacteria which help to keep the gut colonized and thus aid digestion, and can help to prevent both constipation and diarrhoea. If children are having to take antibiotics, these will kill off the good bacteria in the gut, and bio yoghurt can help to replace them.

Yoghurt may be tolerated even by children who are intolerant of cows' milk as the fermentation process aids digestion. Greek yoghurt made from ewes' milk is also useful. Soya 'yoghurt' is an alternative for vegans but unless specifically labelled as 'calcium-fortified', will contain only around 15mg calcium per 100g, as opposed to around 162mg/100g for low-fat natural yoghurt, for example.

See also: Dairy Produce p98, Desserts pp99–100, Food Additives pp114–17, Teeth and Gums pp189–90.

YOGHURT AND FROMAGE FRAIS – NUTRIENTS PER 100G										
	Cals	Tot Fat	Sat Fat	Chol	Protein	Tot Carbs	Sugars	Vits	Mins	Sodium
Whole-milk natural yoghurt	79	3g	1.7g	11mg	5.7g	7.8g	7.8g	B2, B12	calc, iod	80mg
Greek yoghurt	92	6g	3.8g	17mg	4.8g	5g	5g	B2, B12	calc, iod	66mg
Low-fat natural yoghurt	56	1g	0.7g	1mg	4.8g	7.4g	7.1g	B2, B12	calc, iod	63mg
Soya yoghurt, fruit-flavoured	73	1.8g	0.3g	—	2g	13g	12g	E	—	24mg
Fromage frais, natural, 8% fat	113	8g	5.5g	9mg	6g	4.4g	4.1g	A, B2, B12	calc	36mg
Fromage frais, natural, 0% fat	49	trace	trace	1mg	7.7g	4.6g	4.1g	B2, B12	calc	37mg

Y

RECIPES

Although children will eat and enjoy takeaways and ready meals, there are few children who don't appreciate a home-cooked meal. Even for busy working parents, preparing at least some of the children's food from scratch is feasible – there are many quick and easy recipe ideas which are both healthy and packed with 'child appeal'.

Children will always have a few foods they don't like and won't eat but there are so many ingredients to choose from that it isn't hard to give them a really tasty, balanced diet.

To help you choose the right recipes for your own child or children, here are some guidelines on using the recipe section.

RECIPES TO SUIT DIFFERENT AGES

These symbols are a guide to which age group(s) the recipes are suitable for:

6mths+   Suitable for infants over 6 months old

1+   Suitable for children over 1 year old

5+   Suitable for children over 5 years old

11+   Particularly suitable for children over 11 years old, though may also be suitable for children over 1.

Don't make recipes suitable for children over a certain age for younger children as they may contain unsuitable ingredients. For example, infants shouldn't eat soft cheeses, so you wouldn't serve them the

Brie and Tomato Toastie on page 203, which is designed for children over 1).

USING THE SYMBOLS

All of the recipes feature in one or more of the eating plans in Section 1 so that you can see how they might fit into a balanced diet. Each recipe has its own list of symbols to help you choose meals for children with particular needs; a key to the symbols is provided at the bottom of each page. **Note:** Where recipes are designated 'Nut-and-seed-free' this does not include spice seeds such as cumin.

CALORIE COUNTS

Each recipe is also calorie-counted, which may help if your child is prone to overweight. Normal-weight active children do need a lot of calories, however, so many recipes are high in energy to reflect this.

PORTION GUIDELINES

Portion sizes in recipes particularly suitable for infants and pre-school children are smaller than those for older children. If making these recipes for older children, be aware that they will make fewer servings than stated. Indeed, depending on your child's appetite and activity levels, the number of servings from each recipe will vary.

OTHER INFORMATION

Each recipe also tells you which nutrients it supplies in good amounts, and whether the dish can be frozen. I have tried to pick plenty of recipes that will freeze so that you can batch cook to save time.

SOUPS, SNACKS AND DIPS

RED LENTIL AND TOMATO SOUP

 6mths+

Suitable age 6 months+, serves 4–6
Calories per portion: 128 (for 4) 86 (for 6)
Good source of: protein, complex carbohydrate, carotenoids, potassium, iron.
Will freeze.

This colourful soup is simple but full of flavour. For infants, choose a vegetable stock with no added salt, or make your own by simmering 500g total weight of carrot, celery, onion, leek and parsley in 600ml of water for 1 hour; strain and cool. Refrigerate for up to 2 days or freeze.

1 tbsp light olive oil
1 small onion, finely chopped

100g red lentils
150ml unsalted vegetable stock
100ml passata

1 Heat the oil in a saucepan and sauté the onion for 10 minutes, or until softened but not coloured. Use non-extra virgin olive oil so that the flavour won't be too strong.

2 Add the lentils and vegetable stock, bring to a gentle simmer, cover with a lid and cook for 45 minutes, or until the lentils are tender.

3 Add the passata and stir well, allow to cool slightly, then blend the soup thoroughly in an electric blender. Reheat to serve.

Low fat	Low saturated fat	High fibre	Suitable for vegetarians

CARROT AND ORANGE SOUP

 1+

Suitable age 1 year+, serves 4–6
Calories per portion: 120 (for 4) 80 (for 6)
Good source of: vitamins B6, folate, C, E, carotenoids, potassium.
Will freeze.

This bright soup has an appealing colour and a good, thick consistency which makes it easy for infants and young children to eat, and the tangy yet sweet taste will ensure it is a hit.

1 tbsp groundnut oil
1 medium onion, finely chopped
2 medium carrots, peeled and chopped
250g canned chopped tomatoes
juice of 1 large orange
good pinch of ground cumin seeds
good pinch of ground coriander seeds
400ml unsalted vegetable stock
small pinch of salt as necessary

1 Heat the oil in a saucepan and sauté the onion over a medium heat for 10 minutes, until it is soft but not browned. Add the carrots, stir for a minute, then add the rest of the ingredients, excluding the salt. Stir and bring to a simmer, turn the heat down, cover with a lid and cook for approximately 30 minutes, or until the carrots and onions are tender.

2 Allow to cool slightly, then liquidize in an electric blender until smooth. Reheat before serving. Add a very small amount of salt as liked.

Tip: Freeze in individual lidded containers so that the soup can be defrosted as required.

CHUNKY VEGETABLE AND KIDNEY BEAN SOUP

 1+

Suitable age 1 year+, serves 4–6
Calories per portion: 145 (for 4) 97 (for 6)
Good source of: protein, complex carbohydrate, vitamins C, E, potassium, iron.
Will freeze.

Soups are an excellent way to introduce small children to the varied tastes of pulses. Many children who don't like whole kidney beans will enjoy this partially blended soup, while the small, tender vegetable chunks will help to encourage toddlers to accept 'lumps'. See Red Lentil and Tomato Soup, opposite, for home-made vegetable stock.

1 tbsp light olive oil
1 medium red onion, finely chopped
1 medium red pepper, deseeded and cut into
  1cm squares
1 (150g) sweet potato, peeled and cut into
  1cm chunks
300ml unsalted vegetable stock
200g canned tomatoes

200g canned red kidney beans, well drained and
  rinsed, lightly mashed with a fork
small pinch of salt as necessary

1 Heat the oil in a saucepan, add the onion and pepper, and sauté over a medium heat for 10–15 minutes, or until everything is tender and just turning golden.

2 Add the sweet potato and stock, bring to simmer and cook, covered, for 30 minutes. Stir in the tomatoes and mashed kidney beans, return to simmer and cook for a further 10 minutes.

3 Allow the soup to cool a little, then remove half of it and blend in an electric blender. Return the blended soup to the pan, stir in well and reheat before serving, adding a pinch of salt if you like.

Tip: Small children have not developed a taste for salt so, unless you are also serving this soup to older children, just serve it without any extra salt.

Suitable for vegans	Dairy-free	Wheat- and gluten-free	Nut- and seed-free

LENTIL AND VEGETABLE SOUP

Suitable age 1 year+, serves 4–6
Calories per portion: 197 (for 4) 130 (for 6)
Good source of: vitamins B6, C, folate, carotenoids, potassium, iron, selenium.
Will freeze.

'Hiding' healthy foods is one way of ensuring children get their daily requirement of fruit and vegetables. Soups are an excellent method of including green vegetables – this Italian-style soup contains both broccoli and cabbage.

1 tbsp light olive oil
1 medium onion, finely chopped
150g green lentils
2 medium carrots, peeled and finely chopped
100g white cabbage, grated
350ml unsalted vegetable stock
100g broccoli, cut into very small florets
1 medium courgette, grated
small pinch of salt as necessary

1 Heat the oil in a saucepan and sauté the onion over a medium heat for 10 minutes or until soft and just turning golden.

2 Add the lentils, carrots and cabbage, and stir for a minute, then add the stock and bring to a simmer. Turn the heat down, cover and simmer for 45 minutes or until the lentils are tender.

3 Add the broccoli and courgette with a little water if the soup is looking too thick, and simmer for a further 15 minutes, then allow to cool a little.

4 Blend two-thirds of the soup in an electric blender until smooth and return to the pan, stirring thoroughly to combine. Reheat to serve, adding a pinch of salt if you like.

Tip: For all soups or other dishes containing pulses (e.g. lentils, kidney beans) as the main source of protein, serve the soup with a portion of bread – the proteins in the grain complement the proteins in the pulses to form 'complete protein' (see Protein pages 165–6).

CHICKEN SOUP

Suitable age 1 year+, serves 4–6
Calories per portion: 150 (for 4) 100 (for 6)
Good source of: protein, vitamins B3, B6, C, carotenoids, potassium, zinc, selenium.
Will freeze.

Chicken soup has long been regarded as a traditional dish to feed to anyone who is ill or feeling below par, as it seems to have reviving and restorative powers. Indeed, research shows that chicken soup really does boost the immune system and help speed recovery! It is also very tasty.

2 large chicken leg portions (on the bone)
100g swede or parsnip, peeled and cut into
  1cm chunks
2 medium carrots, peeled and cut into
  1cm chunks
1 (200g) old potato, peeled and cut into
  2cm chunks
1 large leek, trimmed, thoroughly cleaned
  and cut into 5mm rounds
2 medium celery stalks, chopped

900ml unsalted vegetable stock
1 tbsp chopped parsley
a little black pepper (optional)
small pinch of salt, if necessary

1 Put all the ingredients except the parsley and salt, into a large saucepan and bring to the boil, then reduce the heat down to a simmer and cover. Cook for an hour and then remove the chicken portions from the saucepan. Allow to cool slightly.

2 When cool enough to handle, remove all the chicken skin and discard. Tear all the flesh off the bones and chop it into small pieces and return the flesh to the soup.

3 Bring the soup back to the simmer and cook gently for 5 minutes, then serve the soup garnished with the parsley, adding a little salt if you like.

Tip: This soup is best served with chunks of bread to mop up the juices.

Low fat	Low saturated fat	High fibre	Suitable for vegetarians

POTATO SOUP

Suitable age 1 year+, serves 4–6
Calories per portion: 170 (for 4) 112 (for 6)
Good source of: complex carbohydrates, potassium.
Will freeze.

1 tbsp light olive oil
1 large onion, finely chopped
400g potatoes, peeled and cut into cubes
400ml low-salt vegetable stock
400ml semi-skimmed milk
a pinch of salt
pepper (optional)

1 Heat the oil in a non-stick saucepan and sauté the onion over a medium heat for 10 minutes or until well softened but not coloured.

 1+

2 Add the potatoes and stir for a minute, then add the remaining ingredients and bring to a simmer. Cover and cook for about 30 minutes, or until the vegetables are tender. Allow to cool slightly.

3 Either whiz the soup for a very short time in an electric blender so that you still have a slightly lumpy texture, or bash with a masher to combine the liquid and potato pieces well. Reheat to serve.

Tip: To vary, try adding one of the following for the last few minutes of cooking: bunch of watercress, stalks trimmed; 100g petit pois (fully defrosted if frozen) and 1 dessertspoon of finely chopped fresh mint; 100g baby spinach.

Note: If no other protein is served at the same meal, add a level tbsp of grated Cheddar cheese to each portion before serving. This will add about 62 calories per portion.

BRIE AND TOMATO TOASTIE

Suitable age 1 year+, serves 1
Calories per portion: 377
Good source of: protein, complex carbohydrates, vitamins A, B1, B2, B3 and B12, folate, calcium, magnesium, iron, selenium.
Do not freeze.

2 large slices of wholemeal bread (each about 30g)
10g (2 tsp) low-fat spread
60g ripe Brie, cut into thin slices
a few drops of balsamic vinegar

1+

1 medium ripe tomato, cut into thin slices
2 basil leaves, chopped

1 Spread the bread with the low-fat spread and arrange the cheese on top. Drizzle the balsamic vinegar over and arrange the tomato slices and chopped basil on top.

2 Top with the remaining bread and toast the sandwich in a sandwich toaster.

Note: For an open sandwich, use one 60g slice of bread, and pop under the grill until the Brie has melted.

CHEESE DIP

Suitable age 1 year +, serves 4–6
Calories per portion: 118 (4) 78 (6)
Good source of: protein, vitamins A, B2, B12, calcium, iodine.
Do not freeze.

This dip is light but tasty and goes well with raw vegetable crudités, home-made crisps or potato wedges. It can also be used as a toast topper or filling for baked potatoes. By using goats' cheese instead of cream cheese, you reduce the total fat content considerably and boost protein content.

 1+

100ml natural whole-milk bio yoghurt
100g soft rindless goats' cheese
2 tsp tomato ketchup
15g finely grated Cheddar cheese
dash of celery salt

To make, simply blend all the ingredients together in a bowl and chill to serve.

Suitable for vegans | Dairy-free | Wheat- and gluten-free | Nut- and seed-free

HOME-MADE BAKED BEANS IN TOMATO SAUCE

Suitable age 1 year+, serves 2–4
Calories per portion: 388 (2) 194 (40
Good source of: protein, complex carbohydrates, carotenoids, potassium, iron.
Do not freeze.

As the recipe uses ready-cooked beans, it is quite quick to prepare and cook – especially if you have batch-cooked some tomato sauce – but contains far less salt and sugar than canned baked beans. These home-made baked beans are great on toast, or with sausages, bacon, ham, baked potato or burgers.

> 400g canned ready-cooked haricot beans
> 1 tbsp light olive oil
> 1 medium onion, finely chopped
> 1 tsp French mustard
> 1 dsp soft brown sugar
> 1 dsp black treacle

juice of ¼ lemon
dash of vegetarian Worcestershire sauce
pinch of salt
1 recipe-quantity of Tomato Sauce (page 237)

1 Preheat the oven to 150°C/gas 2. Drain the haricot beans, rinse them and tip them into a casserole dish.

2 Heat the oil in a saucepan or frying pan and sauté the onion for 10 minutes or until soft and just turning golden. Add the remaining ingredients and stir to combine, bring to a simmer and cook for a few minutes.

3 Pour this sauce over the beans, cover and bake for 1 hour, stirring twice during cooking. When you stir, if the mixture looks as if it is drying out, stir in a little hot water or tomato juice. Adjust the seasoning to taste before serving.

HOME-MADE VEGETABLE CRISPS

Suitable age 1 year+, serves 6
Calories per 35g portion: 150
Good source of: carotenoids, potassium.
Do not freeze.

Although these vegetable crisps are high in fat, they are very low in saturated and trans fats, and their salt content is very, very much lower than that of commercial potato crisps. They also contain more nutrients.

> 200g selection of root vegetables (peeled weight)
>   e.g. parsnip, sweet potato, swede, potato
> sunflower oil or groundnut oil
> sea salt
> black pepper

1 Slice the vegetables into thin strips using a vegetable peeler or a mandolin. Rinse them and dry them thoroughly using kitchen paper.

2 Heat about 5cm of oil in a large saucepan, making sure that the oil comes no higher than halfway up the sides. The oil is hot enough when a small cube of stale bread dropped into it goes golden brown within 30 seconds. Add the vegetables in three or four batches. When golden, remove with a slotted spatula and drain on kitchen paper.

3 Sprinkle with sea salt and pepper, allow to cool, then serve or store in an airtight container.

Note: You can use slices of beetroot, but these are best cooked separately.

Note: For lower-fat crisps you can slice the vegetables very slightly thicker (about 1.5mm), toss them in oil, season and bake on a non-stick heavy-duty baking tray for 30 minutes, turning after 20 minutes. However, these crisps will not be so 'crispy' and are less suitable for a lunch-box, but ideal for home snacking. They will contain approximately 80 calories per serving.

Low fat | Low saturated fat | High fibre | Suitable for vegetarians

PEANUT BUTTER, BANANA AND HONEY TOASTIE

 1+

Suitable age 1 year+, serves 1
Calories per portion: 345
Good source of: complex carbohydrates, vitamins B1, B3, folate, E, magnesium, iron, iodine, selenium.
Do not freeze.

This nutritious snack is filling enough for a small child, or can be used as a snack for older, active children.

1 thick 60g slice of wholemeal bread
1 tbsp smooth peanut butter
1 small banana
1 dsp runny honey

1 Toast the bread under the grill on both sides and then spread one side with the peanut butter.

2 Peel the banana, thinly slice it and arrange evenly over the butter. Drizzle the honey over the top evenly and then pop the bread under the grill for a few minutes until the banana starts to cook. Serve immediately, cut into quarters.

Note: Children at high risk of peanut allergy should not be given peanuts or peanut butter until three years old or, some experts feel, five years old.

Tips: This snack is suitable for vegans if the bread used contains no animal fat. If you have a sandwich toaster, you can use two 30g slices of bread instead of the one large slice and fill them with the peanut butter/banana/honey mixture before toasting.

HUMMUS

 1+

Suitable age 1 year+, serves 4–6
Calories per portion: 210 (4) 140 (6)
Good source of: protein, complex carbohydrates, vitamin E, calcium, magnesium, iron, zinc.
Will freeze; store in fridge 2–3 days.

Hummus is an ideal way to serve pulses to children who might not otherwise be keen: as a dip, on toast, as a sandwich or pitta filler, or stirred into soups and stews.

400g canned chickpeas, drained
juice of 1 lemon
2 tbsp light olive oil
1 tbsp light tahini (sesame seed paste)
1 garlic clove, well crushed (optional)
salt and black pepper to taste

Blend all the ingredients in an electric blender, adding a little water as necessary. Aim for a soft consistency for dips, and slightly thicker for sandwiches, etc.

Note: You can omit the garlic for younger children. Some children are allergic to the sesame seeds in tahini.

Suitable for vegans	Dairy-free	Wheat- and gluten-free	Nut- and seed-free	
				Soups, Snacks and Dips 205

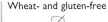

POTATO CAKES

Suitable age 1 year+, serves 2–4
Calories per portion: 292 (for 2) 146 (for 4)
Good source of: complex carbohydrates, vitamin E, potassium.
Will freeze.

These cakes are very straightforward to make and are a good, healthy alternative to chips or ordinary mashed potato. They go well with many foods and are especially nice with bacon, ham, eggs, sausage or fish. You can also add chopped-up cooked green vegetables (e.g. cabbage, spinach, sprouts) to the mixture to make a variation of 'bubble and squeak'.

400g old floury potatoes, peeled and cubed
a pinch of salt
20g butter
black pepper (optional)
1 level dsp finely chopped fresh parsley
small amount of skimmed milk

1 dsp flour
1 tbsp light olive oil

1 Cook the potatoes in lightly salted boiling water until tender. Drain and mash with the butter, parsley, seasoning and a little skimmed milk as necessary (but keep the mixture firm). Allow to cool.

2 When the mash is cool enough to handle, sprinkle the flour on a clean working surface and, using clean hands, form the potato mixture into eight small cakes (be firm about this so that the cakes won't disintegrate when you cook them) and then dust the cakes in the flour.

3 Heat the oil in a non-stick frying pan and, when it is hot, fry the cakes for about 2–3 minutes on each side, until golden. With a spatula, remove from the pan on to kitchen paper and serve.

ROAST MUSHROOM AND TOFU SANDWICH

Suitable age 5 years+, serves 1
Calories per portion: 342
Good source of: protein, complex carbohydrates, vitamins B1, B2, B3, folate, potassium, magnesium, iron, selenium.
Do not freeze.

This sandwich is suitable for vegans if non-dairy spread is used instead of the butter; the recipe will then also be dairy-free. As you need the oven for this recipe, it is a good one to do when the oven is already on for something else. The recipe contains sesame oil, so as some children are allergic to sesame seeds, olive oil could be used as an alternative.

50g slice of firm tofu
dash of light soy sauce
2 tsp sesame oil
1 large flat dark-gilled field or portobello
  mushroom
1 tsp dairy-free spread

dash of lemon juice
a few chopped parsley leaves
pinch of sea salt
1 large flat wholemeal bap
a few salad leaves (e.g. Cos)

1 Preheat the oven to 200°C/gas 6 and brush the tofu slice with the soy sauce and half the sesame oil. Set on a non-stick baking tray and bake for 10 minutes.

2 Meanwhile, sprinkle the remaining sesame oil over the mushroom gills and dot with the butter or spread. Sprinkle on the lemon juice, parsley and sea salt, and add the mushroom to the baking tray. Cook for a further 15 minutes, or until the mushroom is tender and the tofu turning golden and crisp.

3 Halve the bap, arrange the salad leaves on the base, then add the mushroom and tofu slice and close up.

| Low fat | Low saturated fat | High fibre | Suitable for vegetarians |
| ⬇ | ⬇ | ▥ | ✏ |

SALADS

FRUIT AND NUT PASTA SALAD

Suitable age 5 years+, serves 2
Calories per portion: 507
Good source of: protein, complex carbohydrates, essential fats, vitamins B1, B3, C, E, potassium, magnesium. Do not freeze.

Rich in nutrients, this easy salad is a good way to get children to eat nuts and seeds. It can also be made using couscous instead of pasta for a change.

> 100g (dry weight) wholewheat pasta shells
> a pinch of salt
> 1 red apple, cored and chopped

50g almonds
25g pine nuts
2 medium celery stalks, chopped
1 small red pepper, deseeded and chopped
50g red or white seedless grapes, halved
2 tbsp French dressing

1 Cook the pasta in boiling lightly salted water for 10 minutes or until just tender, drain and allow to cool.
2 Add the chopped apple and all the other ingredients to the pasta, stirring well to combine. Serve immediately or keep in the fridge for 24 hours.

EGG AND BACON SALAD

Suitable age 5 years+, serves 2
Calories per portion: 250
Good source of: protein, carotenoids, vitamins A, B1, B3, B6, B12, folate, D, potassium, zinc, iodine. Do not freeze.

Although this dish is not particularly low in fat, it is packed full of vitamins and minerals that all children need for good health. As the bacon contains quite a lot of salt, I haven't added any salt to the dressing, and this brings total sodium down reasonably low. However, because of the salt content, only serve to children over 5.

> 2 medium eggs
> 100g extra-lean back bacon rashers (reduced-salt if possible)
> 100g new potatoes, peeled or scrubbed and boiled until tender
> 1 heart of Little Gem lettuce
> 3 tbsp low-fat bio yoghurt
> 1 tbsp light mayonnaise
> 1 dsp lemon juice
> black pepper (optional)

1 level tbsp chopped parsley
8 cherry tomatoes, halved
50g chestnut mushrooms, thinly sliced
parsley leaves, to garnish

1 Hard-boil the eggs by cooking them for about 8 minutes, run them under cold water, shell and cut into quarters.
2 Grill or dry-fry the bacon until just starting to crisp, let cool a little and cut into strips. Cut the potatoes into bite-sized cubes if necessary. Slice the lettuce heart into thin wedges.
3 Arrange the lettuce in two serving bowls. Mix together the yoghurt, mayonnaise, lemon juice, black pepper and parsley, and add the bacon, potatoes and all but 4 of the tomato halves to the dressing with the egg quarters and mushroom slices, and combine well.
4 Divide the salad into the two serving dishes and garnish with the remaining tomato quarters, halved again, and parsley leaves.

CHICKEN AND PASTA SALAD

 1+

Suitable age 1 year+, serves 2
Calories per portion: 420
Good source of: protein, complex carbohydrates, carotenoids, vitamins B3, B6, E, potassium, selenium. Do not freeze.

This is a cooked salad that can be eaten warm or cold. It is best made with wholewheat pasta, which contains more fibre, B vitamins and minerals than white pasta, but you could sometimes use white pasta for a change.

100g (dry weight) wholewheat penne pasta, or other shape of choice
a pinch of salt
200g chicken breast meat (no skin), cut into large bite-sized pieces
1 tbsp light olive oil
100g beef tomato, cut into 8 wedges
1 medium yellow pepper (about 150g), deseeded and cut into eight
1 small red onion, peeled and cut into 8 wedges

2 tbsp French dressing
a few fresh basil leaves (optional)

1 Cook the pasta in boiling lightly salted water until barely tender (about 10 minutes), drain and cool.

2 Meanwhile, heat the grill to medium-hot. Toss the chicken pieces in the oil and then place on the base of the grill pan. Toss the tomato, pepper and onion in the remaining oil to which you have added 1 tablespoon of the French dressing, and then spread amongst the chicken.

3 Cook the meat and vegetables until turning golden (about 10 minutes), then turn everything over and cook on the other side for a further 6–8 minutes, spooning over any juices. Test a piece of chicken to make sure it is cooked all the way through (when pierced with a knife tip, there should be no pink juices, only clear, and the deepest piece of flesh should not still be pink).

4 Combine the chicken and vegetables with the pasta in a serving bowl, with basil leaves if liked. Drizzle over the remaining oil and serve warm or allow to cool.

Low fat	Low saturated fat	High fibre	Suitable for vegetarians

APRICOT AND BROWN RICE SALAD

Suitable age 1 year+, serves 2
Calories per portion: 360
Good source of: protein, complex carbohydrates, vitamins B1, B3, potassium, magnesium, iron.
Do not freeze.

If properly cooked, brown basmati rice is not at all tough and children enjoy its nutty flavour.

    75g (dry weight) brown basmati rice
    100g canned brown or green lentils, drained
    5cm piece of cucumber, finely chopped
    1 medium celery stalk, chopped

 1+

    50g dried organic ready-to-eat apricots
    1 level dsp finely chopped parsley
    2 tbsp light olive oil
    1 tbsp orange juice
    a pinch of salt
    black pepper (optional)

Cook the rice in boiling water until tender, drain and leave to cool. Combine the rice with the lentils, cucumber, celery, apricots and parsley. Mix the olive oil, orange juice and seasoning and stir into the salad. Serve immediately.
Note: Cooked rice shouldn't be stored for longer than 24 hours and must be stored in a very cool fridge.

TUNA AND CANNELLINI BEAN SALAD

Suitable age 1 year+, serves 2
Calories per portion: 330
Good source of: protein, complex carbohydrates, carotenoids, vits B3, B6, B12, C, D, E, potassium, selenium.
Do not freeze.

    200g canned cannellini beans, drained
    200g tuna canned in water, drained
    2 medium tomatoes, roughly chopped
    4 medium spring onions, trimmed and chopped

 1+

    5cm piece of cucumber, roughly chopped
    several Cos lettuce leaves, roughly torn
    2 tbsp light olive oil
    1 dsp lemon juice
    pinch of salt
    black pepper (optional)

Arrange the beans, tuna, vegetables and lettuce leaves in two serving bowls. Mix together the olive oil, lemon juice and seasoning, and drizzle over the salad before serving.

CHEESY COLESLAW

Suitable age 1 year+, serves 2
Calories per portion: 246
Good source of: protein, carotenoids, vitamins A, B2, B12, folate, potassium, calcium.
Do not freeze

I've taken the fat content of the dressing down low, so we can add some grated hard cheese to give it more calcium and some protein. Serve with a wholemeal bap.

    150g grated white or red cabbage (or a mixture)
    1 medium carrot, peeled and grated
    1 small (50g) onion, grated

 1+

    50g sultanas
    50g Cheddar cheese, grated
    3 tbsp low-fat bio yoghurt
    1 tbsp light mayonnaise
    1 dsp lemon juice
    pinch of salt
    black pepper (optional)

Combine the cabbage, carrot, onion, sultanas and Cheddar cheese in a large serving bowl. Then mix together the yoghurt, mayonnaise, lemon juice and seasoning, and pour over the salad. Combine thoroughly and chill before serving.

| Suitable for vegans | Dairy-free | Wheat- and gluten-free | Nut- and seed-free |

HAM AND RICE SALAD

 1+

Suitable age 1 year+, serves 2
Calories per portion: 298
Good source of: carotenoids, vitamins B1, B3, B6, B12, folate, C, E, potassium.
Do not freeze.

This tasty combination of sweet and savoury flavours, with the added crunch of wild rice, is popular with most children. Remember – cooked rice should not be stored, even in a cold fridge, for more than 24 hours.

75g (dry weight) mixed white and wild rice
100g extra-lean ham, cut into bite-sized chunks
150 slice cantaloupe melon, cut into bite-sized chunks
75g small broad beans, cooked and drained
50g fresh beansprouts
2 tbsp French dressing
1 level dsp fresh chopped mint
1 level dsp fresh chopped parsley

1 Cook the rice according to the packet instructions (approximately 18 minutes), then drain and set aside to cool.

2 In a large serving bowl, combine the cooked and cooled rice with the ham, melon, broad beans and beansprouts.

3 Beat the French dressing with the chopped mint and parsley and then combine with the salad items in the bowl to serve.

Variations: This salad can be made with bulghar wheat for a change, in which case it is not wheat- and gluten-free. You can also use brown basmati rice instead of the white and wild rice.

Low fat	Low saturated fat	High fibre	Suitable for vegetarians

MAIN MEALS

PASTA SHELLS WITH PEPPERS

Suitable age 6 months+, serves 4
Calories per portion: 375
Good source of: complex carbohydrates, carotenoids, vitamin B6, folate, C, E, potassium, iron.
Do not freeze.

To increase the protein content of this pasta dish you can add some grated Parmesan or pieces of mozzarella, or stir in some ricotta, although then the dish will contain dairy produce and won't be suitable for vegans. If serving to infants, mash thoroughly or purée if you prefer.

    1 tbsp light olive oil
    1 red onion, thinly sliced
    2 yellow peppers, deseeded and thinly sliced
    1 garlic clove, well crushed
    1 recipe-quantity Tomato Sauce (page 237)
    salt (optional)

 6mths+

    300g (dry weight) wholewheat pasta shells
    16 small cherry tomatoes, halved
    basil leaves (optional)

1 Heat the oil in a non-stick frying pan and sauté the onion and peppers for 10–15 minutes until soft.

2 Add the garlic and sauté for a few minutes more, then stir in the tomato sauce and simmer for another few minutes, adding a little water if the mix begins to look too dry.

3 Meanwhile, cook the pasta in a large pan of boiling water, lightly salted if liked, for 10 minutes or according to packet instructions, until tender but still firm to the bite, then drain.

4 When the pasta and sauce are cooked, stir the cherry tomato halves into the sauce and pour the sauce over the pasta to serve, garnished with basil leaves if using.

COTTAGE PIE

Suitable age 6 months+, serves 4
Calories per portion: 368
Good source of: protein, complex carbohydrates, carotenoids, vitamins B2, B3, B6, B12, C, E, potassium, iron, zinc.
Will freeze.

I've added baked beans to the basic mince mixture to make it higher in fibre and lower in saturated fat and total fat. I always use organic baked beans in tomato sauce as they taste much nicer and usually contain less salt and sugar than mass-market beans. If serving infants, you could whiz some pie in the blender to remove the lumps.

    1 recipe-quantity Basic Minced Beef (page 220)
    200g organic canned baked beans in tomato
      sauce
    500g old floury potatoes

 6mths+

    10g butter
    1 dsp light olive oil
    50ml skimmed milk
    pinch of salt
    black pepper

1 Preheat the oven to 200°C/gas 6. Lightly bash the beans and mix them into the minced beef mixture, then tip into a deep ovenproof dish.

2 Peel and chop the potatoes, and cook them in boiling water until tender, about 18 minutes. Drain, add the butter, oil, milk and seasoning and mash.

3 Smooth the mashed potato over the top of the mince mixture, ensuring it seals the edges, and bake in the oven for 25 minutes or until the top is golden and the mince piping-hot. Serve warm with a selection of green vegetables.

TRADITIONAL PIZZA

 1+

Suitable age 1 year+, serves 4
Calories per portion: 435
Good source of: protein, carotenoids, vitamins A, B6, B12, folate, C, E, potassium, calcium.
Will freeze before baking.

Home-made pizza is not difficult and contains less saturated fat and sodium than shop-bought ones. Add other toppings – vegetables (e.g. peppers, rocket, spinach or artichokes) or small pieces of lean chicken or fish.

> 225g strong white flour, plus more for dusting
> ½ tsp salt
> ½ tsp easy-blend (quick action) yeast
> 150ml warm water
> 2 tbsp olive oil, plus more for greasing
> 200g red onion, thinly sliced
> 1 garlic clove, well crushed
> 1 recipe-quantity Tomato Sauce (page 237)
> cooking oil spray (optional)
> 100g buffalo mozzarella, thinly sliced
> 1 medium fresh tomato, thinly sliced
> 2 tbsp grated Parmesan cheese
> basil leaves (optional)

1 Sift the flour and salt into a bowl and stir in the yeast. Make a well in the centre and gradually pour in the water and half the oil. Mix with a fork to form a soft dough.

2 Knead the dough on a floured board or kitchen surface for about 10 minutes, until smooth and elastic. Put it aside in a warm place, covered in an oiled bowl, for 1 hour to rise – it should have doubled in size.

3 Meanwhile, make the topping: heat the remaining oil in a non-stick frying pan and sauté the red onion for 10 minutes or until soft, adding the garlic for the last 2 minutes. Stir in the tomato sauce and leave to cool a little.

4 Preheat the oven to 220°C/gas 7 and, when the dough is ready, 'knock it back' and roll out into a circle about 30–35cm in diameter on a lightly floured surface. Transfer to a pizza baking tray or ordinary baking tray (use either non-stick or spray with cooking oil spray or brush with oil) and prick lightly with a fork.

5 Spoon the cooled topping evenly over the pizza, leaving about 1.5cm clear around the edges. Arrange the mozzarella and tomato slices over the pizza and finally sprinkle the grated cheese over the top.

6 Bake for 20 minutes or until the base is crisp and the topping golden. Garnish with basil leaves, if using.

POTATO AND VEGETABLE GRATIN

 6mths+

Suitable age 6 months+, serves 3-4
Calories per portion: 564 (3) 425 (4)
Good source of: protein, complex carbohydrates, vits A, B2, B12, C, E, carotenoids, potassium, calcium, iron, iodine.
Will freeze

This is comfort food for vegetarians – or any children at all – and contains a wealth of vitamins and minerals.

> 400g waxy potatoes and 400g sweet potatoes, peeled and cut into large chunks
> 200g broccoli, cut into small florets
> 1 recipe-quantity Cheese Sauce (page 235)
> 50ml skimmed milk
> handful of small rocket leaves
> cooking oil spray
> 50g Cheddar cheese, grated

1 Preheat the oven to 180°C/gas 4. Parboil the two types of potato until nearly cooked but still firm, drain and leave to cool. Parboil the broccoli florets for 3–4 minutes, then drain. Heat the cheese sauce in a saucepan with the extra milk and then stir in the rocket leaves.

2 When the potatoes are cool enough to handle, slice them thinly and arrange half in the base of a family-sized gratin or baking dish, which you have sprayed with cooking oil spray. Pour over half the warm cheese sauce and then arrange the remaining potato in the dish, followed by the broccoli florets and the remaining cheese sauce. Take care to ensure all the pieces of broccoli are covered with some sauce.

3 Sprinkle over the grated Cheddar cheese and bake for approximately 25 minutes, or until the top is bubbling and golden.

Low fat ⬇ | Low saturated fat ⬇ | High fibre ▥ | Suitable for vegetarians ✎

CHICKPEA AND SPINACH PASTA

 5+

Suitable age 5 years+, serves 4

Calories per portion: 430

Good source of: protein, complex carbohydrates, carotenoids, vitamins B1, B3, B6, folate, C, E, potassium, magnesium, iron, zinc, selenium.

Will freeze, but best fresh.

Chickpeas and spinach marry very well together in this dairy-free pasta dish. You can use any type of pasta, but spirals or large shells work very well. Rocket makes a good alternative to baby spinach to ring the changes.

300g wholewheat pasta of choice (see above)
pinch of salt
30g pine nuts
1 tbsp light olive oil
6 sun-dried tomatoes in oil, drained and chopped, and 1 tbsp of the oil from the jar
200g fresh ripe tomatoes, quartered
1 large garlic clove, peeled and well crushed

200g canned chickpeas, drained
100g baby spinach leaves
black pepper

1 Cook the pasta in plenty of lightly salted boiling water for 10 minutes or according to packet instructions, until tender but still firm to the bite, then drain.

2 Meanwhile, heat a heavy-duty non-stick frying pan, add the pine nuts and toast them – this will take a few minutes, but once they start to go golden they quickly burn, so take care. Remove from the pan and set aside.

3 Add the oils to the pan with the sun-dried and ripe tomatoes, and sauté for a few minutes until the fresh tomatoes are softened and turning golden.

4 Add the garlic and stir until softened, then add the chickpeas, spinach and pepper, and stir until the chickpeas are warmed through and the spinach wilted.

5 Serve the sauce stirred through the cooked pasta, with the pine nuts sprinkled over the top.

Suitable for vegans	Dairy-free	Wheat- and gluten-free	Nut- and seed-free

CHICKEN DIPPERS

Suitable age 1 year+, serves 2–3
Calories per portion: 330 (for 2) 220 (for 3)
Good source of: protein, vits B3, B6, potassium, selenium. Will freeze.

Serve these easy-to-make chicken dippers with a dip either of organic tomato ketchup or a mix of equal parts mayonnaise and bio yoghurt with a little ketchup and lemon juice, or with baked potatoes, Potato Wedges (page 220) and a mixed salad for a main meal.

300g skinless chicken breast fillet
50g plain or wholemeal flour
1 tsp sweet paprika
1 tsp chicken seasoning
1½ tbsp light olive oil

1 If baking the dippers, preheat the oven to 200°C/gas 6. Cut the chicken into strips, each about 2 bites in size. In a plastic bag, mix the flour with the paprika and chicken seasoning. Add the chicken strips and shake to coat well.

2 Now you can either heat the oil in a non-stick frying pan and fry the chicken dippers over a high heat for about 6 minutes, turning once, then drain on kitchen paper. Or, alternatively, you can coat the base of a small non-stick roasting pan with the oil, add the dippers and turn over to coat with the oil and bake in the preheated oven for 15 minutes, or until the chicken pieces are golden and cooked through.

BEEF AND VEGETABLE HASH

Suitable age 6 months+, serves 4
Calories per portion: 260
Good source of: protein, complex carbohydrates, iron, vitamins A, B3, B6, B12, C, carotenoids, potassium, zinc. Will freeze.

For toddlers and pre-school children, this recipe will serve 2–3. You can make your own vegetable stock by simmering 500g total weight mixed celery, carrot, onion, leek and parsley in water for 1 hour then draining.

300g potatoes, peeled and chopped
25g butter (or margarine/oil for dairy-free recipe)
50g (dry weight) red lentils
150ml unsalted vegetable stock
1½ tbsp light olive oil
1 small onion, finely chopped
125g extra-lean minced beef
1 medium carrot, peeled and finely chopped
1 small tender celery stalk, finely chopped
1 large tinned peeled plum tomato, drained and chopped

1 Cook the potatoes in boiling water for 15 minutes or until tender, drain and dry well, then mash with the butter or margarine.

2 Meanwhile, simmer the lentils in two-thirds of the vegetable stock in a small lidded pan until the lentils are tender and the stock has been absorbed, about 30 minutes. Bash the lentils with a fork to mash them a little.

3 While the lentils are cooking, heat half the oil in a non-stick frying pan with a lid and sauté the onion over a medium heat for 10 minutes, until just turning golden. Add the beef, carrot and celery, and stir for another 5 minutes until the meat is browned. Add the plum tomato and the rest of the stock to the pan, bring to a simmer, cover with the lid and cook for about another 20 minutes.

4 Combine thoroughly the lentils and mashed potatoes into the mixture, which should be quite dry.

5 Heat the remaining oil in a non-stick frying pan and add the potato and beef mixture in a flat cake. Fry until golden on the underside, then turn over and fry on the other side to brown lightly. Allow to cool slightly before serving.

Note: For babies aged 6–9 months, purée the mixture in a blender before serving (you may need to add extra water or stock). If freezing, freeze the mixture before frying it and when serving defrost thoroughly before frying. You can also serve the hash mixture without frying it – just reheat in a microwave after blending.

Low fat	Low saturated fat	High fibre	Suitable for vegetarians

VEGETABLE AND BUTTER BEAN HOTPOT

6mths+

Suitable age 6 months+, serves 4
Calories per portion: 142
Good source of: protein, complex carbohydrates, carotenoids, vitamins B1, B3, folate, E, potassium, iron. Will freeze, but not ideal.

Serves 2–3 toddlers or pre-school children. Mash for children under 1 and purée for those under 9 months.

  1 tbsp light olive oil
  1 medium onion, finely chopped
  1 garlic clove, well crushed (optional)
  1 medium (150g) sweet potato and 1 medium
    (100g) parsnip, peeled and cut into small cubes
  80g Savoy cabbage, shredded
  200ml canned chopped tomatoes
  100ml unsalted vegetable stock (see page 200)
  200g canned butter beans (or cannellini), drained

1 Sauté the onion in the oil for 10 minutes until soft. Add the garlic for the last minute or two, if using.

2 Add the sweet potato and parsnip and stir for a minute or two, then add the remaining ingredients and bring to a simmer. Turn the heat down, put the lid on and simmer for 30 minutes, or until everything is tender.

Tip: Garnish with grated cheese for extra calcium and calories, though this no longer makes it a vegan meal.

FISH AND TOMATO BAKE

6mths+

Suitable age 6 months+, serves 4
Calories per portion: 326
Good source of: protein, vitamins A, B2, B3, B12, potassium, calcium, iodine, selenium. Will freeze, but not ideal.

This cheesy fish bake is a great source of calcium.

  450g fillet of cod/coley/haddock, cut into 8 pieces
  cooking oil spray
  2 medium-to-large tomatoes (about 100g)
  1 recipe-quantity Cheese Sauce (page 235)
  4 tbsp stale breadcrumbs
  2 tbsp finely grated Cheddar or Parmesan cheese

1 Preheat the oven to 180°C/gas 4. Arrange the fish pieces in the bottom of a medium-sized gratin dish or small roasting tin sprayed with the oil.

2 Halve one of the tomatoes and deseed it, then chop it into small pieces and scatter around the fish. Cut the other tomato into thin slices and set aside.

3 Pour the cheese sauce evenly over the fish, then arrange the tomato slices on top. Mix together the breadcrumbs and cheese and scatter over the top.

4 Cook in the preheated oven for 20–25 minutes, or until the top of the bake is golden and the fish is cooked through. Serve with new potatoes, or pasta shapes and a selection of vegetables.

| Suitable for vegans | Dairy-free | Wheat- and gluten-free | Nut- and seed-free |

MACARONI AND BROCCOLI CHEESE

 6mths+

Suitable age 6 months+, serves 4
Calories per portion: 456
Good source of: protein, complex carbohydrates, carotenoids, vitamins A, B2, B3, B12, folate, C, potassium, calcium, magnesium, iodine.
Will freeze.

An all-time favourite supper for children, adding broccoli and tomato enhances the nutrition of this dish. Serve with a side salad or vegetables. For infants, mash or purée in a blender.

300g (dry weight) wholewheat macaroni
pinch of salt
200g broccoli, broken into small florets
1 recipe-quantity Cheese Sauce (page 235)
4 tbsp stale breadcrumbs

25g finely grated Parmesan cheese (see Tip)
1 large tomato, thinly sliced

1 Preheat the oven to 180°C/gas 4. Cook the macaroni in very lightly salted boiling water (omit the salt for infants), drain and tip into a baking dish.
2 While the macaroni is cooking, steam the broccoli until just tender and drain. Mix the broccoli with the macaroni and then pour over the cheese sauce, stirring lightly to combine. Mix together the breadcrumbs and cheese and sprinkle over the top of the dish, then arrange the tomato slices around the edges of the dish.
3 Bake in the preheated oven for 25 minutes, or until the top is golden brown and the dish bubbling.
Tip: Use Parmesan cheese in a block, not the ready-grated kind in tubs, which is dry and tasteless.

TURKEY AND VEGETABLE STIR-FRY

 5+

Suitable age 5 years+, serves 2–4
Calories per portion: 376 (2) 250 (3) 188 (4)
Good source of: protein, carotenoids, vitamins B2, B3, B6, B12, potassium, selenium.
Do not freeze.

Stir-fries at home are quick and easy, and they generally contain much less sodium and fat than takeaway or shop-bought versions. Some ready-made stir-fry sauces are low in fat, but most are still too high in sodium. Serve with rice or noodles. Add fresh cashew nuts for an iron-rich addition – in which case the recipe will not be nut-and-seed-free.

1 tbsp groundnut or corn oil
400g turkey stir-fry pieces
2 tsp light soy sauce
100g broccoli florets
100g baby sweetcorn
100g carrot strips
8 spring onions, trimmed and halved lengthways
1 garlic clove, well crushed, OR 1 tsp ready-made minced garlic
2cm piece of fresh ginger, peeled and grated, OR 1 heaped tsp ready-made minced ginger

juice of ½ orange
80ml vegetable or chicken stock (see note)
1 dsp runny honey
1 heaped tsp cornflour or sauce flour

1 Heat the oil in a large non-stick frying pan or wok and stir-fry the turkey pieces over a high heat, sprinkling on half the soy sauce as you do so. When the pieces are golden and nearly cooked (about 3 minutes), remove with a slotted spoon and transfer to a warm dish.
2 Add the broccoli, sweetcorn and carrot to the pan and stir-fry for 2 minutes, then add the spring onions and cook until everything is tender but still firm. (If the mixture looks dry, add a tablespoon of water.) Return the turkey to the pan with the garlic and ginger, and stir-fry for 30 seconds.
3 Mix together the orange juice, stock, honey, cornflour and remaining soy sauce, and pour into the pan. Cook over a high heat for a minute or two, stirring all the time until the mixture thickens slightly, and serve.
Note: Home-made stock contains less sodium, otherwise use low-sodium stock cubes or fresh chilled stock. See page 200 for vegetable stock and page 223 for chicken stock.
Variations: For vegetarians or vegans substitute turkey for Quorn pieces or firm tofu slices.

Low fat | Low saturated fat | High fibre  | Suitable for vegetarians

CHICKEN AND VEGETABLE CURRY

 11+

Particularly suitable age 11+, serves 4
Calories per portion: 245
Good source of: protein, carotenoids, vitamins B3, B6, folate, C, E, potassium, iron, selenium.
Will freeze, but best fresh.

Curries have a reputation as unhealthy high-fat feasts, but if you use good quality oil with plenty of vegetables they can be a very healthy option. Vary the vegetables, and blend and quantity of curry mix according to your family's preferences. Curry mix is a good source of iron.

1½ tbsp groundnut oil or light olive oil
1 large onion, finely chopped
150g cauliflower, cut into small florets
100g green beans, halved
2 garlic cloves, well crushed
400g skinless chicken fillet, sliced
1 tbsp good-quality dry mild curry mix
80g petit pois, defrosted if frozen

400g can of chopped tomatoes
1 tsp garam masala
100ml whole-milk yoghurt
fresh coriander leaves (optional), to garnish

1 Heat the oil in a large non-stick frying pan with a lid and sauté the onion for 10 minutes or until soft. Steam or parboil the cauliflower and green beans for 3–4 minutes until about two-thirds cooked, then drain.

2 Add the garlic to the frying pan and stir for a minute, then push the onion and garlic to the edges and sauté the chicken pieces, turning occasionally, until golden.

3 Add the curry blend to the pan and stir for a minute until the aromas are released. Add the green beans, cauliflower, peas and tomatoes to the pan, stir well, bring to a simmer, turn the heat down and cover. Simmer for 20 minutes, adding a little water if the mixture is too dry.

4 Stir in the garam masala and yoghurt and cook very gently, uncovered, for about 5 minutes. Serve garnished with coriander leaves if using.

Suitable for vegans | Dairy-free | Wheat- and gluten-free | Nut- and seed-free

TUNA, PASTA AND TOMATO BAKE

 6mths+

Suitable age 6 months+, serves 4
Calories per portion: 467
Good source of: protein, complex carbohydrates, carotenoids, vitamins B2, B3, B6, B12, C, D, E, potassium, magnesium, selenium.
Will freeze.

To make this dish dairy-free, omit cheese from the topping and stir the breadcrumbs with 1 dsp light olive oil instead. Suitable for infants if mashed well or lightly blended.

350g (dry weight) wholewheat pasta spirals
pinch of salt

1 recipe-quantity Tomato Sauce (page 237)
400g tuna canned in water, drained
50g Cheddar cheese, finely grated
4 tbsp stale breadcrumbs

1 Preheat the oven to 180°C/gas 4. Cook the pasta in plenty of very lightly salted boiling water (omit the salt for infants) until just tender but still firm to the bite. Drain.

2 Tip the pasta into a suitably sized baking dish. Stir in the tomato sauce and then the tuna. Mix together the cheese and breadcrumbs, and sprinkle over the top. Bake for 20 minutes and serve with a green salad or green veg.

LAMB AND CHERRY TOMATO KEBABS

 5+

Suitable age 5 years+, serves 4
Calories per portion: 312
Good source of: protein, vitamins B2, B3, B6, B12, potassium, iron, zinc.
Do not freeze.

These simple kebabs are tasty and useful for children who don't like large chunks of meat. They can be barbecued as well as grilled, or they can even be cooked in the oven.

700g lean lamb fillet, cut into bite-sized cubes
1 tbsp light olive oil
juice of ½ lemon
1 level tsp each dried chopped rosemary and thyme
1 large garlic clove, well crushed
¼ tsp garam masala (optional)
pinch of salt
8 large cherry tomatoes
4 medium shallots, peeled and halved

1 Place the lamb in a shallow non-metallic dish. Mix together the olive oil, lemon juice, herbs, garlic, garam masala and salt, then pour over the lamb and mix to coat well. Leave to marinate for an hour or two if possible.

2 Heat the grill to medium-high. Coat the cherry tomatoes and shallot halves in the marinade, then thread these and the lamb on 4 kebab sticks (that have been soaked in water). Cook the kebabs for about 10

minutes, turning at least once and basting with the marinade from time to time, until cooked through.

Low fat | Low saturated fat | High fibre | Suitable for vegetarians /

CHICKEN AND MUSHROOM PASTA

 6mths+

Suitable age 6 months+, serves 4
Calories per portion: 223
Good source of: vitamins B2, B3, B6, folate, potassium, selenium.
Will freeze, but not ideal.

This is ideal for using up cooked chicken – or simply poach raw chicken fillet in a little stock until cooked through. May serve only 2–3 toddlers and pre-school children.

125g (dry weight) pasta shapes
50g frozen sweetcorn kernels, defrosted
10g butter
1 dsp light olive oil
80g chestnut mushrooms, sliced (or chopped very small for 6–9-month-olds)
1 garlic clove, very well crushed (optional)
a few fresh thyme leaves (optional)
black pepper (optional)
20g white flour

225ml whole milk
125g cooked chicken meat (no skin), cut into small pieces (or minced for 6–9-month-olds)

1 Cook the pasta shapes in plenty of boiling water for 8 minutes or until just tender, adding the sweetcorn for the last 3 minutes of cooking, then drain.

2 While the pasta is cooking, heat the butter and oil in a non-stick frying pan and sauté the mushrooms over a medium heat, adding the garlic, thyme and pepper after a minute or two. When the mushrooms are just cooked, add the flour to the pan and stir vigorously with a wooden spatula, then gradually add the milk, stirring all the time, until you have a smooth mushroom sauce.

3 Add the cooked chicken pieces, pasta and sweetcorn, and heat through to serve.

Note: If serving to babies under 9 months, blend the meal in an electric blender for a few seconds before serving. If the sauce turns slightly grey, enliven the appearance by sprinkling some fresh chopped parsley over the top to serve.

PRAWN, SALMON AND EGG PIE

 1+

Suitable age 1 year+, serves 4–6
Calories per portion: 603 (for 4) 401 (for 6)
Good source of: protein, complex carbohydrates, vitamins A, B1, B3, B6, B12, folate, D, E, potassium, calcium, magnesium, zinc, iodine, selenium.
Will freeze.

This pie isn't low in fat but it isn't excessively high either, while being extremely rich in a wide range of nutrients. Prawns are low in fat but high in sodium; however, a few as part of a main dish are fine (except for infants). This pie makes a complete meal with a serving of green vegetables.

500g floury potatoes, cubed
300g organic salmon fillet
4 medium eggs
100g peeled cooked prawns
1 tbsp fresh chopped parsley
1 recipe-quantity Cheese Sauce (page 235)
25g butter
50ml skimmed milk

pepper and a pinch of salt
30g grated Cheddar cheese

1 Preheat the oven to 180°C/gas 4. Boil the potatoes until just tender, about 18 minutes.

2 Meanwhile, poach the salmon in water to cover or cook it in the microwave on medium for 3–5 minutes until just cooked but not overcooked.

3 At the same time, boil the eggs until they are hard-boiled (about 8 minutes), rinse under cold water and then shell and quarter.

4 Flake the salmon and arrange it in an ovenproof dish with the prawns, eggs and parsley. Pour over the cheese sauce.

5 Drain the potatoes when they are cooked, then mash with the butter, skimmed milk and seasoning. Spoon or pipe the mashed potato all around the edge of the baking dish on top of the fish mixture and also across the centre.

6 Scatter the cheese over and bake for 30 minutes, or until the top is golden.

Suitable for vegans	Dairy-free	Wheat- and gluten-free	Nut- and seed-free

FISH FINGERS WITH POTATO WEDGES

 1+

Suitable age 1 year+, serves 4
Calories per portion: 244
Good source of: protein, complex carbohydrates, vitamins B3, B6, B12, C, potassium, iodine, selenium. Do not freeze.

Home-made fish fingers usually contain more fish than commercial varieties and the coating contains many fewer additives. Home-made potato chips are a lower-fat alternative to oven chips. Serves 2 for older children.

> 400g baking potato (2 small-to-medium potatoes)
> 1 tbsp light olive oil, plus more for greasing
> 375g fillets of cod, haddock or coley
> 50g polenta
> 1 level tsp fish seasoning
> 1 large egg, beaten

1 Preheat the oven to 200°C/gas 6. Scrub the potatoes well and halve them lengthways, then cut each half into 6–8 long wedges. Dry them well on kitchen paper and then put into a bowl with the oil. Using your hands, coat all the wedges with the oil. Place them on a baking tray, skin sides down, and cook for 30 minutes or until they are cooked through and the outsides are crisp and golden.

2 While the wedges are cooking, cut the cod fillet into 12–16 finger shapes, taking care that all the bones are removed. Pat them dry on kitchen paper. Combine the polenta with the fish seasoning and sprinkle onto a plate. Dip the fingers into the polenta and then into the beaten egg (in a bowl), then back into the polenta again, then place each finger on an oiled non-stick baking tray.

3 Put the fish fingers into the oven when the potato wedges have about 15 minutes' cooking time left. Check a fish finger with the point of a knife to make sure it is cooked all the way through before serving.
Note: If cooking the dish for older children, you can add a little sea salt to the oil and potatoes.

BASIC MINCED BEEF

 1+

Suitable age 1 year+, serves 4
Calories per portion: 200
Good source of: protein, carotenoids, vitamins B2, B3, B6, B12, C, E, potassium, iron, zinc. Will freeze.

This basic minced beef recipe can be used for a great variety of children's dishes, for example: with spaghetti or other pasta (grate some Parmesan over the top); topped with potato for cottage pie; with added chilli, kidney beans and chopped peppers for chilli con carne; in lasagne or moussaka; or as a stuffing for larger vegetables, such as peppers, aubergines or large tomatoes. It can also be served as it is, with accompanying mashed, boiled or baked potatoes, or couscous and side salad or vegetables.

> 1 tbsp light olive oil
> 1 medium onion, very finely chopped
> 1 medium celery stalk, very finely chopped
> 300g extra-lean, good-quality minced beef
> 1 medium carrot, peeled and finely chopped
> 50g chestnut mushrooms, finely chopped
> 200g canned chopped tomatoes
> 150ml gluten-free beef or vegetable stock (see below and page 200)
> 1 tsp dried mixed herbs
> dash of Worcestershire sauce
> black pepper

1 Heat the oil in a non-stick frying pan which has a lid and sauté the onion and celery over a medium heat for 10 minutes, or until well softened.

2 Add the beef and stir until it is browned all over, then add the remaining ingredients, stir thoroughly to combine and bring to a simmer. Cover with the lid, turn the heat down and cook for 45 minutes, or until everything is tender and you have a rich sauce.
Note: To make home-made beef stock, simmer organic beef bones with carrot, onion and celery for 1 hour then drain. To reduce the stock, boil it for 10 minutes, when the flavour will be more concentrated.

Low fat	Low saturated fat	High fibre	Suitable for vegetarians
			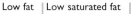

COD, POTATO AND CHEDDAR PIE

6mths+

Suitable age 6 months+, serves 4
Calories per portion: 198
Good source of: protein, complex carbohydrates, vitamins A, B2, B3, B12, D, potassium, calcium, iodine, selenium.
Will freeze.

This is a delicious mixture that most babies enjoy in their first few months of weaning. For toddlers and older pre-school children, the amounts will make 2–3 servings.

> 250g potatoes, peeled and chopped
> 1 small trimmed leek, rinsed and finely chopped
> 150g cod fillet
> 200ml whole milk
> 1 bay leaf
> 25g butter
> 40g Cheddar cheese, grated

1 Cook the potatoes in boiling water for 15 minutes or until tender, adding the leek for the last 8 minutes of cooking time, then drain thoroughly.

2 Put the cod fillet in a frying pan with the milk and bay leaf, bring to a simmer and cook for 8 minutes, or until the fish is cooked through and flakes readily.

3 With a slotted spatula, remove the fish from the pan on to a plate and flake, then mash, being careful to remove any bones which may have been left behind. (For older children you need only flake the fish.)

4 In the frying pan, mash the potato and leek with the butter and cheese and 2 tablespoons of the milk. Stir in the fish and place everything in a small ovenproof dish.

5 Bake for 15 minutes, then cool to warm before serving. Alternatively, heat in a microwave on medium-high for about 3 minutes, making sure the pie is not served too hot.

TUNA AND EGG KEDGEREE

 1+

Suitable age 1 year+, serves 4
Calories per portion: 370
Good source of: protein, complex carbohydrates, vitamins A, B1, B3, B6, B12, folate, D, potassium, magnesium, iodine, selenium.
Do not freeze.

This kedgeree can also be made using white fish, e.g. cod or haddock, or with smoked haddock – although smoked foods shouldn't be served too often. I have used fresh tuna but you could use good-quality tuna steaks canned in water.

> 10g butter
> 1 dsp light olive oil
> 2 shallots, finely chopped
> 200g fresh tuna steak (or canned in water)
> 200g (dry weight) brown basmati rice
> 1 tsp mild (e.g. korma) curry powder (optional)
> 400ml vegetable or fish stock (home-made or
>   good-quality bouillon – check for gluten-free;
>   see page 200 for vegetable stock)
> 75g petit pois, defrosted
> 3 medium eggs
> 1 level tbsp fresh chopped parsley

1 Heat the butter and oil together in a large non-stick frying pan, with a lid, and add the shallots. Sauté the shallots over a medium heat for 6–8 minutes, or until they have softened, and then push to the sides of the pan.

2 Add the tuna steak and cook for 1½ minutes on each side. Remove the tuna with a slotted spatula (leaving the onion in the pan), and flake into bite-sized pieces.

3 Add the rice and curry powder, if using, to the pan and stir it around, then add the stock and bring to the simmer. Turn the heat down, put the lid on and cook gently for 10 minutes, then add the peas to the pan.

4 While the rice cooks, boil the eggs for 8 minutes, rinse under cold water, shell and cut into quarters.

5 When the rice is about 3 minutes from being cooked (total cooking time should be around 25 minutes, but check packet for instructions), return the part-cooked tuna to the rice pan and stir in with most of the parsley, then put the lid back on.

6 Serve with the egg quarters arranged on top and garnished with the remaining parsley.

Tip: The finished kedgeree should be slightly moist and succulent, so if the rice seems too dry towards the end of cooking time, add a little more hot stock to the pan.

Suitable for vegans | Dairy-free | Wheat- and gluten-free | Nut- and seed-free

SALMON AND EGG FLAN

 1+

Suitable age 1 year+, serves 4
Calories per portion: 440
Good source of: protein, vitamins A, B1, B3, B6, B12, folate, D, E, calcium, iron, magnesium, iodine, selenium. Will freeze before baking.

This flan is a good way of getting non-fish lovers to eat their omega-3s.

> 225g wholemeal pastry, plus flour for dusting
> 10g butter
> 1 dsp light olive oil
> 100g shallots (about 5), finely chopped
> 200g fresh salmon fillet, preferably organic
> 2 large eggs
> 100ml whole milk
> squeeze of lemon juice
> 1 level tsp fresh chopped dill (optional)
> 1 level tbsp fresh chopped parsley
> black pepper

1 Preheat the oven to 200°C/gas 6. Roll the pastry out as thinly as you can on a floured surface and use it to line a 20cm metal flan tin. Prick the base, cover with dried haricot beans or similar and bake in the oven for 10 minutes. Remove the beans and cook for another 3 minutes, then allow to cool in its tin. Turn the oven down to 180°C/gas 4.

2 Meanwhile, make the filling: heat the butter and oil together in a non-stick frying pan and sauté the shallots for 8 minutes, or until they are translucent and soft but not coloured. Cut the salmon into bite-sized pieces and add to the pan, stir-frying for another 3 minutes or until the salmon is virtually cooked but still succulent.

3 When the pastry case is cool, tip the salmon and shallot mixture into it and spread evenly over the surface. Beat together the eggs, milk, lemon juice, dill, parsley and pepper, and pour over the fish. Return to the oven and bake for 30 minutes or until the filling is just set and the top lightly browned. Serve warm or cold.

Low fat	Low saturated fat	High fibre	Suitable for vegetarians

SOUTHERN-FRIED CHICKEN

   5+

Suitable age 5 years+, serves 4
Calories per portion: 278
Good source of: protein, vitamins B3, B6, potassium, zinc, selenium.
Will freeze.

It is worth making your own 'Southern-fried' chicken because this version contains much less fat, saturated fat and sodium than the kind of fried chicken you can buy in takeaways or in supermarket packs. Serve it with Potato Wedges (page 220) and salad.

> 80g (8 tbsp) dry breadcrumbs
> 1 tsp chicken seasoning
> 1 tsp dried mixed herbs
> 50g light mayonnaise
> 50g low-fat bio yoghurt

1 tsp French mustard
1 tsp sun-dried tomato paste
8 skinless chicken drumsticks
cooking oil spray

1 Preheat the oven to 180°C/gas 4. In a shallow bowl, mix together the breadcrumbs, chicken seasoning and herbs. In another bowl, mix together the mayonnaise, yoghurt, mustard and tomato paste. Coat each drumstick first with the mayonnaise mix, then dip each one in the breadcrumb mixture.

2 Spray a thick baking tray with the cooking oil spray and place the drumsticks on it. Spray each drumstick lightly too and bake for 45 minutes, or until the drumsticks are golden, turning halfway through. Make sure they are cooked all the way through before serving.

CHICKEN CASSEROLE

    6mths+

Suitable age 6 months+, serves 4
Calories per portion: 268
Good source of: protein, carotenoids, vitamins B3, B6, C, E, potassium, zinc, selenium.
Will freeze.

Boned and skinned chicken thighs make an excellent low-fat casserole which most children like – a casserole is also a good way to introduce a selection of vegetables and these make a good contribution to the day's 'five'. For very young children you can whiz the casserole in a blender.

> 1 tbsp light olive oil
> 1 medium onion, finely chopped
> 1 medium leek, rinsed, trimmed and sliced
> 6 skinned chicken thigh fillets, each cut into two
> 1 level tbsp sauce flour (see note)
> 125g carrot, peeled and sliced
> 125g sweet potato, peeled and chopped
> 1 tsp fresh thyme leaves
> 300ml chicken stock (see note)

1 If planning to cook the casserole in the oven, preheat it to 160°C/gas 3. Heat the oil in a flameproof casserole and sauté the onion and leek over a medium heat for 10 minutes until softened. Push to the sides and add the chicken thigh pieces. Leave them for 2 minutes, without moving, to brown, then turn over with a spatula and brown the other sides.

2 Stir in the sauce flour with a wooden spatula, mixing it in well, and then add the remaining ingredients. Stir again and bring to a simmer. Turn the heat down and cook on the hob or in the oven for 1 hour, or until everything is tender and the liquid is moderately thick. Serve with green vegetables and potatoes or rice.

Note: Sauce flour is available at the supermarket – it is of a very fine texture and helps to prevent lumpiness or a floury taste.

Note: Many stock cubes contain a lot of salt – so, for children, making your own stock may be a good option. Simply simmer a chicken carcass with slices of carrot, onion, celery and leek for 1 hour, then drain. Fast boil to reduce the stock if liked – this will concentrate it and increase the flavour. Otherwise, try to find stock cubes labelled 'low in salt'.

Suitable for vegans | Dairy-free | Wheat- and gluten-free | Nut- and seed-free

TUNA AND POTATO FISHCAKES

Suitable age 6 months+, serves 4
Calories per portion: 242
Good source of: protein, complex carbohydrates, vitamins A, B3, B6, B12, D, potassium, selenium. Will freeze.

Fresh tuna or salmon can also be used to make similar fishcakes, by poaching in water or a water/milk mixture.

> 400g old potatoes, peeled and chopped
> 30g butter
> 4 tbsp milk
> 300g tuna canned in water, well drained

 6mths+

> 1 dsp fresh chopped parsley
> 1 tbsp light olive oil

1 Cook the potatoes in boiling water until tender, about 15 minutes. Drain, add the butter and milk and mash. Stir in the tuna and parsley, and allow to cool.

2 When the mixture is cool, form it into 8 small patties. (For babies under 9 months you may need to blend the mixture for a few seconds before making the patties.)

3 Heat the oil in a non-stick frying pan and sauté the fishcakes for a few minutes each side over a medium hot heat, until they are golden.

VEGETABLE BURGERS

Suitable age 5 years+, serves 4
Calories per portion: 230
Good source of: protein, complex carbohydrates, vitamins B2, B3, folate, E, potassium, calcium, magnesium. Will freeze.

These burgers make a good change from meat burgers – don't be put off by the long list of ingredients as they are actually quick and easy to put together.

> 1½ tbsp light olive oil
> 1 medium (100g) onion, finely chopped
> 1 small carrot (50g), peeled and grated
> 1 garlic clove, finely chopped (optional)
> 1 small canned sweet red pepper, well drained, dried on kitchen paper and finely chopped
> 1 tsp mixed dried herbs
> 1 tsp season-all seasoning
> 1 level tsp ground cumin
> 1 dsp sun-dried tomato purée
> dash of light soy sauce
> 200g canned chickpeas, well drained
> 50g ground almonds
> 1 dsp light tahini (sesame seed paste)
> 50g wholemeal breadcrumbs

1 Heat half the oil in a non-stick frying pan and sauté the onion and carrot over a medium heat for about 8 minutes, or until softened and translucent.

 5+

2 Add the garlic, if using, and the sweet pepper, and stir-fry for another minute or two, then add the herbs, season-all seasoning, cumin, sun-dried tomato purée and soy sauce, and combine well. Turn the heat off and set aside.

3 In a bowl, mash the chickpeas thoroughly with a fork or potato masher (or blend them quickly in a food processor, but be careful not to over-process), then add the ground almonds, the contents of the frying pan and the tahini. Combine well and add the breadcrumbs to make a firm mix (you may need slightly less or more crumbs). Form the mixture into 4 burgers.

4 Brush a griddle, grill or non-stick frying pan with the remaining oil and cook the burgers on a medium high heat for 2–3 minutes on each side, or until golden but not burnt. Alternatively, bake on an oiled baking tray in an oven preheated to 200°C/gas 6 for 10 minutes or until golden.

Variations:
* You can use mashed kidney beans or cannellini beans, or even cooked red lentils, instead of the chickpeas if you like, or a combination of these.
* For children who can't eat nuts, you can omit the ground almonds and instead make up the weight with extra chickpeas plus a scant tbsp of olive oil.
* For children who can't eat seeds, omit the tahini paste and add a little extra sun-dried tomato purée instead.
* For older children, you can add 1 teaspoon chilli sauce to the mixture to make the burgers spicy.

Low fat	Low saturated fat	High fibre	Suitable for vegetarians

HOME-MADE BURGERS

Suitable age 1 year+, serves 4
Calories per portion: 165
Good source of: protein, vitamins B2, B6, B12, potassium, iron, zinc.
Will freeze.

This makes four 'quarterpounders' or eight small burgers for smaller children. Serve with Potato Wedges (page 220) or Home-made Baked Beans (page 204), and salad or vegetables, or in wholemeal baps for a quick lunch.

350g extra-lean minced beef
40g stale breadcrumbs
1 level tsp steak seasoning
2 shallots, very finely chopped
1 level tbsp fresh chopped parsley
1 medium egg, beaten, or 2 tbsp light mayonnaise
1 dsp light olive oil

1 In a large bowl, combine all the ingredients and then, with clean hands, form into round flat patties,

2 Heat a griddle pan or non-stick frying pan and brush with the oil. When very hot, add the burgers and cook for about 5 minutes on each side. Ensure the burgers are cooked all the way through, as underdone beef and partly cooked eggs can be dangerous.

CREAMED PASTA WITH VEGETABLES

 6mths+

Suitable age 6 months+, serves 4
Calories per portion: 245
Good source of: protein, complex carbohydrates, vitamins A, B2, B3, B12, C, potassium, calcium, iodine.
Will freeze.

For toddlers and pre-school children, the recipe will serve 2–3. For babies under 9 months, the finished dish can be lightly puréed in an electric blender or thoroughly mashed.

125g (dry weight) pasta shapes
75g broccoli, cut into florets
50g frozen peas, defrosted
20g butter
20g white flour

225ml whole milk
50g Cheddar cheese, grated
2 whole canned tomatoes, drained and chopped

1 Cook the pasta in boiling water for 8 minutes or until tender but still firm to the bite, then drain. Simmer the broccoli and peas for 5 minutes or until tender, drain.

2 Melt the butter in a small non-stick pan and stir in the flour. Keep stirring until you have a roux (paste). Gradually add the milk, stirring all the time, until you have a smooth white sauce. Stir in the grated cheese.

3 Stir the pasta, broccoli and peas into the cheese sauce, and finally stir in the chopped tomato. Simmer for a minute or two and serve warm.

SPANISH OMELETTE

Suitable age 1 year+, serves 4
Calories per portion: 234
Good source of: protein, complex carbohydrates, vitamins A, B12, folate, C, D, potassium, iodine.
Do not freeze.

Most children enjoy eggs, and this classic mix of potatoes, egg and onion is always popular. If you like, you can add a few cooked petit pois to the egg mixture, or add a little thinly sliced red pepper to the onions. Chopped parsley would also be a good addition. Slices of this omelette also make a very good lunch-box item.

> 400g waxy potatoes, peeled and chopped in half/ left whole, depending on size
> 1 tbsp light olive oil
> 1 medium onion, thinly sliced
> 6 medium eggs
> pinch of salt
> black pepper

1 Boil the potatoes in water until tender, about 18 minutes. Drain and, when cool enough to handle, cut into 5mm slices.

2 Heat the olive oil in a 23cm non-stick heavy-based frying pan and sauté the onion slices over a medium heat for about 10 minutes, or until softened and just turning golden.

3 Beat the eggs in a bowl with 1 tablespoon cold water, adding the salt and pepper seasoning. Tip the potato slices into the frying pan and spread out evenly, then pour the egg mixture over the top.

4 Turn the heat down to medium low and cook the omelette, without touching it, for 5 minutes, or until when you lift the edge with a spatula it looks golden underneath.

5 Meanwhile, heat the grill until very hot. When the underside of the omelette is cooked, flash the pan under the grill to cook and brown the top. Serve warm or cold, cut into 4 wedges.

BEEF AND CARROT CASSEROLE

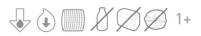

Suitable age 1 year+, serves 4
Calories per portion: 243
Good source of: protein, complex carbohydrate, carotenoids, vitamins B2, B3, B6, B12, C,E, potassium, iron, zinc.
Will freeze.

For a gluten-free diet, check that any beef stock you use contains no gluten – home-made stock will certainly be gluten-free. If serving to younger toddlers, you might like to put the stew through an electric blender for a few seconds to remove any larger lumps. You can serve the stew with a leafy green vegetable, such as broccoli, kale, Brussels sprouts or Savoy cabbage.

> 1 tbsp light olive oil
> 1 large Spanish onion (about 200g), thinly sliced
> 1 large garlic clove, well crushed
> 350g lean braising steak, cut into small cubes
> 250g carrots, peeled and cut into small cubes
> 250g floury potatoes, peeled and cut into small cubes
> 400g can of chopped tomatoes
> approx. 100ml beef stock (see page 220)
> leaves from a few sprigs of fresh thyme OR 1 level tsp dried thyme
> pinch of salt (optional)
> black pepper

1 Preheat the oven to 160°C/gas 3. Heat the oil in a flameproof casserole dish and sauté the onion for approximately 10 minutes over a medium heat, or until soft and just turning golden. Add the crushed garlic and stir for a minute, then add the beef cubes and brown them for a couple of minutes.

2 Add all the remaining ingredients and stir well to combine. Bring to a simmer on the hob and then transfer to the oven for 1½ hours, checking once or twice to make sure that the casserole isn't too dry – if it looks as if it is, add a little extra stock or water and stir well before replacing lid.

3 Serve when the meat and vegetables are tender and you have a rich sauce.

Low fat	Low saturated fat	High fibre	Suitable for vegetarians

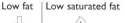

BAKED EGGS AND PEPPERS

Suitable age 5 years+, serves 4
Calories per portion: 186
Good source of: protein, carotenoids, vitamins A, B6, B12, folate, C, D, E, potassium, iodine.
Do not freeze.

This is an excellent lunch or supper dish, rich in vitamin C and very colourful. The peppers when cooked become very sweet and I think for this reason children really enjoy the taste. However, the dish shouldn't be given to small children as it contains partially cooked egg. An accompaniment of good bread is all your child will need.

 1½ tbsp light olive oil
 4–6 mixed peppers (red, orange and yellow are best), deseeded and thinly sliced
 1 medium onion, thinly sliced
 2 large ripe tomatoes, halved and sliced
 1 tsp ground cumin
 pinch of salt
 black pepper
 4 large best-quality eggs
 drizzle of basil-infused olive oil (optional)
 fresh coriander or basil leaves, to garnish

1 Preheat the oven to 190°C/gas 5. Heat the oil in a non-stick frying pan and sauté the peppers and onion over a medium heat for 5 minutes. Turn the heat down and cook, stirring from time to time, for a further 15 minutes, or until the vegetables are soft and lightly golden. Add the tomatoes, cumin and seasoning, stir to combine and cook for a further 5 minutes.

2 Spoon the mixture into 4 individual ovenproof dishes and make a well in the centre of each. Break an egg into each well and, if using, drizzle a little basil oil over the yolk of each one.

3 Cover with foil and bake for 12 minutes or until the eggs are lightly set but the yolks are still runny. Garnish with basil or coriander leaves to serve.

SALMON FISHCAKES

Particularly suitable age 11 years+, serves 4
Calories per portion: 333
Good source of: protein, complex carbohydrates, omega-3s, vitamins B1, B3, B6, B12, D, E, potassium, iodine, selenium.
Will freeze, preferably before cooking.

Quick to make and very tasty, these fishcakes are popular with children of all ages, although the high chilli content may make them unsuitable for small children. If you would like to make a similar recipe for youngsters, you can simply omit the chilli and add some sun-dried tomato paste instead. Serve with baked potatoes and green vegetables or a green salad.

 400g old floury potatoes, roughly chopped
 pinch of salt
 400g organic salmon fillet
 50ml light mayonnaise
 1 rounded tbsp flour
 2 red chillies, seeds removed and very finely chopped
 handful of fresh coriander leaves, stalks removed and roughly torn
 1 tbsp light olive oil

1 Boil the potatoes in lightly salted water until tender. At the same time, poach the salmon fillet in water (or microwave on medium high) for 3 minutes or until two-thirds cooked.

2 Flake the salmon. When the potatoes are cooked, drain them and mash fairly lightly with the mayonnaise, leaving a few small chunks of potato for texture.

3 Sprinkle the flour on a board. In a bowl, combine the potato mixture with the salmon, chillies and coriander. Using clean hands, form into 8 patties, placing each on the floured board as you make it. When all the cakes are prepared, turn them over to coat the other sides with flour.

4 Heat the oil in a non-stick frying pan and fry the cakes over a medium heat for 3–4 minutes, or until the undersides are golden. Turn them with a spatula and fry the other side for a further 3 minutes to brown lightly.

GREEK CHEESE AND SPINACH PIE

 1+

Suitable age 1 year+, serves 4
Calories per portion: 355
Good source of: protein, carotenoids, vitamins B12, folate, C, E, potassium, calcium.
Will freeze (before baking).

This pie makes a delicious snack or main meal with the addition of salad or vegetables.

600g fresh spinach
125g feta cheese
125g cottage cheese or 8%-fat fromage frais or ricotta
pinch of freshly grated nutmeg
2 medium eggs, beaten
black pepper
8 sheets of filo pastry
cooking oil spray
1½ tbsp light olive oil

1 Preheat the oven to 180°C/gas 4. Thoroughly rinse the spinach and put it in a large saucepan with only the water clinging to the leaves. Cover and cook over a medium heat until it is cooked. Drain well and press out as much liquid as you can. Put the spinach in a sieve and press with the back of a wooden spoon and then dry in strong kitchen paper.

2 Beat the two cheeses together in a bowl, then combine with the spinach, nutmeg, egg and pepper.

3 You need a shallow baking dish just a little smaller than the filo sheets. Spray the base with cooking oil, lay 3 sheets of the filo in the base and brush the top layer with half the oil. When the spinach mixture is cool, spread it over the filo and then top the pie with the remaining filo layers and use the last of the oil to glaze. With a sharp knife, score the pastry into quarters, so that when it is cooked it will be easy to cut and serve.

4 Bake for 40 minutes or until the top is crisp and golden. Serve hot or cold.

Low fat ⬇ | Low saturated fat ⬇ | High fibre ▦ | Suitable for vegetarians ✎

CHICKEN AND VEGETABLE PIE

 1+

Suitable age 1 year+, serves 4
Calories per portion: 400
Good source of: protein, carotenoids, vitamins B3, B6, folate, E, potassium, iron, magnesium, selenium.
Will freeze (before baking).

This pie is a delicious energy-giving dish and a slice will give one portion of the day's fruit and vegetables. Find good-quality wholemeal pastry which is made with vegetable oils – you then have a good source of iron, magnesium and vitamin E.

1 tbsp light olive oil
1 large leek, rinsed, trimmed and cut into 5mm rounds
350g skinless chicken breast fillet, cut into bite-sized pieces
2 medium carrots (about 150g), peeled and cut into 1cm cubes
50g French beans, halved
50g petit pois
1 tbsp sauce flour (see Note, page 223)
100ml hot whole milk, plus a little more to glaze
100ml chicken or vegetable stock

1 level tbsp fresh chopped parsley
200g wholemeal pastry, well chilled

1. Preheat the oven to 200°C/gas 6. Heat the oil in a non-stick frying pan and sauté the leek over a medium heat until softened. Add the chicken fillet pieces and sauté until light golden.

2. Meanwhile, steam or boil the carrots, beans and peas in the stock for 3 minutes until cooked but still with a little bite. Set aside (but don't drain).

3. Add the sauce flour to the chicken and leek and stir well with a wooden spatula to combine, then pour in the milk gradually, stirring all the time, to thicken.

4. Add the vegetables, chicken stock and parsley, and stir thoroughly to combine. Bring to a simmer and then tip the mixture into a suitably-sized pie dish (about 1 litre) into which you have put a pie funnel, and allow to cool a little.

5. Roll out the pastry to fit the pie and place on top of the dish, pressing the edges down well and trimming as necessary. Make a small hole in the centre over the pie funnel. Glaze the pastry with the milk and bake for 30 minutes or until the top is browned.

CHICKEN ENCHILADAS

 5+

Suitable age 5 years+, serves 4
Calories per portion: 580
Good source of: protein, carotenoids, vitamins B3, B6, C, E, potassium, calcium, selenium.
Will freeze, but best eaten fresh.

A great favourite with teenagers, though younger children may like them too, in which case you might like to use mini tortillas to reduce the calorie content somewhat.

1 tbsp light olive oil
1 red onion, thinly sliced
1 red pepper, deseeded and thinly sliced
1 medium courgette, topped, tailed and thinly sliced
1 large garlic clove, well crushed
400g skinless chicken fillet, cut into thin slices
100g Cheddar cheese, grated

8 (40g) wheat tortillas
1 recipe-quantity Tomato Sauce (page 237)

1. Preheat the oven to 180°C/gas 4. Fry the onion, pepper and courgette in the oil over a medium heat for about 10 minutes, or until everything is soft and turning golden, adding the garlic for the last 2 minutes.

2. Push the vegetables to the edges of the pan and add the chicken fillet. Sauté for 5 minutes or until the chicken is golden and cooked through, then stir in half the Cheddar cheese and mix everything together well.

3. Place one-eighth of the mixture on each tortilla and roll them up, then place them side by side snugly in an ovenproof dish. Pour over the tomato sauce, sprinkle the remaining cheese over the top and bake in the oven for 20 minutes or until the top is bubbling and the enchiladas are piping hot.

Suitable for vegans	Dairy-free	Wheat- and gluten-free	Nut- and seed-free

DESSERTS AND BAKES

BANANA SPLIT

Suitable age 1 year+, serves 2
Calories per portion: 180
Good source of: vitamins B2, B6, B12, C, potassium, calcium, iodine.
Do not freeze.

2 small bananas, peeled and halved lengthways
100g fresh strawberries
50ml Greek yoghurt
2 scoops of frozen yoghurt
1 tbsp fresh strawberry coulis (see note)

 1+

1 Arrange the banana halves in an oblong dish. Chop half of the strawberries quite small and scatter over.

2 Spoon the Greek yoghurt over the top, then add the frozen yoghurt. Halve the remaining strawberries and arrange on top. Finally, drizzle over the strawberry coulis. Children over 5 can have chopped nuts sprinkled on top.
Note: Most supermarkets stock good-quality coulis. To make your own, simply purée strawberries in a blender, then push through a sieve and stir in icing sugar to taste, adding water to thin to the desired consistency.

FRUIT FOOL

Suitable age 1 year+. serves 2
Calories per portion: 175
Good source of: vitamins A, B2, B12, folate, C, potassium, calcium, iodine.
Do not freeze.

Higher in fruit and lower in fat and sugar, this fruit fool makes a healthier alternative to commercial fruit yoghurts,

1 large fresh ripe peach
100g raspberries

 1+

20g icing sugar
100g Greek yoghurt
100g 8%-fat fromage frais

Cut two slices off the peach and reserve. Peel and chop the rest and purée in a blender with the raspberries and half the icing sugar. In a bowl, combine the yoghurt and fromage frais with the remaining icing sugar until smooth. Stir in the fruit mixture and divide between two dishes. Garnish with the peach slices and chill for 30 minutes.

SUMMER FRUIT COMPOTE

Suitable age 1 year+, serves 4
Calories per portion: 80
Good source of: carotenoids, vitamin C.
Will freeze (but loses texture).

This compote is a very rich source of vitamin C and contains a range of powerful antioxidants.

200g strawberries, sliced
100g blueberries

 1+

100g blackcurrants
50g redcurrants
50g sugar

Preheat the oven to 170°C/gas 3½. Mix together all the fruits in a baking dish and sprinkle over the sugar and 1–2 tablespoons water. Cover and bake for 30 minutes or until the fruits are tender. Use as a topping for ice cream or yoghurt, with cereal for breakfast or serve with other fruits.

Low fat	Low saturated fat	High fibre	Suitable for vegetarians

FRESH FRUIT TRIFLE

 1+

Suitable age 1 year+, serves 4
Calories per portion: 210
Good source of: vitamins B2, B6, folate, potassium, calcium, iodine.
Do not freeze.

This trifle contains around half the fat and calories of normal trifle, and makes an excellent occasional treat.

100g Madeira cake
150g raspberries
1 level tbsp icing or caster sugar
1 large banana
150g low-fat custard
150g 8%-fat fromage frais
whole raspberries, to decorate

1 Crumble the Madeira cake into the base of 4 glass dessert dishes.

2 Put the raspberries into a bowl with the icing sugar and a tablespoon of water, and cook on a medium heat for approximately 2 minutes or until the icing sugar is melted and you have some juice from the raspberries. Spoon this over the cake.

3 Peel the banana, thinly slice and divide between the 4 dishes. Beat together the custard and fromage frais till smooth, then spoon evenly over the top of the trifles. Decorate with the raspberries and chill for 30 minutes before serving.

Note: Other fruits can be used in the trifle – poached rhubarb is nice, or you could use seedless satsumas, or canned apricots in juice, chopped.

PLUM CRUMBLE

 5+

Suitable age 5 years+, serves 4–6
Calories per portion: 400 (4) 267 (6)
Good source of: carotenoids, vitamins B1, B3, B6, E, potassium, magnesium, selenium.
Will freeze (best frozen before baking).

A crumble is never going to be a low-calorie affair, but this one contains a long list of important nutrients, so makes a nutritious pudding in winter.

800g ripe red plums
40g sugar
½ tsp ground cinnamon
125g wholemeal flour
50g butter or vegan margarine
40g soft brown sugar
40g chopped mixed nuts

1 Preheat the oven to 180°C/gas 4. Stone and quarter the plums and mix them in a baking dish with the sugar and cinnamon. Sprinkle over 1 tablespoon of water.

2 Using your hands, mix together the flour and butter or margarine until it resembles breadcrumbs, then stir in the sugar and nuts and sprinkle over the fruit.

3 Bake for 45 minutes or until the topping is golden and the juice begins to bubble up around the sides.

Suitable for vegans | Dairy-free | Wheat- and gluten-free | Nut- and seed-free

BAKED BANANAS

Suitable age 1 year+, serves 4
Calories per portion: 140
Good source of: vitamin B6, potassium.
Do not freeze.

This easy fruity pudding is very low in fat and contains lots
of fibre. Serve with Greek yoghurt or low-fat custard.
Open in front of the kids so they can enjoy the aromas!

> 4 small-to-medium bananas
> 40g sultanas

2 tbsp orange juice
2 tbsp maple syrup

1 Preheat the oven to 200°C/gas 6. Peel the bananas
and lay each on its own piece of foil. Mix the sultanas
with the orange juice and leave to soak for a few minutes.
Stir in the maple syrup and pour it all over the bananas.

2 Wrap the parcels up loosely so that there is an air
pocket in each but the foil is tightly sealed. Place on a
baking tray and bake for 15 minutes.

PANCAKES

Suitable age 1 year+, serves 4
Calories per portion: 240
Good source of: protein, complex carbohydrates,
vitamins A, B1, B2, B3, B6, B12, folate, D, potassium, calcium,
magnesium, iodine, selenium.
Will freeze.

Though high in calories, pancakes filled with fresh, tinned
or stewed fruit make a relatively healthy pudding.

> 150g wholewheat flour
> 2 medium eggs

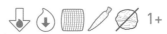

250ml semi-skimmed milk
1½ tbsp groundnut or sunflower oil

1 Sieve the flour into a bowl and make a well in the
centre. Beat the eggs and milk together and combine
with the flour using a fork or hand mixer, until smooth.

2 Heat a non-stick frying pan over a high heat, coating
the base with a little oil. Add one-eighth of the
mixture and swirl it around to cover the base. Cook for
1–2 minutes, then flip over and cook the other side for 1
minute. Remove to a warmed plate and repeat.

DATE LOAF

Suitable age 1 year+, makes 10 slices
Calories per slice: 155
Good source of: potassium, iron, calcium.
Will freeze.

This nice moist, sticky low-fat loaf is also high in fibre.
Serve it as it is or spread it with a little butter or spread.
This loaf will keep for 3 days in an airtight container.

> 225g self-raising flour
> pinch of salt
> 30g soft brown sugar
> 75g sultanas
> 100g semi-dried dates, chopped
> 30g golden syrup

3 tbsp malt extract
150ml semi-skimmed milk

1 Preheat the oven to 170°C/gas 3½. Oil a 1-litre cake
or loaf tin and line with baking parchment. Mix the
flour and salt in a bowl, then add the sugar, sultanas and
dates, and stir well.

2 Warm the syrup, malt extract and milk in a saucepan
until everything is melted. Pour the liquid into the flour
mixture and stir thoroughly to combine, adding a little
extra milk, if necessary, to achieve a dropping consistency.

3 Turn into the cake tin and bake for 1–1¼ hours or
until a skewer comes out clean. Turn out and leave to
cool, then wrap and freeze or store in an airtight tin.

Low fat  | Low saturated fat | High fibre | Suitable for vegetarians

APPLE MUFFINS

Suitable age 1 year+, makes 12 muffins
Calories per muffin: 145
Good source of: vitamin E, calcium.
Do not freeze.

  125ml semi-skimmed milk
  4 tbsp groundnut or sunflower oil
  1 large egg
  100g soft brown sugar
  2 dessert apples
  125g self-raising flour
  50g wholemeal flour
  1 tsp each baking powder and mixed spice

 1+

1 Preheat the oven to 180°C/gas 4 and put 12 muffin cases in a muffin tin. In a large bowl, beat the milk, oil, egg and sugar together. Peel, core and very finely chop or grate the apples and add to the milk mixture, stirring well.

2 In another bowl, mix together the two kinds of flour, baking powder and spice. Make a well in the centre and gradually combine the milk mixture with the flour.

3 Spoon the muffin mix into the muffin cases and bake for 20 minutes, or until they are golden and risen. Transfer to a wire rack to cool and then store in an airtight tin for up to 2 days.

FRUIT AND NUT COOKIES

Suitable age 5 years+, makes 30 cookies
Calories per cookie: 107
Good source of: vitamins A, B1, B3, B6, B12, folate, D, E, magnesium, iron.
Do not freeze.

For children with a nut allergy, substitute 75g rolled oats for the peanut butter. For vegan children use vegan margarine instead of the butter.

  cooking oil spray
  125g vegetarian margarine
  150g golden caster sugar
  1 medium egg
  75g wholemeal flour
  75g plain white flour
  ½ tsp baking powder
  pinch of salt
  125g crunchy peanut butter
  100g sultanas
  75g chopped dried ready-to-eat apricots

1 Preheat the oven to 190°C/gas 5 and spray two heavy-duty non-stick baking sheets with the oil.

2 Combine the fat, sugar, egg, flour, baking powder, salt and peanut butter until well mixed, then stir in the sultanas and apricots. Spoon the mixture on to the baking sheets in 30 small spoonfuls, leaving enough room so they won't touch during cooking.

 5+

3 Bake for 15 minutes. Allow to cool a little, then place on wire racks to finish cooling. Store in an airtight tin.

Suitable for vegans | Dairy-free | Wheat- and gluten-free 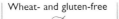 | Nut- and seed-free

FRUIT CAKE

Suitable age 1 year+, makes 12 slices
Calories per slice: 197
Good source of: vitamins B1, B3, B6, potassium, calcium, iron, magnesium, selenium.
Will freeze.

This teabread tastes rich but is low in fat and makes a good lunch-box addition or after-school snack. For children over 5 you could add some chopped almonds or hazelnuts.

50g chopped dried apricots
50g chopped stoned prunes
225g seedless raisins
150g dark sugar
300ml weak brewed tea
a little vegetable oil for greasing
125g wholemeal flour
125g white self-raising flour
1 tsp baking powder

1 level tsp mixed spice
2 medium eggs, beaten
125ml runny honey

1 Mix all the fruit and the sugar together with the tea and leave to stand for several hours.

2 Preheat the oven to 180°C/gas 4, oil a 1-litre loaf tin or cake tin and line with baking parchment.

3 In a large mixing bowl, mix together the flours, baking powder and spice, then add the fruit mixture, the eggs and the honey and stir well to combine. Spoon into the prepared baking tin and smooth down the top.

4 Bake for 1–1¼ hours or until the cake is cooked through so that when a skewer comes out of the centre it is clean. Leave to cool and then turn out, wrap and freeze or store in an airtight tin. It will keep like this for several days.

CARROT CAKE

Suitable age 1 year+, makes 12 slices
Calories per slice: 198
Good source of: complex carbohydrates, carotenoids, vitamins B1, B3, B6, magnesium, selenium.
Will freeze.

The novelty of baking a cake using vegetables appeals to children, and is a clever way of including them in their diet. If you like, you can make a reasonably low-fat topping for this cake by beating together 225g 8%-fat fromage frais (in which case the recipe isn't dairy-free), a little runny honey and lemon juice. Keep the cake in a fridge if you use a topping.

cooking oil spray
225g wholemeal self-raising flour
1 tsp ground cinnamon
2 medium eggs
4 tbsp runny honey
100g soft brown sugar
100ml groundnut or sunflower oil
225g carrot, peeled and grated
1 tbsp lemon juice

1 Preheat the oven to 180°C/gas 4 and spray a 1-litre loaf tin with cooking oil spray then line it with baking parchment.

2 Sieve the flour with the cinnamon and return any large bits of flour in the sieve to the mixing bowl. Beat together the eggs, honey, sugar and oil and add the carrots then the lemon juice. Stir this mixture into the flour until well combined, and spoon into the prepared tin, then level off the top.

3 Bake for 25 minutes or until a skewer comes out clean from the centre. Leave to cool in the tin for a few minutes, then remove and leave to cool completely on a wire rack. Wrap and freeze or store in an airtight tin for a few days.

| Low fat | Low saturated fat | High fibre | Suitable for vegetarians |

BANANA BREAD

Suitable age 1 year+, makes 12 slices
Calories per slice: 187
Good source of: vitamins A, B1, B3, B6, B12, folate, D, E, potassium, magnesium, selenium.
Will freeze.

There are plenty of nutrients in this delicious bread, which you can wrap and freeze, or it will keep for a couple of days in an airtight tin.

cooking oil spray
225g wholemeal flour
125g soft brown sugar
pinch of salt
½ tsp ground cinnamon
2 ripe bananas
150ml orange juice

2 medium-to-large eggs, beaten
5 tbsp groundnut or sunflower oil

1 Preheat the oven to 180°C/gas 4 and spray a 1-litre loaf tin with the cooking oil spray.

2 In a mixing bowl, combine the flour, sugar, salt and cinnamon. In another bowl, mash the bananas and then combine them with the orange juice, followed by the eggs and oil. Tip the banana mixture into the flour mixture and combine thoroughly.

3 Pour the mix into the loaf tin and smooth over the top. Bake for 45 minutes or until a skewer comes out of the centre clean. Wrap and freeze or store in an airtight tin – it will keep for several days.

SAUCES

CHEESE SAUCE

 6mths+

Suitable age 6 months+, serves 4
Calories per portion: 190
Good source of: protein, vitamins A, B2, B12, potassium, calcium, iodine.
Will freeze.

This sauce can be used in many savoury dishes and is particularly good for children because of its high calcium content. Using skimmed milk for children over 5 would further reduce the fat, saturated fat and calorie content. For infants and young children, don't add salt. If you replace the cheese with 3 tablespoons chopped parsley, you have a delicious low-fat parsley sauce which is good with all types of fish or ham.

20g unsalted or lightly salted butter
25g plain flour
400ml semi-skimmed milk

1 tsp Dijon mustard
white pepper
75g grated Cheddar cheese
pinch of salt (except for infants)

1 Melt the butter in a non-stick saucepan and add the flour. Off the heat, combine with a wooden spoon and then cook over a medium heat for 2 minutes.

2 Gradually pour in the milk (preferably warm or at least at room temperature), stirring all the time, until you have a smooth sauce. Add the mustard and pepper, and then stir in the cheese. Add a little salt as necessary (taste to check).

Suitable for vegans | Dairy-free | Wheat- and gluten-free | Nut- and seed-free

VEGETABLE SAUCE

 6mths+

Suitable age 6 months+, serves 4
Calories per portion: 168
Good source of: carotenoids, vitamins B6, C, E,
potassium.
Will freeze, but best served fresh.

This is a fairly light sauce, containing small chunks, which is
useful in summer with pasta or as a light lasagne filling. For
infants, purée the sauce in a blender.

- 2 tbsp light olive oil
- 1 large red onion, fairly finely chopped
- 1 garlic clove, peeled and well crushed
- 2 small or 1 large red pepper, deseeded and
  fairly finely chopped
- 1 medium courgette, topped, tailed and fairly
  finely chopped
- 1 small aubergine (about 100g), topped, tailed
  and fairly finely chopped
- 100ml low-salt vegetable stock
- 1 recipe-quantity Tomato Sauce (opposite)
- basil leaves (optional)

1 Heat the oil in a non-stick frying pan which has a lid
and sauté the onion for about 5 minutes.

2 Add the garlic and pepper, and sauté for a further 5
minutes, then add the courgette and aubergine and
stir for a minute. Add the stock and bring to a simmer,
cover with the lid and cook gently for about 20 minutes
or until all the vegetables are soft.

3 Stir in the tomato sauce and basil leaves, and cook,
uncovered, for about 20 minutes or until the sauce
has reduced to a nice thick consistency.

Low fat | Low saturated fat | High fibre | Suitable for vegetarians

TOMATO SAUCE

 6mths+

Suitable age 6 months+, serves 4
Calories per portion: 70
Good source of: carotenoids, vitamins C, E, potassium.
Will freeze.

It is useful to make this sauce in bulk for children as it can be used on its own with pasta or as a base in so many recipes – several of which are in this book.

1 tbsp light olive oil
1 medium onion, finely chopped
1 garlic clove, peeled and well crushed
400g can of good-quality chopped tomatoes
1 dsp sun-dried tomato paste or tomato purée
1 tsp brown sugar
juice of ½ lemon
a little salt (see note)
black pepper

1 Heat the oil in a non-stick frying pan which has a lid and sauté the onion for 10 minutes, or until soft and translucent but not turning golden.

2 Add the garlic and stir for a minute, then add the remaining ingredients. Stir well, bring to a simmer, turn the heat down, put the lid on and leave the sauce to cook for 15 minutes.

3 Take the lid off and continue cooking for 15 minutes more or until the sauce has reduced and is rich and darkened in colour.

Note: Add no salt for infants and young children.
Variations:
*Add chopped fresh herbs to taste (e.g. basil, thyme, oregano).
*Add finely chopped fresh chillies with the garlic.
*Add extra garlic and sliced black olives for older children to use with pasta.

LENTIL RAGU

6mths

Suitable age 6 months+, serves 4–6
Calories per serving: 280 (for 4) 189 (for 6)
Good source of: protein, complex carbohydrates, carotenoids, vitamins C, E, potassium, iron.
Will freeze.

Although children sometimes prefer red lentils, you can also use brown or green lentils for this ragu, which would increase the mineral content and would provide more B vitamins. The ragu is good with pasta, baked potatoes or rice, and also makes a good vegetarian filling for lasagne or moussaka. If serving to infants, purée the sauce in a blender until smooth.

1½ tbsp olive oil
1 Spanish onion, finely chopped
175g red lentils
1 garlic clove, peeled and well crushed
1 large celery stalk, finely chopped
100g mushrooms, cleaned and finely chopped
1 medium carrot, peeled and finely chopped
100ml low-salt vegetable stock
1 recipe-quantity Tomato Sauce (see above)

1 Heat the oil in a non-stick frying pan which has a lid and sauté the onion for 10 minutes or until softened and just turning golden.

2 Add the lentils, garlic and vegetables to the frying pan, and stir for a minute or two. Then add the vegetable stock and tomato sauce, stir well and bring to a simmer. Turn the heat down, put the lid on the pan and cook gently over a low heat for 40 minutes or until you have a rich sauce.

Suitable for vegans | Dairy-free | Wheat- and gluten-free | Nut- and seed-free

DRINKS

APPLE SMOOTHIE

 1+

Suitable age 1 year+, serves 2
Calories per portion: 114
Good source of: vitamin C, potassium.
Do not freeze.

Making fruit smoothies (which include the whole fruit) rather than juice (which leaves the solids, and thus much of the plant phytochemicals behind) is a healthier way to serve juice drinks. Smoothies are a delicious substitute for milkshakes.

2 ripe kiwi fruit
3 rings of fresh or canned pineapple, chopped

1 Golden Delicious apple
about 100ml apple juice

1 Peel the kiwi fruit, roughly chop and place in a blender with the chopped pineapple.
2 Peel and core the apple, then chop it finely. Add to the blender with a small amount of the apple juice. Blend until you have a smooth purée, then add the rest of the apple juice and blend again. If the mix is too thick, add more juice until you get the right consistency. Chill and serve.

Low fat | Low saturated fat | High fibre | Suitable for vegetarians

BERRY AND BANANA MILKSHAKE

Suitable age 1 year+, serves 2
Calories per portion: 170
Good source of: vitamins A, B2, B12, C, potassium, calcium, iodine.
Do not freeze.

This drink is high in vitamins and calcium and doubles as a snack. It is very popular with most youngsters.

 1+

1 large ripe banana
125g ripe strawberries, sliced
1 tbsp fresh strawberry or mixed berry coulis
300ml whole milk

Peel the banana, chop and put in blender with the strawberries and coulis. Purée and then add the milk and blend again until thick and frothy. Chill and serve.

PEACH AND MANGO SMOOTHIE

Suitable age 1 year+, serves 2
Calories per portion: 122
Good source of: carotenoids, vitamins B3, C, E, potassium.
Do not freeze.

You need to make sure the mango is really ripe, otherwise it won't blend smoothly and the recipe won't work. The peaches should also be ripe and juicy, to maximize the flavours. You can buy cans of skimmed coconut milk at the supermarket, alternatively it's very simple to skim your own – simply buy an ordinary can, leave it to stand for 24 hours, open carefully without shaking and remove the coconut cream from the top. The remaining milk will be skimmed.

 1+

1 average ripe mango
2 ripe peaches
100ml orange juice
100ml skimmed coconut milk

1 Peel the mango and cut off the flesh from around the stone. Chop the flesh and place in a blender. Halve, stone and peel the peaches, chop them and add to the blender with half the orange juice, then purée until smooth.
2 Add the remaining orange juice and the coconut milk to the blended fruit and purée again until you have a smooth drink. Chill and serve.

YOGHURT SMOOTHIE

Suitable age 5 years+, serves 2
Calories per serving: 180
Good source of: protein, vitamins B2, B12, folate, C, potassium, calcium, iodine.
Do not freeze.

This naturally-sweet smoothie makes a nice change from a milkshake and if you use good-quality bio yoghurt, the smoothie will help soothe an upset digestive system and restore beneficial gut bacteria after illness or antibiotics. You can also use pineapple (fresh or canned in its own juice) instead of pear for a change. Leave out the ground almonds for children who suffer from nut allergies.

 5+

1 ripe Comice pear
125g raspberries
300ml low-fat bio yoghurt
1 tbsp ground almonds
1 dsp runny honey

1 Peel, halve and deseed the pear, and cut it into small chunks then place in blender. Add the raspberries and some of the yoghurt, and blend until smooth.
2 Add the almonds, honey and rest of the yoghurt, and blend again. Chill before serving.

Suitable for vegans | Dairy-free | Wheat- and gluten-free | Nut- and seed-free

APPENDIX 1:
NUTRIENT SOURCES

This list of selected good sources of the major vitamins, minerals, phytochemicals and essential fatty acids is not exhaustive – there are many other foods in which the nutrients may be present – but the foods listed are some of the best sources likely to be eaten by children. Recommended daily amounts of all the vitamins and minerals will be found in the A–Z under Minerals pages 148–9 and Vitamins pages 194–6.

VITAMINS

VITAMIN A (RETINOL AND EQUIVALENTS)

Food (all per 100g)	Amount (µg)
Lambs' liver	19,700
Chicken livers	10,500
Liver pâté	7,300
Liver sausage	2,600
Butter	958
Double cream	779
Polyunsaturated margarine	675
Egg yolk	535
Cheddar cheese	364
Goats' cheese	333
Sour cream	330
Brie	297
Mozzarella (soft type)	258
Greek yoghurt	115
Herring	44
Rainbow trout	29
Salmon	13

BETA-CAROTENE AND CAROTENOID EQUIVALENTS

(6µg beta-carotene is equivalent to 1µg retinol)
All foods raw unless otherwise stated.

Food	Amount (µg)
Carrots	12,472
Spring greens	8,295
Sweet potatoes	3,930
Red peppers	3,840
Spinach	3,535
Squash, orange-fleshed	3,270
Kale	3,145
Cantaloupe melon	1,765
Watercress	2,520
Cos lettuce, average	1,025
Papaya	810
Mango	696
Mangetout	695
Courgettes	610
Broccoli	575
Peas, frozen, boiled	571
Tomatoes	564
Plums, average	376
Swede, boiled	350
Brussels sprouts, boiled	320

VITAMIN B1 (THIAMIN)

Food	Amount (mg)
Meat extract (e.g. Bovril)	9.7
Yeast extract (e.g. Marmite)	4.1
Vegeburger	2.4
Special K	2.3
Vegetable pâté	2.1
Sunflower seeds	1.6
Cornflakes	1.2
Wholewheat pasta, raw	0.99
Pork fillet, raw	0.98
Bacon, lean, grilled	0.98
Tahini	0.9
Fruit'n'Fibre	0.9
Black-eye beans, dried	0.87
Ham, lean	0.8
Peas, fresh, boiled	0.74
Peanuts and raisins	0.69
Brazil nuts	0.67
Red kidney beans, dried	0.65

VITAMIN B2 (RIBOFLAVIN)

Food	Amount (mg)
Yeast extract (e.g. Marmite)	11.9
Lamb's liver	5.6
Special K	2.7
Weetabix	1.4
Ready Brek	1.4
Nori seaweed	1.3
Cornflakes	1.3
Rice Krispies	1.3
Liver pâté	1.2
Muesli	0.7

Food	Amount (mg)
Camembert cheese	0.52
Eggs	0.47
Cheddar cheese	0.39
Goat's cheese, soft	0.39
Low-fat fromage frais	0.37
Low-fat fruit yoghurt	0.29

VITAMIN B3 (NIACIN)

Food	Amount (mg)
Yeast extract (e.g. Marmite)	64
Lambs' liver	20
Special K	30
Tuna, fresh	17
Tuna, canned in oil, drained	16.1
Weetabix, Ready Brek	15.3
Cornflakes	15
Peanuts, fresh	13.8
Peanut butter	12.5
Chicken or turkey breast	10.7
Pheasant meat	9.2
Lambs' kidneys	9.1
Rabbit	8.4
Bacon, lean, grilled	7.2
Salmon, fresh	7.2
Pork fillet, raw	6.9
Ham, lean	6.5
Muesli	6.5
Chicken nuggets	6.3
Salmon, canned, drained	5.9
Chicken, leg meat	5.6
Sardines canned in tomato sauce	5.5
Lamb, lean, raw	5.4
Duck, lean, raw	5.3
Beef, lean, raw	5
Haddock	4.4
Chicken burger	4.3
Sunflower seeds	4.1
Herring	4.1
Cod	2.4

VITAMIN B6 (PYRIDOXINE)

Food	Amount (mg)
Special K	3.3
Branflakes	2.3
Ready Brek	1.7
Muesli	1.6
Yeast extract (e.g. Marmite)	1.6
Turkey, light meat	0.81

Food	Amount (mg)
Tahini (sesame seed paste)	0.76
Salmon, fresh	0.75
Squid	0.69
Walnuts	0.67
Venison	0.65
Hazelnuts, peanuts	0.59
Peanut butter	0.58
Pheasant	0.57
Pork fillet, raw	0.54
Beef fillet, raw	0.53
Lambs' liver	0.53
Bacon, lean, grilled	0.52
Chicken, breast	0.51
Tuna canned in oil, drained	0.51
Rabbit	0.5
Herring	0.44
Haddock	0.39
Sardines, canned in tomato sauce	0.35

VITAMIN B12

Food	Amount (µg)
Lambs' liver	83
Lambs' kidneys	54
Nori seaweed	27
Mussels	22
Sardines, canned in oil, drained	15
Pilchards, canned in tomato sauce	13
Herring	13
Liver pâté	12
Rabbit	10
Prawns	8
Egg yolk	6.9
Tuna, canned in oil, drained	5
Salmon, fresh	4
Duck, lean meat	3
Whole egg	2.5
Cheddar cheese	2.4
Lamb, fillet, raw	2
Turkey, dark meat	2
Beef fillet, raw	2

FOLATE

Food	Amount (µg)
Yeast extract (e.g. Marmite)	2,620
Chicken livers	1,350
Bran Flakes, Cornflakes, Rice Krispies, Special K	330
Black-eye beans, cooked	210

Lambs' liver	207	Spring greens, lightly boiled	77
Asparagus, boiled	173	Kale, lightly boiled	71
Weetabix, Ready Brek	170	Brussels sprouts, lightly boiled	60
Baby spinach, raw	114	Red cabbage, raw	55
Brussels sprouts, boiled	110	Mangetout, stir-fried	51
Peanuts, fresh	110	Broccoli, lightly boiled	44
Tahini	99	Baby sweetcorn, lightly boiled	39
Liver pâté	99	White cabbage, raw	35
Kale, cooked	86	Mangetout, lightly boiled	28
Spinach, cooked	81	Cauliflower, lightly boiled	27
Cabbage, raw	75	Spinach, baby, raw	26
Hazelnuts, fresh	72	Courgettes, raw	21
Cashew nuts, fresh	68	Sweet potato, baked	20
Spring greens, cooked	66	Cabbage, average, lightly boiled	20
Peanuts and raisins	66	Tomatoes, raw	17
Walnuts	66	Potatoes, new, boiled	15
Broccoli, cooked	64	Potatoes, baked, flesh and skin	14
Lettuce	55	Peas, frozen, boiled	12
Courgettes, mixed vegetables	52	Chips, oven, baked	12
Green beans, cooked	48	Potatoes, old, boiled	6
Peas, frozen, boiled	47		
Leeks, cooked	40		
Wholewheat bread	40		

VITAMIN C (ASCORBIC ACID)

Food	Amount (mg)
FRUIT	
Guava	230
Blackcurrants, stewed	115
Strawberries, raw	77
Papaya	60
Kiwi fruit	59
Lemons	58
Oranges	54
Clementines	54
Mangos	37
Nectarines	37
Grapefruit	36
Raspberries, raw	32
Peaches	31
Satsuma, tangerine	27
Fruit salad, home-made	27
Melon, cantaloupe	26
Mandarins canned in juice	20
VEGETABLES	
Red peppers, raw	140
Yellow peppers, raw	130
Green peppers, raw	120

VITAMIN D (CHOLECALCIFEROL)

Food	Amount (µg)
Cod liver oil	210
Red salmon, canned, drained	23.1
Cod's roe, fried	17
Herring, fresh, grilled	16.1
Pilchards, canned in tomato sauce	14
Sardines, fresh, grilled	12.3
Trout, fresh, grilled	9.6
Salmon, pink, canned, drained	9.2
Mackerel, fresh, grilled	8.8
Special K	8.3
Margarine, average, all types	7.9
Tuna, fresh	7.2
Salmon, fresh	5.9
Sardines, canned in oil, drained	5
Egg yolk	4.9
Bran Flakes	4.2
Tuna, canned in brine, drained	3.6
Tuna, canned in oil, drained	3
Tuna pâté	2.9
Eggs, whole	1.8

VITAMIN E (TOCOPHEROLS)

Food	Amount (mg)
Wheatgerm oil	137
Sunflower oil	49.2

Safflower oil	40.7
Sunflower seeds	37.8
Polyunsaturated margarine	32.6
Hazelnuts, fresh	25
Sun-dried tomatoes in oil, drained	24
Almonds, fresh	24
Rapeseed oil	22
Cod liver oil	20
Corn oil	17.2
Mayonnaise, retail	16.9
Soya oil	16
Groundnut (peanut) oil	15.1
Pine nuts	13.6
Popcorn, plain	11
Vegetable ghee	10.3
Peanuts, fresh	10
Low-fat spread (not polyunsaturated)	8
Brazil nuts, fresh	7.2
Marzipan, retail	6.1
Potato crisps, average	6
Peanuts and raisins	5.6
Tomato purée	5.4
Olive oil	5.1
Peanut butter	5
Trail mix	4.5

MINERALS

CALCIUM (CA)

Food	Amount (mg)
CHEESE	
Parmesan	1,025
Edam	795
Cheddar	739
Processed cheese slices	610
Cheese spread, plain	498
Mozzarella, soft	362
Feta	360
Brie	256
Goats'-milk cheese, soft	133
OTHER DAIRY PRODUCE	
Whole-milk yoghurt, natural	200
Sheeps' milk	170
Low-fat yoghurt, natural	162
Low-fat yoghurt, fruit	140
Choc ice	140
Custard, ready-made	140
Greek yoghurt	126

Skimmed milk	122
Semi-skimmed milk	120
Whole milk	118
Fromage frais, 8% fat	110
Goats' milk	100
Ice cream, dairy, vanilla	100
Cream, single	89
Rice pudding, ready-to-eat	88
Fromage frais, low-fat	87
FISH	
Whitebait fried in oil	860
Sardines canned in oil, drained	500
Fish paste	280
Crab, canned, drained	120
Prawns, peeled	110
Fish fingers	92
PULSES	
Tofu, steamed	510
Soya flour	210
Soya milk, calcium-enriched	89
Soya beans, cooked	83
Red kidney beans, cooked or canned	71
Beanburger, retail	69
Baked beans in tomato sauce	53
Chickpeas, cooked or canned	46
Hummus	41
Soya milk, non-calcium-enriched	13
NUTS AND SEEDS	
Tahini (sesame seed paste)	680
Almonds, fresh	240
Brazil nuts	170
Hazelnuts	140
Nut roast	72
Trail mix	69
Marzipan, retail	66
Peanuts, fresh	60
Peanuts and raisins	54
Peanut butter	37
BREADS AND CEREALS	
Ready Brek	1,200
Rice Krispies	453
White self-raising flour	350
All Bran	340
Naan bread	187
White bread	177
White plain flour	140
Pitta bread, white	138
Wholemeal bread	106

Special K	70	Skimmed milk	29
Pasta, white, dry weight	64	Milk chocolate	30

FRUIT AND VEGETABLES

Figs, dried, ready-to-eat	230
Okra, stir-fried	220
Watercress	170
Spinach, raw	170
Spinach, lightly cooked	160
Kale, lightly cooked	150
Spring greens, lightly cooked	75
Broad or green beans, lightly cooked	56
Parsnip, boiled	50
White cabbage, raw	49
Onions, fried in oil	47
Mangetout, lightly cooked	46
Instant mashed potato with milk	44
Celery	41
Broccoli, lightly cooked	40
Peas, frozen, boiled	35
Carrots, raw	34
Cabbage, average, lightly cooked	33

MISCELLANEOUS

White chocolate	270
Milk chocolate	220
Digestive biscuits, plain	92
Cornetto ice cream cone	84
Non-dairy ice cream, vanilla	72

IODINE (I)

Food	Amount (µg)
Fish paste	310
Haddock	250
Choc ice	160
Mackerel, grilled	150
Egg yolk	140
Cod	110
Fish fingers	110
Parmesan cheese	71
Chocolate mousse	66
Whole-milk yoghurt, natural	63
Eggs, whole	53
Goats'-milk cheese, soft	51
Low-fat fruit yoghurt	48
Greek yoghurt	39
Low-fat natural yoghurt	34
Dairy vanilla ice cream	32
Whole milk	31
Semi-skimmed milk	30

IRON (FE)

Food	Amount (mg)

MEAT

Black pudding	12.3
Lambs' kidneys, fried	11.7
Lambs' liver, fried	7.7
Liver pâté	5.9
Venison	5.1
Meat paste	4.7
Beef, lean	2.7
Steak and kidney pie	2.7
Duck, lean	2.4
Corned beef	2.4
Pheasant	2.2
Beefburger (no bun)	1.7
Lamb, lean	1.4

CEREALS AND GRAINS

Branflakes	24.3
Special K	23.3
Ready Brek, Weetabix	11.9
All Bran, Fruit'n'fibre	8.8
Cornflakes, Rice Krispies	7.9
Pot barley, dry weight	6
Muesli	5.8
Poppadum	4.4
Wholemeal flour	3.9
Wholewheat pasta, dry weight	3.9
Chocolate fudge cake	3.1
Wholemeal bread	2.4
Fruit cake	2.1

VEGETABLES, PULSES, SPICES

Curry powder, dry mix	58.3
Seaweed, dried, nori	19.6
Lentils, brown or green, cooked	3.5
Tofu, steamed	3.5
Soya beans, cooked	3
Red kidney beans, cooked	2.5
Lentils, red, cooked	2.4
Chickpeas, cooked	2.1
Spinach, raw	2.1
Kale, lightly cooked	2
Beansprouts, fresh	1.7
Peas, boiled	1.5
Spring greens, lightly cooked	1.4
Baked beans in tomato sauce	1.4

Broccoli, lightly cooked	1

FRUIT, NUTS AND SEEDS

Tahini (sesame seed paste)	10.6
Sesame seeds	10.4
Pumpkin seeds	10
Peaches, ready-to-eat dried	6.8
Sunflower seeds	6.4
Cashew nuts	6.2
Pine nuts	5.6
Figs, ready-to-eat dried	3.9
Raisins	3.8
Trail mix	3.7
Apricots, ready-to-eat dried	3.4
Hazelnuts	3.2
Peanut butter	3.1
Peanuts and raisins	3.1
Almonds, fresh	3
Prunes	2.6

MAGNESIUM (MG)

Food	Amount (mg)
Brazil nuts	410
Sunflower seeds	390
Tahini (sesame seed paste)	380
Sesame seeds	370
Pine nuts	270
Almonds	270
Soya mince, dry	270
Cashews, fresh	250
All Bran	240
Peanuts, fresh	210
Peanut butter	180
Hazelnuts, walnuts	160
Puffed wheat	140
Mixed nuts and raisins	133
Shredded Wheat	130
Poppadoms	121
Weetabix, Branflakes, Ready Brek	120
Pasta, wholewheat, dry weight	120
Nut roast	113
Lentils, green or brown, dry weight	110
Okra, stir-fried	110
Chocolate, plain	89
Vegeburger	80
Licorice Allsorts	76
Marzipan, retail	68
Wholemeal bread	66
Spinach, raw	54

Quorn pieces	37

POTASSIUM (K)

Food	Amount (mg)

NUTS

Peanuts and raisins	824
Pine nuts	780
Almonds	780
Hazelnuts, cashews	730
Sunflower seeds	710
Peanut butter	700
Peanuts, fresh	670
Brazil nuts	660
Trail mix	620
Tahini (sesame seed paste)	580

FRUIT

Apricots, ready-to-eat dried	1,380
Sultanas	1,060
Raisins	1,020
Figs, ready-to-eat dried	890
Prunes, ready-to-eat	760
Currants	720
Dates, dried	700
Avocado	450
Banana	400
Kiwi fruit	290
Blackcurrants, stewed	290
Plums	240
Cantaloupe melon, grapes	210
Apples	120

VEGETABLES AND PULSES

Baked potato, flesh and skin	630
Chips, oven, baked	530
Soya beans, cooked	510
Courgettes, stir-fried	490
Okra, stir-fried	480
Red kidney beans, cooked	420
Onion, fried	370
Parsnips, boiled	350
Mushrooms, fried	340
Brussels sprouts, lightly cooked	310
Baked beans in tomato sauce	310
Sweet potatoes, boiled	300
Potatoes, old, boiled	280
Chickpeas, cooked	270
Potatoes, new, boiled	250
Tomatoes, raw	250
Spinach, cooked	230

Peas, cooked	230
Mixed leaf salad, average	220

SELENIUM (SE)

Food	Amount (µg)
Brazil nuts	254
Lambs' kidneys, fried	209
Peanuts and raisins	170
Lentils, green or brown, dry weight	105
Tuna, canned in oil, drained	90
Lambs' liver	62
Tuna, fresh	57
Sunflower seeds	49
Sardines, canned in oil, drained	49
Lentils, green or brown, cooked	40
Sardines, fresh, grilled	38
Plaice	37
Herring	35
Cashews, fresh	34
Pilchards in tomato sauce	30
Cod	28
Haddock	27
Salmon, fresh	26
Prawns, peeled	23
Fish fingers	23
Wholewheat pasta, dry weight	16
Pork, lean	13
Wholemeal bread	7
White bread	6

ZINC (ZN)

Food	Amount (mg)
MEAT, FISH AND DAIRY	
Oysters	8.3
Beefburger, grilled	6.1
Lambs' liver	5.9
Crab, canned, drained	5.7
Corned beef	5.5
Parmesan cheese	5.1
Beef, lean	4.1
Cheddar cheese	4.1
Venison	3.9
Edam cheese	3.8
Lamb, lean	3.3
Turkey, dark meat	3.1
Liver pâté	2.8
Processed cheese slices	2.6
Bacon, back, grilled	2.5
Prawns, peeled	2.2
Pork, lean	2.1
VEGETARIAN	
Wheatgerm	17
Poppy seeds	8.5
Quorn pieces	7
Pumpkin seeds	6.6
Pine nuts	6.5
All Bran	6
Cashews, fresh	5.7
Tahini (sesame seed paste)	5.4
Sesame seeds	5.3
Pecans	5.3
Sunflower seeds	5.1
Brazil nuts	4.2
Lentils, green or brown, dry weight	3.9
Soya flour	3.9
Peanuts, fresh	3.5
Almonds, fresh	3.2
Lentils, red, dry weight	3.1
Puffed wheat	2.8
Ready Brek	2.7
Branflakes	2.5
Wholemeal bread	1.6

PHYTOCHEMICALS

PHENOLIC COMPOUNDS (FLAVONOLS)
ANTHOCYANINS
Found in: Blueberries, blackberries, blackcurrants, cherries, cranberries, grapes (black), strawberries, raspberries, red-tinged leaves.
Action: Antioxidant, anti-inflammatory.

CATECHINS (FLAVANOLS)
Found in: Apples, chocolate, cocoa, tea (green/black), pears, wine.
Action: Antioxidant, heart protection.

FLAVANONES
Found in: Citrus fruits, prunes, cashew nuts.
Action: Antioxidant, cholesterol-lowering.

FLAVONES
Found in: Artichokes, celery, lemons, parsley, peppers, olives, oranges.
Action: Antioxidant, anti-cancers.

QUERCETIN
Found in: Apples, citrus fruits, grapes, lettuce (red-tinged), onions, tea.
Action: Anti-cancer, skin-protecting, cataract prevention, anti-hay fever.

RUTIN
Found in: Citrus fruits.
Action: Antioxidant, heart health.

OTHER PHENOLS
CAPSAICIN
Found in: Chillies, peppers.
Action: Antioxidant, pain killer, anti-inflammatory, cholesterol-lowering.

COUMARINS
Found in: Citrus fruits, green tea, leafy green vegetables, parsley.
Action: Help prevent blood clotting, anti-cancer.

CURCUMIN
Found in: Corn, mustard, turmeric.
Action: Antioxidant, anti-inflammatory.

ELLAGIC ACID
Found in: Black and red berries, cherries, grapes, pecans, walnuts.
Action: Anti-cancer.

RESVERATROL
Found in: Red grape juice, red wine.
Action: Antioxidant, protects heart.

CAROTENOIDS
ALPHA-CAROTENE
Found in: Avocado, carrots, corn, red peppers, squash, tomatoes.
Action: Antioxidant, anti-cancer.

BETA-CAROTENE
Found in: Carrots, dark leafy greens, sweet potatoes, red peppers, cantaloupe melon.
Action: Anti-cancer, immune-booster, eye health, skin health.

CRYPTOXANTHIN
Found in: Red, orange and yellow fruits.

Action: Heart health.

LUTEIN
Found in: Dark leafy greens, peas, rhubarb, squash.
Action: Eye health.

LYCOPENE
Found in: Tomatoes, pink grapefruit.
Action: Anti-cancer, anti-heart disease.

ZEAXANTHIN
Found in: Lettuce, spinach, spring greens, sweetcorn.
Action: Eye health.

PHYTO-OESTROGENS
COUMESTROL
Found in: Beansprouts
Action: Anti-inflammatory.

ISOFLAVONES
Found in: Soya and soya products, and other pulses.
Action: Heart health, possible breast cancer risk reduction.

LIGNANS
Found in: Flax seeds, whole grains, berries.
Action: Possibly anti-breast cancer.

OTHERS
GLUCOSINOLATES
Found in: Broccoli (sulphoraphanes), cabbage (indoles), cauliflower, kale, sprouts (sinigrin).
Action: Anti-cancer.

LENTINEN
Found in: Exotic mushrooms, e.g. shiitake
Action: Immune-boosting, anti-cancer.

PHYTOSTEROLS
Found in: Soya beans, nuts, seeds, whole grains.
Action: LDL cholesterol-lowering.

SULPHIDES
Found in: Garlic, onions, leeks.
Action: Antioxidant, anti-bacterial, anti-cancer, heart and circulation protection.

ESSENTIAL FATTY ACIDS

There are two fats essential for the maintenance of health and development in humans that cannot be manufactured in the body, both of which are polyunsaturated fats. One is linoleic acid, which is the 'head' of the omega-6 group of fatty acids and which can be converted in the body into the omega-6s 'lower down' in the group. The other is alpha-linolenic acid, which is the 'head' of the omega-3 group of fatty acids, which can be converted in the body into the omega-3s 'lower down' in this group.

Within the omega-3 group are two special 'long-chain' fatty acids found mainly in fish – eicosapentaenoic acid (EPA) and docosahexaenoic acid (DHA). Although, in theory, these can be made in the body from alpha-linolenic acid, it is thought that this process may be blunted by various factors, and research shows that if EPA and DHA are eaten regularly there are several health benefits. Adequate intake of these fatty acids in children has been shown to be linked with improved brain power and concentration, protection against heart disease and the maintenance of a healthy blood cholesterol profile, while also helping to minimise the effects of eczema, asthma, food allergies, dyslexia and dyspraxia, autism and behavioural problems such as attention deficit hyperactivity disorder (ADHD).

It is also thought that the balance of intake of omega-6s and omega-3s is important – most children get too much omega-6s in their diets and not enough omega-3s; the British Nutrition Foundation recommended in 2002 that young people should double their consumption of omega-3 oils. For vegetarians and vegans the main non-fish source of omega-3 oils is linseed (flax seed) oil, although walnuts and walnut oil also contain good amounts.

The tables below and opposite give the main sources of the omega-6 group via linoleic acid, of the omega-3 group via alpha-linolenic acid, and of EPA and DHA.

SOURCES OF OMEGA-3 'LONG-CHAIN' FATTY ACIDS, EPA AND DHA (g/100g)

FOOD	EPA	DHA
Anchovies	0.5	0.9
Herring	0.51	0.69
Herring roes, soft	0.2	0.38
Kipper	1.15	1.34
Mackerel	0.71	1.10
Pilchard in tomato sauce	1.17	1.2
Salmon, canned in brine, drained	0.55	0.86
Salmon, fresh, farmed	0.6	1.2
Sardines, canned in oil, drained	0.89	0.82
Trout	0.23	0.83
Tuna, fresh	0.4	1.2
Tuna, canned in oil, drained	0.06	0.27

OMEGA OILS – CONTENT IN SELECTED FOODS

FOOD	OMEGA-6 GROUP (g/100g)	OMEGA-3 GROUP (g/100g)
Vegetable ghee	9.12	0.19
Vegetable suet	11.81	0.18
Butter	0.95	0.46
Margarine, soft, not polyunsaturated	9.48	2.44
Margarine, soft, polyunsaturated	33.26	0.09
Margarine, soya	29.9	3.51
Low-fat spread, not polyunsaturated	4.27	1.54
Cod liver oil	2.6	1.1
Corn oil	50.4	0.9
Olive oil	7.5	0.7
Groundnut (peanut) oil	31	0
Linseed (flax seed) oil	15	53.1
Rapeseed oil	19.7	9.6
Safflower oil	73.9	0.1
Sesame oil	43.1	0.3
Soya oil	51.5	7.3
Sunflower oil	63.2	0.1
Walnut oil	58.4	11.5
Blended vegetable oil	23.2	6.5
Chicken skin, cooked	6.23	1.02
Pork fat	6.98	0.73
Duck, meat and fat	5.69	0.69
Tofu mayonnaise	12.83	2.38
Almonds	10.19	0.27
Brazil nuts	25.43	0
Flax seeds	5.7	14
Pine nuts	24.9	0.8
Pumpkin seeds	21.58	0.13
Sesame seeds	25.35	0.15
Sunflower seeds	28	0.09
Broccoli	0.04	0.1
Cauliflower	0.2	0.8
Green beans	0.2–0.5	0.2–0.6
Spinach	0.2	0.9

APPENDIX 2:
GROWTH CHARTS / BMI

You can get a good indication as to whether or not your child is a reasonable bodyweight by checking out the Growth Charts (opposite) and/or by working out his or her Body Mass Index (BMI) and checking the result against the table below.

GROWTH CHARTS

Pick the correct chart for your child's age and sex. Now simply weigh him or her in kilograms and then, using a ruler, check off that weight against your child's age. The nearer your child's weight is to the central, fiftieth percentile line, then the nearer average weight he or she is. The further below this average line, the more underweight he or she is, and the higher above the line, the more overweight. But note that these charts don't take into account large variations in height, so if your child is particularly taller or shorter than average you should also check out the BMI as further confirmation.

BODY MASS INDEX (BMI)

The following instructions will enable you to calculate your child's BMI:
• Write down your child's height in metres (this is height in inches multiplied by 0.025).
• Square this result (multiply the figure by itself, e.g. 1.25m x 1.25m) using the calculator.
• Write down your child's weight in kilograms (weight in pounds divided by 2.2; e.g. 100lb = 45.5kg).
• Now divide the weight in kg by the height in metres squared. The result is your child's BMI.
• Finally check off your child's BMI against the ages listed in the panel, right. If the BMI is more than that listed, your child is overweight.

Note: The BMI chart below is adapted from the Institute of Child Health and the International Obesity Task Force. The growth charts opposite are based on those produced by the National Center for Health Statistics in the USA.

BMI CHART – YOUR CHILD IS OVERWEIGHT IF HE / SHE IS		
AGE, YEARS	BOYS, BMI OVER	GIRLS, BMI OVER
2	18.4	18
3	17.9	17.6
4	17.6	17.3
5	17.4	17.1
6	17.6	17.3
7	17.9	17.8
8	18.4	18.3
9	19.1	19.1
10	19.8	19.9
11	20.6	20.7
12	21.2	21.7
13	21.9	22.6
14	22.6	23.3
15	23.3	23.9
16	23.9	24.4
17	24.5	24.7
18	25	25

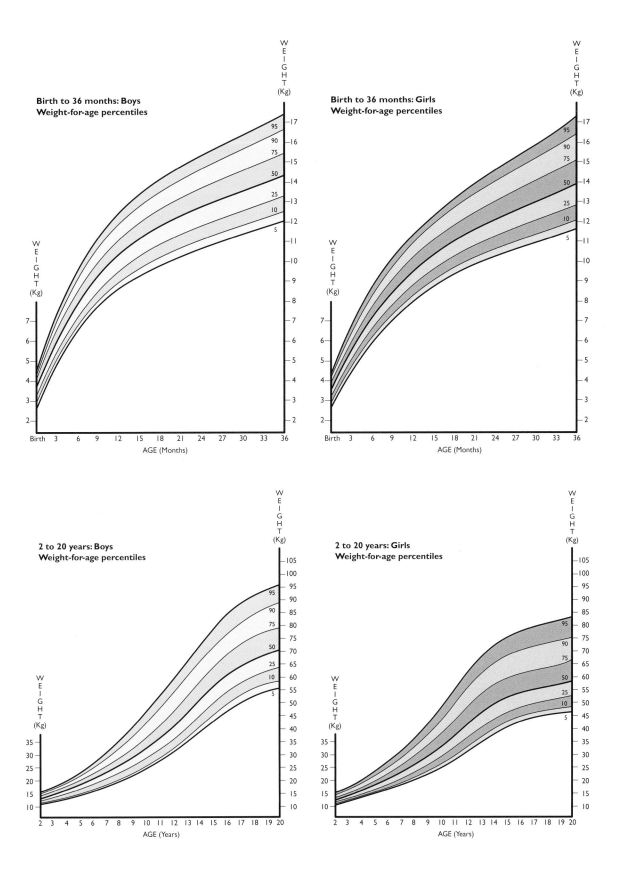

Birth to 36 months: Boys
Weight-for-age percentiles

WEIGHT (Kg)

95
90
75
50
25
10
5

WEIGHT (Kg)

Birth 3 6 9 12 15 18 21 24 27 30 33 36
AGE (Months)

Birth to 36 months: Girls
Weight-for-age percentiles

WEIGHT (Kg)

95
90
75
50
25
10
5

WEIGHT (Kg)

Birth 3 6 9 12 15 18 21 24 27 30 33 36
AGE (Months)

2 to 20 years: Boys
Weight-for-age percentiles

WEIGHT (Kg)

95
90
75
50
25
10
5

WEIGHT (Kg)

2 3 4 5 6 7 8 9 10 11 12 13 14 15 16 17 18 19 20
AGE (Years)

2 to 20 years: Girls
Weight-for-age percentiles

WEIGHT (Kg)

95
90
75
50
25
10
5

WEIGHT (Kg)

2 3 4 5 6 7 8 9 10 11 12 13 14 15 16 17 18 19 20
AGE (Years)

Appendix 2: Growth Charts / BMI   251

APPENDIX 3: CONTACTS AND REFERENCE

HEALTH ORGANISATIONS

ALCOHOL CONCERN

Waterbridge House, 32–36 Loman Street, London SE1 0EE

Tel: 020 7928 7377

Email: contact@alcoholconcern.org.uk

Web: www.alcoholconcern.co.uk

ALLERGY UK

Deepdene House, 30 Bellegrove Road, Welling, Kent DA16 3PY

Tel: helpline 020 8303 8583

Email: info@allergyuk.org; web: www.allergyfoundation.com

THE ANAPHYLAXIS CAMPAIGN

PO Box 275, Farnborough, Hampshire GU14 6SX

Tel: helpline 01252 542 029

Web: www.anaphylaxis.org.uk

NATIONAL ASTHMA CAMPAIGN

Providence House, Providence Place, London N1 0NT

Tel: helpline 0845 701 0203; other 020 7226 2260

Web: www.asthma.org.uk

HYPERACTIVE CHILDREN'S SUPPORT GROUP

71 Whyke Lane, Chichester, W. Sussex PO19 7PD

Tel: 01243 551 313

Email: contact@hacsg.org.uk; web: www.hacsg.org.uk

CancerBACUP

3 Bath Place, Rivington Street, London EC2A 3JR

Tel: helpline 0808 800 1234; general enquiries 020 7739 2280

Web: www.cancerbacup.org.uk

INSTITUTE OF CHILD HEALTH

30 Guildford Street, London WC1N 1EH

Tel: 020 7242 9789

Email: info@gosh.nhs.uk; web: www.ich.ucl.ac.uk

COELIAC UK

PO Box 220, High Wycombe, Bucks HP11 2HY

Tel: helpline 0870 444 8804; office 01494 437 278

Email: diet@coeliac.co.uk; web: www.coeliac.co.uk

DIABETES UK

10 Parkway, London NW1 7AA

Tel: 020 7424 1000

Email: info@diabetes.org.uk

Web: www.diabetes.org.uk

THE DYSLEXIA INSTITUTE

Park House, Wick Road, Egham, Surrey TW20 0HH

Tel: 01784 222 300

Email: info@dyslexia-inst.org.uk

Web: www.dyslexia-inst.org.uk

BRITISH DYSLEXIA ASSOCIATION

989 London Road, Reading RG1 5AU

Tel: 0118 966 2677

Email: admin@bda-dyslexia.demon.co.uk

Web: www.bda-dyslexia.org.uk

THE DYSPRAXIA FOUNDATION

8 West Alley, Hitchin, Herts SG5 1EG

Tel: helpline 01462 454 986; general enquiries 01462 455 016

Web: www.dyspraxiafoundation.org.uk

EATING DISORDERS ASSOCIATION

103 Prince of Wales Drive, Norwich NR1 1DW

Tel: youth helpline 0845 634 7650

Email: helpmail@edauk.com

Web: www.edauk.com

NATIONAL ECZEMA SOCIETY

Hill House, Highgate Hill, London N19 5NA

Tel: eczema info 0870 241 3604; office 020 7281 3553

Email: helpline@eczema.org

Web: www.eczema.org

BRITISH HEART FOUNDATION

14 Fitzhardinge Street, London W1H 6DH

Tel: infoline 08450 708070; office 020 7935 0185

Email: internet@bhf.org.uk; web: www.bhf.org.uk

OBESITY RESOURCE INFORMATION CENTRE

22 Apex Court, Woodlands, Bradley Stoke, Bristol BS32 4JT

Tel: 01454 616 798

Email: oric@endocrinology.org

Web: www.aso.org.uk

NUTRITION AND FOOD ORGANISATIONS

BRITISH DIETETIC ASSOCIATION
5th Floor, Charles House, 148–149 Great Charles Street,
Queensway, Birmingham B3 3HT
Tel: 0121 200 8080
Email: info@bda.uk.com
Web: www.bda.uk.com

BRITISH NUTRITION FOUNDATION
52–54 High Holborn, London WC1V 6RQ
Tel: 020 7404 6504
Email: postbox@nutrition.org.uk
Web: www.nutrition.org.uk

THE FOOD COMMISSION
94 White Lion Street, London N1 9PF
Tel: 020 7837 2250
Email: enquiries@foodcomm.org.uk
Web: www.foodcomm.org.uk or www.parentsjury.org.uk

THE SOIL ASSOCIATION (organic food)
Bristol House, 40–56 Victoria Street, Bristol, BS1 6BY
Tel: 0117 929 0661
Email: info@soilassociation.org
Web: www.soilassociation.org

THE VEGETARIAN SOCIETY
Parkdale, Dunham Road, Altrincham, Cheshire WA14 4QG
Tel: 0161 925 2000
Email: info@vegsoc.org
Web: www.vegsoc.org

GOVERNMENT DEPARTMENTS AND INFORMATION

DEPARTMENT OF HEALTH UK
Richmond House, 79 Whitehall, London SW1A 2NS
Tel: 020 7210 4850
Email: dhmail@doh.gsi.gov.uk
Web: www.doh.gov.uk

FOOD STANDARDS AGENCY UK
Aviation House, 125 Kingsway, London WC2B 6NH
Tel: 020 7276 8000
Email: helpline@foodstandards.gsi.gov.uk
Web: www.foodstandards.gov.uk

FOOD AND DRUG ADMINISTRATION USA
Center for Food Safety and Applied Nutrition
5100 Paint Branch Parkway, College Park, MD 20740-3835
Tel: free infoline 1-888-723-3366
Web: www.cfsan.fda.gov

FOOD AND NUTRITION INFORMATION CENTER USA
National Agricultural Library
10301 Baltimore Avenue, Beltsville, Maryland 20705
Tel: 301 504 5755
Email: webmaster@nal.usda.gov
Web: www.nal.usda.gov/fnic

FOOD STANDARDS AUSTRALIA AND NEW ZEALAND
Boeing House, 55 Blackall Street, Barton Act 2600,
Canberra, Australia
Tel: 612 62 71 2222
Email: info@foodstandards.gov.au
Web: www.foodstandards.gov.au

PUBLICATIONS

The Food Magazine, published monthly by The Food Commission which campaigns for the right to safe, wholesome food. For subscriptions, see details, left, for the Food Commission.

The Nutrition Bulletin, published quarterly by The British Nutrition Foundation. For subscriptions, see details, left, for the BNF.

The American Journal of Clinical Nutrition, published monthly by the American Society for Clinical Nutrition Inc. For subscription details visit their website on www.ajcn.org/cgi or email secretar@ascm.faseb.org or tel: 301 530 7038.

RECOMMENDED BOOKS
Eating Problems in Children – Information for Parents by Claudine Fox and Carol Joughin (Gaskell, 2002)

The Food our Children Eat – How to Get Children to Like Good Food by Joanna Blythman (Fourth Estate, 1999)

Fast Food Nation by Eric Schlosser (Penguin, 2002)

The Complete Guide to Healing Foods by Amanda Ursell (Dorling Kindersley, 2000)

Kids' Food for Fitness by Anita Bean (A & C Black, 2002)